D1565803

THE PROBLEM OF DEMOCRACY
IN THE AGE OF SLAVERY

ANTISLAVERY, ABOLITION, AND THE ATLANTIC WORLD

R. J. M. Blackett and James Brewer Stewart, Series Editors

THE PROBLEM OF

DEMOCRACY

IN THE AGE OF

SLAVERY

GARRISONIAN ABOLITIONISTS & TRANSATLANTIC REFORM

W. CALEB McDANIEL

LOUISIANA STATE UNIVERSITY PRESS
BATON ROUGE

Published by Louisiana State University Press
Copyright © 2013 by W. Caleb McDaniel
All rights reserved
Manufactured in the United States of America
First printing

DESIGNER: Michelle A. Neustrom
TYPEFACE: Whitman
PRINTER: McNaughton & Gunn, Inc.
BINDER: Acme Bookbinding

LIBRARY OF CONGRESS CATALOGING-IN-PUBLICATION DATA

McDaniel, W. Caleb (William Caleb), 1979–
    The problem of democracy in the age of slavery : Garrisonian abolitionists and transat-
lantic reform / W. Caleb McDaniel.
        p. cm. — (Antislavery, abolition, and the Atlantic world)
    Includes bibliographical references and index.
    ISBN 978-0-8071-5018-4 (cloth : alk. paper) — ISBN 978-0-8071-5019-1 (pdf) — ISBN
978-0-8071-5020-7 (epub) — ISBN 978-0-8071-5021-4 (mobi) 1. Antislavery movements—
United States—History—19th century. 2. Slavery—Political aspects—United States—History—19th century. 3. Democracy—Philosophy. 4. Garrison, William Lloyd, 1805–1879.
5. Phillips, Wendell, 1811–1884. 6. American Anti-Slavery Society. 7. Abolitionists—
United States—Biography. I. Title.
    E449.M473 2013
    326'.8092—dc23

                                                                            2012027975

Portions of chapter 7 first appeared in "Repealing Unions: American Abolitionists,
Irish Repeal, and the Origins of Garrisonian Disunionism," *Journal of the Early Republic* 28,
no. 2 (2008): 243–69. Copyright 2008 Society for Historians of the Early
American Republic. Used by permission.

The paper in this book meets the guidelines for permanence and durability of the Committee
on Production Guidelines for Book Longevity of the Council on Library Resources. ∞

For Brandy
and my parents

Republics exist only on the tenure of being constantly agitated. . . . If the Alps, piled in cold and still sublimity, be the emblem of Despotism, the ever-restless ocean is ours, which, girt within the eternal laws of gravitation, is pure only because never still.

—WENDELL PHILLIPS, 1852

It is no real paradox to affirm that a man's love of his country may often be gauged by his disgust at it.

—JAMES RUSSELL LOWELL, 1875

CONTENTS

ACKNOWLEDGMENTS

This book began as a dissertation at Johns Hopkins University under the direction of Ronald G. Walters and Dorothy Ross. I could not have asked for better guides into the worlds of abolitionism, American cultural and intellectual history, and academic life.

Today it is impossible for me to return to Ron's scholarship on the antislavery movement without noticing countless ways in which his thinking has informed my own; it would be just as impossible to calculate his influence on these pages—not to mention the many, many drafts that came before them. Dorothy's interest in and support for my work has also been invaluable. I have returned to her searching comments on my dissertation many times over the past several years to help me find my way forward in the revision process. Her equally generous comments on the final draft of the book manuscript challenged me in all the right ways and proved essential to the finished product. Most importantly, both Ron and Dorothy offered me friendship and the feeling that I was their colleague from the beginning of my time as their student. Their belief in the historian I could be has made me the historian I am, but I still aspire to be more like the historians they are.

At Johns Hopkins, it was also my good fortune to learn from Christopher Brown, Michael Johnson, and Paul Kramer, each of whom helped to shape the lines of inquiry that led to this book. For reading parts or all of the dissertation and sharing advice along the way, I'm grateful as well to David Bell, Jane Dailey, Thomas Izbicki, Pier Larson, Phil Morgan, Ken Moss, Bill Rowe, Erica Schoenberger, and Judy Walkowitz. I could not have finished the dissertation without the intellectual camaraderie and feedback of my fellow graduate students, especially Joe Adelman, Matthew Bender, Michael Henderson, Katherine Hijar, Marguerite Hoyt, Kate Jones, Tara Kelly, Jason Kuznicki, Kimberly Lynn, Lars

Maischak, Bonnie Miller, Ethan Miller, Catherine Molineux, Clare Monagle, Kate Moran, Sarah Mulhall, Kate Murphy, Greg O'Malley, and Kyle Planitzer.

I am deeply honored that this book is appearing in a series edited by James Brewer Stewart and Richard Blackett, two of my scholarly heroes. From the day we met in 2004, Jim has been a tireless friend of this project, and those who know Jim will realize that "tireless" is the right word for him. For his comments on earlier versions of this work and for our many conversations on Phillips, Garrison, and abolitionism then and now, I am extraordinarily grateful. Hopefully I will have many opportunities to pay forward the collegiality and generosity that I cannot fully repay to him. Richard is the sort of scholar who always seems to discover and take the "new turn" in the historiography decades before everyone else; that's why his support for this book, his advice about archives, his comments on an earlier draft, and his friendly questions about when it would be finished have meant so much. Most of all, Jim and Richard have modeled for me how to take history seriously while still having fun doing it.

Shortly after I finished at Hopkins, Robert K. Nelson and Amanda Bowie Moniz did me the honor of reading the dissertation and sending me their reflections on it; their comments influenced my revisions more than they may realize. My good friend Kent Dunnington read chapters of the first complete draft as I finished them, providing helpful insights and moral support. Conversations with François Furstenberg at conferences, in Montreal, and in Houston helped me figure out what I was trying to say and encouraged me to say it. Richard Huzzey's comments on the penultimate draft were hugely helpful, and Edward Rugemer's report on the final draft and help at earlier stages proved invaluable. Rand Dotson and Lee Sioles helped shepherd the project to publication at LSU, and Stan Ivester made the copyediting process a pleasure.

Many other scholars also contributed to my thinking by commenting on conference papers, sending me citations and sources, sharing their work, providing encouragement, or listening patiently as I tried to talk through unformed ideas. In particular, I would like to thank Leslie Butler, Enrico Dal Lago, Douglas Egerton, Roy Finkenbine, David Gellman, Luke Harlow, Martha Hodes, Mischa Honeck, Daniel Walker Howe, Ari Kelman, Gale Kenny, Jane Landers, Brian Luskey, Tim Marr, Matthew Mason, Angela Murphy, Rich Newman, Jim Oakes, Lewis Perry, David Quigley, John Quist, Timothy Roberts, Stacey Robertson, Tamara Thornton, Sean Wilentz, Julie Winch, and Joseph Yannielli. I'm also grateful to the organizing committee of the Wendell Phillips Bicentennial Committee, including Amy Aiséirithe, John Stauffer, and Donald Yacovone, for giving me the opportunity to share my thoughts about Phillips before a friendly audience. Amy, whose forthcoming book will provide a much-needed and thorough examination of Garrisonian abolitionists during the Civil War, also graciously read a draft of the manuscript and offered helpful feedback. Bertram Wyatt-Brown shared generously of his hospitality and his expertise in the history of abolitionism, and his interest in my project sustained me at several crucial moments.

The History Department at Rice University provided a wonderfully collegial environment in which to complete the book. The Mosle Fund for junior faculty in the School of Humanities supported research in the final stages. My department chairs, Martin Wiener and Lora Wildenthal, also provided research funding and a teaching release near the end of the project, as well as comments on parts of the manuscript. A brief conversation with Carl Caldwell about an early version of what is now chapter 6 totally reoriented my thinking about the book, and his encouragement after reading the entire manuscript helped get me to the finish line.

John Boles's hospitality and enthusiasm made me feel welcome in Houston from the beginning, and conversations with Ussama Makdisi and Jack Zammito helped me think more broadly about my work. Special thanks are due to Randal Hall and Bethany Johnson for their friendship and interest in the project. I'm also particularly grateful to a faculty writing group that read a much earlier version of chapter 1 and has provided many stimulating conversations since then; in particular, my thanks to Lisa Balabanlillar, Alex Byrd, Anne Chao, Stephanie Camp, T. J. Fitzgerald, Rebecca Goetz, Maya Soifer Irish, Moramay Lopez-Alonso, Kate De Luna, Cyrus Mody, Aysha Pollnitz, and Kerry Ward. Paula Platt, Anna Shparberg, and Rachel Zepeda cheerfully provided whatever I needed, even when asked at the last minute. I also thank doctoral students Zach Dresser, Blake Earle, Mercy Harper, and Allison Madar for their vital assistance with research and editing.

Colleagues at the University of Denver provided a great deal of professional, intellectual, and personal support at an earlier stage of this project, and I'm especially thankful to Susan Schulten, Carol Helstosky, and Ingrid Tague. I'm also grateful to the then dean of the School of Arts, Humanities, and Social Sciences, George Potts, for funding an important research trip in 2007 that served as the basis for the expansion of the manuscript beyond the scope of the dissertation.

Several friends opened their homes to me on my research trips, including John Pittard, Rahul Nair and Haimanti Roy, and David Stockton and the late

Jim Farnsworth. For their hospitality in Manchester and London during my brief visits there, I'm grateful to David Brown, Adam Smith, and Brian Ward. The heroic staff at the Houghton Library at Harvard, the John Rylands Library in Manchester, the New-York Historical Society, and the Boston Public Library in Copley Square, especially Eric Frazier and Sean Casey, deserve special thanks for pulling countless boxes of abolitionist letters and answering requests by email after I left.

My friends and family members seemed to sense that it is not always polite to ask a book its stage. But throughout the long process of writing this volume, they were steadfast in their support, interest, and love. My thanks especially to Michael and Luci Bell; James Denham; Whitney Fleming; David and Amy Fuller; Mark and Jennifer Lackey; David and Sara Pybus; Steve and Chelsie Sargent; and Chris and Jenny Thompson; my siblings Bonnie Crumpton, Travis McDaniel, and Conner McDaniel; my grandparents Bettie McDaniel, and Bob and Yvonne Clayton; and my mother- and father-in-law Bill and Gayle Hunt.

Mere words do not seem sufficient to thank my parents, Jim and Pam McDaniel, both for loving me and for instilling in me a love of learning. The sacrifices they have made for my education and enrichment—including a crossing of the Atlantic at an early age—are too many to recount here, but their unfailing support and guidance still supply the model for what I hope to provide my own children, Ellery and Carter. Ellery would have preferred me to write a book about outer space, but I hope that someday she and Carter will read this, too. Perhaps they will conclude, as Maria Weston Chapman told her children, that it is good to become cosmopolitan early in life and to see the world as their country. But most of all, I hope that by the time Ellery and Carter are able to read and understand this they will already know how much I love them both.

I suspect that no one will be happier to see this project come to an end than Brandy McDaniel. But I am certain that no one's support was more important to its completion than hers. Over the roughly ten years that I have been working on this book in various forms, she consoled, commiserated, encouraged, and listened, but most of all, she loved. During my extended absences at archives and my long hours at the computer, Brandy never doubted that I could do this and gave me countless pep talks when I did have doubts. From beginning to end, this book is hers. More importantly, so is its author.

THE PROBLEM OF DEMOCRACY
IN THE AGE OF SLAVERY

INTRODUCTION

O
n April 14, 1865, hours before Abraham Lincoln sat down for the last time at Ford's Theater in Washington, D.C., the famous abolitionist William Lloyd Garrison sat down for the first time in Charleston, South Carolina. More than three decades before, Garrison had founded the Boston *Liberator*, a newspaper dedicated to universal, immediate slave emancipation. In 1833, he helped found the American Anti-Slavery Society (AASS), a group devoted to the same goal. And by the time he went to Charleston, Garrison had served as the society's president for over twenty years. Only in the last few, however, had emancipation changed from a despised, minority opinion to the official policy of federal armies in a cataclysmic civil war. With the war now ending and a constitutional amendment to abolish slavery awaiting ratification, Garrison had come to Fort Sumter to attend a flag-raising ceremony at the invitation of Lincoln's administration.[1]

Undoubtedly Garrison's emotions about the trip were difficult to express, and not only because he met recently emancipated slaves, one of whom pressed a ten-dollar bill into his hand. Garrison's emotions were also stirred because he could now celebrate a country he had long regarded with deep disillusionment— even disgust. That disillusionment had two main causes. Four million of Garrison's countrymen had been considered chattel property just three years before. But the abolitionists who had worked for three decades to abolish this evil met with nearly unremitting hostility, even in the "free states" of the North. Garrison once confessed to feeling more at home in Britain, which abolished slavery in its West Indian colonies only two years after he started his paper, and as recently as 1860, Garrison had objected to having the American flag wave over his head. Now, five years later, he literally helped pull the Star-Spangled Banner up the flagpole at Fort Sumter, accompanied by his friend of thirty-two years, British abolitionist George Thompson.[2]

Thompson was also at his side two years later when Garrison was toasted in London at a public breakfast held in his honor. It was Garrison's fourth trip to Great Britain, and among the crowd were other British abolitionists who had supported Garrison for two decades or more. There was Richard Davis Webb, a Dublin printer. There was the lawyer William Shaen, longtime associate of William Henry Ashurst, who had once served as the London correspondent for the *Liberator*. These were two of the many reformers whom Garrison could recognize on sight. But dotting the crowd were also many internationally famous reformers, including John Bright, the meeting's chairman; Victor Schoelcher, the French abolitionist; and John Stuart Mill, member of parliament for Westminster, author of *On Liberty*, and a leading figure for liberal thinkers on both sides of the Atlantic.[3]

Before 1867, Garrison and Mill had never met, and at first glance they had little in common. One was a lifelong printer and agitator, the other a statesman and philosopher. Garrison was the son of an alcoholic father and pious mother who never received much formal education; Mill, who was raised in the shadow of famous English philosophers like his father James Mill and the utilitarian Jeremy Bentham, learned to read classical Greek at the age of three. But Mill knew about Garrison. In the 1830s, he had read about American abolitionists in the essays of the English writer Harriet Martineau. Mill had also followed Garrison's career as an advocate of women's rights, and he shared Garrison's abhorrence of chattel slavery. It was thus only with slight exaggeration that Mill wrote, in 1865, that he had always regarded Garrison's band of abolitionists "as the élite of their country, not to say of their age."[4]

Two years later in London, Mill gave a laudatory speech in honor of Garrison, only a few days after the two men had shared a private moment at the House of Commons. At a special meal with members of parliament, Garrison sat next to Mill. And according to the journal of Frederick W. Chesson, who knew both men, Mill told Garrison upon "shaking hands with him, that there was no man in the world he was better pleased to see." He later invited Garrison to visit his vacation home in France.[5]

Garrison proved unable to accept Mill's invitation. But Garrison had already crossed the English Channel earlier in the month, and he returned to Paris a few weeks later for an international antislavery conference. There he received another round of congratulations from European reformers like the Russian exile and anti-serfdom reformer Nicholas Tourgeneff and the French liberal Edouard

Laboulaye, who reminded Garrison of his old friend Charles Follen, the German American exile. And between his two trips to the continent, Garrison also visited twice with Giuseppe Mazzini, the famous Italian revolutionary.[6]

Garrison and Mazzini had met twenty years before, and a few days after their final meeting the Italian sent Garrison a friendly note expressing his regard, accompanied by a photograph of himself. Garrison, in turn, later wrote a fond memoir of his "personal friendship" with Mazzini. The abolitionist acknowledged that his and Mazzini's "fields of labor were widely apart, and our modes of action in some respects diverse." But the differences between Mazzini and himself, Garrison claimed, were slighter than the similarities: "we cherished the same hostility to every form of tyranny, and had many experiences in common."[7]

In that single, telling line, Garrison opened a revealing window onto the world he had known for fifty years: a world in which American abolitionists were connected to a transatlantic host of reformers as diverse as Thompson, Follen, Chesson, Mazzini, and Mill. This book places the story of Garrison and his movement within that wider world, and in so doing explains how and on what terms one of American history's most radical critics came to stand beneath the flag.

The primary experience that Garrison, Mill, and Mazzini had in common was that of being antislavery in an age of slavery. But they also defended democracy in an age of aristocracy, monarchy, and doubt about democracy's future. These experiences differed, however, according to location, or what Garrison called each man's "field of labor."

All three reformers lived through an epochal transformation in world history: the abolition, in about one hundred years, of a transoceanic system of slavery that had thrived since the fifteenth century. Between the American and Haitian revolutions of the late eighteenth century and the Brazilian abolition of 1888, millions of African-descended people held as slaves in the Western hemisphere became free in the eyes of the law, while observers on both sides of the Atlantic came to regard slavery as antithetical to human progress. But during these dramatic changes, abolitionism remained more unpopular in America, and for longer, than in Europe.[8]

In Mill's England, Parliament abolished British West Indian slavery in the 1830s, after which many Britons considered being antislavery synonymous with being British. In Europe itself, chattel slavery had largely disappeared as a legal institution by the time that New World African slavery began, so reformers like Mazzini never lived in the sort of slave societies that grew up across the Atlantic. In the post-revolutionary United States, by contrast, the federal government gave numerous protections to a powerful southern planter class, enabling slavery to expand rapidly in space and scale. American slavery proved so resilient that only civil war succeeded in destroying it.[9]

Even emancipations outside the antebellum United States often strengthened the hand of slavery's defenders there. After the lengthy wars that ended slavery in Haiti, American slaveholders argued that merely discussing abolition would provoke apocalyptic bloodshed. British abolitionists and their few American allies countered by pointing to the British West Indies as a "mighty experiment" in emancipation that proved its safety and wisdom. But that strategy faltered in the face of racism, American Anglophobia, fears of insurrection or sectional strife, and discouraging economic growth in the post-emancipation Caribbean.[10]

The small minority of Americans who demanded immediate emancipation thus remained on the defensive throughout the first five decades of the nineteenth century. Even antislavery politicians like Lincoln suggested that American slavery could only end gradually and might well survive until the 1890s or beyond, while more radical abolitionists like the "Garrisonians"—as members of the AASS were known—faced threats, ostracism, and even physical violence. So it was no wonder that abolitionists looked to England as a safer haven where they could "breathe freely," as Garrison put it. Temporary exile in Great Britain provided resources, refuge, and respite from an age of slavery whose end was not yet assured.[11]

The fate of democracy was also far from assured when Garrison's career began. By 1855, more than half a century after French and American revolutionaries created self-governing republics, democratic governments were still few and feeble on both sides of the Atlantic, and the enemies of democracy—monarchs, aristocrats, and their conservative defenders—still clung tightly to the reins of power in almost every state. Clandestine networks of agitators like Mazzini tried to revive popular revolution in Europe after 1815, but most members of these groups were forced to live in exile, and in their new homes they still often aroused suspicion for their radical views. Even when French revolutionaries succeeded in overturning another monarch in 1830, the French electorate grew only to around 200,000 men—a number representing less than 1 percent of the whole population.[12]

Elsewhere, universal suffrage remained as controversial as the idea of immediate emancipation in the United States. In the United Kingdom, parliamentary reformers modified the composition of the electorate with the passage of the Reform Act of 1832. But by 1848, despite a massive decade-long Chartist movement calling for universal manhood suffrage, the number of Englishmen who could vote still hovered consistently at just under 20 percent of all adult males in England. Another broadening of the franchise would not occur until a second Reform Bill in 1867, whose merits Garrison heard being debated in the House of Commons before he lunched with Mill.[13]

In the United States, by contrast, universal white manhood suffrage was the law in most states by 1855, making the country an unusual experiment in political democracy. Just as many European and American writers turned to the British West Indies or Haiti to observe the effects of slave emancipation, scores of European travelogues, essays, and books about American democracy appeared in the decades when abolitionists were most active. Alexis de Tocqueville's *Democracy in America,* published in 1835 and 1840, was only the most famous. As Mill noted in the first of his two reviews of that book, the United States was "usually cited by the two great parties which divide Europe as an argument for or against democracy. Democrats have sought to prove by it that we ought to be democrats; aristocrats, that we should cleave to aristocracy, and withstand the democratic spirit."[14]

Yet even in the antebellum United States, "the democratic spirit" remained contested and limited; all of its gains were hard-won. As historian Kyle Volk notes, after their own revolution Americans continued to debate "the boundaries to the democratic creed of majority rule, the rights of minorities and their proper place in policymaking, and whether 'the people' could ever be too involved in popular self-government," as well as "whether public policy should always reflect public opinion." Many Americans in the Whig Party still admired England's small electorate and property qualifications for voting. And even the most ardent Jacksonian Democrats were only willing to follow the democratic tendency so far—to the point of political equality for adult white men.[15]

The idea of completely unlimited and equal suffrage was, in short, still a radical notion in the world abolitionists knew, even to some abolitionists. In 1843, for example, the political abolitionist James Birney nearly lost the presidential nomination of the Liberty Party after some indiscreet public remarks deploring that, "since the time of Mr. Jefferson, what is called democracy has been on the increase." Birney was sure that "no people . . . can advance in moral refinement and true civilization under the univ[ersa]l Suffrage." These were not the views of Garrisonians or most Liberty Party members, but outbursts like Birney's showed that "democracy" was not incontrovertible even among American reformers. As historian Daniel Feller notes, for a nineteenth-century American democrat surveying the world at large, "there was reason, in the 1830s and even later, to believe that issues we now consider settled by then were in fact not settled."[16]

In short, when Garrison launched his *Liberator* in 1831, democrats were largely on the defensive everywhere but in the United States, while abolitionists were on the defensive everywhere but in Great Britain. The map of places where a democrat could breathe freely was almost the photographic negative of those where abolitionists felt at ease. For American abolitionists, the embattled situation of democrats abroad raised fears that the tendency of the times could veer back toward tyranny and away from universal freedom, notwithstanding emancipation's recent gains. Conversely, for those struggling for democracy in Europe, the persecution of abolitionists in the United States seemed to threaten their own success, since conservatives like Sir Robert Peel could point to recent mobs and anti-black riots in the United States as arguments against "experiments" in "popular Government." As the French abolitionist Victor Schoelcher wrote in a Garrisonian publication, it was "an incalculable danger to the democratic idea, both now and hereafter, that the most democratic people existing should be holders of Slaves!"[17]

As Schoelcher realized, events in the nineteenth-century Atlantic World made it difficult for anyone to debate about slavery without also debating the legitimacy of different forms of government. But for abolitionists, the age of slavery exposed problems with both aristocracy *and* democracy, with rule by the few as well as rule by the many. On the one hand, abolitionists understood slavery as it existed in the American South as antithetical to democracy. Slavery denied the democratic premise of human equality. It disfranchised millions of black men and women, who in some parts of the South outnumbered whites. And it empowered a small landed class of slaveholders, a "Slave Power" that exerted aristocratic control in Congress and legislated in the interests of the planter class.

On the other hand, the unpopularity of abolitionism and the persistence of slavery in the United States also revealed problems with democracy. Slavery survived partly thanks to the votes of congressmen and electors in northern states where slavery had ended after the revolution. At the state and municipal levels, laws that benefited slaveholding aristocrats, repressed northern abolitionists, and discriminated against free black communities were often ratified by electoral majorities or their representatives. And what anti-abolitionists could not accomplish by law they often achieved through violence or harassment that was tolerated by elected officials. Mobs like the one that disrupted a meeting of abolitionist women in Boston in 1835 and led Garrison through the streets by a rope seemed, as one *Liberator* headline put it, to provide "Another Argument for Sir Robert Peel" that majority rule in the United States had not been an unqualified good.[18]

These realities made abolitionists acutely aware of the problem of democracy: majorities could be unjust, immoral, selfish, and unconcerned about the oppression of others. Democratic procedures could even allow enfranchised groups to deny minorities the very same rights they already enjoyed. Surveying American politics on the eve of the civil war, the leading Garrisonian orator, Wendell Phillips, concluded that "the weakness of a Democracy is that, unless guarded it merges in despotism." Abolitionists like him, more than most Americans, appreciated how easily "a Democrat . . . will harden into a despot," and how difficult it was for a minority to protect itself. But given this awareness, how could they answer the Peels of the world who doubted "the democratic principle"?[19]

The problem of justifying democracy despite its potential for despotism is not an easy one to solve; indeed, it continues to vex liberal political theorists even in the present. Often democracy is minimally defined as a procedure for fair political decision-making, yet even so-called procedural democrats acknowledge that the decisions of a majority may be wrong or even anti-democratic. As Amy Gutmann and Dennis Thompson put it, "numerical might does not make a decision morally right. Majorities have a moral right to govern only because minorities do not." Liberal democracy needs protections for minority groups and individual rights that cannot be overruled by majorities, but debating procedures and deciding the limits of majority rule often expose even deeper moral disagreements. Some theorists, including Gutmann and Thompson, argue that greater democratic participation and conversation can deal with these disagreements. But debate continues over how to justify and create ground rules for deliberation in a way consistent with procedural fairness and the principles of autonomy and equality on which democratic procedures are based.[20]

Similar debates on the legitimacy of democracy began during the age of slavery, before struggles to establish democratic procedures had even been settled beyond doubt. Indeed, abolitionists pondered similar questions together with many European contemporaries. When Phillips declared that democracy could merge with despotism, he paraphrased directly from the writings of Tocqueville, whose books on American democracy Phillips read closely and cited often. Mill also read Tocqueville's volumes as soon as they appeared and spent two decades puzzling over how to shield democratization in England from the dangers of majoritarian tyranny.[21]

Like them, Garrisonians saw the problems with the democratic procedure of majority rule. But unlike many European writers on democracy, Garrisonians sought ways to correct democracy's weaknesses without sacrificing its procedures—the representative institutions and voting rights which American democrats had fought hard to win. Many of Tocqueville's admirers, including Mill, sometimes entertained the idea of placing limitations on suffrage to keep immoral or incompetent majorities from running amok, or favored a mixture of aristocracy and democracy. Garrisonians, on the other hand, typically grew up believing that the United States government provided a model for the world, and even their conversions to abolitionism did not entirely destroy that faith.

While in Scotland during his second transatlantic tour, for example, Garrison affirmed "the superiority of the American form of government over every other now existing in the world." Frederick Douglass, the famous African American abolitionist who allied with Garrison in the early 1840s, likewise told British audiences that, "aside from slavery I regard America as a brilliant example to the world. Only wash from her escutcheon the bloody stain of slavery, and she will stand forth as a noble example for others to follow." Similar statements can be found scattered throughout the Garrisonians' writings. Wendell Phillips even declared that "I have full faith in democratic institutions" and identified the antislavery movement with "the Democratic principle."[22]

These expressions of faith in democratic institutions and principles are noteworthy because Garrisonians are best known among historians of abolitionism for their own refusal to vote. For various reasons, including religious beliefs and interpretations of the Constitution, members of the American Anti-Slavery Society decided after 1840 not to cast ballots, even for antislavery parties like the Liberty Party, founded in 1840, or the Free Soil Party, founded in 1848. Instead, Garrisonians relied exclusively on strategies intended to change public opinion, like holding meetings, publishing tracts, circulating petitions, and delivering speeches.

Abolitionists who did join the Liberty Party and the Free Soil Party often criticized these Garrisonian non-voters for an irresponsible lack of faith in democratic procedure, and many historians have leveled the same charge. In 1845, for example, Charles Sumner urged his friend Phillips to reconsider his refusal to vote, since abolitionists could not afford to lose any means of influence for the slave. "I think that you would *speak* in favor of an alteration of the Constitution, why not *act* in favor of it?" Sumner asked. "Take your place among citizens, & use all the weapons of a citizen in this just warfare."[23]

Other critics of Garrisonian non-voting were less charitable and accused Garrison of caring more for his own moral purity than for abolition. They viewed Garrison's style of agitation, which at one point included his public burning of the Constitution, as proof of a blind zeal that could not distinguish at all between what was good in American institutions and what was bad. As one critic lamented, members of Garrison's society seemed to take "the 'backing out' principle" to extremes. "Their plan of navigating our poor misguided ship is to renounce helm, roles, compass, anchor, all, jump overboard and scream!"[24]

Historians have also often seen Garrisonians as self-righteous separatists who backed out instead of pitching in, adopting a "remarkably passive plan of action." On this view, Garrison led his small band of followers into a "detour" or "moral dead end . . . a seemingly endless pursuit of self-purification that mistook the avoidance of politics for progress." He and his disciples "privileged the purification of the individual soul, the conversion of individual hearts and minds against slavery and other worldly corruptions, over the practical result of abolition." In short, to many historians, the classic image of Garrison is of an impractical, "radically antinomian" religious reformer obsessed with moral perfectionism, rather than a political activist. By refusing to vote at all, he and his allies allegedly showed a "contempt for ordinary politics" that came close to contempt for the democratic process itself.[25]

The Garrisonians' own self-professed faith in democratic institutions has been further obscured by a long tradition in American democratic theory that began not long after emancipation. In the last years of the nineteenth century, many American intellectuals began to deprecate the sort of religious and moral absolutism that could lead someone to burn laws and spurn ballots. These thinkers saw the inflexibility of abolitionists like Garrison and Phillips as inimical to the pragmatism that reformers needed in a complex modern world, where uncertainty and pluralism were facts of life. Indeed, already by the 1860s, Garrison's stock was falling among some of the young liberals who admired Mill, a philosopher who loved to synthesize seeming opposites into subtle wholes. Moncure Conway, a Unitarian who briefly joined Garrison's movement in the 1850s, breezily remembered the editor as the leader of a religious sect who refused to work with other abolitionists—in contrast to Conway himself, who considered himself more open-minded and "knew good people on both sides."[26]

Despite these common criticisms, however, Garrisonians unquestionably believed in democracy. Indeed, their focus on altering public opinion required as much faith in democratic procedures as the decisions of other abolitionists to vote, because Garrisonians assumed that majority rule allowed changes in public opinion to direct policy. Moreover, despite their voluntary decisions to refrain from voting, Garrison and his allies did not call for others to be deprived of their votes. By advocating equal political rights for women and black Americans, they demonstrated a more expansive view of suffrage than many antislavery voters. Garrisonians also echoed the hopes of Schoelcher and their European friends that the democratic idea would spread to other countries, and they hated American slavery partly because it robbed the United States of the role they assumed it should play as a global exemplar of democracy in action. When Garrison hoisted the flag at Fort Sumter at the end of the Civil War, he rejoiced that slavery had perished, but like Lincoln, he was also relieved that government of, by, and for the people had not.

Still, Garrisonians could not forget the weaknesses of democracy, its potential drift toward despotism; they knew firsthand what it meant to be a moral minority in an age when slavery and racism still had numbers on their side. Though remembered for their own inflexibility, they themselves knew the damage done by a bad idea when held by an unreflective and unbending majority. Throughout the antebellum period, therefore, Garrisonians often meditated not only on the problem of how to abolish slavery, but also on how to solve the problem of democracy that their ideas and experiences made plain. To make American democracy safe for the world, they had to do more than abolish American slavery; they had to articulate the habits of mind and social practices that would keep future democratic majorities from abusing their power in new ways.[27]

Garrisonian abolitionists wanted to make democracy work, and the key to that, they believed, was to couple majority rule and democratic procedures with constant *agitation* by at least some citizens outside of political institutions. But while this emphasis on agitation as essential to democracy was ultimately the thing that most endeared Garrisonians to Mill, it was not a self-evident truth to Americans at the time. By the time Garrison founded the *Liberator*, many conservatives and radicals alike viewed agitation by private clubs and extra-parliamentary movements as possible threats to the rule of law, which democratic citizens should control through more orderly forms of civic participation like jury duty and voting. Surveying the United States of the 1830s, Supreme Court Justice Joseph Story spoke for many American thinkers in deploring "Ultraism" and the "restless spirit of innovation and change—a fretful desire to provoke discussions of all sorts." Many others criticized abolitionist agitation more explicitly as a threat to the harmony of the Union, which—as the world's mighty experiment of democracy—had to be preserved even at the expense of discussing divisive ideas.[28]

In short, most antebellum Americans assumed that what made the United States a democracy were its political institutions and procedures, not the extent to which unpopular views could be expressed. But Garrisonian abolitionists preached that dissent was as necessary in a democracy as suffrage, representative institutions, or the rule of law. While certain of their own moral rectitude, they also articulated a defense of constant deliberation and free inquiry that later democratic thinkers might have recognized. Because other deeply held views had been proved wrong in the past, and because passive conformity favored political tyranny, Garrisonians believed, in Phillips's words, that "unintermitted agitation" was essential to self-government—a controversial point in their day, but an important one in the history of American democratic thought.[29]

Wendell Phillips best summarized the Garrisonians' vision of democracy in 1852, when he compared popular government to an "ever-restless ocean," its waves constantly agitated and never still. Phillips returned to that image frequently. But the ocean was more than a metaphor for abolitionists. Garrisonians also crossed the actual ocean frequently, revealing the transnational dimensions of American reform and the extent of transatlantic networks even in an era of nation-building and civil war.[30]

As historian C. A. Bayly and others have shown, the nineteenth century witnessed the birth of a nascent "international civil society" and the rise of transnational "networks of information and political advocacy which, though less obvious than the rising national and imperial state, [were] no less important." Abolitionists experienced these realities in their everyday lives thanks to revolutions in transportation and communications technology that knit the Atlantic World together and astonished their contemporaries. By the end of Garrison's life, one American abolitionist marveled to the Irish abolitionist Richard Davis Webb about the incredible "wilderness of waters" over which their letters always crossed. Yet "our regular, constant, almost daily intercourse by steam mail-vessels" had led these distant friends to "accept it as a matter of course!"[31]

Like the generations after them, abolitionists compared their experiences to the generations before them and concluded that it was a small world after all. Over the course of Garrison's five eastward Atlantic voyages, the length of his trips in days trended steadily downward: 21, 25, 15, 10, 11. The first westward crossing Garrison ever made, in 1833, took 42 days by sail; his last return from Europe, in 1877, took 10 days by steam. Those contrasts struck abolitionists as proof that "the oceans that divided us, have become bridges to connect us," as Frederick Douglass put it in 1848. The year before, Douglass had completed his own first Atlantic crossing, which introduced him to a vibrant community of reformers who had corresponded with American abolitionists for a decade or more.[32]

Transatlantic travel and correspondence also brought American abolitionists into close contact with a wide range of reform movements, including Irish Repeal, Corn Law Repeal, and Chartism. As Douglass pointed out after his first tour of Great Britain, many of the British reformers whom abolitionists knew identified with "the democratic element in British politics"; they sympathized with European exiles like "Louis Kossuth and Mazzini, and with the oppressed and enslaved, of every color and nation, the world over." And through these friends abolitionists joined dense, overlapping networks that spanned the Atlantic Ocean.[33]

For a sense of how complex these networks could become, it is enough to consider one exchange between Mazzini and several of Garrison's allies before the Civil War. In 1855, Mazzini wrote a note to the Bristol Unitarian and abolitionist George Armstrong, telling him that "we are moving along the same path," and reporting that he had conveyed a note from Armstrong to Kossuth, the Hungarian revolutionary. Mazzini had received Armstrong's note through Ashurst, a mutual friend of Garrison and Mazzini. Mazzini had then passed the note to Kossuth's Italian secretary, whom he knew. Finally, in a postscript to Armstrong, Mazzini asked for the address of the Boston abolitionist Maria Weston Chapman, one of Garrison's closest allies, who by then had moved to Paris and had met Mazzini in London. Armstrong, for his part, copied and sent the whole correspondence to Samuel May Jr., a Massachusetts Unitarian who had met Armstrong on an abolitionist tour in England.[34]

Close attention to these networks is crucial not just for mapping the nineteenth-century Atlantic World of reform, but also for understanding Garrisonians. Like the later Progressive intellectuals studied by historian James Kloppenberg, the abolitionists' ideas were "shaped within a transatlantic community of discourse rather than a parochial national frame of reference," and many of their strategies and premises make sense only within the larger context of the Atlantic World. For example, Garrisonians partially modeled their strategy of agitating public opinion from outside Congress on successful extra-parliamentary reform movements overseas, like Daniel O'Connell's crusade for Catholic emancipation in Ireland or Richard Cobden's struggle against the Corn Laws. They viewed setbacks for abolitionists in America as setbacks to democracy abroad partly because this is what their own correspondents affirmed. And finally, focusing on the extent of their transatlantic networks makes clearer why Garrisonians so often described themselves not only as democratic agitators, but also as citizens of the world.[35]

Garrison made his own cosmopolitan ideals clear in the famous motto that he published on every issue of the *Liberator*: "Our Country is the World—Our Countrymen are all Mankind." But between 1831 and 1865, this motto and its variants also became a mantra for Garrison's allies on both sides of the ocean. George Thompson cited it in a speech in Calcutta in 1843. Charles Follen called it "our watchword from the beginning." Douglass claimed Garrison's motto as his, too. And when Chapman moved to Paris she told Pease that she had gone partly to teach her daughters to "to become cosmopolitan . . . & to be able to say with an experimental feeling, 'My Country is the World My Countrymen are all Mankind.'" In 1867, Garrison's friend and ally Henry Clarke Wright, who spent five years in Europe in the 1840s, inscribed the title page of the forty-seventh volume of his personal diary with the words: "Henry C. Wright. Citizen of the World."[36]

Becoming "cosmopolitan," in short, mattered greatly to Garrison and his allies. When Garrison's sons published a four-volume memorial biography of their father, they described "Our Country is the World" as his "favorite motto" and printed it on the title page of each book. The motto was printed on memorial cards distributed at Garrison's funeral. And it is engraved on the southern side of the Garrison statue that sits near the Boston Public Library in Copley Square, where Garrison's voluminous correspondence with European reformers was deposited after the Civil War.[37]

Like their insistence on agitation, the Garrisonians' cosmopolitanism often made them unpopular in their day. Many Americans during and after the

American Revolution had once believed that ideals like cosmopolitanism, world citizenship, and universal benevolence were good things; loving the world was not incompatible with loving their country. But the early nineteenth century brought with it hardening notions of national loyalty that put pressure on these ideals. As Tocqueville noticed when he toured the country in 1830s, Americans tended towards an "irritable patriotism" that bristled at any criticism from foreigners. "Our Country, Right or Wrong"—a popular antebellum slogan—captured the way that many Americans thought about patriotism.[38]

Garrisonians, however, believed both that democracy, like an ocean, should be ever-restless, and that crossing the ocean was good for democracy. They were wary about the dangers of too much national pride in a democracy like theirs, a concern that was both reinforced by their transatlantic experiences and echoed by transatlantic writers. Contemporary European liberals like Mazzini and Mill also criticized the sort of nationality that encouraged "senseless antipathy to foreigners," and they too defended a vision of democracy in which unpopular or foreign ideas would not only be tolerated but seen as essential to the health of any nation. Placing Garrisonians alongside and within the personal networks of European reformers therefore makes clearer the origins and nature of their own ideas about democracy and patriotism, while also revealing intellectual and practical connections between their agitation at home and their activities abroad.[39]

In sum, the Garrisonians' participation in transatlantic debates about democracy, slavery, and nationalism, reveals abolitionists both as transatlantic agitators and as transatlantic *thinkers*. Although abolitionists usually did not think of themselves primarily as intellectuals, they fit David Hollinger's capacious definition of intellectuals as a community of people who exchange ideas, ask shared questions, and probe the "points of contact between minds." Words mattered to Garrisonians not just as weapons, but also as carriers of ideas. And close readings of their speeches, letters, and pamphlets reveal abolitionists to be appropriate subjects for nineteenth-century intellectual history.[40]

To say Garrisonians were thinkers is not, however, to deny they were activists. On the contrary, Garrisonians were goal-oriented activists who wanted to change politics from without. Although they did not vote or run for office, Garrisonians were extra-parliamentary activists who followed political events closely, thought strategically, and assumed their agitation would have political effects. To be sure, this depiction again differs from the typical view of Garrisonians as reformers who cared little about political outcomes. Historians usually do concede that Garrison "eventually adopt[ed] a strain of . . . pragmatism," but this transformation is typically seen as a late development brought on by the antebellum sectional crisis or the Civil War, "when events overwhelmed his perfectionism." Rather than making a total break from the past, however, Garrisonians were always more interested in politics than is often assumed. Their tack was never one of total withdrawal from political engagement.[41]

Instead, like a later generation of transatlantic liberals studied by historian Leslie Butler, Garrison and other abolitionists "confronted what they considered national flaws with a strategy of dissent and reform rather than a willful retreat from public life." Throughout their careers Garrisonians were politically engaged thinkers, or profoundly reflective activists, neither of which was an oxymoron in the world they knew. Indeed, whether it is ever appropriate for historians to observe a strict distinction between political "activists" and "intellectuals," recent scholars have made clear that such a distinction often broke down in the nineteenth-century Atlantic World. In the European context, historians and political theorists have recently rediscovered "agitators" like Mazzini or Cobden as complex political thinkers, too. Mill has been redescribed as both a sophisticated thinker and an engaged politician. On the other side of the Atlantic, figures once thought of as disengaged intellectuals, like Emerson, Henry David Thoreau, and Margaret Fuller, are now recognized as agitators.[42]

Garrisonians, likewise, were agitators informed by ideas, which were in turn informed by their agitation. Their experiences as a persecuted minority raised a set of shared intellectual questions that they tried to answer in ways that accounted for their experiences. Simultaneously, however, they never ceased to follow political events, to care deeply about their effectiveness, or to consider how well their extra-parliamentary tactics were influencing politics. And despite their criticisms of national pride, they remained vitally concerned with the reputation of American democracy in the world at large, convinced that love for country and shame for country were not incompatible feelings.[43]

Part I of this book begins with Garrison as a teenager, following him through his conversion to abolitionist work and the origins of his transatlantic reform networks. These chapters proceed chronologically, but they emphasize the continuities and persistent ideas that linked the adolescent Garrison of 1818 to the transatlantic abolitionist of 1854. Among the most important of these continuities were Garrison's belief in the special mission of the United States as a republican model to the world, and a related belief that "public opinion" had special power to change American institutions. Those beliefs coexisted with, rather than being supplanted by, the views for which Garrisonians are still better known.

Having discussed the experiences of Garrisonian abolitionists up to 1854, I turn in Part II to the intellectual problems that these experiences posed. These chapters are organized more synchronically. They emphasize the ways Garrisonian ideas resembled and were sometimes informed by transatlantic thinkers and activists like Tocqueville, Mazzini, Mill, O'Connell, Cobden, the Chartists, and the British allies of Garrisonian abolitionists introduced in Part I.

Part III then returns to the chronological narrative, picking up with the democratic revolutions that rocked Europe in 1848 and following Garrisonians into the Civil War, when many new tensions suddenly appeared between longtime allies like Garrison and Phillips. With this tripartite structure, which turns from events to ideas and back to events, I hope to convey something of how Garrisonians themselves turned back and forth between their experiences as transatlantic abolitionists and their ideas about democracy, "public opinion," nations, cosmopolitanism, and the United States. Reasoning in light of their experiences, they also interpreted experiences in light of their ideas.

For the purposes of this book, "Garrisonians" were those members of the American Anti-Slavery Society who remained with the society after a famous split in its ranks in 1840. Yet even on that definition, Garrisonians were a diverse lot. They resist generalization partly because they themselves resisted strict criteria for membership in the AASS. After 1844, Garrisonians in the AASS were somewhat more united by their identification with the motto "No Union with Slaveholders" and their refusal to vote. But they remained divided on a range of questions about violence, theology, capitalism, and much else. When drawing generalizations about Garrisonians, I have thus tried to note significant exceptions to the rule.

My primary focus, however, is on those Garrisonians who belonged to the organization early enough to experience the schism of 1840, who embraced its non-voting tactics during all or most of the 1840s and 1850s, and who then supported the Union war effort and participated in political campaigns after 1861. I have chosen this focus in order to show why postwar scenes like Garrison's trips to Charleston and London were more explicable than they may appear, but my focus does mean paying less attention to Garrisonians who left the AASS long before 1861, or who joined long after 1840, or who were uncomfortable with wartime views like Garrison's—a broad spectrum that includes figures like Parker Pillsbury, George Bradburn, Stephen Foster, Abby Kelley, John A. Collins, and many black abolitionists. On the other hand, I sometimes discuss reformers not typically treated as Garrisonians, like Frederick Douglass. Though he made the decision to support political candidates for election a decade earlier than Garrison and Phillips, he too remained a non-voting "disunionist" throughout the 1840s and thus went through the same transformation they did at a more accelerated rate.

Throughout the book, however, my two main characters are William Lloyd Garrison and Wendell Phillips—two figures who at first seem almost as different as Garrison and Mill. Phillips descended from one of the wealthiest families in Boston's history and was educated at elite schools like Boston Latin and Harvard; Garrison was an ink-stained printer who was viewed as a vulgar fanatic by most Bostonians of Phillips's rank. While it was Garrison who eventually met Mill and Mazzini, it was Phillips who read works by the likes of Mill and Tocqueville and synthesized their arguments with the outlook of Garrison's band.

Despite their differences, each of these men built a life that would not be intelligible apart from the other. Phillips credited Garrison's influence with making him "a better man" and marveled to his friend in 1846 "that our slightly different paths lead always to the same point." After Garrison's death, Phillips confessed that "no words can adequately tell the measureless debt I owe him, the moral and intellectual life he opened to me. I feel like the old Greek who, taught himself by Socrates, called his own scholars 'the disciples of Socrates.'" While Garrison remained the president of the AASS for most of its career, Phillips became the society's leading intellectual and orator—a man so closely identified with Garrison by outsiders that they were seen as inseparable. Together, they helped define the boundaries of Garrisonian abolitionism in the antebellum period, and despite disagreeing on some points, Garrison never seriously objected to any argument Phillips made until the Civil War.[44]

I have chosen to tell a focused narrative of the Garrisonians' movement not because it is the only story that could be told, but because it helps to demonstrate how the age of slavery raised questions for abolitionists about democracy and agitation, too, including questions that persisted for Americans, reformers, and democratic theorists well beyond emancipation. Even the famous rupture between Phillips and Garrison at the end of their careers, discussed in Part III, serves this larger goal. In 1863 and 1864, their lifelong friendship was riven by a sharp disagreement that divided the AASS itself into warring camps. Yet these wartime quarrels emerged from shared questions that long predated and long outlived the specific causes of dispute.

In particular, Phillips and Garrison had spent decades defending the agitation of public opinion both as a necessary, permanent feature of democracy and as an effective way to change politics in a democracy from the outside. Their alliance broke not on those two points, on which they always agreed, but on two unresolved questions that this agreement had obscured: When could and should politicians guide public opinion, instead of the other way around? And how could extra-parliamentary agitators or politicians ever be sure what the state of public opinion was? Those questions remained open after their particular age of slavery had closed, and they persisted for American reformers who lived outside the period covered by this volume. But to later generations of reformers, Garrisonians also bequeathed a cosmopolitan patriotism, a persevering faith in democracy despite its flaws, and a belief in the importance of ever-restless agitation; how and why they did so is the subject of this book.

I

ORIGINS

THE EDUCATION OF
WILLIAM LLOYD GARRISON, 1818–1833

On July 5, 1824, William Lloyd Garrison—then an eighteen-year-old journalist with Federalist inclinations in politics and Romantic tastes in poetry—delivered a patriotic oration in Newburyport, Massachusetts. It did not sound at all like the speech of a future Constitution-burner. On the contrary, like most Fourth of July orators, Garrison described the United States "government [as] the most enlightened, the most liberal, and the most virtuous on earth." The American Revolution was "the pole-star of attraction,—the splendid, immaculate guide,—to all other nations, in their career after freedom." In view of these facts, any American who was not filled "with patriotic ardor" was "a slave indeed—a monster."[1]

Such lines reveal a Garrison now hardly recognizable, given the reputation he soon earned as a fierce critic of the Union. Yet long before—and even long after—Garrison declared the world was his country, threatened disunion, and burned the Constitution, he assigned the United States a special role as a republican model for the world. Two years before this speech, Garrison had already described the United States as "a model which no other nation under heaven can boast its equal, for correctness of sound republican principles." And even in 1828, on the eve of his conversion to abolitionism, Garrison wrote and publicly read a poem that lauded American institutions: "our deeds and examples are laws to mankind."[2]

Garrison's youthful boasts about the nation partly mark the great distance he had traveled by the time he burned the Constitution thirty years later, on a different Fourth of July. His conversion to abolitionism would eventually make Garrison critical of American vanity; indeed, as early as 1829, Garrison had decided that "the moral and political tendency of this nation is downward," and such censures only became more severe once Garrison became an abolitionist—a transformation as rapid as it was unexpected. When July 4, 1830, arrived, Garrison had just spent seven weeks in a Baltimore jail for accusing a Newburyport merchant of being a trader in slaves. By the next Fourth of July, he was editing the *Liberator*, and one year after that he already had a transatlantic reputation as an uncompromising abolitionist who described the Constitution as a document "*dripping . . . with human blood.*" By the time Garrison made his first Atlantic crossing in 1833, the patriotic apprentice from Newburyport had been reborn as a radical.[3]

Yet Garrison did not simply doff his youthful ideas about the United States, fold them up, and lay them aside as he began his radical career, like grave-clothes left behind at a resurrection. Even in his first antislavery speech, on July 4, 1829, Garrison described the Fourth as "a proud day for our country" that had given "an impulse to the world, which yet thrills to its extremities." These views died hard, if they ever died at all. On the very day in 1854 when Garrison torched the Constitution, he first delivered a speech praising the Fourth of July as "the greatest political event in the annals of time."[4]

Garrison made such statements because of his belief in republican government, which predated and outlived his abolitionism. As a young man he credited the American Revolution with "vindicat[ing] the omnipotence of public opinion over the machinery of kingly government" and for "[shaking], as with the voice of a great earthquake, thrones which were seemingly propped up with Atlantean pillars." In 1854 he still believed that the principles of the American Revolution demanded the "eternal dethronement" of all despots everywhere. Even in 1865, as the Civil War drew to a close, Garrison rejoiced that Americans could finally fulfill their high calling as "world-wide propagandists in the cause of human liberty and republican institutions, through the power of a glorious example."[5]

The roots of these wartime ideas about the nation lay as far back as the 1820s, the decade when Garrison first learned to see Americans as "worldwide propagandists." In fact, far from being dislodged by his conversion to abolitionism in 1829, Garrison's idea that the United States should be a model for the world played an underappreciated role in spurring his abolitionism in the first place. Garrison's youthful patriotism was not incidental to his abolitionism but integral to it, and his formative years as an apprentice propelled and directed much of his later career.

THE PATRIOTIC PRINTER'S APPRENTICE

Garrison spent most of the 1820s learning the trade of newspapermen, but in that process he forged deep-seated beliefs about the United States and the world. In 1818, on the eve of his thirteenth birthday, Garrison became an apprentice at the Newburyport *Herald*, edited by Ephraim Allen. Lloyd—as his family and friends called him—was quickly promoted to office foreman, and in that position, Garrison spent the next seven years learning both to print news and to read it like an editor. As he learned to mine the "exchanges"—the newspapers that circulated postage-free among early American editors—Lloyd probably spent as much time scanning newspapers as composing them, thereby gaining an eclectic but thorough education in the affairs of the world.[6]

In many other ways, too, the *Herald* was Garrison's door to education. Before 1818, his schooling was confined primarily to religious tutoring from friends of his Baptist mother. Christian faith and the King James Bible remained deeply imprinted on Garrison for the remainder of his life, and in Newburyport, Lloyd became known as a serious young man who pored over sermons and religious tracts and never missed church. But at the *Herald*, Garrison's reading habits also expanded from the sacred to the secular. Allen introduced him to Shakespeare, Sir Walter Scott, and Lord Byron, and young Lloyd developed a voracious appetite for this new literature—especially the poetry.[7]

Working at the *Herald* also baptized Garrison into the political culture of New England Federalism, for Allen belonged to a Newburyport elite that was trying to save the dying Federalist Party. Allen gave his young foreman access to his large library of writings by Federalist heroes like Fisher Ames, and Lloyd rapidly absorbed their views. Later, when editing his own paper for the first time, he selected a Federalist slogan for the masthead: *"Our Country—Our Whole Country—And Nothing But Our Country."*[8]

Lloyd's education was never confined to the canons of high Federalism, however. Allen's office was also awash with exciting foreign news. Simón Bolívar was completing a victorious campaign for Latin American independence from Spanish colonial rule. The year 1821 witnessed an uprising against Austrian rule in Naples and the beginning of a decade-long struggle for Greek independence from Ottoman rule. In 1820, Spanish liberals demanding constitutional government unsettled the power of conservative monarch Ferdinand VII. And the Greeks' eventual, hard-won independence from the Ottoman Empire coincided with another revolution in Paris in July 1830.[9]

These reports charged Garrison's imagination with the idea that a new age of liberty was underway. Nor was he the only American transfixed by political upheavals abroad. As the nation's semi-centennial approached, Americans were still seeking to demonstrate the legitimacy of their own revolution, and many were eager to conclude from the news they read that "the popular cry throughout Europe, is, for forms of government more liberal," as the *Herald* put it in 1821. Americans were equally eager to take credit for this growing "popular cry" and seized on any evidence that Europeans regarded them as a model.[10]

In May 1821, for example, the *Herald* reprinted an editorial from Liverpool which declared that "Austria may triumph over Naples, but America remains a great and inextinguishable beacon, to direct our hopes." A few months later, the *Herald* reprinted an equally gratifying "Extract from a Letter from an American Gentleman Travelling in Europe." The unnamed "American gentleman" had visited the French Chamber of Deputies and witnessed the Marquis de Lafayette praising "the happy government" of the United States, and young Lloyd may well have read the American's conclusion while arranging it in a case of types: "Our system of government occupies greatly the attention of the European governments —wherever their statesmen see a necessity for reform or alterations, they look to see how things are organized with us."[11]

But news from abroad also provided sobering evidence that Europe's crowns and crosiers remained powerful and secure. The Neapolitan revolt against Austrian rule failed. A Polish revolt against Russian rule was crushed at the end of the decade. The 1820 revolution in Spain was undone when French troops, with backing from Austria and Russia, invaded the country. Each of these events pointed to the growing power of the "Holy Alliance" of Russia, Austria, and Prussia, a trio of absolutist governments dedicated to repressing popular revolution in Europe. But even within non-allied countries, liberal reformers began the 1820s under the gun. At the Peterloo Massacre of 1819 in Manchester, England, soldiers fired on an outdoor meeting of parliamentary reformers.

Reports about all these events appeared in the pages of the *Herald,* and Allen also reprinted extracts from liberal English periodicals denouncing the Holy Alliance and its "detestable principles," teaching Lloyd a way of looking at the world at large. Before long, the teenaged apprentice had decided to put what he was learning to use as a writer. In May 1822, Garrison began to slip essays under the door of Allen's office, hiding his identity and secretly delighting when his articles were printed.[12]

The first essays Lloyd published, signed with the pseudonym "An Old Bachelor" or "A.O.B.," were humorous satires. But once he obtained access to the *Herald*'s pages, Garrison quickly graduated to more serious topics. Indeed, of the approximately fourteen communications that he published in the *Herald* between May 1822 and May 1823, half concerned political events abroad. In July 1822, "A.O.B." published a three-part series on "South America." A brief August piece noted rumors of war between Russia and Turkey. Finally, Garrison published a series of three long articles titled "A Glance at Europe," which analyzed the intervention of the Holy Alliance in putting down the Spanish revolution.[13]

Clearly, while immersing himself in Newburyport politics, Garrison was also learning to glance abroad, and what he saw was a world-historical moment as significant as the Age of Revolutions that created the United States. "No time, perhaps, has ever been more interesting to freemen than the present," he noted, pointing to South America, Mexico, and Greece. "The world, at the present juncture, presents a very interesting crisis," in which the spirit of "*Liberty*" was struggling almost everywhere for the "emancipation" of those "yet under the iron yoke of tyranny." The recent invasion of Spain by French armies, for instance, struck Garrison as part of a much larger "contest" between "Despotism" and "the friends of reform throughout Europe and America."[14]

Yet like many patriotic Federalists primed to celebrate the nation's semicentennial, Garrison believed that events unfolding in South America and elsewhere confirmed the superior virtue and foresight of the republicans who founded the United States, which remained, in his view, the model for nations still in their "infancy." Other revolutions were praiseworthy insofar as they "followed the example of the United States," and Garrison hoped "the inhabitants of South America" would "take the United States as a fair and beautiful model by which to direct and govern the affairs of their country."[15]

But if such statements were unexceptional for a young Federalist, in other ways Garrison's articles ranged beyond those of his master's party. When Garrison argued that "the government of the United States [should] be more energetic" in its foreign policy, he aligned less with provincial Federalists than with a new generation of politicians like Henry Clay, who argued that American diplomats should take advantage of European turmoil by recognizing South America's revolutionary governments and forming a hemispheric alliance as a "counterpoise to the Holy Alliance." "An Old Bachelor" contended, similarly, that North and South Americans were natural allies in the struggle against

Old World despotism and should ultimately cooperate as if they were "but one government."[16]

Garrison's first articles also reveal a young man who was beginning to imagine himself not just as a Federalist, but as part of an ocean-spanning group: "the friends of reform throughout Europe and America." This global cloud of witnesses "ardently" hoped for the success of the period's revolutionaries, Garrison wrote, and he identified with them wholeheartedly. Some other Federalists, by contrast, saw recent events as premonitions of the anarchy and bloodshed they associated with the French Revolution. In 1821, one of these more conservative partisans published two articles in the *Herald* which dismissed American criticisms of the Holy Alliance and even defended it as a reasonable league for maintaining law and order.[17]

Garrison's own articles were different. The "Unholy Alliance," he warned, had already proved its determination to wage a "war of extermination *upon the rights and privileges of men*" with "barbarian legions" of "mercenary soldiers." These "Royal Banditti" had forged a "grand engine of destruction, by which . . . to dig up and destroy the seeds which Liberty has planted," and Lloyd was especially concerned about "the Russian Autocrat," who was building an "unwieldy, overgrown empire" capable of crushing resistance even without the help of Austria and Prussia.[18]

Although Garrison continued to toe the Federalist party line on domestic politics, such ideas sounded more like the pronouncements of the Republican administration of James Monroe, who announced the Monroe Doctrine during Lloyd's apprenticeship. In the years between Lloyd's debut as a writer and his debut as a public speaker, Monroe not only recognized Mexico and the new South American states; he and his secretary of state, John Quincy Adams, began publicly rebuking the Russian czar and declaring that New World governments "differ[ed] from Europe in the fundamental principles upon which their respective Governments are founded." Such statements from Washington were not universally approved by Federalists at the time and represented a departure from Monroe's own earlier foreign policy. But they closely resembled the views of "An Old Bachelor."[19]

Indeed, Lloyd seemed to wish that the United States would embrace its role as the leader of a free world and lead the fight against Russia's evil empire and its Allies. In 1824, when Garrison finally rose to deliver his first, patriotic Fourth of July address, he centered his oration on a survey of the recent "convulsions of South America, of Spain, and of Greece" and the lessons they offered "the friends of reform." Speaking to a small audience of the Franklin Debating Club, a young men's group that he helped found, Garrison traced setbacks recently suffered by revolutionaries in these countries primarily to the brutal power of the "leagued Banditti" of the Holy Alliance and France, the Allies' "miserable dupe." Hewing closely to his earlier articles, Lloyd again singled out the "Russian Autocrat," without whom "the Holy Alliance is feeble and helpless," for special censure. But he also expressed renewed faith that "the SPIRIT OF LIBERTY" was rising throughout the world, and his speech began and ended with predictions that "the icy-fetters of old despotism" would soon melt in the blaze of the American "torch," which had already "illumined, electrified, and warmed the world!"[20]

HEROES OF TWO CONTINENTS

Any adherent of the Monroe Doctrine could also cheer these patriotic lines, but Garrison's ideas about Europe probably owed less to the influence of Washington politicians than to the reading he was doing in his spare time. As an apprentice, Lloyd developed a special penchant for the Romantic poetry of Lord Byron and his disciples, whose verses also became lenses through which to see the news of the world.

Byron himself was a guilty pleasure for pious young men like Garrison because of the poet's reputation for infidelity. But Garrison loved the cadences and content of Byronic verse nonetheless. In addition to reading works like *Childe Harold's Pilgrimage,* he even began a lifelong habit of composing poetry, including an early poem entitled "The Shipwreck" that was a transparent homage to Byron. Lloyd, like many young men of his age, was entranced by the death-defying exploits conjured by Romantic poets, who returned again and again to stories of storm-tossed voyages and heroic adventures in the service of freedom. Many years later his sons even remembered Garrison frequently quoting from memory Byron's apostrophe to "The Ocean."[21]

Contemporary revolutions were also frequent subjects in the poetry Garrison admired, which helps explain why Lloyd never favored the present European order over revolution. In April 1825, for example, when Garrison published an ode pseudonymously in the *Herald,* immediately above it was another author's poem "To Greece"—one of countless examples in which contemporary poets took up Greece as a theme. Garrison himself followed suit in a poem he later wrote from the perspective of a Grecian youth "fired with Freedom's flame," and in his 1824 Fourth of July address Garrison excerpted one of Byron's own poems on Greece. His earlier "Glance at Europe" articles were also studded with snippets of verse, including "The Pleasures of Hope" by Thomas Campbell, which warned despots around the world that their days were numbered: "Tyrants! in vain ye trace the wizard ring; / In vain ye limit Mind's unwearied spring: / What! can ye lull the winged winds asleep, / Arrest the rolling world, or chain the deep?"[22]

Poems like this one left impressions still evident years later. But poetry did more than convey and confirm Garrison's perceptions of world politics; it also gave Garrison models of individual heroism that he could use to construct new images of himself. In the early 1820s many young men saw the heroes of works like *Childe Harold's Pilgrimage* not just as fantastical entertainments, but as exemplars to follow in real life. Indeed, Byron deliberately blurred the line between poems and newspapers when he famously traveled to Greece and joined its struggle for independence, eventually dying there in 1824. Byron's story transfixed young devotees like Garrison who imagined themselves on the ramparts, too, and some young Americans—including future abolitionist Samuel Gridley Howe—actually followed Byron to Greece.[23]

Garrison did not. But he read news of Byron's martyrdom as it filtered into the *Herald*'s pages and reportedly fantasized about going to Greece himself. More important than his specific plans, however, is the evidence that the lines between reading and reality often seemed to blur in Garrison's youth. Certainly that was the case in the summer of 1824, not only because of Byron's adventures but also because another larger-than-life hero stepped out of the newspapers at the same time: the Marquis de Lafayette, friend of George Washington and French hero of the American Revolution, returned to the United States for the first time in forty years.[24]

Lafayette's reputation as a hero of the American Revolution prompted national pageantry and public welcoming ceremonies on an unprecedented scale. Eighty-thousand New Yorkers thronged the streets of the city to greet Lafayette when he disembarked in August, and huge crowds greeted him in every city Lafayette visited on his thirteen-month tour. Countless Americans donned Lafayette boots and hats in their returning hero's honor, and Congress assembled in joint session to hear the great man speak. But for young men like Garrison, Lafayette came both as a representative of America's past and as a figure from Europe's present. At the time of his visit he was a leader of France's embattled liberal forces and a sharp critic of the continent's monarchists.[25]

No wonder, then, that Lloyd caught the Lafayette fever only a few weeks after his address to the Franklin Debating Society. After all, Lafayette was a foe of the Holy Alliance that Garrison hated. He was a hero of the revolution that Garrison believed had illumined the world. And he was a European who endorsed Americans' special mission to model republican institutions. The United States would yet "save the world," Lafayette told Congress on New Year's Day, paying the nation a compliment that must have gratified young Garrison. Moreover, the Marquis offered Garrison an embodiment of the heroes in his favorite poems. At Garrison's age, a young Lafayette had risked his life, left his home, and crossed an ocean on a mission for liberty, much like Bryon, and by 1824 Garrison was already dreaming of emulating such men.[26]

On the rainy night of August 31, 1824, those dreams led Garrison to join a large crowd that waited into the night to welcome Lafayette to Newburyport. As the general approached from Ipswich, cannons were fired, rockets were launched, and bells were pealed on the outskirts of town, despite what local reports described as "extreme[ly] unfavourable" weather. By prearranged signal, all the residents along Lafayette's route illuminated their houses simultaneously, revealing "an arch, thrown across State-Street, [that] presented the following inscription:—'The Hero of two Continents.'" Sixty years later, Garrison's sons recalled their father's fond retellings of what happened next. Upon seeing the crowd, a visibly moved Lafayette urged the drenched crowd to seek shelter, and when he invited them to return in the morning and shake his hand, the star-struck Lloyd was "one of the multitude" who did just that.[27]

After he met Lafayette, Lloyd continued his apprenticeship for another sixteen months. But the young man's eagerness to glimpse the Nation's Guest sums up much of what he had learned during his years at the *Herald*. By the time Lafayette arrived, Garrison habitually read the latest news from across the Atlantic. He had honed personal views about transatlantic events that were similar to those of Lafayette and the nation's leaders. And although Garrison had never traveled farther than the distance between Baltimore and Newburyport, he had learned to imagine himself as part of an intercontinental community of liberal reformers. For young Lloyd, the latest dispatches from Greece or Gran Colombia evoked an exciting global drama in which even a teenager in small-town New England could participate by writing pseudonymous columns, delivering speeches, and composing Byronic poems.

He had also learned that the drama could be reversed, however; the world was not yet saved. Much depended, Lloyd believed, on whether new revolutionaries had the mettle of the Americans' founding generation and could keep their fires burning for other friends of reform. The failure of the Neapolitans to win independence from Austria had been all the more disastrous, he thought, because it encouraged the Holy Alliance to intervene in Spanish affairs not long after. In other early columns, Lloyd warned the leaders of the South American republics that, if they did not implement "just government," their failures would "be a great detriment to liberty" in Europe. "For these several years past, the eyes of all Europe, nay of the whole world, have been turned towards South-America," he noted. But for just that reason, if South Americans did not "wipe off the stains already accumulated against them," tyrants would point "the finger of scorn" and "say to *their* slaves, with contempt, 'Behold the blessings of Liberty.'"[28]

When Garrison wrote those lines, he did not yet believe it possible that his own country could encourage European tyranny. He admitted the nation had vices, and in 1825 he conceded, in one of his last *Herald* articles, that Americans were sometimes, "perhaps, too vain." But Garrison emerged from his apprenticeship more impressed by the republic's virtues. "Our vanity is pardonable," Lloyd concluded as he embarked on an independent printing career. The "great and glorious" republic, like Allen's ambitious printer, was still "young, ardent, aspiring, [and] going forward 'on the full tide of successful experiment.'"[29]

PATRIOTIC SHAME AND THE DANGERS OF THE NATION

Garrison learned many things as an apprentice, but abolitionism was not one of them; he said very little about slavery before 1828. In 1826, while editing his own paper for the first time, Garrison did conclude a glowing Fourth of July editorial by noting that a few "dark shades" blighted the nation, singling out "SLAVERY" as one such "curse." But overall, when Garrison used the word "slave" in the 1820s, it was usually to refer to the subjects of kings.[30]

Even after his apprenticeship, Garrison did not immediately move into antislavery work. Instead, he quickly took over three small newspapers, leaving each one almost as quickly. Lloyd's life did not acquire real direction until he moved to Boston in 1827 and encountered the preaching of reform-minded New England ministers like Lyman Beecher. Their sermons quickened Lloyd's piety and directed the young man to support the temperance and peace movements. The energetic work of evangelical reformers and preachers in Boston was especially important to Garrison for two reasons: it gave him a way to combine the sober faith he had learned from his Baptist upbringing with his interest in political and social affairs, and it fired him with the thought that God's spirit was active and abroad in the United States, judging the country's sins while also transforming it in preparation for Christ's eventual return. But while each of these movements changed Garrison—his growing pacifism, for example, tempered his youthful admiration for armed revolutionaries—neither made him an abolitionist. In his writings, breaking the bonds of drink still took priority over breaking the bonds of slaves.[31]

Something had clearly changed, however, by July 4, 1829, when Garrison delivered a provocative antislavery speech at Boston's Park Street Church. Now he suddenly painted a startlingly dark picture of a nation bound for destruction. If emancipation of slaves in the South were long delayed, Garrison now said, "the nation will be shaken as if by a mighty earthquake," with scenes of blood and chaos surpassing those of the Haitian Revolution, and "the terrible judgments of an incensed God will complete the catastrophe of republican America."[32]

Those lines showed Garrison already in the throes of a dramatic transformation from an apprentice in 1825 to a leading member of two radical abolitionist organizations by 1833. Within months of his first antislavery speech, Garrison would join Quaker abolitionist Benjamin Lundy in Baltimore as coeditor of an antislavery paper. Still, even as he became an abolitionist, the young man who had recently caught Lafayette fever continued to imagine himself as part of a global community battling the Holy Alliance. This self-image was only reinforced by Lundy, Garrison's first abolitionist mentor, who showed Garrison that many of the foreign icons he already loved, like Bolívar and Lafayette, were also abolitionists. While some other young Americans had followed Byron literally to Greece, Garrison found in the abolitionist movement his own way to fulfill long-simmering fantasies of joining the global battle for liberty. While imprisoned in Baltimore in 1830, he wrote at least three Byronic sonnets about his plight.[33]

Lundy had been trying for years to vitalize a national antislavery movement with his newspaper, the *Genius of Universal Emancipation*, and he immediately made an impression when the two men met in March 1828 at a gathering arranged by Garrison's employer. Garrison soon began to praise the *Genius* in the pages of the *Philanthropist*, a temperance newspaper he was editing at the time, and Lundy returned these compliments by mentioning his new proselyte in the pages of the *Genius*. For the rest of the year, Garrison admired Lundy from afar. Even after he moved from Boston later that year to take a new editorial post in

Bennington, Vermont, Lloyd studied the *Genius* and spoke of joining Lundy as its editor.[34]

In short, by the time Garrison did move to Baltimore, he owed much of his education about abolitionism to his long-distance apprenticeship to Lundy. Nonetheless, part of Lundy's special appeal to Garrison stemmed from the persistence of the patriotic and Romantic ideals that Lloyd had learned long before, as well as from the specific things he and Lundy had in common.

First, Lundy entered journalism around the same time as Garrison, so he knew the rituals of the trade they shared, like the practice of mining the exchange piles for transatlantic news. The *Genius*, founded in 1821, often carried the latest dispatches from Latin America, Poland, and Greece, and much like other contemporary newspapers, Lundy depicted revolutionaries like Bolívar as heroes. Like Lloyd in Newburyport, Lundy also cited recent events in Spain, Greece, and Europe as evidence that "Monarchy totters on its foundations, and is nodding to its fall." But Lundy, like Lloyd, also worried that the thrones of the world would not go down easily. In one issue, he reprinted a speech on the Holy Alliance by the British antislavery statesman Lord Henry Brougham which depicted the Allies as a "set of despots leagued together against the liberties of the human race," echoing Garrison's own concerns.[35]

Lundy also shared Lloyd's patriotism and a deep veneration for the Declaration of Independence. Its claims that "all men are created equal" and enjoyed inalienable rights appeared prominently on the masthead of the early issues of the *Genius,* and like Garrison, Lundy believed these phrases had world-historical implications. He viewed the spate of revolutions spreading in Europe and South America as "effects" of the "ball of political reformation" that the American Revolution had "put in motion."[36]

In short, Lundy's view of European politics was much like that of "An Old Bachelor," with two crucial differences. First, Lundy emphasized that supporting transatlantic "friends of reform" required becoming an abolitionist. In 1822, the *Genius* published a pseudonymous "Address to the Youth of the U. States" which declared that "no truly great or good man has ever enrolled his name among the advocates for human bondage," while the ranks of slavery's opponents were filled with "illustrious defenders of freedom." The "history of Poetry" also proved that "genius is inimical to slavery," continued the author, posing a series of questions for his "youthful countrymen": "Does the desire for honest fame kindle enthusiasm in your hearts? Would you have your names inscribed on ever-during tablets, with those of orators, patriots, sages, and poets? Then, rally round yon stainless banner that flows on the breezes of liberty." In subsequent issues, Lundy built upon this early "Address" by showing just how many of the era's luminaries opposed human bondage—Bolívar, Lafayette, and more.[37]

Lundy's *Genius* also distinguished itself by claiming that slavery was weakening the influence of America on Europe's political reformation, though here Lundy capitalized on a long tradition of antislavery argument that was revived by the Missouri Crisis of 1819–21. That well-known crisis began when New York Congressman James Tallmadge submitted a proposal to ban slavery from the new state of Missouri. Over the next two years, this plan sparked a political firestorm made all the more intense by Tallmadge's opening confession that he acted out of deep concern for the reputation of the United States abroad. Citing an antislavery letter he received from an Englishman, Tallmadge told Congress that "I felt the severity of the reproof; I felt for my country." "On this subject the eyes of Europe are turned upon you," he reminded his fellow representatives, and "the enemies of your Government, and the legitimates of Europe, point to your inconsistencies."[38]

By citing European opinion about American slavery, Tallmadge mined a rich vein of antislavery rhetoric that stretched to the American Revolution, when many writers on both sides of the Atlantic attacked slavery as a stain on the nation's honor. George Washington himself owned several antislavery pamphlets that stressed this theme, and after England and the United States abolished the transatlantic slave trade, national honor continued to be a sensitive point in diplomatic debates about slavery. Occasional pamphlet wars broke out when American newspaper editors caught wind that transatlantic writers were criticizing the hypocrisy of the United States.[39]

In one sense, then, the Tallmadge thesis—that slavery was being used by European enemies of republicanism—merely gave new life to an old idea, but Tallmadge also placed the relationship between slavery and the nation's reputation squarely in the explosive realm of policymaking. The result, however, was not the one he desired. Missouri was admitted as a slave state in 1821, and the lesson many Americans learned from the crisis was that slavery was a subject best left alone in order to preserve national harmony. Nevertheless, Tallmadge showed a new generation of antislavery writers like Lundy how to combine patriotic sentiment with sharp critiques of American slavery. After founding the *Genius* in 1821, Lundy devoted column space in three early issues to reprinting

Tallmadge's 1819 speech, and in each subsequent volume Lundy made international testimony a central theme. One of his first issues reprinted a newspaper report about an American who had visited a coffeehouse in Vienna, deep in the Holy Alliance, and heard an Austrian exclaiming "shame! shame!" while reading a local paper. When the American inquired about the outburst, he was mortified to learn that the Austrian had been reading about slavery in Virginia.[40]

Lundy continued in this vein by regularly taking notice of antislavery articles and speeches by Bolívar, Lafayette, and other internationally famous figures in the 1820s, including Daniel O'Connell, the leader of a movement for Catholic rights in Ireland. He also highlighted the antislavery edicts of newly independent Latin American republics and contrasted revolutions abroad with slavery at home. In one essay, Lundy even predicted that "the mighty force of *Public Opinion*" sweeping down from the American North would soon join forces with the antislavery republics of Latin America to surround "the fiend of slavery" and drive him off the continent.[41]

That prediction showed Lundy was initially optimistic about the death of slavery. But much depended on whether South and North America would align against the institution, and the passing of years made that seem less and less likely. In Congress, southerners stymied attempts to recognize the independence of Haiti or to curtail slavery in the District of Colombia. In 1826, southern congressmen even defeated a proposal by John Quincy Adams to send an American delegation to a pan-American conference being organized by Bolívar, just because black delegates from Haiti would likely be present.[42]

Still, Lundy carried on. He used Panama as new evidence that slavery was preventing the United States from performing its role as a leader of American anti-colonial states, and he continued to use variations on the Tallmadge thesis in attempts to elicit shame. One typical piece of correspondence published in September 1827, after Lundy had moved to Baltimore, summarized his favorite themes: slavery was affixing "a reproach and a stigma" to "our envied happy land"; the country was "becom[ing] a stink and a bye-word to less enlightened nations"; and Americans had been "put to shame" by "our younger sister republics of the South."[43]

These arguments did not persuade southern congressmen opposing Adams, but they certainly caught Garrison's attention when he and Lundy finally met the following year. After all, Lundy's attempts to mobilize American shame began from premises Garrison shared. As early as 1822, Lloyd had warned that embarrassments to republicanism in one country could injure republicans elsewhere. Now, in reading and talking with Lundy, Garrison was forced to consider that his own countrymen were the ones stigmatizing republicanism abroad.

Indeed, in the weeks surrounding the two men's first meeting, the *Genius* contained several typical articles describing slavery or the slave trade as "a foul and scandalous stain on our government" that attached great "odium" to the country "in the estimation of enlightened foreigners," a fact that "must inevitably . . . degrade our national character in the eyes of the world." An April issue printed an article comparing American slave regulations to those of "the Turks," and another scorned Americans for pretending to sympathize with "suffering Europeans" without sparing a thought for "the Blacks." In June Lundy also reprinted an article by English abolitionist James Cropper, which bluntly stated "that negro slavery is an evil which the United States must look in the face. To whine over it is cowardly; to aggravate it, criminal."[44]

Finally, on July 12, 1828, Lundy published a letter which offered a sobering assessment of American slavery in light of current events "throughout the world." Its writer had never submitted anything to the *Genius* before, but the letter, originally intended for publication on the Fourth of July, rehearsed themes so familiar to Lundy that they were almost formulaic. "The liberal and enlightened minds of Europe exultingly point their countrymen to the example of the United States of America," argued Lundy's new correspondent, while "the minions of royalty are literally watching for evil, and rejoice whenever a fit occasion offers to brand our country and its institutions with opprobrious epithets." American slavery "has furnished an enduring theme of reproach" among the enemies of republican government, making it essential to speedily remove "this foul blot from our national character."[45]

Here was a letter so perfectly pitched to a reader like Garrison that it could have been written by Garrison himself, and it very well might have been his work. It was signed "W.L." and closed with a lengthy quote from Campbell's "The Pleasures of Hope," the same poem Garrison quoted in one of his last *Herald* essays. But whether "W.L." was William Lloyd or not, subsequent months showed how much he had learned from letters like this one. In the *Philanthropist* Garrison now published articles calling for an end to slave trading in the District of Columbia so that "the reproach which is affixed to us as a nation may be forever taken away," adding in another public letter that the "reputation of the nation is involved in the controversy." And in March 1829, Garrison wrote an antislavery poem, later reprinted in the first volume of the *Liberator* as "The Fourth of July," which depicted a personified Liberty blushing with shame "in this her sanctuary and home."[46]

The clearest evidence of Lundy's impact came, however, in Garrison's Park Street Church address on July 4, 1829, which first fully revealed the ideas animating him since the previous March. The central reason Garrison gave for his new commitments was summarized in the speech's title: "the *Dangers of the Nation.*" The nation now faced the literal danger of "armed and desperate" slaves seizing their own freedom, Garrison believed. But more figurative dangers were no less serious and were possibly more immediate—especially the dangers posed to the nation's reputation. "Every Fourth of July," Garrison said, Americans assembled to hear the Declaration of Independence recommended to "the admiration of the world." Yet the outrageous "contradiction [that] exists between our creed and practice" led Garrison to the climax of his speech: "I am ashamed of my country." The first Fourth had been a glorious day worthy of the world's compliments, Garrison told his listeners, but now, he "could not, for my right hand, stand up before a European assembly, and exult that I am an American citizen, and denounce the usurpations of a kingly government as wicked and unjust," or else "the recollection of my country's barbarity and despotism would . . . cover my cheeks with burning blushes of shame."[47]

Such statements suggest how quickly Garrison was learning to imitate Lundy's style—and he kept learning after moving to Baltimore and becoming co-editor of the *Genius* in September 1829. In this new role, Garrison published on the progress of antislavery reform abroad, noting that "the efforts of the friends of abolition, in Great Britain, absolutely put to shame every thing that is doing in this country." He printed an editorial by a minister commenting on similarities between slaveholders and "the lordly Turk." And Garrison also participated in the paper's frequent coverage of liberal figures abroad. He published news about Lafayette's attempts to rally anti-monarchical forces in France, and he noted a speech by O'Connell which denounced American slaveholders and compared Washington unfavorably with Bolívar. "However mortifying the concession may be to our vanity, as a people," Garrison noted, there was no way to deny that Washington was a slaveholder, which "must seal up the lips of the American people, and cover them with confusion and shame."[48]

These were remarkable concessions from a young man who, in his first speech five years before, lauded Washington as the country's "political Saviour," the man who had "severed" the "chains" of Americans when "he found us en-slaved." Yet these earlier views were also important precursors to Garrison's conversion. His newfound outrage about the nation drew power from the high station to which he and patriotic abolitionists like Lundy assigned it in the first place. Propelled to Baltimore partly by his patriotic shame, Garrison would learn there how to mobilize such shame in others.[49]

BLACK ABOLITIONISTS AND THE BIRTH OF THE LIBERATOR

The dangers to his nation helped spur Garrison to a new career as an abolition-ist, but they did not make him an advocate of immediate emancipation. In his Park Street Church address, Garrison endorsed gradual emancipation and the plans of the American Colonization Society (ACS), a well-connected organiza-tion which advocated the removal of manumitted slaves to the African colony of Liberia. Garrison was beginning to doubt colonization by the time he joined the *Genius*, but even then he accepted colonization societies as useful in the larger antislavery cause, a position that followed Lundy's own toleration of coloniza-tionists' plans. Garrison did not definitively reject those plans until a series of transformative encounters with free black abolitionists who pushed Garrison beyond Lundy's mentorship.[50]

Nevertheless, Garrison did not jettison all of Lundy's lessons; on the contrary, Garrison and his new allies continued to make the mobilization of shame a cen-terpiece of their own antislavery appeals. It was also through Lundy that Garri-son first became aware of publications like *Freedom's Journal*—an African Ameri-can newspaper founded in 1827—and Lundy's personal connections introduced Garrison to active groups of black abolitionists in Baltimore, Philadelphia, and Boston. Even Garrison's first editorial in the *Genius* showed that their views were making an impact on him. He noted, for example, that the preferences of "our free coloured people" posed a probably insuperable obstacle to the plans of the ACS.[51]

These doubts about colonizationism only grew over the next year. By Janu-ary 1830, if not earlier, Garrison had read and pondered David Walker's *Appeal to the Colored Citizens of the World*, an incendiary pamphlet whose author had served as a subscription agent for *Freedom's Journal*. Walker ended his *Appeal* with a long chapter attacking the ACS, and Garrison soon encountered other black abolitionists who echoed Walker's arguments. While visiting Pennsylvania with Lundy sometime in the summer of 1830, Garrison met the wealthy black

Philadelphian and Revolutionary War veteran James Forten, a staunch anti-colonizationist who soon became one of Garrison's most important patrons.[52]

Not long after, Garrison resolved to return to Boston and build an anti-colonizationist movement around a new paper: *The Liberator*. His very first issue, published on New Year's Day in 1831, offered a full recantation of his very brief career as a colonizationist, and for the next year and a half, he opened the *Liberator* to numerous African American writers who made the case for immediate emancipation without colonization. Finally, in June 1832, Garrison released a 238-page pamphlet entitled *Thoughts on African Colonization*, which collated his own arguments over the past year with dozens of anti-colonization resolutions adopted by meetings of free black northerners. Three years after his first anti-slavery address, Garrison's rebirth as an "immediatist" was complete.[53]

This transformation represented more than a rethinking of the pace or process of emancipation, however. His contacts with free people of color also pushed Garrison to a broader attack on racial prejudice. From men like Forten, Garrison learned that free black northerners were not the "aliens and foreigners, wanderers from Africa" that often appeared as stock characters in colonizationist literature. Rather, he now saw, they professed deep "attachment to this country," the land of their birth and a nation for which some, like Forten, had literally fought "during our revolutionary struggle." Patriotism became a bridge for Garrison's tentative crossings of the color line, for even the severest critics of white Americans, like Walker, expressed a belief that the United States was still worth saving. "What a happy country this will be, if the whites will listen," Walker noted in a paragraph that Garrison quoted in his *Thoughts*. "What nation under heaven, will be able to do any thing with us, unless God gives us up into its hand?"[54]

Testimonies like Walker's convinced Garrison that colonizationists were motivated by "unchristian prejudices . . . against a sable complexion," encouraging him to widen his indictment of racial prejudice in the North. In his twelfth issue, Garrison called a Massachusetts law banning interracial marriage "preposterous," and not long after, he described marriage between blacks and whites as "proper and salutary." Garrison also opened his columns to black writers who offered their own "thoughts on color" and made the case for racial equality. Meanwhile, these arguments, combined with the fact that the agents of the *Liberator* included black men, made Garrison a lightning rod for criticism in northern states, where he and his allies would often be accused of racial "amalgamation."[55]

Garrison became even more controversial after Nat Turner's famous slave revolt of August 1831, which killed dozens of white men, women, and children in Virginia. Many contemporaries connected these scenes of terror to the recent appearance of abolitionists like Garrison and Walker, and Garrison hardly dispelled their fears with his reaction to the revolt. While disclaiming a desire for violence, Garrison argued that, if the American Revolution was justified, so too were uprisings by slaves. The gruesome reprisals that followed the revolt only demonstrated further the depraved character of the nation. Slaves in the South received enough encouragement to revolt from "across the ocean" and from the revolutionary rhetoric that resounded every Fourth of July without needing his encouragement, said Garrison. But such language revealed just how far Garrison had diverged from Lundy, whose reaction to Turner's revolt dwelt more on the slaves' "butchery" and "bloody rage" than on the power and hypocrisy of white Americans.[56]

Nonetheless, there were still many continuities between Lundy, Garrison, and his new black allies, who used shaming arguments much like the Quaker's. Forten shared many of Garrison's assumptions about the influence of the United States on the world, and Walker also made the contrast between the American Revolution and slavery one crux of his attack on colonizationism. His *Appeal* ended by reproducing key passages from the Declaration of Independence and offering them up for the inspection of "the whole world." Just as Lundy had printed articles by European liberals like O'Connell to embarrass Americans, Walker also praised the British as the "best friends [of] the coloured people"; compared American slavery with the "barbarity of the Turks"; and warned that slaveholders would not be able to hide their crimes "from the rest of the world" by collecting funds for "the Greeks, Irish, &c."[57]

Garrison, meanwhile, continued to use the global reputation of the nation as a way to mobilize sentiment against colonizationism. When colonizationists argued that whites would never be able to change their own prejudices, Garrison rejected these assertions as "libels upon the character of my countrymen" and pointed to the treatment of people of color in Europe as proof that interracial harmony was possible. "[I]t is proclaimed to the world by the Colonization Society, that the American people can never be as republican in their feelings and practices as Frenchmen, Spaniards or Englishmen!" Garrison exclaimed. "My countrymen! is it so? Are you willing thus to be held up as tyrants and hypocrites for ever? as less magnanimous and just than the populace of Europe? No—no!

I cannot give you up as incorrigibly wicked, nor my country as sealed over to destruction."[58]

Clearly Garrison had not given up the rhetoric he learned at the *Genius,* and his anguished address to "my countrymen" suggests how much of his own love for country had survived his growing disgust with it. Even in 1832, Garrison retained his assumption that Americans should be more "magnanimous and just" than "the populace of Europe." And he clung to the hope held out by Walker that the United States could become a happy country.

These continuities between Lundy's rhetoric and Garrison's were only strengthened by circumstances overseas, for the founding of the *Liberator* coincided with another wave of revolutions. Between 1829 and 1832, Greek revolutionaries won the nation's independence from the Ottoman Empire, bringing to an end the protracted struggle that had killed Byron. In July 1830, liberal forces in France overthrew their monarch, King Charles X. The next month, an uprising in the Netherlands began, eventually resulting in Belgian independence. Later in 1831, Polish soldiers rebelled against Russian rule in the so-called November Revolt. Then, the following year, Parliament passed the Reform Bill of 1832, encouraging a popular abolitionist movement that had been growing in size and strength through all these episodes.[59]

Garrison certainly noticed these events, announcing in his first issue of the *Liberator* that "Europe has just begun to feel the upheavings of the earthquake which is to overthrow its strong towers, and the heat of a fire which is to melt every chain." "The empires of the old world are in travail with liberty," he told potential subscribers, "and revolution is marching onward with an earthquake step, and thrones are crumbling to the dust, and fetters are everywhere falling." These upheavals struck Garrison and his new allies as auspicious signs. "When we . . . hear of almost every nation fighting for its liberty," Forten told the *Liberator,* "is it to be expected that the African race will continue always in the degraded state they are now?"[60]

Forten's answer was "No," as was Garrison's. In a speech to multiple groups of "free people of color" in June 1831, Garrison declared that "the signs of the times" in Europe promised "sudden changes in the condition of the oppressed. . . . [T]he wave of revolution is dashing in pieces ancient and mighty empires—the hearts of tyrants are beginning to fail them for fear." The times were no less stirring as the second volume of the *Liberator* began. "The Spirit of Liberty . . . is abroad with power" and "shaking the world," Garrison said in his first editorial of 1832. Indeed, the signs now suggested that "thrones" and "hereditary titles" were doomed to destruction. There would be "no cessation of revolutionary movements . . . until personal thralldom be broken" and "every government be elective and republican."[61]

In these and similar statements, Garrison stressed the revolutionary newness of immediatism, but nothing was more familiar than his desire for "elective and republican" government or his attempt to place American antislavery within a transatlantic context. Like Lundy, Garrison continued to publish testimonies from European abolitionists like O'Connell and Lafayette that slavery was "a dark spot on the face of the nation" that embarrassed those fighting against the Holy Alliance. And he still turned the most recent wave of European revolutions into opportunities for mobilizing patriotic shame. Only two weeks after the Turner revolt, when a huge crowd of Bostonians, including Garrison's once-favorite minister Lyman Beecher, gathered in Faneuil Hall to praise Polish rebels, Garrison denounced "patriotic hypocrites" who praised "Frenchmen, Greeks, and Poles" while excoriating Turner, who deserved "no more censure than the Greeks in destroying the Turks, or the Poles in exterminating the Russians." Garrison later argued that by pledging themselves to assist the South in suppressing slave insurrections, the northern states had become just like the "Holy Alliance."[62]

By thus comparing an enslaved rebel to a European freedom fighter and the American republic to European despotism, Garrison challenged many Americans' most basic ideas about what made their nation unique. Yet even in doing so, Garrison retained his belief that American institutions were at least freer and more open to change than the kingly and aristocratic governments that still plagued the "Old World." Indeed, that was why Garrison relied exclusively on the tools of "public opinion" as he began his crusade. From the start Garrison regularly announced that "the great work of national redemption" could be accomplished "through the agency of moral power—of public opinion—of individual duty," a three-pronged set of means that historians have sometimes too quickly reduced to the single phrase "moral suasion."[63]

Garrison's faith in "moral power" and "individual duty" were undergirded by his brief prior experience in reform movements whose evangelical ethos took for granted that "moral influence, widely and wisely disseminated, is productive of beneficial results." But Garrison's faith that abolitionists should mobilize "public opinion" also rested, as Garrison explained in 1833, on the fact that "ours is a representative Government, subject to the will of the people." He was confident as he began his crusade that "public opinion is the lever of national reform."[64]

That confidence in "public opinion," which many of those who rallied to the *Liberator* shared, rested on two main pillars: first, a widespread belief that the American Revolution had created a government ruled by "the omnipotence of public opinion," as Garrison put it in his Park Street address, and second, a local myth that slavery had been abolished in Massachusetts exclusively by means of "public opinion." Drawing on both those views, one of Garrison's early Massachusetts allies, Robert B. Hall, affirmed in March 1832 that "it is our high privilege to live in the most favored part of a land, pre-eminently distinguished by the special smiles of Heaven . . . under a government, the mildest and most equitable upon earth; enjoying all the rights and immunities of free citizens; and uncontrolled in the formation and expressions of our opinions." These privileges, Hall explained, were the reason why all Americans rejoiced to "see the thrones of despots tottering to their foundations and crumbling to decay" overseas, and they also gave Hall confidence that "the force of public opinion" would remedy the "monstrous evil" that still blighted their "favored land."[65]

Hall's confidence in the power of public opinion in the United States was typical of the New England immediatists with whom Garrison associated at the time: one "Man of Color" who wrote to the *Liberator* affirmed that "public opinion is a masterly engine," while another reader argued that all abolitionists had to do was "to produce a sufficient change in public opinion to put an end to slavery." Later still, in an 1834 series of lectures defending Garrisonian immediatism, Boston minister Amos A. Phelps approvingly cited Lyman Beecher's own judgment that "no nation ever possessed the opportunities and the means that we possess" for effecting "reformations" through "the medium of a rectified public opinion." All of these statements echoed Garrison's own frequent assurances that abolitionists would "conquer through the majesty of public opinion." All that was required was "an entire revolution in public sentiment," and the rest would soon follow: "better conduct . . . contrition for past crimes . . . a reparation of wrongs . . . a healing of breaches . . . a quiet, improving, prosperous state of society!"[66]

As a printer Garrison was also confident that revolutions in public sentiment would begin with the printed word, a faith that may have been Allen's most important bequeathal to his apprentice. But a second continuity from his apprenticeship also carried Garrison into his new career: his youthful tendency to imagine himself as part of a worldwide community of "friends of reform." That Romantic tendency had not abated in all the changes between 1828 and 1831, nor had Lloyd's love for poetry. On the contrary, while editing his first newspaper, Garrison went out of his way to solicit verses from John Greenleaf Whittier, later a celebrated poet and abolitionist whose first published poem, "The Exile's Departure," appeared in Garrison's Newburyport *Free Press*. In the typically Romantic style that Garrison loved, Whittier's poem depicted a Byron-like patriot from Ireland saying goodbye to his homeland after having fought for its liberty, and in future years, Garrison would also forge friendships with other poets who shared his tastes.[67]

Lloyd's continued love for poetry—which he published in a weekly department in the *Liberator*—signified a larger truth: conversion to abolitionism had only amplified his aspiration to live like the heroes he read about in newspapers and Romantic poems. Even the new motto he selected for the masthead of the *Liberator*—"Our Country is the World—Our Countrymen are Mankind"—sent two messages at once. It trumpeted the editor's startling new commitments to ending slavery and combating racial prejudice. But it also encapsulated Garrison's old, familiar claims of kinship with liberal heroes in other countries; he surely knew that "the Liberator" was a nickname that many contemporaries used to refer to Bolívar and to O'Connell.[68]

In short, the young man who shook Lafayette's hand still imagined himself as part of a transatlantic host fighting for freedom and "elective and republican" governments and still often blurred the lines between poetry, the news, and his own life. When writing to three of his staunchest black supporters in 1831, for example, Garrison dramatically assured them that he was ready to die "to achieve your complete emancipation, and to promote the happiness of my country," much like Byron had laid down his life for liberty. Garrison's letter cited "the inspiring words of the poet" and quoted Lord Byron's belief that "they never fail who die / In a great cause." In the same letter, Garrison paraphrased a line from "To the Memory of the Spanish Patriots," by Thomas Campbell, another of his favorites: "The martyr's blood's the seed of Freedom's tree."[69]

Garrison had not yet shed a drop of blood for his views, of course, but he clearly believed he had found the "great cause" that could compare to Byron's sacrifices for Greece, or to Lafayette's for America. Perhaps that was why, in an address to the "colored people" that same summer, Garrison also inserted a quote from a recently published ode to the 1830 French Revolution:

> A voice on every wave,
>   A sound on every sea!
> The watch-word of the brave,
>   The anthem of the free!
> From steep to steep it rings,
>   Through Europe's many climes,
> A knell to despot Kings,
>   A sentence on their crimes. . . .

As a budding immediatist, Garrison continued to hear the revolutionary voice on "every wave" and "every sea," and in 1833, that thought would continue to propel him as he made his own first passage across the ocean's waves.[70]

THE TROUBLOUS OCEAN OF
TRANSATLANTIC ABOLITIONISM, 1833–1840

arrison's first time crossing the Atlantic Ocean shared one thing with all his future crossings: sea-sickness. On May 1, 1833, his New York–to–Liverpool packet ship had not even cleared the bay before Garrison's stomach was "vanquished" by "a petty tumult among the waves!" Thirteen years later, after five more crossings of "the restless deep," Garrison confessed that "I shall never get reconciled to the ocean. Though I am fond of agitation, it does not run in that line."[1]

Garrison nevertheless saw his first Atlantic crossing as "providential," nausea aside. He spent several mornings discussing Parliament's West Indian emancipation bill at the Guildhall Coffee House in London. He "procur[ed] a large collection of anti-slavery documents, tracts, pamphlets and volumes" to use as "ammunition" at home. He helped combat a representative of the American Colonization Society who was in England raising funds. He met leading British abolitionists like Cropper, O'Connell, and William Wilberforce, all of whom signed statements against colonizationism. And most importantly of all, he met abolitionist lecturer George Thompson, who became a lifelong friend and a lynchpin in future transatlantic networks.[2]

Yet for Garrison, the significance of his first Atlantic crossing went beyond these achievements. For a young man who swooned to Romantic poems about heroism and revolution, crossing the ocean was also a journey of imagination and self-fashioning. Though he traveled to England instead of to Greece, Garrison was finally fulfilling his own Byronic dreams. Before setting sail, the young editor wrote several letters modeled on typical Romantic poems about seafaring and the ocean. In one, he imagined himself standing on a high mountaintop and surveying the world below. He could see "the flames of a thousand burning [African] villages fearfully reddening the wide heavens." As he turned to gaze on the Atlantic expanse he would soon cross, "the troublous ocean throws aside its blue curtain, and reveals to my vision an African golgotha,—the bodies of the dead, men, women, and babes, tracking the paths of the slave ships, and numerous as the waves that chant their requiem."[3]

Such lines were the latest examples of Garrison's tendency to read himself into Romantic poems, whose narrators often found themselves alone on mountains, reflecting with anguish on the evils of the human world below. Images of the "troublous ocean"—shipwrecks, suffering travelers, and storms—were also common motifs in this poetry, and Garrison's vision of the Atlantic as an African "golgotha" echoed earlier antislavery poets and their grisly evocations of the slave trade. Now, by repeating those images, Garrison cast himself as a heroic traveler willing to brave both the physical dangers and moral terrors of an ever-restless ocean. "Unto the winds and waves I now commit / My body," Garrison wrote in a shipboard sonnet, bidding adieu to "my much beloved yet guilty country." He knew his "resting place may be the watery pit," but his "deathless soul" would confront the peril undaunted.[4]

These were not the words of a man who believed that going to England was only about fundraising or gathering tracts; they were the words of a man who imagined himself as the liberty-loving patriot in "The Exile's Departure," or like Lafayette, the Hero of Two Continents who also crossed an ocean on a mission for freedom. But those exalted visions inevitably led Garrison to exaggerate the newness of his trip. He was far from the first abolitionist to see the value of obtaining British support, and although his *Thoughts on African Colonization* had earned Garrison a transatlantic reputation, by the time he arrived the black New Yorker Nathaniel Paul and the English abolitionist Charles Stuart were already working to undermine the Colonization Society. Although Garrison's trip created new transatlantic abolitionist networks, in the beginning he followed in the wake of others.[5]

Garrison could take credit for one innovation, however: before leaving England, he persuaded George Thompson to lecture on abolition in the United States. Other abolitionists were not all convinced of its wisdom, yet this new tactic flowed from Garrison's earlier beliefs about the United States and his experiences attempting to mobilize patriotic shame. He was confident a visit from Thompson would succeed because he continued to believe that Americans would respond to appeals to "public opinion," especially from foreigners.

In the years to come, that belief was sorely challenged by a violent anti-abolitionist backlash provoked by Thompson's visit; crossing the ocean on anti-slavery missions would be more "troublous" than Garrison or Thompson realized in 1833. Nonetheless, Garrison's belief that foreign appeals could mobilize patriotic shame proved as difficult to extinguish as his aversion to sea travel. After Thompson was forced to return to England in 1835, Garrison and other abolitionists did not stop building transatlantic networks or soliciting rebukes from abroad. In the coming years, Garrison's first voyage became the first of five round-trips, and Thompson's became the first of three. Soon, new immediatists also followed in their wakes, including Wendell Phillips, who became one of Garrison's most important new allies in the late 1830s and eventually gained a transatlantic reputation of his own.

BRITISH ABOLITIONISTS AND MORAL LAFAYETTES

Garrison's 1833 trip to England was one of the first projects undertaken by the New England Anti-Slavery Society (NEASS), a group founded in the winter of 1832 by local activists who rallied around the *Liberator*. From the beginning, however, the NEASS was a tiny group, because, as Unitarian minister Samuel J. May quickly learned, supporting Garrison meant social proscription.

May, like Garrison, was initially a colonizationist, knew Lundy, and founded a local auxiliary of the ACS in Brooklyn, Massachusetts, on the same day that Garrison delivered his 1829 address at Park Street Church. But in October 1830, May traveled to Boston and heard several lectures by Garrison, who was raising money for the *Liberator*. Soon thereafter, May recommended Garrison, whom he regarded as "a providential man," from his pulpit. In doing so, however, he alienated his congregation and most of his family. His parents went to their graves still recoiling from their son's association with Garrison.[6]

Other early white allies of the NEASS had similar experiences, including Oliver Johnson, David Lee Child, his wife Lydia Maria Child, and May's cousin Samuel Sewell. The NEASS was a controversial and pioneering organization because of its rejection of colonization, its grassroots tactics, and, especially, its interracial ethos. The society was founded in the African Meeting House in the heart of Boston's black community, and it quickly encouraged radical new collaborations between white and black abolitionists.[7]

Few New Englanders were willing to join such a group, but those who did shared some of the strategic assumptions that Garrison had learned from past antislavery writers. They, too, made the mobilization of shame a mainstay of abolitionist rhetoric. In 1831, for example, May delivered a sermon castigating American audiences for sympathizing with Greece and Poland in their struggles against Turks and Russians, while ignoring how "we ourselves are implicated with the oppressors." Even now "a stinging reproach is often sent home to us from abroad; and we deserve it all." Three years later, May delivered a Fourth of July address that again lingered on the descent of the nation: "Genius of America! Spirit of this republic! . . . The tyrants of the earth cry out to thee, and say—Aha! aha! 'Art thou become like unto us?'" These lines, in turn, became the epigraph for one of Whittier's early antislavery poems, which also blasted Americans for demanding freedom for the Greeks and Poles: "Will not the scorching answer come / From turbaned Turk, and scornful Russ: / 'Go, loose your fettered slaves at home, / Then turn and ask the like of us!'"[8]

David Lee Child also frequently said that slaveholding America deserved "the contempt of the world," but unlike others he had lived the Byronic dream of fighting in a European revolution. In 1823, while serving as a secretary for the American legation in Portugal, Child traveled to Spain to enlist with the liberal constitutionalists who were then fighting against the invading armies of French monarchists, memories he could summon ten years later at the annual meeting of the NEASS. "How small and contemptible must we appear in the eyes of enlightened and impartial foreigners!" Child exclaimed. In the same year, his wife, Lydia Maria Child, put an actual face on these "enlightened and impartial foreigners" in her famous *Appeal in Favor of the Class of Americans called Africans*, which soon became a touchstone text for immediatists. In 1833, Child told readers about a Brazilian man she knew who had been harassed on a Massachusetts steamship because of his color. "You Americans talk about the Poles!" the Brazilian declared. "You are a great deal more Russian than the Russians."[9]

In short, New England immediatists in the early 1830s drew, like Garrison, from a deep well of shaming rhetoric. And despite their reputations as dangerous supporters of "amalgamation" who threatened the racial order, Garrison's allies also believed they could change public sentiment in New England, both by pointing to foreign rebukes and by joining with elite black New Englanders to support projects of "elevation" within free black communities like the construction of schools.[10]

Old England seemed like an obvious place to seek support for these new projects. After all, abolitionists there had a long history of organized protest stretching back to the campaign against the slave trade in the 1780s and 1790s, and in recent decades, popular mobilization had flooded Parliament with antislavery petitions. While American abolitionists still lacked the beginnings of a national organization, British abolitionists had organized a new Agency Committee in the summer of 1831 solely for the purpose of advocating emancipation in the West Indies. In the fall of 1832 Garrison began receiving "cheering letters" from these "British philanthropists," and NEASS president Arnold Buffum soon became convinced that "Garrison in England will do the cause more good in 3 months than in 12 in America." Garrison, for his part, had no doubts about "what my reception will be in that country." "The British abolitionists waste no ammunition," he told May. "When I see what they are doing, and read what they write, I blush to think of my own past apathy."[11]

The admiration of American abolitionists for "coadjutors in England" only increased after Garrison's return, thanks to Parliament's passage of its West Indian emancipation bill in 1833, a pivotal legislative victory that spurred the founding of the American Anti-Slavery Society (AASS), the first interstate organization devoted to immediate emancipation. The society's Declaration of Sentiments, composed by Garrison in December 1833, professed the group's solidarity with "the friends of liberty all over the world." Arthur Tappan, the society's first president, expressed the view of many members when he predicted that "the impulse given to the cause by the movements in England would . . . aid us greatly here."[12]

From the beginning, the AASS placed the British example at the center of its work. It appointed a secretary of foreign correspondence, a significant post held in its early years by Garrison and William Jay, son of famous jurist John Jay. Abolitionists also quickly established an annual ritual that lasted through the remainder of the antebellum years: on every First of August—the anniversary of the day in 1834 when West Indian emancipation went into effect—abolitionists gathered in large numbers to celebrate the event, staging a subversive alternative to the Fourth of July.[13]

But the act of British emancipation presented American abolitionists with problems as well as opportunities. Parliament's initial act struck Garrison and other abolitionists as deeply flawed: it compensated planters, and it required freed slaves to remain apprenticed to their owners for six years. Reporting from England on the bill's passage, Garrison lamented that the West Indian planters' lobby in Parliament managed, through "colonial chicanery," to thwart the will of "the British people" for total emancipation. "It is not an example for us to imitate, but a precedent for us to shun."[14]

Garrison's concern about the bill was lessened, however, after a renewed popular campaign to abolish the apprenticeship system succeeded in 1838. He and others also remained more impressed by the mass protests that British abolitionists mounted before 1833 than by the compromised bill that resulted. Garrison was especially struck by the mobilization of British women who sent numerous massive petitions to Parliament. Garrison viewed these efforts as exemplary models, especially since most abolitionists still believed the people's voice would be harder to stymie in the United States. There, he and others were sure, reformers could rely on the omnipotence of public opinion even more than in Britain, where aristocrats retained the power to thwart the popular will.[15]

Yet the success of British emancipation also created problems for American abolitionists in the arena of public opinion. Slaveholders perceived conspiratorial, ulterior motives behind the British Empire's antislavery policies, and West Indian emancipation sparked a more militant form of proslavery rhetoric from American southerners. Even northerners often proved receptive to these arguments because of deep strains of Anglophobia in antebellum culture. West Indian emancipation occurred while Andrew Jackson, an inveterate hater of England, occupied the White House, and his supporters were easily convinced that England's embrace of abolition was an attempt to destroy the Union, incite slave insurrections, ruin the American economy, or do all of the above. For decades, American abolitionists would constantly battle the impression that they were really the tools of a hostile British Empire.[16]

British abolitionists foresaw this future unfolding even in 1833. Having already battled against Anglophobia in earlier attempts to cooperate with French abolitionists, many veteran English reformers were reticent when Garrison first proposed an American visit by George Thompson, one of the chief orators for the Agency Committee. Not only did such a tour seem like a departure from the strategy of building free black institutions designed to demonstrate respectability; it also seemed to invite conspiracy theories about British interference. When Garrison proposed a tour by Thompson at the home of the genteel British abolitionist Thomas Fowell Buxton in 1833, Buxton objected with a prescient question: "would not there be strong prejudices excited against him, on account of his being an Englishman?" Cropper likewise wondered whether English abolitionists would be "stepping out of our proper place in paying Agents to travel in the United States."[17]

Such a trip would certainly be unprecedented, for even American abolitionists had rarely entertained the idea. In the mid-1820s Lundy printed a letter calling on abolitionists to "induce Lafayette to come to America and engage in the abolition of *slavery*," but nothing came of this "Lafayette Plan." Meanwhile, English abolitionists had never contemplated sending a paid agent to America. Even when Thompson finally crossed the Atlantic in 1834, his trip was funded primarily by members of newly founded abolitionist organizations in Glasgow and Edinburgh instead of by leaders in London. In all future years, no abolitionist would ever travel to the United States as official representative of an English antislavery society.[18]

Nonetheless, Garrison was optimistic about his Thompson plan. He began to publicize Thompson's "contemplated visit" in March 1834, and later that month, Thompson told Garrison, in a letter signed "your Atlantic friend," that he planned to sail for New York towards the end of May. After that, he would "consult with your society and act as you may deem best."[19]

By that time, Thompson and Garrison already had begun an instinctive friendship. Separated in age by only eighteen months, both men had broken with more conservative antislavery reformers to take up immediatism. Both were educated informally and built careers as professional agitators. Thompson, like Garrison, also saw his antislavery work as part of a larger movement for liberty around the world, and after Garrison returned to the United States, the Englishman spent time lecturing not only to abolitionists, but also on behalf of Polish exiles from the December 1830 uprisings against Russian rule. The two young abolitionists had so much in common that Garrison, who married Helen E. Benson after returning to the United States, hoped Thompson and his wife would stay with the Garrisons in their new cottage. Later, Lloyd and Helen would name their firstborn son George Thompson Garrison.[20]

Garrison's enthusiasm about Thompson's tour was prompted by more than friendship, however. The tour made sense strategically according to the logic of the Tallmadge thesis and the mobilization of shame. Here, it seemed, was a way to bring foreign antislavery testimony directly to American audiences instead of waiting for distant figures like O'Connell or a stranger like Child's Brazilian friend to speak out. Garrison's own youthful memories of Lafayette's tour taught him to believe that Americans would pay attention to European visitors, for better or for worse, and his announcements of Thompson's visit in the spring of 1834 show that he had the "Hero of Two Continents" on his mind. In March Garrison wrote that his friend's American tour deserved comparison with "the spectacle of the chivalrous Lafayette's embarkation for this country."[21]

The same reasoning explained why Garrison and others were excited by the appearance of another new ally in the spring of 1834—Charles Follen. Follen, who was born Karl Follen in Germany, had immigrated to the United States in 1824, arriving on the same packet ship that carried Lafayette across the Atlantic a few months before. Ten years later, he was the first professor of German at Harvard, an active new member of the NEASS, a vice-president of the fledgling AASS, and a perfect example of what Garrisonians hoped Thompson could be when he arrived.[22]

Follen exemplified the views that American abolitionists had long attributed to liberal Europeans about their country; before leaving Germany, he called America a "promised land," but soon after his arrival, he grew dismayed by the model republic's pervasive racism. By the end of 1833, Follen had read Child's *Appeal* and heard of Walker's, and he had married the American-born Eliza Lee Cabot, an active member of the Boston Female Anti-Slavery Society, founded in October 1833. Finally, in March 1834, Follen made his first public speech as an abolitionist, in the same month when Garrison announced Thompson's upcoming visit. Two months later, after Follen spoke at a meeting of the NEASS, Garrison wrote excitedly to his future brother-in-law that an overflow crowd of 1,500 people had turned out to hear the German's "excellent speech."[23]

Garrison's excitement stemmed both from Follen's high social standing in Boston and from his European past. Follen was a highly respected Cambridge intellectual and prominent Unitarian minister, and he was also no ordinary immigrant: Follen had fled Germany because of his connection to radical groups whose mission was to assassinate conservative figures, and he came to the United States after spending several years in exile in Europe. During that time Follen even befriended Lafayette—who was instrumental in helping Follen secure a position in Cambridge. It was no wonder, then, that Follen immediately struck Garrison as an invaluable ally. As English writer Harriet Martineau later put it, here was both a "victim of the Holy Alliance" and an "American abolitionist" who "declined to prosper as an American by flattering the nation's sin." Such a figure was rare indeed at the time, and Garrison wanted him to appear at more abolitionist gatherings. In May, Follen again drew a standing-room-only crowd in Salem, and later that spring, the officers of the NEASS enlisted him to help draft the society's inaugural "Address to the People of the United States."[24]

It was a wise invitation, for in this "Address," Follen played perfectly the role that American abolitionists had long imagined for enlightened Europeans. He credited the American Revolution with kindling "the extinguished lamp of liberty" abroad. But he also spotlighted the pall that slavery had thrown over the republic's reputation. Now, Follen warned, England "goes before us as a torch-bearer, leading the way to the liberation of mankind." "Shall the United States, the free United States, which could not bear the bonds of a King, cradle the bondage which a King is abolishing?"[25]

With questions like these, Follen was already demonstrating to New England immediatists the potential power of having a liberal European on their platforms, increasing their confidence that Thompson would soon rouse American audiences to shame as well. Indeed, Garrison believed that Follen and Thompson together could be the abolitionist movement's "moral Lafayettes," to borrow a phrase he later used to describe Thompson. Thompson's "errand of mercy" to this "vaunted land of liberty" would be full of "sublimity" and "moral heroism," Garrison predicted a week after one of Follen's speeches. In the *Liberator*, he commanded the "billows" he had crossed the year before to "be gentle . . . and ye winds, propitious," for a "nobler freight was never borne to our shores."[26]

"THE REIGN OF TERROR"

The winds and waves soon gave Garrison his wish, safely depositing Thompson in New York in September 1834. His troubles began on shore. Thompson immediately commenced a series of antislavery lectures in the North, echoing arguments like Follen's at many early stops. America, he said, was "peculiarly an anointed cherub" and a nation "peculiarly blessed." But "all eyes were now turned toward the United States of America, to see if that land of Liberty, of Republicanism, of Bibles, of Missions, of Temperance Societies, and Revivals, would direct her matchless energies to the blessed work of enfranchising her slaves, and elevating her entire colored population."[27]

Unlike Follen's similar comments, however, Thompson's speeches raised a firestorm of protest and violence in the North. Thompson was harassed from the beginning by mobs and threats from local committees that they would not tolerate a "foreign emissary" in their town. Indeed, the tour soon became a focusing point for a broader wave of anti-abolitionist violence that peaked between July and October 1835. That summer there were 109 riots in the United States, 35 of which targeted abolitionists directly. Five were directed at Thompson himself. In Lowell, for instance, a rowdy crowd threw brickbats at the building where Thompson was speaking, barely missing the orator's head. In Concord, New

Hampshire, the house where Thompson was staying was attacked, and Whittier, who was mistaken for the Englishman, was assaulted with rotten eggs.[28]

In September 1835 a gallows also appeared outside Garrison's door. But the most troubling riot came on October 21, 1835, when a large mob disrupted a meeting of the Boston Female Anti-Slavery Society after rumors that Thompson would be appearing there. When Thompson did not show, an angry group instead led Garrison through the streets of Boston by a noose. He was only spared, according to one account, when some members of the mob identified Garrison as an American and took him to the city jail for his own protection.[29]

Despite its unprecedented ferocity, immediatists initially reacted to this surge of violence with old arguments, still hoping they would arrest the onslaught. Reaching for the familiar weapon of shame, Garrison "blush[ed]" for the way his countrymen were treating Thompson and expressed horror that antiabolition riots had taken place not in "Hindostan" or Paris but in "a land boasting of its liberty." "Is it a thing to be told in Europe to our honor, that such a man as Thompson is sneeringly published here as a 'foreign emissary,'" asked another anguished abolitionist. Thompson himself encouraged this rhetoric by writing to Garrison, shortly after he escaped harassment in New York, that he would soon send Garrison details that would "bring another blush for your country upon your cheek."[30]

Garrison and others also reiterated the comparison Garrison had drawn between Lafayette and Thompson. If American patriots had no problem welcoming the former in 1824, Garrison argued, they should have no objection to Thompson. "What had Lafayette to do with the quarrel about liberty between us and the mother country?" he asked one critic in September 1835. "Shall we apply to him the infamous epithets which you have cast upon our *moral* Lafayette?" Abolitionists still hoped to shame Americans with arguments like the ones Thompson himself was making.[31]

Yet the ground immediatists stood on had shifted violently between Garrison's and Thompson's Atlantic crossings. By the time he arrived, the Anglophobic fallout from West Indian emancipation was in full swing, and anti-abolitionists, drawing on earlier proslavery interpretations of the Haitian Revolution, were warning Americans that, when distant agitators talked about emancipation, slave insurrections were sure to follow. By the beginning of 1835, white Americans were primed to see Thompson's visit as the first of a series of events that would result in apocalyptic bloodshed, and the fact that one of Thompson's earliest speeches was on the subject of "Santo Domingo" did not help his case. After hearing Thompson speak in Philadelphia in the spring of 1835, veteran abolitionist Roberts Vaux could tell where things were tending: "The idea of *foreign* interference is very exciting, and the enemies of emancipation will not fail to turn it to the best account."[32]

The violence against Thompson was also part of a larger backlash against the rise of the AASS in the North, sparked especially by increasingly public interactions between white immediatists and people of color. The perception that abolitionists were racial "amalgamationists" had already led to mob violence even before Thompson's arrival. In July 1834, massive anti-abolitionist riots in New York City erupted when black and white members of the AASS gathered to observe the Fourth of July, and the news that "amalgamationists" were now inviting British interference only exacerbated this mounting hostility. On November 5, 1835, just before Thompson returned to England, Garrison witnessed an angry procession of protestors marching by the anti-slavery offices in Boston carrying "a large board, on which were drawn two figures, quite conspicuously—viz. George Thompson and a black woman. Over the head of Thompson were the words 'The Foreign Emissary,'" while the black woman was pictured asking him, "'When are we going to have another meeting, brother Thompson?'" According to Garrison the crowd later took the poster outside the city limits to use it for target practice.[33]

Other anti-abolitionists also increasingly linked the outrage of British interference with racial amalgamation. Edward Clay's 1839 cartoon "Practical Amalgamation," which depicted a Garrison look-alike proposing marriage to a woman of color, also depicted a portrait of O'Connell on the wall behind the illicit lovers. And in 1835, then-senator and future-president John Tyler reinforced the equation in a speech in Virginia. Holding up a copy of an AASS pamphlet, Tyler expressed outrage that slaveholders appeared like "demons" on the cover, while next to some slaves appeared "Arthur Tappan, Mr. Somebody Garrison, or Mr. Foreigner Thompson, patting the greasy little fellows on their cheeks and giving them most lovely kisses." The AASS was not only a "powerful combination" backed by "a foreign emissary," Tyler concluded; it was subversive of the proper relations between whites and blacks.[34]

Clearly, by November 1835, when Thompson quietly boarded a homeward ship, any hopes of his being a second Lafayette were gone. He left more firmly united in friendship with Garrison than ever. But the mobs had shown that future American audiences would not be receptive to "foreign interference." Just before leaving, Thompson confessed that he looked forward to being once again "upon the billows—less turbulent & cruel in their most angry form" than the mobs that had chased him away.[35]

These reactions did not take immediatists entirely by surprise, of course. Nonetheless, American abolitionists *were* caught off guard by the virulence of the backlash against Thompson's tour. Bostonians that Garrison had once respected now scorned him as a dangerous fanatic and questioned his patriotism. In Washington, President Jackson made thinly veiled jabs at Thompson and other antislavery "emissaries from foreign parts" in his annual address to Congress, while popular writers now described the Garrisonian fanatic as "opposed to all patriotism" and "false to his native land." Meanwhile, in the same year as the Boston mob, emboldened Charlestonians publicly burned abolitionist propaganda sent to southern cities by the AASS. News of bounties on the heads of Garrison and Tappan flew northward with the sparks of flaming tracts.[36]

Together these episodes formed part of a concerted campaign to silence all discussion of emancipation forever. In the aftermath of Thompson's tour, southern politicians like John C. Calhoun and James Henry Hammond argued that even abolitionist speech was a danger to the country, and they succeeded in convincing both chambers of Congress to pass an infamous rule banning abolitionist petitions from being read in Congress—the "gag rule." Even Follen found himself increasingly harassed; in 1837, his association with abolitionists cost him his job at Harvard, forcing the German into yet another exile.[37]

By 1836, the *Liberator* warned of a "reign of terror" across the North, and subsequent events lent credence to the idea. In 1837, Elijah Lovejoy, an antislavery newspaper editor in Illinois, was shot down while taking up arms in his own defense. The following year, a more typical mob in Philadelphia torched Pennsylvania Hall—a structure intended for abolitionist events—while city officials stood by, one of many actions intended to destroy abolitionist property and disrupt their meetings. Meanwhile, anti-abolitionists increasingly took the arguments made against Thompson's "foreign interference" and turned them on native-born abolitionists, too. In 1837, while abolitionist Charles C. Burleigh toured Pennsylvania for the AASS, he dodged rotten eggs and charges of being a "foreign agent" simply because he hailed from the distant climes of Connecticut. In the end, Garrison's grand idea to make Thompson a moral Lafayette had backfired in just the ways that London abolitionists had feared.[38]

ONCE MORE ONTO THE SEA

The Boston mob of October 1835 gave Garrison new enemies, but it also brought him closer than he had ever been to the martyrdoms of Byron and other revolutionary heroes. Thompson's tour sharpened Garrison's old images of himself as part of a global liberal movement, in which victories for his enemies were victories for despotism everywhere. While spending the night in prison after the mob, Garrison scrawled a short poem on the walls of his cell, with a sarcastic but telling inscription: "Cheers for the Autocrat of Russia, and the Sultan of Turkey!"[39]

The 1835 mobs also left deep scars on Garrison's memory, however, and the experience of being led through the streets by a rope made him permanently sensitive to any perceived attempts to "gag" him. Over the next few years, as a growing number of abolitionists began criticizing Garrison, he tended to see the specter of the Boston mob and the flames of Pennsylvania Hall looming behind his critics. The effects of the "reign of terror" would be measured partly in painful schisms among abolitionists themselves.

Even so, the "reign of terror" did not halt transatlantic abolitionism. Several American abolitionists quickly followed Garrison across the Atlantic, beginning with the free black abolitionist Robert Purvis—James Forten's son-in-law—who visited Scotland and forged ties between Philadelphia abolitionists and the groups that financed Thompson's tour. In 1838 another Philadelphian, the Quaker abolitionist Edward M. Davis, crossed the ocean armed with letters of introduction and was welcomed by Thompson and O'Connell at the House of Commons. The following year, abolitionists from Oberlin College in Ohio dispatched two men to England to raise funds. These trips also bracketed a fifteen-month European tour by David Lee Child, who reported to abolitionist publications back home that he now found a much different attitude in Europe than in the 1820s, when he had gone to Spain to fight the Holy Alliance. "At that time, the face of a liberal European would brighten at the name of 'American,'" Child said, but no longer.[40]

While Child and others crossed the Atlantic, several American abolitionists also traveled south to the Caribbean, hoping to make abolitionist contacts and study the effects of emancipation. James Thome and Horace Kimball made a November 1836 journey to investigate the post-emancipation colonies of Antigua, Barbados, and Jamaica for the AASS. Two years later, three other abolitionists—Burleigh, Lewis Gunn, and black Philadelphian Robert Douglas, Jr.—traveled to Haiti, where they discovered portraits of Garrison hanging in the meeting rooms of the "Haytien Abolition Society" in Port-au-Prince. Maria Weston Chapman—a co-founder of the Boston Female Anti-Slavery Society and one of Garrison's most trusted supporters since the Boston mob—also made an extended visit to Haiti with her husband and arranged to exchange abolitionist publications with contacts there.[41]

Meanwhile, several British abolitionists reversed the direction of these trips by stopping in the United States on their way home from the Caribbean. In 1839, English abolitionist John Scoble delivered a few lectures sponsored by the AASS while returning home from his own fact-finding mission to the West Indies. Around the same time, Irishman Richard R. Madden, who had been appointed as a judge in Cuba to prosecute illegal slave trading, also traveled to New York, where he testified on behalf of a group of illegally captured Africans in the famous *Amistad* case.[42]

In short, both American and British abolitionists continued to venture abroad, in spite of the "reign of terror." Three main reasons explain why. First, Thompson had brought new converts and organizations into the movement. Many prominent American abolitionists, like Chapman, Henry Clarke Wright, Angelina Grimké, and Sarah Pugh, were first stirred to action by hearing Thompson speak or by meeting him personally. Others, like Francis Jackson, Edmund Quincy, Henry Ingersoll Bowditch, and Wendell Phillips, were so appalled by the mobs that harassed Thompson and other abolitionists that they soon joined the front lines themselves. These individual conversions were also part of a broader growth in the membership of antislavery societies, which well exceeded 100,000 northerners by 1840. And because Thompson's tour had been funded in part by women abolitionists in Scotland, his visit also helped catalyze the growth of American women's antislavery societies. Those results could not help but encourage abolitionists to believe that their existing strategies, including their solicitation of "foreign interference," were bearing some fruit.[43]

Secondly, Thompson had at least forced national politicians to discuss abolitionists, the very thing they had hoped to avoid. Southerners even acknowledged that few things concerned them more than the abolitionists' Atlantic crossings. In a notorious 1836 speech, Calhoun warned southerners that the "war which the Abolitionists wage against us" was not a war of "arms," but a war of words that aimed to debase slaveholders "in our own estimation, and that of the world in general." Hammond agreed and went further in warning about the abolitionists' potential effectiveness abroad. "In England and in France, the developments of popular sentiment are all against us," he said in a speech reprinted in the *Liberator*. "The denunciations heard there reverberate throughout our own country," and time would show that this "growing hostility" would not be "speedily checked." "Agents are lecturing, papers are circulating, societies are forming, and thousands continually joining them," Hammond also said. "It seems as if the world will soon be on fire."[44]

Abolitionists seized such admissions as evidence that their tactics could still be effective. While addressing abolitionists in Port-au-Prince, Burleigh specifically cited Calhoun's 1836 speech as a reason why the Haitians should "bring to bear on the American slave system and its upholders, [the] withering scorn and righteous indignation of the civilized world," for this was "the very thing they most of all dread—even now." Another contretemps in 1839 reinforced Burleigh's points. That year, at a First of August celebration, O'Connell denounced George Washington as a "slaveholding hypocrite" and then described the American ambassador to England, Virginian planter Andrew Stevenson, as a "slave breeder." Stevenson bristled, and soon rumors reached the United States that the ambassador had challenged O'Connell to a duel, sparking a motion, even in the gagged House of Representatives, for an investigation of the rumors.[45]

In short, even after 1835 abolitionists had strategic reasons for continuing ties with "moral Lafayettes." The reaction to Thompson taught abolitionists that their Atlantic crossings had the power to win new sympathizers, while provoking their opponents to lash out in Congress, to threaten duels, or even to cross the Atlantic themselves. In 1836, Robert J. Breckinridge of Kentucky was piqued enough by Thompson's lectures to travel all the way to Glasgow just for a five-day public debate with him. Supporters of both debaters declared victory, but the more important lesson, for abolitionists, was clear: few things were more certain to break their opponents' silence than transatlantic attacks.[46]

Above all, however, American abolitionists continued to cross the ocean because the forces pulling them to Great Britain were stronger than the forces that pushed them away. After 1833 the most powerful empire in the world was committed to emancipation in its wealthiest colonies, and American abolitionists immediately grasped that the British Isles now beckoned as safe havens and points of leverage in an otherwise hostile world. For black abolitionists, the importance of British emancipation was especially obvious, since Britain and Canada extended protection not only to the speech but also to the security of free black men and women. Black abolitionists like James McCune Smith, who was educated as a doctor in Glasgow after being denied admission to medical schools in the United States because of his color, were especially quick to echo Walker's earlier declaration that the English were the best friends of black Americans. But white abolitionists, too, were encouraged by the more hospitable venues for speech that an overseas trip provided.[47]

British abolitionists, meanwhile, talked more about their American friends after 1834. Once at home, Thompson lectured widely about his treatment abroad, and his speeches, together with the essays of well-known English writer Harriet Martineau, cultivated special admiration for the men and women targeted by the Boston mob of 1835. While staying in Follen's Boston home in 1835, Martineau witnessed the treatment of abolitionists and began a lifelong friendship with Chapman, prompting her to write about her experiences in 1838 for the influential English liberal journal the *Westminster Review*. Martineau's "The Martyr Age of the United States," soon published as a pamphlet, painted a saintly portrait of Garrison and his allies, particularly the numerous women emerging as leaders and rank-and-file members of the abolitionist movement.[48]

In short, abolitionists now had more than just a safe haven in Britain; they had an audience. Their newfound publicity also made possible new interpersonal ties. Americans like Chapman began corresponding with Scottish abolitionists like Jane Smeal and Mary Wigham, as well as with Elizabeth Pease, an English Quaker in Darlington who quickly became an indispensable figure in the expanding networks of correspondence among British and American abolitionists. As early as 1837, British women also began sending contributions for annual fundraisers run by abolitionist women in America, a yearly ritual that soon became a crucial ligament in abolitionists' transatlantic networks. By 1839, female antislavery societies in Sheffield, Manchester, and elsewhere were exchanging friendly addresses with women abolitionists in the United States.[49]

Clearly, if Thompson's attackers had hoped to deter "foreign interference," the unintended result was to draw British and American abolitionists together. But in retrospect this was an unsurprising result. For several reasons, British readers and abolitionists were already directing greater attention to events in the United States by the time Garrison crossed the Atlantic. First, the 1830s marked the beginning of a decades-long boom in Anglo-American travel literature that one historian has dubbed the "travel wars." After Frances Trollope's 1832 book *Domestic Manners of the Americans* became a bestseller, British authors flooded the transatlantic book market with travelogues critical of American society, prompting American writers to publish a slew of rejoinders.[50]

These "travel wars" were a boon to publishers, who tried to keep up with demand for books like Alexis de Tocqueville's two-volume *Democracy in America* (published in 1835 and 1840) and Charles Dickens's *American Notes* (1842). But the "travel wars" also had uses for abolitionists; often they informed British readers about slavery and supplied abolitionists with more transatlantic testimonies. In 1835, English reformer Edward Strutt Abdy published a three-volume American travelogue, to the delight of abolitionists who reprinted his sections on slavery. And two years later, Martineau followed with a multivolume work called *Society in America,* introducing even more readers to the arguments of her abolitionist friends in Boston.[51]

Meanwhile, in 1839 British abolitionists founded two new organizations with transnational aims. The first was the British India Society (BIS)—an organization in which Thompson and Pease played leading roles. In 1838, Pease's father concluded that the British Empire could hasten the abolition of slavery by encouraging a viable free-labor economy in India, and in 1838, he shared the rudiments of his plan with O'Connell while riding on a train to a First of August celebration. The following summer, he joined with his daughter and Thompson to form the BIS, and before long the society had garnered endorsements from many abolitionist leaders. Pease also directed informative letters about the BIS to numerous sympathetic American abolitionists, including Davis, Phillips, and Chapman.[52]

A second important organization established in 1839 was the much longer-lived British and Foreign Anti-Slavery Society (BFASS), founded by Birmingham Quaker Joseph Sturge and other veteran abolitionists "to open an active correspondence with the abolitionists in America, France, and elsewhere, and to encourage them by every means in our power." Over the next five years leaders of the BFASS sent representatives to meet with abolitionists in Holland, Denmark, France, Spain and Portugal, and these activities, more than any other single development, greatly encouraged American abolitionists to hope that, despite the troubled beginnings of transatlantic immediatism, smoother sailing was ahead.[53]

THE MOTHER COUNTRY'S PULL

Great Britain always remained the preferred destination for antebellum American abolitionists abroad, and despite their occasional trips to continental Europe, Haiti, or Africa, they had few foreign correspondents there. Most abolitionists— with the exception of highly educated leaders like Phillips, Chapman, and Follen —could only speak English, and that reality created language barriers to cooperation with other national antislavery movements, which were weak anyway in comparison with the British. In 1836, leaders of the NEASS (now renamed the Massachusetts Antislavery Society) underlined the point by rejoicing that West Indian emancipation was accomplished by "a people speaking the same language . . . with ourselves."[54]

Yet such statements hinted at other perceived affinities that explain abolitionists' special attraction to Britain. Although many antebellum Americans were ardent Anglophobes, many were also Anglophiles who celebrated the "mother country" and developed elaborate national histories that located the origins of American institutions in the distant English past. Like a densely woven double-helix, Anglophilia and Anglophobia sat near the molecular center of American culture, helping to determine the shape of individual lives and institutions ranging from churches to political parties. For decades after independence, Americans forged their sense of themselves through complex patterns of rivalry and identification with England.[55]

Abolitionists were no exception. As former Federalists, abolitionists like Garrison and the Childs had been nurtured by a party that defined itself in opposition to Francophilic Republicans. Indeed, the very fact that abolitionists dubbed the anti-abolition backlash a "reign of terror," in allusion to the French Revolution, revealed how deeply rooted that upbringing remained. In an age of transatlantic revivalism, the evangelicals and Quakers who joined the abolitionist crusade also looked on coreligionists in Britain as close sisters and brothers, while some elite abolitionists hailed from families who prided themselves on lineages stretching back to the Puritans.[56]

Two especially Anglophilic abolitionists were the well-heeled Bostonians Edmund Quincy and Wendell Phillips—two of Garrison's most important allies by 1840. The Quincys knew (thanks to research assistance from family friend John Adams) that one of their ancestors was present at the signing of the Magna Carta, and in 1833, Edmund Quincy spent the summer preparing for his family's bicentennial celebration of their arrival in America. Two years earlier, as Garrison began the *Liberator,* Phillips was at Harvard College immersing himself in David Hume's *History of England* and writing senior essays connecting the first English settlers of New England to a long line of English heroes like Edmund Burke, Cromwell, and the Magna Carta's signers. In his first years after graduation, as a young lawyer bored with his practice, Phillips conducted painstaking genealogical research to trace his own family tree back to the Puritans.[57]

Phillips and Quincy, like many of their class and region, were also connected by blood and myth to American Revolutionaries. As the sons of Boston's first and second mayors, Phillips and Quincy (whose grandfather was a revolutionary pamphleteer) were weaned on stories about the city's role as the cradle of liberty, and their reactions to the "reign of terror" were strongly affected by those stories. The event that finally pulled Phillips from the sidelines of the antislavery movement was a meeting held in Faneuil Hall—a sacred space in American revolutionary lore—after the murder of Lovejoy. When the attorney general of Massachusetts rose at that meeting to compare Lovejoy's murderers to the patriots of the Revolution, a horrified Phillips gestured towards the portraits of Adams, John Hancock, and James Otis that hung on the walls and declared that "the glorious mantle of Revolutionary precedent could never be thrown over the mobs of our day."[58]

Americans like Phillips and Quincy saw little contradiction between their veneration of such fallen patriots and their celebrations of the Pilgrims and Cromwell, however. American revolutionaries were heroic, they believed, because they perfected a story of English liberty that long predated them. As Americans and Anglophiles, abolitionists like Phillips thus had little difficulty weaving new English heroes like Thompson into a rich tapestry that already included both Americans and Englishmen. Indeed, Phillips's sense of American history as an extension of English history contributed to his optimism that West Indian emancipation would inevitably influence the United States. As Phillips explained in two 1842 letters to transatlantic friends, he viewed "'English Dissent' . . . in its various forms [as] the parent of modern liberty" and the "mother . . . [of] modern change." Therefore, Phillips continued at a First of August celebration, British emancipation was a case of a powerful "parent" rebuking its "child." "In the name of three million slaves among us, let us thank God that that nation was our mother country—the glass of our public opinion—the source of our literature and our religion."[59]

On both sides of the Atlantic, speeches like these cemented new tactical ties with stories that made the adhesion between transatlantic abolitionists seem inevitable. Thompson told the Edinburgh Emancipation Society how rewarding it had been "to become acquainted with men in a distant country, having one common language and one common ancestry." He brought home an address from American female abolitionist societies to the "Ladies of Great Britain" which likewise began by declaring that "you, as well as ourselves, claim kindred with . . .

the puritan mothers of New England." Such lines also echoed David Lee Child's 1834 oration celebrating British emancipation, which began with a brief history of "our ancestors." "There are probably few of us here," Child mused, "who are not descended" from "the body of the English nation" that had endured centuries of feudalism before giving birth to modern freedom and "the first settlers of New-England."[60]

Here and elsewhere, white abolitionists often failed to note that the black abolitionists so crucial to the immediatist movement could not claim descent from "the body of the English nation." But even abolitionists of African descent often imaginatively wrote themselves into the stream of English history, creating a mythic genealogy for black Anglophiles that was no less imaginative than the suggestion of white Americans that they were somehow the heirs of the Magna Carta. White and black abolitionists alike had powerful reasons to connect themselves to antislavery England with ties of historical memory and myth.[61]

Nonetheless, abolitionists diverged from antebellum patterns of Anglophilia and Anglophobia in two important respects. First, the abolitionists' pantheon of heroes reflected their peculiar antislavery commitments, resulting in the exclusion of some figures whom others venerated and the inclusion of others whom most Americans preferred to forget, like Toussaint L'Ouverture, the hero of the Haitian Revolution. Writing to the Chapmans while they were in Haiti, Quincy went so far as to say that "if [he] were a sentimental traveller [he] would far sooner make a pilgrimage to the tomb of Toussaint than to Mount Vernon." Likewise, Child followed his musings on "the free spirit of England" and its influence across centuries with a section praising "the case of St. Domingo" and crediting Toussaint for making the island "prosperous and the people happy" until Napoleon attempted to reinstate slavery in 1802. In short, American abolitionists drew around their movement a variegated mantle, in which English heroes like Cromwell bumped elbows both with American patriots and freedom's newest champions, white and black.[62]

Secondly, antislavery commitments shaped the abolitionists' unique perceptions of Anglo-American ties in the present. Immediatists began their work at a moment when many literary nationalists—even those who admired England— were troubled by the influence of English tastes and titles on American readers. They recognized that the print culture of the early republic was awash with more British books, newspapers, and periodicals after 1776 than before. Savvy American printers took advantage of the new nation's lax international copyright laws by reprinting transatlantic articles and books with abandon, thereby both creating and supplying a boundless American appetite for cheap British works. For American publishers and readers, the borders of the nation actually became more permeable as they became politically rigid.[63]

Thus, when Phillips praised the "mother country" as "the source of our literature," that observation had as much to do with the actual state of transatlantic publishing as it did with Anglophilia. While southerners could gag petitions to Congress or single out abolitionist publications for burning, abolitionists knew it would be impossible for their enemies to dam the ocean of British print. American abolitionists told their new transatlantic allies that the influence of "the public opinion of England" on America was mightier than they realized. "The chapter of Dickens on Slavery was perhaps more extensively read than any tract on the subject ever published," noted the Massachusetts Anti-Slavery Society (MASS) in one of its annual reports. "Every body reads English newspapers and periodicals." Though the connection of the United States to England was "no longer *colonial*," continued the same report, "it is still, in a very important sense, *provincial*. She is our metropolis after all, to which we look for the fashion of our thoughts as well as of our coats."[64]

These were statements published in 1847, but abolitionists were keenly aware of the facts many years before. In 1839 Phillips emphasized to Thompson that, because England was "the fountain-head of our literature," "the slightest censure, every argument, every rebuke on the page of your Reviews strikes on the ear of the remotest dweller in our country. . . . You have influence, where we are not even heard." Phillips thanked God that "in this, the sceptre has not yet departed from Judah—that it dwells still in the land of Vane & Milton, of Pym and Hampden, of Sharp, Cowper & Wilberforce."[65]

Such lines showed how seamlessly mythology and strategy merged in the thinking of abolitionists. Battered by mobs and charges of "foreign interference," they remained hopeful that Americans' connections to "the land of Vane & Milton" would give "public opinion" in England special influence. National myths, historical memory, present realities, and new interpersonal ties also focused Garrisonians' attentions on the "mother country" and inspired confidence "that the sentiments and feelings of the British nation . . . cannot fail to be diffused among us, their literature being intimately blended with our own." But much of this hope also continued to rest on a faith in the unique responsiveness of American institutions to "public opinion."[66]

CONFLICT AND CONTINUITY IN
TRANSATLANTIC ABOLITIONISM, 1840–1854

The 1840s proved to be an even more active decade of transatlantic abolitionist networking than the previous one, but the decade opened with setbacks. Nathaniel Paul—the black abolitionist who had battled colonizationism in England from 1832 to 1836—died in 1839. Then, in January 1840, Charles Follen was killed in a steamship accident off the coast of New York, depriving abolitionists of a promising link to European liberals and unconverted New Englanders who admired the cultured German.

Meanwhile, even as the ocean took Follen to his rest, abolitionists' transatlantic networks were being battered by intense, internecine quarrels over religion, political strategy, and the role of abolitionist women. These conflicts reached a high-water mark in the summer after Follen's death, when a divisive meeting of the AASS split the society in two. Only a few weeks later, at a contentious London meeting known as the "World's Convention," disagreements between American abolitionists also divided British abolitionists. Garrison emerged from these schisms in control of the AASS, but by 1841 the organization had been severely reduced by mass defections to the abolitionist Liberty Party, led by James Birney, and a new organization founded by the evangelical abolitionist Lewis Tappan.[1]

Many abolitionists shared blame for these conflicts. But at the root of the 1840 splits were different strategic and ideological conclusions about what should be done in the aftermath of the "reign of terror." Memories of mob violence encouraged "Garrisonian" loyalists to insist on unfettered freedom of speech and agitation at a time when others believed abolitionists should focus on slavery and avoid other controversial topics—creating a tactical gap that proved impossible to bridge. Nonetheless, transatlantic abolitionist networks expanded, multiplied, and diversified in the decade after 1840, even as they divided. An unprecedented number of black abolitionists, including Frederick Douglass, Charles Lenox Remond, and William Wells Brown also crossed the Atlantic in these years, skillfully navigating among abolitionist factions and helping to ensure the continued vitality of transatlantic abolitionism. And when Thompson returned for a second American tour in 1851, American abolitionists were more intimately connected to Europeans by ties of acquaintance, travel, and correspondence than ever before.[2]

Unfortunately, these networks only made anti-abolitionists more convinced than ever that Garrisonians were self-righteous, rootless fanatics who did not love their country. One 1847 satire on "World's Conventions," published in New York, pictured a gathering of "worthless humbugs from abroad" who enjoyed puffing themselves up "like bladders filled with wind," while another typical screed, published in 1851, described abolitionists as "philanthropic slough-hounds that are tracking patriotism to its death"—reformers who "set up philanthropism as their supreme deity, and fall down before their rotten god, and worship!" If Garrisonians could not abide the evils of their country, sneered Massachusetts minister George Putnam in 1847, they should "seek a better place to live."[3]

Even Garrison's abolitionist critics grew increasingly severe as the 1840s went on, especially when he began to preach that the Constitution was a proslavery document and that northerners should demand a dissolution of the Union with the South. Some former defenders of Garrison thought of the adoption of "No Union with Slaveholders" as the official motto of the AASS in 1844 as a turn "to the right-about-face." Others wondered how "disunionists" like Garrison and Phillips could consistently remain in the United States, paying taxes and enjoying citizenship, while refusing to support the Constitution. To Garrisonians, meanwhile, such questions sounded too much like Putnam's suggestion that they love their country or leave it. "I was born here," observed a testy Phillips in 1844. "I ask no man's permission to remain."[4]

Yet these conflicts also obscured many continuities in Garrisonian abolitionism even after the schism of 1840. First, Garrisonians expanded their transatlantic networks because they still believed that "moral Lafayettes" could mobilize Americans' shame. Writing from England in 1840, Remond declared that abolitionists were trying to annihilate American slavery so that "not a vestige remains to remind the future traveller, that such a system ever cursed our country, and made us a hissing and a by-word in the mouth of every subject of every Monarch, King, Queen, Despot, Tyrant, Autocrat and Czar of the civilized and uncivilized world!" Likewise, when Garrison returned for a third trip to England in 1846, he repeated his long-held faith that foreign "testimony against American slavery" was one of the best ways to "swell that tide of moral indignation, which, rising like a deluge, shall ultimately sweep the foul system of slavery from the earth."[5]

This resilient faith in public opinion was rooted partly in a faith in the inevitability of universal human progress as moral sentiments gradually improved. As historian David Brion Davis has shown, the workings of divine providence, as manifested in British emancipation, convinced many on both sides of the Atlantic of a "new human ability—the ability of an enlightened and righteous public to control the course of events." Garrisonians likewise believed that because "the Public Opinion of Christendom is the true Law of Nations," "the rebuke of national sins by foreigners, whether uttered in the midst of the guilty nation by the lips, or borne to them on the wings of the press," was still "the mightiest instrument for the regeneration and progress of Society."[6]

Garrisonians also continued to believe, however, that institutions in their own country were especially responsive to "public opinion." As Douglass explained to a Dublin audience shortly after his first Atlantic crossing, "public opinion in America boasts that it is almost omnipotent, and to a great extent this is true; it makes and unmakes laws—it establishes and overturns the customs of society." This was precisely why Douglass still believed that "the influence of public opinion would do much for the slave." Douglass, like many others, would eventually part ways with the AASS in the early 1850s, opting instead to join abolitionists who entered electoral politics. But in his 1845 statements about the peculiar power of public opinion in America, he echoed an assumption that Garrisonians retained, even as critics charged them with deserting the country.[7]

THE SCHISMS OF 1840

The World's Convention of 1840 is best remembered for its divisiveness, but American abolitionists were initially optimistic about the meeting. The idea for the convention belonged to Joshua Leavitt, editor of the official AASS newspaper, the New York *Emancipator*. In March 1839, he called for a "GENERAL ANTI-SLAVERY CONFERENCE" to be held in London to coordinate ties between British abolitionists and abolitionists elsewhere, and BFASS leaders quickly endorsed Leavitt's idea. American abolitionists spent the remainder of 1839 looking forward with high hopes to the meeting. In a famous poem that was printed in the

Liberator and reprinted by the BFASS, Whittier christened it "the World's Convention," while Edward M. Davis told Elizabeth Pease that the convention would be the "greatest [sic] moral light of our times."[8]

Davis crossed out his superlative suffix, but his enthusiasm was typical. Almost a year before the meeting, Angelina Grimké Weld told Pease that, although she often felt, "like thyself, ready to despair of my Country," she "rejoice[d] in the prospect of the World's Convention to be held in England next Spring." Unitarian minister William Ellery Channing, a recent convert to antislavery, likewise hoped the London Convention would be "the sign of a new era." Philadelphia abolitionists predicted that the convention would finally vanquish the "absurd cry of 'foreign interference' in reference to aught which concerns the welfare of man."[9]

Yet disagreement lurked beneath this apparent unity. First, by 1839 many American abolitionists were troubled by Garrison's increasingly caustic criticism of northern churches and clergymen who refused to dissociate themselves from slavery. In 1836, Garrison published a series of editorials denouncing the influential ministers Lyman Beecher and Leonard Bacon for having advised northern ministers not to preach abolitionism. His attacks on clerical authority and church doctrines like the sanctity of the Sabbath increased the next year after he came into contact with the radical "perfectionist" John Humphrey Noyes, who preached a post-millennialist gospel of withdrawal from organized religion. Soon, the appeal of Noyes's perfectionism was also reinforced by a burgeoning friendship with Henry Clarke Wright, another discontented clergyman with heterodox theological ideas.[10]

The closer Garrison grew to figures like Wright and Noyes, the more concerned leaders of the AASS became, especially when Garrison began using *The Liberator* to discuss topics like clerical authority and "non-resistance," a radical brand of Christian pacifism. In 1838, Wright joined with Garrison, Chapman, and Quincy to form the New England Non-Resistance Society, whose agents not only denounced all violence as un-Christian but argued that human governments which relied on the threat of violence were sinful and illegitimate. By 1839 Garrison had concluded that it was even a sin to vote.[11]

Garrison's support for the equal participation of men and women in reform organizations also offended a growing number of abolitionists. In 1837, when Sarah and Angelina Grimké, two sisters from a South Carolina slaveholding family, began delivering abolitionist lectures in the North to mixed assemblies of men and women, Garrison defended their practices and soon began arguing that women could hold official positions in mixed antislavery societies. To many abolitionists, however, Garrison's seeming disregard for social and scriptural conventions about women's roles risked further alienating potential evangelical converts to abolitionism.[12]

These disagreements first led to organizational schisms in 1839, when a group of abolitionist clergymen formed the Massachusetts Abolition Society as a rival to the MASS. In the same year, some political abolitionists in the AASS began preaching the duty of abolitionists to vote, partly in an effort to purge the organization of non-resistants. Deriding "non-resistance" as "no-governmentism," these reformers joined the Liberty Party and began supporting abolitionist candidates for election. Meanwhile, dissensions in the ranks of the Boston Female Anti-Slavery Society led to its own dissolution in April 1840, the same month in which Liberty Party activists met in Albany to nominate Birney for president.

The climactic confrontation between Garrison and his critics came the following month at the annual meeting of the AASS. Following a renewed effort by New England abolitionists to elect female officers, a large number left the meeting to found the American and Foreign Anti-Slavery Society, which provided a home to evangelicals like Lewis Tappan who were fed up with Garrison but unprepared to join the Liberty men. Around the same time, Leavitt and the *Emancipator* also left the AASS, leaving the Garrison-controlled society financially depleted, deprived of its newspaper, and dominated by members from New England, Pennsylvania, and Ohio.

The "World's Convention" in London would soon be roiled by stormy conflicts, too. All the major American factions sent large delegations to London, and the Garrisonian delegations from Massachusetts and Pennsylvania included women. Officials in the BFASS tried to clarify in May that only men would be admitted. But since the Pennsylvania delegation of women had already sailed for London by that time, British officials were left to wring their hands about what the Garrisonians would do when they arrived. One critic, Gamaliel Bailey, hoped that "unfavorable winds" would delay "Garrison with his troop of males and females . . . till the convention is over."[13]

Bailey almost got his wish. Garrison set sail for London immediately after the AASS meetings, accompanied by Remond and New Hampshire abolitionist Nathaniel P. Rogers, a fellow non-resistant. But because of unfavorable winds, Garrison's party missed the meeting's first several days, only to learn upon their arrival that women were only "admitted as *Visitors*." The American women had unsuccessfully protested their exclusion before the convention, and a few male delegates, allied with Garrison and led by Phillips, had used the first day of the meeting to demand the recognition of the American women. But Phillips's resolutions were overwhelmingly rejected; Garrison could register his own protest only by sitting with the excluded women, whose number included Philadelphians Lucretia Mott, Sarah Pugh, Mary Grew, Elizabeth Neall, and Abby Kimber.[14]

Despite their outrage, Garrisonians tried to make the most of the two-week convention. Over five hundred delegates attended the sessions, where they heard addresses by O'Connell and Thomas Clarkson, as well as detailed reports on abolitionism and slavery in Africa, the Americas, the Caribbean, and the Islamic world. When they could, Garrisonian delegates also spoke up in support of points they agreed with. On the third day, Henry B. Stanton—who opposed the inclusion of women at the conference despite the presence of his wife, future suffragist Elizabeth Cady Stanton, in the galleries—rose to emphasize the importance of bringing "the literature of the world" to bear on American slavery, and Phillips seconded Stanton's remarks. Even the most popular American abolitionist tracts probably would "not be read by one in a thousand persons," Phillips said. But when their contents were mentioned "in the *Edinburgh* [Review]," they were more likely to be read in America. "The fact is, although we have declared independence of Queens and Parliaments, that we are yet in contented vassalage to the genius of the mother country."[15]

Such statements showed that American abolitionists still agreed about the tactical logic that led to the London conference. Nonetheless, the exclusion of women from the convention inaugurated a decade of bad feelings between Garrisonians and their critics on both sides of the Atlantic. BFASS officers Scoble and Sturge showed which party they preferred by accompanying Birney and Stanton on a lecture tour after the convention. But the full effects of their decision would not be felt until that fall, when American John A. Collins arrived in England to raise funds for the now-diminished AASS. The society's coffers had been almost fatally weakened by the loss of wealthy patrons like Tappan and a staggering decline in the readership of the *Liberator*, which lost five hundred subscribers in the year after the schism, in addition to another few hundred subscriptions that had to be terminated because of delinquent payments. But English abolitionists almost universally shut their doors and purses to Collins and Remond, who remained in Britain and toured in support of the AASS.[16]

If further proof was needed that BFASS leaders had thrown their support to Tappan's "new organization," it came in 1841, when Sturge traveled to the United States and avoided Garrisonians. Two years later, when the BFASS convened a second international conference on slavery in 1843, Tappan and Leavitt attended, while Garrison and his allies were not invited. Such slights inspired deep resentments against BFASS leaders among Garrisonians that rankled all the more because British abolitionists had been such a source of inspiration. "How melancholy it is to lose all respect for such men as the London Com[mitt]ee," Phillips lamented to Pease in May 1841. "How much two years ago I looked up, how reverentially, to such names as Scoble and Sturge—but then I had not seen them." At the "World's Convention," Garrisonians' glowing image of British abolitionism collided with experience, and the resulting wreckage would wash up on both shores of the ocean for years.[17]

FREEDOM OF SPEECH AND THE SOURCES OF SCHISM

All parties in the great schism tended to exaggerate the uniformity of their critics, however, and to overstate the damage of division. Garrisonians branded all of the abolitionists who left the AASS as agents of "New Organization" and cast their critics as members of a malicious conspiracy determined to silence them. Conversely, Garrison's critics tended wrongly to trace every controversial position he took to the heresies of Noyes and non-resistance.[18]

In reality, Garrison's "new organization" critics were a diverse lot. Many evangelical abolitionists were troubled equally by his non-resistance views, his attacks on the clergy, and his position on the "woman question." But others who supported expanding women's roles in antislavery societies could not brook non-resistance or believed Garrison's attacks on the clergy, while just, were unwise. For still others, it was Garrison's decision not to vote, not his theology, that was counter-productive. Conversely, not every Garrisonian shared Garrison's views on the clergy or non-resistance. Critics often failed to distinguish between the various other reasons that AASS members gave for not voting, and frequently missed the numerous ways Garrison himself diverged from Noyes.

Abolitionists also overlooked what seems clearer in retrospect: external pressures were as responsible as internal factionalism for causing the schism. All of the main players in 1840 had experienced the "reign of terror": Tappan's house had been ransacked and his furniture torched in the streets during the 1834 New York riots, Birney had a printing press destroyed and his office vandalized by a mob in Cincinnati in 1836, and memories of the Boston Mob of 1835 remained fresh in the minds of Garrison and his allies. But because they had learned different lessons from it, the common experience of being attacked ultimately drove abolitionists apart instead of drawing them together.[19]

On the one hand, anti-abolitionist furor convinced Garrisonians that slavery could not be dismantled without addressing other evils—like violence, conservative theology, and opposition to women in public—that directly fueled or failed to prevent the mobs. To men like Birney and Tappan, on the other hand, anti-abolitionist violence and legislative obstacles like the "gag rule" suggested the need for more prudent tactics, focused on political maneuver, church reform, and carefully delimited publicity efforts. Meanwhile, Garrison concluded that the mob of 1835 and the "gag rule" of 1836 were united by one aim—to silence talk about radical ideas—and in subsequent years he interpreted other attempts to quiet him as fruits of the same spirit.

In 1837, for example, when a group of antislavery ministers published a "Clerical Appeal" criticizing the *Liberator*'s harsh language, Garrison sensed a polite but no less determined attempt to "gag" him again. So when his evangelical allies decided not to rebut the "Clerical Appeal," they planted seeds of suspicion that grew over the coming years. An aging Lundy, for example, publicly criticized Garrison's "erratic" tendency to "meddle with other subjects" and "force them into the anti-slavery controversy." Tappan similarly told Garrison privately that the *Liberator* had introduced questions "that had better not have been discussed," using language "not in accordance with . . . the gospel."[20]

In response to such criticism, Garrison consistently pointed out that the *Liberator* was not the official journal of any antislavery organization, and that by trying to press on all members a duty to vote, his critics were the ones forcing rigid doctrines on the AASS. Garrison also maintained that other abolitionists in the AASS could continue to vote, so long as they did not abridge his right to say that voting was a sin *for him*. As historian Aileen Kraditor has observed, the "crucial issue" in the debates of 1839 and 1840, for Garrison, was protecting New England abolitionists' "freedom of speech and advocacy."[21]

That belief also helps explain why Garrisonians reacted strongly to what seem like slight matters. For reasons that their critics never quite understood, Garrisonians were especially outraged by the decision of AASS officers to transfer control of the *Emancipator* to a local New York society just prior to the schism. But they interpreted the transfer as another sign of how far Garrison's critics would go to keep certain conversations closed.[22]

Garrisonians drew similar conclusions on the first day of the "World's Convention," when an officer of the BFASS read a statement declaring "that no topics of a foreign and irrelevant character may be introduced to divide our attention." Even more shocking, though, was the argument made by several other English delegates that to admit women would contravene "the custom of this country." One British delegate argued that "English ladies and English gentlemen are accustomed to consider what takes place on this side of the water, just as American ladies and American gentlemen consider what takes place their side the water." Garrisonians should have understood the call for delegates according to "English phraseology."[23]

To Garrisonians, these arguments sounded too much like the complaints of "foreign interference" they had heard at home. At issue was not national custom, retorted Phillips, but a "matter of conscience." Besides, making a final appeal to national "custom" vitiated the convention's own raison d'être, since by that logic, slaveholders could also claim that slavery was a local "custom," too. Both before and during the meeting, Garrisonians stressed that theirs was a "World's Convention," in which appeals to local custom should have little weight. But English abolitionists responded that the conference had always been intended as a BFASS meeting with guests; the title of the "World's Convention," they argued, was a "poetical flourish" that had no bearing on the meeting's composition.[24]

These attempts to put a lid on further discussion only made Garrisonians stew; many began referring to the "pseudo" or "so-called" World's Convention, for, as one Garrisonian put it, "a *World's* Convention we can no longer term it." Phillips reported to the *Liberator* that BFASS organizers had "persisted in giving an exclusively *English* character to the meeting." And Garrison wryly remarked that he had been "sent over to this country to attend what was to be called the World's Convention," but had not been able to find it.[25]

These complaints about the convention's name have often been overlooked because historians tend to call it the World Anti-Slavery Convention, despite the fact that BFASS organizers always used "the General Anti-Slavery Convention" as its official name. But given the long shadow cast by the "reign of terror," it is easy to see why the name mattered to Garrisonians. The attempt of BFASS officials to gag Garrisonians by appeal to national custom sounded all too familiar. Rogers went so far as to say, in a speech reprinted in the *National Anti-Slavery Standard*, the new official journal of the AASS, that "I would sooner trust our enterprise in the hands of our pro-slavery mob, than with the Committee of the British and Foreign Anti-Slavery Society."[26]

Such gibes did not, of course, mollify Garrison's critics, especially when Rogers was assigned to the editorial chair at the *Standard*. Whittier, who now sided with the Liberty Party, wrote a typically heated response: British abolitionists, Whittier said, were sincere reformers who had come to London expecting to discuss emancipation, not "Yankee doctrines of Equality, or sexless Democracy." Tellingly, Whittier also drew special attention to Rogers's comparison of the BFASS with proslavery mobs, replying sarcastically that "I am not aware how far the 'pro-slavery mob' of Concord [New Hampshire] and vicinity has improved since 1835," but if Rogers had "been, like myself, the target of its brick bats," he would not have compared the mob's leaders to British abolitionists. The wounds inflicted by the Thompson mobs clearly remained very fresh, affecting perceptions on all sides of the schism.[27]

A NEW CIRCLE OF FRIENDS

Just as the anti-Thompson mobs had not killed transatlantic abolitionism, however, Garrisonians' transatlantic ties actually grew stronger after 1840. Reflecting on friendships made in London, Philadelphia delegate Sarah Pugh concluded just before her return home that while not "all we hoped for has been realized . . . we have gained much more than we dared to expect." After the convention, Garrisonians "commune[d] face to face" with longtime correspondents, attended meetings of the BIS, traveled to Scotland and Ireland, and spent long hours with supporters like Pease, who had over a dozen social meetings with Lucretia Mott alone. Through shared meals, afternoon teas, rambling parlor conversations, and overnight stays in British homes, abolitionists made previously abstract ties newly tangible.[28]

Garrisonians also forged new ties at the convention with the few delegates who supported women's inclusion. Among the more prominent of these supporters was the influential statesman and Unitarian John Bowring, who was well known as a supporter of causes ranging from Greek independence to parliamentary reform. Meanwhile, Garrisonians' visits to Scotland netted them staunch allies like the iconoclastic Church of Scotland minister Patrick Brewster of Paisley. Over the next several years women's antislavery organizations aligned with Garrison appeared in Glasgow, Edinburgh, Kirkcaldy and Perth.[29]

But the most important new friends Garrisonians made at the "World's Convention" were William Henry Ashurst and Richard Davis Webb. Ashurst, a radical lawyer, joined Phillips in arguing for women's inclusion at the meeting, and thereafter his household became a central node in the new transatlantic Garrisonian networks that developed after 1840. At his northeast London home, Muswell Hill, Ashurst presided over a circle of Unitarians involved in many radical movements. Ashurst's daughters, for example, were feminists and quickly established friendships with Garrisonian women, especially after Emilie and Eliza Ashurst happened to cross paths with Elizabeth Neall and other Pennsylvania delegates on the continent. Meanwhile, Ashurst became the regular London correspondent to the *Liberator* until his death in 1855, publishing over 130 dispatches between 1842 and 1854 under the pseudonym "Edward Search."[30]

Dublin—the home of Richard Davis Webb—joined Muswell Hill as another new locus of Garrisonian sympathy. Webb, an acerbic Quaker printer and member of the Hibernian Anti-Slavery Society (HASS), traveled to the convention hoping to meet American abolitionists, and afterwards he hosted many of them in his home. There they met two other leaders of the HASS, the Unitarian merchant James Haughton and a draper named Richard Allen. Soon no British abolitionist, with the possible exceptions of Pease and Thompson, became a more prolific transatlantic correspondent than Webb, who was also a regular columnist for the *National Anti-Slavery Standard* between 1846 and 1859.[31]

These English and Irish abolitionists had various reasons for supporting Garrisonians. Many had already formed glowing impressions from Martineau's writings; Webb confessed that he considered himself "most fortunate" to enjoy "the actual society of so many men & women, any one of whom I would have been rejoiced to get a glimpse of through a telescope." British Garrisonians also tended to be Quakers and Unitarians who were tolerant of unorthodox religious views. Finally, Garrisonian supporters hailed from provincial antislavery societies that were already chafing at the haughty oversight of BFASS leaders even before the Americans arrived. After Pease, Allen, and Webb all lodged futile protests with London about its refusal to endorse John A. Collins, Garrisonian allies in Dublin, Edinburgh, and Glasgow made formal breaks with the BFASS. By the end of 1841, there was an identifiable group of British abolitionists who thought of themselves as "Garrisonite."[32]

Over the next two decades, these British Garrisonians helped build an "elaborate communications network," composed first of newspapers. By January 1841, Webb's household received the *Liberator,* the *National Anti-Slavery Standard,* the *Non-Resistant,* the *Herald of Freedom,* and the *Pennsylvania Freeman,* and, as Mott noted in a letter to the Webbs in 1843, this "abundant access to our Anti-Slavery papers" ensured they were extraordinarily well informed about American activities. In 1844, Sydney Howard Gay, then serving as editor of the *Standard*, told Webb that he believed Irish abolitionists were "as cognizant [of the affairs of American abolitionists] as if you daily visited the A.S. [Anti-Slavery] Office in Boston."[33]

Meanwhile, British abolitionists forwarded to America newspapers like the Dublin *Freeman's Journal,* the *British Friend* (founded by Garrison's Scottish ally William Smeal), and liberal sheets like *Douglass Jerrold's Journal* and *The People's Journal.* These and other British papers were not "so much read as devoured" by American friends, as one put it to Webb shortly after arriving home. But the interest of British Garrisonians in American newspapers was, if anything, more intense. "You are my authors," Webb told Rogers in November 1840 after receiving a bundle of *Liberators* and *Standards.* "I almost read my eyes out so that they are only now getting the better of the wasting I gave them."[34]

Private correspondence was a second—and perhaps the most important— material in the Garrisonians' transatlantic networks. So many letters flew back and forth between American and British Garrisonians that obtaining a precise count is difficult, but an extremely conservative estimate would place the number in the thousands, not including the numerous letters that abolitionists on either side of the Atlantic wrote to compatriots about transatlantic friends. Moreover, because correspondents usually treated letters as open communications, these missives were often forwarded, published, excerpted in other letters, or read aloud in groups, extending their reach. In many letters, intimacy between correspondents was only deepened by factional gossip, as each report on the latest quarrel, divulged "entre nous," helped to create a new "us."[35]

The open character of Garrisonians' private correspondence meant that even abolitionists who remained on one side of the Atlantic often became friends with abolitionists on the other. A case in point was Quincy's voluminous correspondence with Webb, which lasted for decades even though the two men could have only met, if they met all, in 1868, when Webb first visited the United States. Pease also corresponded with Chapman and her sisters long before they met. "I almost feel as tho' we had met," Chapman's sister Anne Warren Weston told Pease, who in turn wrote that because she had "conversed together so much" with Phillips "respecting thyself & other Boston friends, I seem unable to realise the fact that we are personally unknown." When preparing to meet a longtime transatlantic correspondent, new introductions rarely occurred between total strangers. Though Chapman met Pease "face to face" for the first time in 1851, she had been "long known in the spirit."[36]

As such statements reveal, letters and newspapers became more than conduits for information; they were also aids to the imagination that enabled distant friends to cope with long separations. James Haughton told Massachusetts abolitionist Samuel May Jr., whom he met in 1843, that receiving a newspaper from him "shows me that I am not forgotten by you," adding that he "reciprocated . . . for a similar purpose, to let you know that your short visit to us lived in our remembrance." While the gross number of British abolitionists who actually subscribed to American prints seldom, if ever, rose into the triple digits, their qualitative value was incalculable. "How near it makes you feel to us," Mott wrote the Webbs, "to read your comments on such recent transactions as are recorded in the Liberator!" Abby Kimber agreed: when reading papers sent by Webb, "I look round almost expecting to see you at my elbow."[37]

Virtual presence was still no substitute for face-to-face meetings among friends, of course, but these were also remarkably common between 1839 and 1855. In that period there was always at least one "old organization" American in Britain or Europe continuously. Some, like Chapman and Wright, made extended tours abroad that lasted half a decade or more, enabling them to create what one abolitionist called a "European branch" of the Garrisonian clique. Meanwhile, in addition to reinforcing friendships, these extended stays introduced abolitionists to a variety of radical and liberal reformers in the Atlantic World of the mid-nineteenth century. Deeply involved in their own local reform movements, British Garrisonians often introduced visiting friends to Chartists, Irish nationalists, and even European revolutionaries living in exile in Paris or London.[38]

For example, the Ashursts were the closest English friends of Giuseppe Mazzini, whose frequent presence at their home enabled him to meet several Garrisonians. Wright described a memorable Sunday afternoon of conversation at Muswell Hill with the Ashursts and their company, which included the socialist Robert Owen and Webb's brother James, as well as Mazzini. "We gathered into a convention, or council, under a magnificent beech tree, in front of the house," Wright recorded, and talked over "the affairs of mankind." The talk continued late into the day, when Mazzini stayed to give Italian lessons in the parlor.[39]

As Garrisonian travelers like Wright made the rounds to Muswell Hill, Dublin, Glasgow, and Darlington, these visitors increased the "intimate relations" between "Trans-Atlantic brethren." Conversely, though trips by British Garrisonians to the United States were much fewer, Thompson visited America again in 1851 and was followed by Ashurst in 1853. These and like visits helped create a "tangible tie of brotherhood" between "Abolitionists of the Old World" and "those of the New," and Garrisonians greeted visitors both as "living epistles" who could report on mutual friends, and as brokers of new relationships. For example, when Samuel May Jr., a Unitarian minister and Garrisonian from Leicester, Massachusetts, visited England in 1843 to rally Unitarians there against slavery, he won several new allies for the AASS, like the Unitarians Mary Carpenter and the Bristol abolitionists Mary Estlin and her father John B. Estlin, a prominent ophthalmologist who opened his home to many Garrisonian visitors, including black abolitionists Frederick Douglass and William Wells Brown.[40]

The Atlantic crossings of black American abolitionists also increased significantly after 1840. Several black abolitionists who were allied with Garrison, including Douglass, Brown, Remond, and others, spent more than a year abroad, and their visits proved especially crucial in shoring up ties between British and American abolitionists. For white British reformers, meeting black lecturers created a unique sense of connection to the American cause, as Isabel Jennings, leader of a group of Garrisonian women in Cork, made clear in a letter to Chapman. "It is very hard for me to think that 'tis far short of two years since we felt that Americans were our brethren—and not the inhabitants of a world with which we had no feelings in common," Jennings wrote. But Remond made her feel a new closeness to American "brethren." While she had "*read*" Martineau's writings on abolitionism before meeting him, those writings were not truly "*felt*" until after C. L. Remond's visit."[41]

As Jennings's comments showed, black abolitionists helped reenergize the commitment of Garrisonians abroad, both by captivating audiences with the details of their harrowing experiences and by publicly praising British abolitionists. At the conclusion of his narrative about his five years in Europe, for example, Wells Brown singled out Estlin as a "model Christian" whose "many acts of kindness" were done "without any regard to sect, color or country." Though black abolitionists themselves were sometimes caught up in the factional strife between "old" and "new" organizations, too, they played important mediating roles between the various parties, often pushing white allies like Estlin to be more inclusive.[42]

In short, although Garrisonians left the World's Convention with new enemies abroad, they also returned home with a "choice circle of friends" and a new set of names—Pease, Webb, Allen, Haughton, and Ashurst—written on "the tablets of our hearts." Those names only multiplied and became more deeply inscribed over the next dozen years. As May Jr. told Estlin in 1846, "it is *one of my greatest pleasures* to receive a letter from my Bristol correspondents." Webb likewise told one of his American friends, "I look on some of you as more than ordinary cousins and acquaintances." Abolitionists sometimes even named actual family members after foreign friends. Having already named his firstborn after Thompson, Garrison named one of his daughters Elizabeth Pease. Conversely, Thompson named children after Pease and Garrison, and a daughter born to British Unitarian Francis Bishop just after Garrison's 1846 trip to Britain was named "Caroline *Garrison* Bishop."[43]

CONTINUITIES

Transatlantic Garrisonian networks would also be strained after 1840 by new internal dissensions, but American and British abolitionists forged deep and lasting bonds that shaped their strategic thinking, provided material and moral support, and encouraged their sense of themselves as cosmopolitan reformers who were not hidebound by local "custom" like the leaders of the BFASS. Garrison's critics saw things differently, however, and usually dismissed the Garrisonians' transatlantic networks when mentioning them at all. Writing to Tappan after the World's Convention, Birney reported that Garrison had done little more than spout his "peculiar views" and "fantasies," pointing to a London speech he had given on the need for a universal language. Likewise, when Garrisonians on both sides of the Atlantic later embraced "disunionism"—demanding that the North dissolve the Union if slavery was not immediately abolished—Tappan saw it as a senseless "crusade against this country & the principal part of the best abolitionists in England and the U.S." In return, Garrisonians frequently mobilized transatlantic networks to attack "new organization" and defend their own interpretation of the 1840 schism.[44]

Yet such criticisms obscured important continuities in Garrisonian strategy. When Garrison traveled to England in 1846, for example, his goals were much like those he had in 1833: to gather antislavery pamphlets and urge British journalists to criticize American slavery. Garrisonian visitors to Europe also continued their familiar attempts to mobilize patriotic shame. While traveling on the continent in 1844, for example, Wright told the *Liberator* about a Polish woman who, upon learning that Wright was an American, asked if he was a slaveholder. Wright made the obvious point, like so many abolitionists before: "the United States, as a nation, has become a hissing and a scorn in Europe."[45]

What changed after 1840 was that Garrisonians could count on many new voices to tell this old story. In England, Estlin repeated the arguments of Lafayette, Thompson, and Tallmadge's English correspondent by warning American readers of "the effect of their Slave institutions upon public opinion in this, and other European countries." James Haughton, George Armstrong, and other new friends likewise informed Americans that their "blotted escutcheon [was] the scorn of the world" and urged them to "WIPE OUT THE SHAME."[46]

The growing number of black American lecturers who traveled to England after 1840 sounded many of the same basic themes. The most famous was Douglass, who escaped from slavery in 1838 and began speaking at New England abolitionist meetings in 1841. When Douglass traveled to the British Isles for the first time in 1845, he showed an exceptional facility with the rhetoric of patriotic shame; no one proved more incisive about the stains on the nation. In Ireland, for example, Douglass declared that he wanted Americans to "know that a slave had stood up in Limerick and ridiculed their democracy and liberty." "Liberty under a monarchy," he told another British audience, "is better than despotism under a democracy."[47]

In Douglass's hands, however, this well-worn rhetoric became sharper and more searing. For example, when Douglass told British audiences that "he was not prepared to say that he entertained any great respect for America," a line that drew "a laugh," he deployed a mordant wit that similar words could not convey when spoken by white Americans. Still, Douglass's speeches were continuous with a long tradition of shaming rhetoric. To an audience in Scotland, for instance, he compared the slaves to the Poles in Russia, and he embraced the same logic abolitionists had long used to justify Anglo-American cooperation. Thanks to the travel wars and the ease of steam passage, Douglass told his British audiences, "tourists were constantly going over" the Atlantic, making international opinion especially powerful. Americans were "vain of their institutions," he explained, and "sensitive in the extreme to the opinions entertained of them in European countries."[48]

In the 1840s, then, black and white Garrisonians abroad shared at least one common aim, even when some well-known conflicts emerged between them. They wanted to draw a "moral cordon" around the United States, in Richard Blackett's felicitous phrase, and direct international scorn at American slavery. What they discovered after the schism was not a new agenda so much as new means for pursuing old aims.[49]

One such new method was the composition of signed international addresses from different British groups to their American counterparts. This strategy had precedents in the active petition campaigns that abolitionists mounted in the 1830s, as well as in canonical abolitionist literature like Angelina Grimké's 1836 *Appeal to the Christian Women of the South*. The idea of internationalizing this "appeal" genre emerged early in the history of transatlantic immediatism; before Thompson made his first trip to the United States, he mailed Garrison a "memorial" drafted by British abolitionists which "we have some thoughts of getting signed as a national document and forwarded to the U. States." But international addresses of this sort were most widely used in the fifteen years after 1840.[50]

For example, in 1841 a group of Glasgow workingmen adopted an address that Garrisonians then published for the view of American workingmen. This was followed in 1842 by an Irish address, signed by O'Connell, Irish temperance reformer Theobald Mathew, and thousands of others, and in 1843 by an address from British Unitarians to "Their Ministerial Brethren" in America, organized by Samuel May Jr. Women's abolitionist groups also gathered signatures for several transatlantic addresses; in 1847 alone, four Scottish women's groups affiliated with Garrisonians composed antislavery addresses to American women that, combined, bore more than 55,000 names.[51]

After 1840 Garrisonians also sought new ways to monitor the actions of slaveholders abroad, having learned from episodes like the Stevenson-O'Connell affair that confronting Americans on British soil could stir public opinion back home. Among the "tourists" whom Douglass said were "constantly going over" the Atlantic were many southerners and their sympathizers, and Garrisonians frequently mobilized their "choice circle of friends" and European representatives to expose any proslavery statements they made while abroad. Two publicity campaigns mounted by Garrisonians—one against the Evangelical Alliance and one against the Free Church of Scotland—also attempted to shame British organizations that accepted donations or memberships from proslavery Americans.[52]

Abolitionists also found new purposes for old activities like the large fundraising "fair" that Garrisonian women organized every Christmas. These antislavery fairs, held in the major cities of the North, provided crucial financial support for abolitionist activities. But the fairs, which at their height lasted for as many as ten days, were also propagandistic events that publicized abolitionism to a diverse cross-section of northerners shopping for holiday gifts. This was especially true of the preeminent fair run in Boston by Chapman and her sisters, which raised thousands of dollars for the AASS and grew significantly in the 1840s—largely thanks to the help of British women who annually sent large boxes of items for sale.[53]

Indeed, a huge proportion of Garrisonians' transatlantic correspondence at the end of each year concerned "boxes" for the fair, which were stuffed with consumer goods like Tartan shawls and tablecloths from Scotland, *papier-mâché* ornaments and knitted curtains from England, and an array of statuary, textiles, china, and stationery collected from various places in Europe. These donations were often responses to the appeals of black abolitionist lecturers like Douglass and William Wells Brown, who paired his famous panorama of American slavery, which he exhibited in Britain in the early 1850s, with an appeal for fair items. By the late 1840s, organizers began to solicit European contributions for the fair as early as the previous spring and summer.[54]

Once the fair finally arrived, its organizers emphasized the "world-embracing" networks behind it. At one fair a placard displaying the *Liberator*'s motto—"Our Country is the World"—was placed at the entrance, while a bust of John B. Estlin was displayed at another; American flags were deliberately excluded from the decorations. After the fair, too, organizers described it in the press as a "microcosmic" event that exhibited all the variety of the world. "The world is like the sea-anemone," said one fair report for 1846: "any part of it, however small, has the capacity of becoming a complete model of the whole; and truly and well does this little world in Faneuil Hall show forth a larger one."[55]

Abolitionists agreed, however, that the merchandise sold gave the most visible evidence of the world beyond the fair. Chapman used a contact she had made while in Haiti to secure hammocks for sale, and after her household moved to Paris in 1848, Chapman and her sisters expanded the fair's European offerings. The Westons also used social contacts in Switzerland and Germany to secure rare items like foreign books, oil paintings, bronzes, busts, ivory carvings "peculiar to Baden," and Bohemian glass. Pease and others sent autographs by O'Connell and reform luminaries; Webb sent books like Gustave de Beaumont's travelogue about Ireland and Proudhon's history of the French Revolution; and the Estlins donated some locks of hair from the Indian reformer Ram Mohun Roy, whom Estlin had treated during his final days in Bristol. These curiosities and stylish European items were especially useful for attracting general shoppers to the fair. In a letter to Mary Carpenter in 1845, Samuel May noted that "English, Scotch, & Irish donations to the Fair" gave it "its greatest pecuniary value, and much perhaps most of its éclat," a judgment confirmed by others.[56]

More importantly, these foreign goods continued to call attention to the "moral cordon" surrounding the United States. Both Douglass and Brown asked for fair contributions not only "for their pecuniary value," as Douglass put it, "but on account of the sympathy they displayed." Others explained that by displaying European goods and testimonies against slavery, abolitionists could impress upon fair visitors that "though anti-slavery is unpopular in America, it is not so the wide world through." And the Garrisonians' European friends made the same point by contributing essays, poems, and short stories to the *Liberty Bell*, a gift book edited by Chapman and sold each year at the Boston bazaar. From 1841 to 1849, Martineau appeared as an author in all but one issue of the *Bell*, and Bowring appeared in all but three. Webb, Pease, Carpenter, Haughton and others wrote frequently, and Frederika Bremer, the radical Swedish feminist, and Lady Byron, the poet's widow, also appeared. Finally, beginning in the late 1840s, thanks to the connections of English friends like the Ashursts and the relocation of Chapman to France, the *Bell* boasted pieces by Mazzini and Elizabeth Barrett Browning, who spent time with the Weston sisters in Paris, as well as by the Russian exile Nicholas Tourgeneff and the Polish exile Alexander Holinski, who also donated $120 to the 1847 bazaar.[57]

More than just a fundraiser, then, the fair represented a continued effort to represent abolitionism as both a *national* movement (the Boston fair was publicized as the "National Anti-Slavery Bazaar" and was often held in Faneuil Hall) and an *international* movement in which British abolitionists remained particularly active as "witnesses to America." In this way, the fairs were end-of-year counterparts to abolitionist celebrations of West Indian emancipation on the First of August each summer, though they arguably placed the movement on an even more cosmopolitan footing with their goods from France and Germany and essays by sympathizers from Italy and Poland.[58]

The First and the fairs, each in their own way, both represented the continuation of strategic assumptions about the special connection between England and the United States. In 1846, for example, Douglass told an English audience that "you have an influence on America that no other nation can have." And Garrisonians continued to believe in the influence of public opinion, both in general and particularly in the United States. As an unsigned article in the *Liberator* put it, Garrisonians were confident that "no individual men or women, however high or low—no individual states or nations, whether young or old—can escape the judgment of public opinion. Russia, Austria, Prussia, shrink from its inflictions," while "the United States and Great Britain are still more amenable to its power."[59]

In sum, the schisms of 1840 exposed deep and real differences between Garrisonians and other groups. The debacle of the "World's Convention" also increased Garrisonians' determination to support the widest range for free speech and agitation. Nonetheless, the continuation of transatlantic networks after 1840 showed the continuation of two beliefs that long predated the "World's Convention" and long outlived it, too: if they could marshal international public opinion to their side, they could almost certainly change public opinion in the United States, where "public opinion" was omnipotent; and if they could change American public opinion, their triumph would be sure.

II

IDEAS

THE PROBLEM OF PUBLIC OPINION

etween 1830 and 1854, Garrisonians were transformed from unknown Americans into an infamous, tightly knit movement with dense connections to European reformers. But Garrisonians remained a diverse lot: no single theology or socioeconomic marker united all members of the AASS, who sometimes struggled to keep their community intact. Garrisonians generally could draw on at least two commonalities, however: a hope that nonviolent agitation would change society in the future, and a set of experiences that made them feel embattled in the present. From these two group traits emerged a third: a habit of reflecting on and critically discussing their ideas and their experiences. Their careers as agitators made them *thinkers,* too.[1]

As thinkers, Garrisonians wrestled with intellectual problems that were widely discussed on both sides of the Atlantic, and that went beyond the problem of slavery itself. First and foremost, their experiences almost inevitably led Garrisonians to confront philosophical questions about the role of public opinion in a democracy like the United States. Indeed, as Garrisonians reflected on their history after the 1830s, many were led to ponder the central question of democracy itself: Was a society in which public opinion was omnipotent always preferable to the alternatives?

Much of the Garrisonians' strategic thinking rested on their faith in the power of public opinion. Both Garrison and Douglass had, at different times, called public opinion "omnipotent" and rejoiced in its rule. That faith even served as a slender piece of common ground with their factional adversaries, for all of whom influencing "public opinion" remained a strategic goal. Even political abolitionists who actively sought to win elections after 1840 saw their pursuit of political office partly as a means of reaching "public opinion" and generating discussion both inside and outside of Congress. Joshua Giddings described the

Free Soil Party, which formed in 1848 with the support of some Liberty Party activists, as a movement that sought to *"correct public opinion, not . . . control political action."*[2]

Yet Garrisonians, even more than other abolitionist groups, believed American public opinion was deeply corrupt, which made its omnipotence troubling, too. Garrisonians understood themselves as a "trampled minority" opposed by sizable majorities both outside and within the abolitionist movement. So they had ample reason to "distrust public opinion," as one abolitionist report put it, even though (or precisely because) they believed in its power.[3]

In retrospect, this ambivalence about public opinion is evident in the earliest texts that Garrisonians wrote. In *Thoughts on African Colonization*, Garrison predicted that "an enlightened and energetic public opinion" could reform the country, but he also admitted that black Americans were, in the meantime, weighed down by "the massy shackles of law and of public opinion." Was public opinion, then, a coercive master or a force for good? The "reign of terror" of the 1830s, far from settling that question, only raised it with new force, especially since anti-abolitionists often described their riots and "gag rules" as legitimate expressions of "public opinion." George Thompson concluded that in America "the minority [was] prostrate before the majority," which was free to "perpetrate every enormity in the name of *'public opinion.'* 'PUBLIC OPINION,'" he bemoaned, "is at this hour the *demon of oppression.*"[4]

Thompson was far from the only contemporary to believe that public opinion could, at some hours, be a demon—the source of "terrors" instead of reform. Indeed, the idea that the public was vulgar and wrong, and that mere "opinion" was something often rooted in irrational prejudice, were commonplaces among thinkers on both sides of the Atlantic. Both ideas lay behind the motto that Garrison chose for one of his first newspapers: "Reason shall prevail with us more than Public Opinion." And for many European commentators, the experience of the abolitionists in the 1830s only strengthened a common association of opinion with unreason.[5]

In his famous entry into the "travel wars," for example, Charles Dickens scoffed at southerners who told him that public opinion curtailed the mistreatment of slaves. "Public opinion!" Dickens jeered in his *American Notes*. "Why, public opinion in the slave States *is* slavery, is it not? . . . Public opinion has made the laws," while at the same time "public opinion threatens the abolitionist with death, if he ventures to the South; and drags him with a rope about his middle, in broad unblushing noon, through the first city in the East"—an allusion to the Boston mob of 1835.[6]

Since he had actually been at the other end of that rope, Garrison could not easily disagree with such critiques. Few Americans better grasped how easily and how long a depraved majority could shackle a minority that was in the right. Indeed, that recognition sometimes led Garrisonians right to the edge of the idea that democracy was fundamentally flawed as a system of government. "Is it republicanism to say, that the majority can do no wrong?" Garrison asked in his Park Street Address. "Then I am not a republican. Is it aristocracy to say, that the people sometimes shamefully abuse their high trust? Then I am an aristocrat."[7]

Garrison did not reason from those questions, as an Englishman like Dickens might, to support for a more aristocratic government. But he and other abolitionists were certainly aware that American slavery made a strong argument against their system of government. In one 1847 editorial, Garrison noted that many contemporary writers believed "republican governments, as now constituted," were not "just, protective, and beneficent," since "the doctrine that might is right, when the majority obtain the reins of power," could become "as essentially despotic in principle, as that of the divine right of kings." The United States seemed to prove the point.[8]

Because they knew these arguments and appreciated their force, Garrisonians faced the task of showing why slavery was wrong, while simultaneously maintaining that rule by public opinion was right. Wendell Phillips, for example, frequently defended the Garrisonians' claims that public opinion would ultimately demolish slavery. At the end of an 1852 speech, he even exclaimed, "All hail, Public Opinion!" Yet in the very next breath Phillips acknowledged that public opinion was a "dangerous thing under which to live." The same "Public Opinion" that ruled one day in favor of abolition could, on the next day, hound abolitionists to death. Three years later, on the twentieth anniversary of the Boston mob, Phillips remembered the mob teaching him "what a republican government really is" and observed "what a miserable refuse public opinion has been for the past twenty years!" Herein lay the problem of public opinion: though potentially a moral resource, it was often a miserable refuse. The first task for Garrisonian thinkers was therefore twofold: to defend a society and a movement based on the power of public opinion while at the same time showing how to mitigate its undeniable terrors.[9]

Although many Garrisonians addressed that fundamental problem, over the course of the antebellum decades they came to slightly different answers. Two major Garrisonian positions on the problem of public opinion emerged. For one set of Garrisonians, the idea of "non-resistance" focused attention on the individual and institutional obstacles that kept an otherwise "enlightened and energetic" public opinion from moving in the right direction. Wendell Phillips, on the other hand, considered the problem of public opinion from the vantage of his often-overlooked admiration for the works of Alexis de Tocqueville. Reasoning from Tocqueville's arguments and his own experiences, Phillips came to some similar conclusions as non-resistants, who believed God worked with them to lead public opinion in the right direction. But, with Tocqueville's help, Phillips also developed his own more bracing critique of public opinion itself as a force whose natural tendency was not to move at all, but to stay at rest—a critique with long-lasting implications for the Garrisonians' movement.

PHILLIPS, TOCQUEVILLE, AND
THE PROBLEM OF PUBLIC OPINION

By the 1840s and 1850s, Wendell Phillips, the well-read and Harvard-educated orator, was widely considered the movement's leading public intellectual. Garrison always remained the chief provocateur and agenda setter for the AASS, but after the "World's Convention," Phillips took up the challenge of making Garrisonians intelligible to the world outside. In the early 1840s, he authored two important pamphlets that laid out the society's positions on the Constitution and voting, and he made himself ubiquitous as a speaker at antislavery meetings and northern lyceums. There Phillips was renowned for translating dense pamphlets like *Can an Abolitionist Vote or Take Office under the United States Constitution?* into electrifying orations that attracted the curious and the converted alike. Indeed, Garrisonians themselves often turned to Phillips to help them understand the society's positions, and very few disagreed with the answers he gave.[10]

Phillips based his ideas, however, on a broader base of reading than most Garrisonian agitators possessed. In particular, Phillips brought to the problem of public opinion a remarkable familiarity with the insights of Alexis de Tocqueville, whose two-volume *Democracy in America*, published in 1835 and 1840, provided the era with its most searching examination of the potential dangers of a society built on public opinion. Unlike typical conservatives who focused their critiques of democracy on the incompetence of the common people to rule, Tocqueville's masterwork argued that a majoritarian society was dangerous not because of the composition of any given majority, but simply because it offered no refuge to any minority or individual who was oppressed. Drawing on his reading of this book, which few other Garrisonians read closely, Phillips developed a theory of democratic agitation that gave Garrisonians powerful new ways to understand their movement.

Both Phillips and Tocqueville wrote at a time when "public opinion" was still a relatively new and undefined concept on both sides of the Atlantic; that was both its appeal and part of its problem. English and French writers first began referring to "public opinion" or "opinion publique" in the second quarter of the eighteenth century. But at that time the phrase connoted older notions of "opinion" as a vague social force that governed fashions, reputations, and collective mores. Not until the latter half of the eighteenth century did "public opinion" take on an explicitly political connotation in England, France, and the United States.[11]

During the era of the American and French revolutions, political actors and Enlightenment thinkers on both sides of the Atlantic began for the first time to invoke "public opinion" as an independent, extra-governmental tribunal to which aggrieved groups could seek redress from absolute rulers. It was frequently associated with the press and civil society, but some democratic radicals used "public opinion" to refer more generally to the popular will. Still others defined "public opinion" not as the opinion of the whole public, but as the outcome of deliberation by well-informed men of letters. Meanwhile, as the nineteenth century began, some conservatives cited "public opinion" to defend monarchism and aristocracy.

One of the few things on which most contemporaries could agree was that "public opinion" seemed to have almost irresistible power. That made even some radical democrats and republicans concerned that "public opinion" was too vulnerable to error or manipulation by powerful elites to make it reliable as a sole basis for government. During the French Revolution, Jacobins began to speak of "public opinion" pejoratively as a cacophony of individual opinions and factions, reflecting a long-standing view that excessive diversity of opinion in a society invited factionalism and disintegration. The sense that "public opinion"—however defined—was becoming more powerful only heightened these anxieties about discord. Post-revolutionary thinkers throughout the Atlantic World agreed that "public opinion" was a force to be reckoned with in the modern world—perhaps an invincible one—yet few praised it outright.[12]

Still, the term "public opinion" appeared often in transatlantic political discourse after 1820, partly because it was so pliable. Many contemporary English reformers, including abolitionists, parliamentary reformers, and advocates of free trade, sought to build support for their causes by citing "public opinion," exploiting the term's multiple meanings in the process. To appeal to aristocratic members of Parliament, reformers often associated "public opinion" with the reasoned deliberations of an educated, respectable, and enterprising "middle class." Simultaneously, invoking the sovereignty of "public opinion" enabled "middle class" reformers to appeal to popular radicals who understood the term as a challenge to aristocratic rule itself. Conservative English aristocrats, on the other hand, still tended to view "public opinion" either as a homogeneous mass or a heterogeneous mess of individual opinions. Both possibilities made them afraid.[13]

In the republican United States, reformers also gave "public opinion" a wide range of meanings. They, like Europeans, often referred to it as an indomitable force. "This is an age," wrote immediatist William Jay in 1837, "in which public opinion has snatched the sceptre away from kings and senates, and reigns an imperious and absolute despot. She may, indeed, be influenced, but not resisted." But in general, Americans, including abolitionists, embraced democratic notions of "public opinion" as a politically sovereign amalgam of all the people's views. Douglass, for instance, defined public opinion as nothing more than "an aggregate of private opinions," and for Phillips, democracy entailed "the most unfettered wildness of thought; it presupposes the most unchecked individualism of opinion."[14]

Nonetheless, abolitionists also sometimes described public opinion as the product of rational deliberation—opinions reached by careful and well-informed thought. No Garrisonian was more gripped by this ideal than Phillips. In his 1852 speech "Public Opinion," Phillips argued forcefully that "the great American idea" was "the omnipotence of 'thinking men,'" and throughout the address, Phillips associated public opinion with the ideas of the "thinking, reading men" of a nation. The primary fountains of public opinion, he argued, were "the school-houses, the school-books, the literature, and the newspapers."[15]

Yet unlike many transatlantic thinkers on the subject, Phillips did not distinguish the "thinking men" of the United States from the masses or regard "public opinion" as a way to keep democracy in check. Though Phillips sometimes spoke of the opinion of the "middle classes" in Britain, he did not view "public opinion" in the United States as the special preserve of any class, thanks to widespread literacy and the nation's teeming newspapers and schools. The American masses, he believed, *were* thinkers and readers.

These were remarkable conclusions for a man like Phillips, born into a Federalist family of mind-boggling wealth and educated at Boston's most elite schools. Phillips was groomed from an early age to imagine himself as part of a natural aristocracy more qualified to govern than the unwashed democratic mobs that flocked to the banners of Thomas Jefferson and Andrew Jackson in the early nineteenth century. But even as a Harvard undergraduate in the early 1830s, Phillips rejected the idea that his education and rank set him apart from the so-called "rabble who know nothing." In one of his student essays, Phillips argued that mass literacy was enlightening all. Now that "the works of the learned" were no longer "sent to be neglected on the shelves of academies," but instead were "scattered" abroad by the printing press, they were "read of all men" and improved "the Many" instead of only "the Few."[16]

Such views enabled Phillips to avoid the problem that troubled so many European conservatives who worried about "public opinion," for in the United States, he believed, almost all opinions were at least partially the products of deliberation and thought. Twenty years after his senior essays at Harvard, Phillips even declared that a republic was by definition "an educated community, where ideas govern;—ideas stamped into laws by the majority, and submitted to by the minority." These points reappeared frequently, too, in his abolitionist career, often in the form of vivid metaphors. Once, Phillips contrasted the nineteenth-century United States with the old feudal "days of nobles and knights," when "a hundred men-at-arms" could best whole armies of peasants thanks to their training and costly armor. Just as the invention of gunpowder had made armor and swordplay pointless, Phillips said, the invention of the printing press meant that "the statesman is no longer clad in the steel of special education."[17]

Phillips knew, of course, that not all Americans were educated or literate. Even so, when he praised the "reading" and "thinking" people of the nation, his intent was the opposite of those who believed that only a small minority was equipped to participate in public life. "The accumulated intellect of the masses," declared Phillips, "is greater than the heaviest brain God ever gave to a single man." Indeed, far from deprecating their competence, Phillips praised their "democratic tendencies" and rejoiced that "the age of the masses has come." He even endorsed the democratic dictum, "'*Vox populi, vox Dei*'—the voice of the people is the voice of God."[18]

Phillips also endorsed the principle of majority rule, despite his role as an unpopular agitator who, like all members of the AASS after 1844, refused to vote. In an 1865 speech on the Maine Liquor Law, which many Americans opposed, Phillips argued that, as soon as the law had obtained "the decided, unmistakable sanction of a majority" and was "put upon the statute-book," at that moment the "reluctant minority" were obliged to submit. Opponents could agitate the question again and turn "public opinion" against temperance statutes, Phillips said. But once a minority was "voted down," "the era of *public opinion* is finished," and "the era of legislation has come,—the time when the minority sits down and obeys."[19]

Phillips undoubtedly found it easier to embrace majority rule in the case of temperance, which he supported, than in the case of proslavery laws, which he abhorred. Yet Phillips consistently described "the duty of the minority to submit" as "that constitution of things which God has ordained." When overruled by a majority, an abolitionist could stop voting and refuse to obey any law he thought immoral or unjust. But in a republic he would have to "submit to all the penalties which my disobedience . . . brings on me." When "the majority have said the thing shall be so," then "a minority has no right to rebel." Even when the majority was in the wrong, as on the issue of slavery, a minority's duty was to reopen discussion on the matter and try "to convert" public opinion to its side.[20]

In short, thanks to the printing press and republican institutions, Phillips did not fear that rule by "public opinion" would empower people incapable of reasoned deliberation. Nor did Phillips fear that the multiplicity of opinion in a democratic society was a danger to social cohesion. Instead, Phillips followed the idea of popular government to the extremes that most troubled conservative Europeans and Americans: now that the printing press had done "for the mind" what "gunpowder did for war," "every reading man" was the "judge" of even the greatest statesman. "Every thoughtful man, the country through, who makes up an opinion, is his jury to which he answers, and the tribunal to which he must bow."[21]

Still, although Phillips was not impressed by the usual objections to rule by "public opinion," he did believe that it presented problems of a different kind. The most troubling features of a democratic, republican society, he thought, were those identified by Alexis de Tocqueville—who began his famous tour of the United States while Phillips was completing his senior year at Harvard. In the United States, Tocqueville found a society where the essence of democracy—the sovereignty of the majority—had been taken to greater lengths than anywhere else, and he was sympathetic to much of what he saw. Yet according to Tocqueville, democracy as practiced in America also raised serious dangers that Phillips found troubling, too.[22]

One was that a popular majority, once endowed with suffrage and sovereignty, would elect mediocre officials. To illustrate the problem, Tocqueville pointed particularly to the House of Representatives and asserted that "the most talented men in the United States are very rarely placed at the head of affairs." Tocqueville attributed this to the fact that even educated and literate voters were usually too concerned with subsistence to have the time or means to conduct research about their elected officials. Moreover, when American voters did deliberate, they tended to judge candidates by the polestar of egalitarianism—Americans' most treasured ideal. Even when they possessed good information about candidates, they shunned any candidates who gave even a whiff of elitism. The result, Tocqueville curtly reported, was that "universal suffrage is by no means a guarantee of the wisdom of the popular choice."[23]

But these complaints were among the least of Tocqueville's concerns. The greater danger in American democracy was that it gave majorities free rein to pursue their interests to the exclusion of all others. In the United States, the majority possessed so much "actual authority" and "moral influence" that "no obstacles exist which can impede, or so much as retard its progress, or which can induce it to heed the complaints of those whom it crushes upon its path." "When an individual or a party is wronged in the United States" by a majority, Tocqueville asked, "to whom can he apply for redress?" The legislature, the executive branch, the police, the judicial system, and even "public opinion," all represented the will of the majority. In every aspect of government and society, the American majority enjoyed unlimited power, a state of things that was "fatal in itself and dangerous for the future."[24]

Here Tocqueville raised the specter that made him most famous: American democracy raised up few barriers to a "tyranny of the majority." In an important footnote in his first volume, Tocqueville also gave a telling illustration of how the American majority could already be as tyrannical as any despot. While visiting Pennsylvania, he asked a white citizen there why he had not seen "a single Negro" on election day, even though in that state some had the right to vote. The Pennsylvanian explained that "the Negroes . . . voluntarily abstain" from being present at elections because "the majority entertains very strong prejudices against the Blacks, and the magistrates are unable to protect them in the exercise of their legal privileges." To Tocqueville this situation boggled the mind: "What, then, the majority claims the right not only of making the laws, but of breaking the laws it has made?" Such episodes showed how "the germ of tyranny" could take root and grow, even in a democratic republic.[25]

The danger of a majoritarian tyranny was compounded, in Tocqueville's view, by the fact that political sovereignty also gave majorities presumptive authority even in the sphere of "public opinion." Americans so worshipped the majority, he explained, that minority viewpoints were rarely even expressed. When authors did venture to "step beyond" the mainstream opinion, they were immediately ostracized and forced back into line by their "overbearing opponents." Indeed, Tocqueville argued that "the display of public opinion in the United States" offered the clearest evidence of how far "the power of the majority" extended in the country. "I know of no country," he concluded, "in which there is so little true independence of mind and freedom of discussion as in America." Even the most absolute despots in the Old World could not suppress the publication of radical doctrines to the extent possible under American democracy. "As long as the majority is still undecided," Tocqueville claimed, "discussion is carried on; but as soon as its decision is irrevocably pronounced, a submissive silence is observed."[26]

Tocqueville amplified this theme in the second volume of *Democracy in America*, published in 1840, which closed by predicting that the equality of condition and political rights in a democracy would end by pressing almost all individuals into the same mold. The result would be a society of conformity and apathy in which "the most original minds and the most energetic characters cannot . . . rise above the crowd" and the nation is reduced to "nothing better than a flock of timid and industrious animals." Content to cede power to government and society so long as they remained formally democratic, individuals would find themselves imperceptibly and "gradually losing the faculties of thinking, feeling, and acting for themselves." If, as James Kloppenberg puts it, Tocqueville's "first volume focuses on his fear that majority tyranny will stifle dissent," the second volume revealed a darker fear: that as democracy advances "there will be no dissent to stifle but only conformity."[27]

Taken as a whole, Tocqueville's *Democracy in America* expressed some familiar concerns about majority rule, yet it also represented a subtle departure from standard European critiques of democracy. For Tocqueville, democracy was not dangerous because it empowered a rabble incapable of deliberation; its danger lay in giving the numerical majority absolute power in every arena of life. Democracy was not dangerous because it gave free rein to an infinite number of discordant views, but instead because it muffled individual thought and bred conformity. Unlike most European writers, Tocqueville noted, he was "not so much alarmed at the excessive liberty" in the United States "as at the very inadequate securities which exist against tyranny."[28]

Few reviewers at the time grasped this subtle critique, but a few contemporary thinkers were deeply impressed. One was John Stuart Mill, who credited Tocqueville with having a decisive impact on his thinking and began a long correspondence with the Frenchman after writing a favorable review of his first volume. In one letter, Mill explained how glad he was to find a kindred thinker who saw that "the real danger in democracy . . . is not anarchy or love of change," but rather "stagnation and immobility."[29]

Phillips, too, would find a kindred thinker in Tocqueville, not least because his grimmest observations comported so well with the experiences of abolitionists. Yet Tocqueville also posed some difficult questions for Phillips's republican faith. After all, Phillips's faith in majority rule depended on his assumption that "the era of legislation" would always be preceded by an "era of public opinion"— of thinking and the discussion of the widest possible range of views. Tocqueville, however, described a more frightening possibility: that democracy stifled talk and slowly homogenized "public opinion." In Tocqueville's bleakest images of the American future, the problem would not be getting a majority to sit down and obey, but getting a minority to stand up. Ultimately that became Phillips's greatest worry, too.

"THE DANGERS OF OUR FORM OF GOVERNMENT"

Tocqueville and his work were familiar to abolitionists in the United States, partly because he also worked with French abolitionists after returning to Paris and wrote a report on French colonial slavery mentioned at the 1840 "World's Convention." At least some Garrisonians read *Democracy*, too. Follen, for example, reportedly spoke often of his agreement with Tocqueville that there was "little true independence of mind and freedom of discussion" in America. But few Garrisonians studied Tocqueville's work more closely than Phillips. Phillips's first biographer, abolitionist Thomas Wentworth Higginson, later remembered that his lectures "drew habitually from but few books, Tocqueville's 'Democracy in America' being among the chief of these," and Phillips's frequent quotations from Tocqueville confirm this recollection.[30]

The many abolitionists who heard Phillips's speeches certainly would have had little trouble seconding Tocqueville's ideas, even if they had not read him as closely as Phillips. Garrisonians' own experiences, after all, seemed to confirm a great deal of what Tocqueville said. They knew that only a few years after Tocqueville wondered why black voters abstained from the polls in Pennsylvania, white voters totally disfranchised blacks there. Not long after that, in 1842, a temperance parade organized by black abolitionists in Philadelphia was violently attacked by a mob, leading to three days of rioting in which black churches and homes were burned while elected officials dragged their feet.[31]

Garrisonians denounced the 1842 riot as the latest proof of how precarious the safety of black minorities was even in the "free" states. Henry Clarke Wright noted that Philadelphia's "CLERGY, and CHURCHES, and CITY AUTHORITIES" had all refused to speak out in clear denunciation of the rioters; instead, they and the city's newspapers blamed the victims for instigating the violence. Meanwhile, a local court granted a petition to have a temperance hall used by the black marchers demolished, after the petitioners alleged that the building was a "nuisance" to the neighborhood. In view of these events, local black abolitionists like Robert Purvis could only conclude that "the bloody *will* is in the heart of the community to destroy us." "I am convinced," Purvis sadly told Wright, "of our utter and complete nothingness in public estimation."[32]

Readers of the *Liberator* became sadly familiar with such tragedies, which seemed to confirm Tocqueville's observations about the power of public opinion in every arena of American life. Every year the antislavery press published a litany of similar horrors that Garrisonian orators and editors could conjure up at any time with barely a word—Pennsylvania Hall, Cincinnati, the "Boston mob," Chatham Street chapel, Prudence Crandall. These assaults on free blacks or their white allies were also especially troubling because they could not be blamed on the Union or the Constitution—whose compromises Garrisonians often blamed for the perpetuation of slavery in the South. Instead they showed the ease with which northern majorities and public officials could abuse their power, just as Tocqueville warned.[33]

When Phillips first read Tocqueville is uncertain, but when he did, memories of countless outrages like the one in 1842 clearly shaped his reading. In 1860, for example, Phillips thought of Tocqueville when yet another anti-abolitionist mob in Boston violently disrupted an antislavery meeting, all while the mayor remained passive. In a speech after the disturbance, Phillips began by musing that Americans had inherited "a government which, after two hundred years, is still the wonder and the study of statesmen," thanks to its "universal suffrage," "the eligibility of every man to office," and the principle that "the majority rules, and law rests on numbers, not on intellect or virtue." But while Phillips still believed that this was "a sound rule" that best served "freedom and progress," it also threatened freedom, because it encouraged Americans to "practically consider public opinion the real test of what is true and what is false." "Tocqueville has noticed," he added, "that practically our institutions protect, not the interests of the whole community, but the interests of the majority."[34]

Tocqueville's other concerns about democracy were also uncomfortably persuasive to Phillips, like his warning about the propensity of the people to choose poor representatives. In the same 1860 speech, Phillips pointed to Boston's mayor as a proof of what "Tocqueville has hinted" about Americans' tendency to elect "common men" who were subservient to mainstream prejudices. But to Phillips, the most notorious of these mediocre statesmen, and the one who brought Tocqueville's warnings most to mind, was Daniel Webster.[35]

Webster was one of the country's most respected politicians and a staunch defender of New England at the height of his career; he was even Phillips's own ideal statesman in his Harvard days. But on March 7, 1850, Webster delivered an infamous speech endorsing a strengthened Fugitive Slave Law as part of a larger package of compromises with slaveholders. Thereafter Webster became, for Phillips, the epitome of Tocqueville's incompetent American leader—a politician who was the slave of the majority instead of a tribune of liberty. In a particularly damning speech in 1859, which called for the removal of Webster's statue from the grounds of the Massachusetts State House, Phillips claimed "to see written all over his statue Tocqueville's conclusion from his survey of French and American Democracy,—'*The man who seeks freedom for anything but freedom's self, is made to be a slave!*'"[36]

Despite Webster's apostasy, Phillips still clung to the hope that the march of ideas and the power of "public opinion" would sweep small-minded, compromising men like Webster into the dustbin of history. Yet Phillips's hopes were chastened by Tocqueville's warnings of majoritarian tyranny, especially given how frequently Garrisonians witnessed the attempted repression of free speech.

The "gag rule" in Congress could only have been passed, they thought, because abolitionists were the "minority, the weaker party, and under the ban of popular proscription." Even Phillips's inaugural abolitionist speech—on the murder of Elijah P. Lovejoy—echoed Tocqueville's concern about the dangers that democracy posed to free discussion. In that speech, he noted with horror that a Boston clergyman had recently defined "republican liberty" as the "liberty to say and do what the *prevailing* voice" of the community will "allow and protect." Phillips retorted that he would rather have "the despotism of the Sultan, where one knows what he may publish and what he may not, rather than the tyranny of this many-headed monster"—a majority that could deprive "the individual and the minority of their rights" at whim.[37]

Such statements suggest why Phillips turned so often to Tocqueville's first volume in his speeches. Yet as the antebellum period wore on, Phillips also grew fearful of the future Tocqueville sketched in his second volume, in which there would not even be dissent to stifle, only conformity and moral stagnation. Webster troubled Phillips for just that reason: he seemed to demonstrate how easily a republican citizen and statesman could gradually lose the capacity for independent thought. At one time, Phillips knew, Webster had been renowned for his bravery in standing up to southerners, especially in his famous 1830 speech denouncing the "nullification" movement. Yet twenty years later, Webster weakly submitted to southern demands for a Fugitive Slave Law. The only explanation Phillips could find was that Webster had been nothing but a follower of majority opinion all along. He never "had an original idea," Phillips charged in 1859, only "borrowed" ones.[38]

Phillips attributed this flaw mostly to Webster's being a politician. But the roots of his fall also seemed to go deeper. As Phillips noted, contemporary politicians in Britain, possessing all the faults of their kind *plus* an upbringing as aristocrats, had proved willing to reject the prevailing opinions of their class and think new thoughts. In his 1859 attack on Webster's statue, Phillips pointed explicitly to the English Tory leader Sir Robert Peel who, despite being "just like" Webster in many respects, bucked expectations as prime minister by embracing controversial reforms. By contrast, all of Webster's "steps, crab-like, were backwards."[39]

Webster's backsliding was all the more troubling because it seemed symptomatic of a broader American malaise—a general tendency to borrow ideas. Phillips illustrated the problem with an anecdote that drew chuckles from his audience: "In the country once," said Phillips, "I lived with a Democrat who never had an opinion on the day's news till he had read the Boston Post." Thankfully, he added, most Americans found "such close imitation" to be "a little too hard" and preferred "doing their own thinking." But in candid moments, Phillips feared that true independence of thought was becoming rarer all the time. Even in 1859, Phillips's barbs at Webster's "crab-like" career drew hisses from audiences in Boston—suggesting how difficult it was even for New Englanders to question their leaders and think for themselves.[40]

Thus, only a year after his optimistic speech about the power of "Public Opinion," Phillips gave a more sobering assessment of the "desperate odds" that abolitionists faced: "the press, the pulpit, the wealth, the literature, the prejudices, the political arrangements, the present self-interest of the country, are all against us. . . . The elements which control public opinion and mould the masses are against us. We can but pick off here and there a man from the triumphant majority," which gave little thought to its own positions. Abolitionists still had "facts for those who think, arguments for those who reason," Phillips said. But he sensed, like Tocqueville, that the reading and thinking people of the nation were sinking into stagnation, indifference, and conformity. The audience with which abolitionists had to deal was increasingly composed not of "confused intellects" that needed convincing, but of "sluggards" and "dead hearts" that needed to be "awakened" and "quickened."[41]

As much as abolitionists had to fear from "gag rules" and mob violence, Phillips ultimately came to fear nothing so much as this pervasive passivity—"the habitual caution which treads on eggs without breaking the shells." Looking back on the past decade in 1859, Phillips worried that Americans had too often "held back" from fulfilling their role as a thinking people. Instead, they had showed "all the timidity of the Old World." "It seems to me that, on all questions, we dread thought," Phillips said, "we shrink behind something," refusing to "sail outside" of the mainstream or "attempt to reason outside of . . . [its] limited, cribbed, cabined" ideas.[42]

In short, Phillips saw the same worrisome progression that Tocqueville had foreseen—a gradual slide into an America in which everyone was a little Webster, bereft of original thoughts and moved by "compulsion or calculation, not by conviction." That was why the fall of his one-time senator portended so much evil. "I read in this [life] one of the dangers of our form of government," Phillips concluded in 1859, before adding a fitting paraphrase of *Democracy in America*.

"As Tocqueville says so wisely, 'The weakness of a Democracy is that, unless guarded, it merges in despotism.' Such a life is the first step, and half a dozen are the Niagara carrying us over."[43]

Phillips fully grasped the dangers of democracy outlined by Tocqueville. But he never proposed to solve these problems by making government or society less democratic. This was partly because Phillips thought it impossible to turn back the tide of democratization represented by the printing press and the spread of suffrage. Reverting to aristocracy would be as absurd as showing up for a gun-fight in a suit of armor, an absurdity also underscored by another of Phillips's favorite metaphors. "You may sigh for a strong government, anchored in the con-victions of past centuries, and able to protect the minority against the majority, —able to defy the ignorance, the mistake, or the passion, as well as the high pur-pose, of the present hour," mused Phillips; "you may prefer the unchanging *terra firma* of despotism; but still the fact remains, that we are launched on the ocean of an unchained democracy." The following year, Phillips reaffirmed that "this is the lesson of our history,—that the world is fluid; that we are on the ocean; that we cannot get rid of the people, and we do not want to."[44]

Nonetheless, Phillips's encounter with Tocqueville's work, together with his own experiences, did convince him that democratic procedures alone could not guarantee justice. Having institutions controlled by public opinion did not make the liberties of the people "necessarily safe," said Phillips, turning once again to Tocqueville's observations that "fifty years before the great [French] revolution, public opinion was as omnipotent in France as it is to-day, but it did not make France free." From this, Phillips concluded that "you cannot save men by ma-chinery." Saving men from the dangers of democracy required "eternal vigilance" instead.[45]

Eternal vigilance, in turn, required three things: individual thought, constant agitation, and education. First, to counteract democracy's drift towards confor-mity, Phillips stressed "the importance of free individual thought,—the ques-tioning of whatever came before us." In a democracy, individuals were too of-ten "bullied by institutions"—churches, courts, and the like—into surrendering free thought, an argument also made by Phillips's Boston contemporary Ralph Waldo Emerson. One way to combat that tendency, Phillips declared, was "simply this,—Stand on the pedestal of your own individual independence, summon these institutions about you, and judge them."[46]

Agitation was as important as self-reliance, however. Unless public opinion was constantly stirred by dissenting opinions, Phillips believed, new and minority viewpoints would quickly sink and disappear altogether—a point he made most vividly by returning to his image of democracy as an ocean. "If the Alps, piled in cold and still sublimity, be the emblem of Despotism," he quipped in 1852, "the ever-restless ocean is ours, which, girt within the eternal laws of gravitation, is pure only because never still."[47]

Yet just as the "machinery" of democracy could not by itself create a good state of society, agitation alone would not make democracy safe. Eternal vigilance required, thirdly and finally, *education*. In a democracy, Phillips asserted in 1859, "God has set us this task: 'If you want good institutions, do not try to bulwark out the ocean of popular thought, educate it.'"[48]

By stressing that popular thought needed to be educated, Phillips was only partly referring to things like literacy. Phillips did assume that learning to read was essential to the thinking that self-government required. "We live under a government of men—and morning newspapers," he said, in which powerful editors were "more really Presidents of the United States than Millard Fillmore." That made learning to read essential to political participation, broadly defined. For the same reason, Phillips often took time, throughout the antebellum sectional crisis, to lecture on temperance reform. In his view, drunkenness, like illiteracy, interfered with the deliberative duties of a republic's reading and thinking people. In a country with "democratic institutions, where the law has no sanction but the purpose and virtue of the masses," Phillips said in 1863, it was important to keep "the hearts of the people" clear.[49]

Sobriety and literacy were also important because ignorant and immoral citizens were less likely to think for themselves. The ability to read was no guarantee of independent thought, of course, as illustrated by the man who did not form an opinion until he read the Boston *Post*. Nevertheless, the lack of education posed a greater danger to independent thinking, Phillips believed, because it made the ignorant prime targets for the manipulation of demagogues and conniving authority figures.

Few experiences proved that point better, in Phillips's view, than the opposition of Boston's Irish immigrants to abolitionists there. Garrisonians tried to reach out to Boston's Irish in 1842 by publicizing a large antislavery Irish address, signed by O'Connell and thousands of other Irish citizens. But the reaction to the address proved to be uniformly hostile. After attending a local Irish meeting in 1842, Phillips was appalled by how quickly the mass of immigrants believed the charges of their community leaders that the address had been forged. Phillips blamed this not on "the poor people who flung up their hats & shouted" when the abolitionists were denounced, but on their ignorance. The Irish themselves were "true metal" and "fit for great things," Phillips told Richard Allen, but they were "an illiterate mass in general" and therefore "under the control of those few among them who have education or those who act as their lawyers or the few who court office by begging their votes." Lack of education made it impossible for abolitionists to "get between them & their leaders."[50]

Despite these concerns, for Phillips "education" always signified more than book-learning or temperance. Literacy and sobriety were morally neutral, like "public opinion" itself, and could be used to good or bad ends. Often enough, those who were most highly educated were the most inveterate opponents of abolition. As Phillips noted in 1860, one of the ironies of the recent mob violence at the Tremont Temple was that "white men, having enjoyed the best book education," had mobbed the platform to silence some black abolitionists "whose only education was oppression and the antislavery enterprise!"[51]

The kind of education that Americans really needed, Phillips believed, was one that would make them concerned with the rights and welfare of all instead of only being concerned about themselves: "it is our interest to educate this people in humanity, and in deep reverence for the rights of the lowest and humblest individual that makes up our numbers." *Selfishness* was the form of ignorance that Americans most needed to unlearn, Phillips thought, revealing another point on which he and Tocqueville agreed. In a series of chapters on "individualism," Tocqueville argued that in the United States "the interest of man is confined to those in close propinquity to himself," and even neighbors "become indifferent and as strangers to one another."[52]

In the United States, Tocqueville also believed, "individualism" was hastened and worsened by the intense, pervasive concern for making money and enjoying material comforts. "Carefully to satisfy all, even the least wants of the body, and to provide the little conveniences of life, is uppermost in every mind," especially since Americans seemed to believe that anyone could acquire a fortune. Tocqueville worried that Americans would be consumed by the pursuit of material goods "till, in snatching at these lesser gifts, men lose sight of those more precious possessions which constitute the glory and the greatness of mankind."[53]

Phillips echoed these concerns in 1852 when he noted that "a man is always selfish enough for himself" but was rarely "willing to sacrifice his own character for the benefit of his neighbor." He also shared Tocqueville's concern that the American mind was slowly being debased and clouded by "mechanical routine" and materialism. It was difficult to convert northerners to abolitionism, he argued, because all they saw were profits from trade with the South. The Tremont Temple disturbance in 1860 was "a case of men undertaking to join in public debate and preside over public meetings, whose souls are actually absorbed in pricing calico and adding up columns of figures." Like Tocqueville, he wondered whether the "industrial energy" of the nineteenth century was really an unmixed blessing, and urged that the only way to prevent anti-abolitionist mobs was to "educate" the people and their magistrates "more thoroughly. Teach them the distinction between duties and dollars."[54]

The problem of selfishness was even more troubling for Phillips than it was for Tocqueville, however. Tocqueville ultimately argued that Americans mitigated the evil effects of "individualism" by banding together in voluntary associations and by embracing "the principle of interest rightly understood," which Tocqueville defined as the idea that concern for each was in the interest of all. Tocqueville considered this principle sound and urged that all Americans be "educated" in the truth that "it is the interest of every man to be virtuous."[55]

Phillips agreed with this dictum only to an extent. Like Tocqueville he predicted that "in time, the selfishness of one class neutralizes the selfishness of another," and he also believed abolitionists should appeal to the self-interest of their listeners when they could. Yet Phillips was less sanguine that virtue could be saved solely by such appeals. "The ideas of justice and humanity" were always fighting "against the organized selfishness of human nature," he explained. Men were not likely to extend rights to women out of a belief that it would benefit them, nor was it easy to show white men why granting rights to people of color was in their own interest. The reality was that "the slave question halts and lingers, because it cannot get the selfishness of men on its side." Abolitionists had to educate white men and women in "disinterestedness" and make them "interested, indignant, enthusiastic for others, not for themselves."[56]

The primary goal of what Phillips referred to as "education" was therefore disinterestedness. Even a school education was "not simply books," Phillips explained; it was a means of lifting people outside of their "narrow and sordid" interest in material gain and making them active citizens concerned with the rights of all. What Phillips intended by the term "education" were all the ways to "win men from cares that eat out everything lofty" and stimulate them to be vigilant for the good of the community.[57]

By that definition, Phillips often said, the antislavery agitation was itself a form of education. "There are men who prate about 'nationality,' and 'the empire,' and 'manifest destiny,'—using brave words, when their minds rise no higher than some petty mass of white States making money out of cotton and corn," Phillips declared. So when abolitionists, women, or people of color ascended northern platforms to speak of liberty and rights, they became more than agitators—they were "teachers of American Democracy" who called Americans to a higher "idea of American nationality . . . collecting on the broad bosom of what deserves the name of an empire, under the shelter of noble, just, and equal laws, all races, all customs, all religions, all languages, all literature, and all ideas." Convincing Americans mired in cotton and corn, prejudice and self-interest, to accept this idea would be difficult, Phillips knew. But, as a reflective reader of Tocqueville and his own experiences, he also believed that only such education and agitation could avert the dangers inherent in the American form of government.[58]

THE SCHOOL OF ATHENS

Phillips's speeches between 1837 and the beginning of the Civil War reveal a rigorous and reflective mind at work on important questions about public opinion and democracy itself. Nor was he alone. In fact, his responses to Tocqueville and his ideas about "the ever-restless ocean" of an agitated democracy were very close to the ideas of his contemporary John Stuart Mill, another transatlantic thinker whom Phillips read and admired.

Because of his famous 1859 essay *On Liberty,* Mill has often been remembered exclusively as a defender of the absolute good of individual liberty and the importance of protecting it from any interference by state or society. But more recent commentators have offered a convincing, fuller portrait of Mill as a theorist of democracy and social relations. That portrait makes it easier to understand why Phillips praised Mill, on the eve of the Civil War, as one of the "largest brains" and "profoundest thinkers" in Europe.[59]

The first thing Phillips and Mill had in common was Tocqueville. As it did for Phillips, Tocqueville's work crystallized for Mill his own worries about the dangers of a tyranny of the majority and a future of mass conformity; even *On*

Liberty can be seen partly as a response to questions Tocqueville had posed, and their influence on later works like *Considerations on Representative Government* is even clearer. In many essays, including *On Liberty*, Mill emphasized the value of individual independence and autonomy partly because he, like Phillips, viewed them as essential bulwarks against the tendency of democratizing societies to breed conformity and squash dissent.[60]

Like Phillips, too, Mill did not view liberty as a license for individuals to pursue their own interests in total disregard for neighbors, provided only that they did not harm one another. His ideal society was rather one in which individuals actively participated in public life instead of shrinking from it. Citizens also had a duty, he believed, to present reasons and arguments for their views and to listen to arguments for others. Indeed, many of Mill's specific ideas about parliamentary reform were designed to protect dissenting viewpoints and ensure that all ideas were "fully, frequently, and fearlessly discussed."[61]

Finally, Mill believed that a society in which political consent was formed through rational deliberation, either within legislative assemblies or in civil society itself, would improve individual citizens. Like Tocqueville and Phillips, Mill worried that economic pursuits and selfish concerns were too easily turning his contemporaries inward and away from the "common interest." But, also like Phillips, he saw democratic politics and discussion as a "school of public spirit" that would teach a disinterested regard for others and the public good—without which no individual life could really be elevated or complete. Political participation would lift ordinary people who had done "nothing in their lives but drive a quill, or sell goods over a counter" out of their self-interested pursuits and towards public goods. For that reason, even in his reviews of Tocqueville, Mill argued that social and moral progress lay "not [in] the patching of the old worn-out machinery of aristocracy" but in figuring out how to ensure "the instruction of the democracy."[62]

Mill's solution, in the words of one writer, was to spend his life arguing "in favour of publicity, equal representation and freedom of discussion as basic conditions for democratic political freedom." And no part of his work made those principles clearer than his frequent descriptions of Athens as the model republic of the ancient world. For Mill the touchstone of Athenian democracy was the *agora*, the marketplace in which all citizens could join in rational discussions of the public business, and many of the schemes of electoral and parliamentary reform he supported were attempts to recreate those conditions.[63]

Phillips also shared Mill's admiration for Athens, and for the exact same reasons. In an 1859 speech on "The Education of the People," Phillips contrasted the ancient civilization of Egypt, which "kept its knowledge for priests and nobles," with the "democratic" civilization of Greece, which "busied itself with every man in the market-place, day by day." In Athens, the "scholar" like Pericles "thought life wasted if he did not hear, at the moment, the echo and the amen to his labors in the appreciation of the market-place. The Greek trusted the people," Phillips concluded, and "our civilization takes its shape from the Greek." In a true democracy like the Athenian model, "government . . . is a school" in which all participated in rational deliberation and discussion and were encouraged by that process to curb their natural selfishness.[64]

In another speech that same year, Phillips recalled the ancient story of Anacharsis, who witnessed a debate in the forum of Athens and saw the vote that followed. Anacharsis concluded that under Athenian liberty, "wise men argue causes, and fools decide them." Phillips implied that the same was true in the United States, where the present generation of elected officials like Webster were often "fools." But he took reassurance in the fact that even "unruly Athens," where the "caprices of the mob" could overturn the wisdom of the wisest, "probably secured the greatest human happiness and nobleness of its era" because it allowed open discussion. "Now my idea of American civilization is," said Phillips, "that it is a second part, a repetition of that same sublime confidence in the public conscience and the public thought which made the groundwork of Grecian Democracy."[65]

Like Mill, however, Phillips believed that the Athenians' system demanded much of its citizens, particularly those who dissented from the majority. Liberty and virtue were preserved in Athens only because its noble-minded citizens, instead of cloistering themselves, followed the example of Socrates and Demosthenes and sought to educate their contemporaries. This was precisely the role, Phillips believed, that abolitionists now had to perform in the United States: "Our object for twenty years has been to educate the mass of the American people up to that level of moral life which shall recognize that free speech . . . is God's normal school, educating the American mind, throwing upon it the grave responsibility of deciding a great question, and by means of that responsibility lifting it to a higher level of intellectual and moral life."[66]

For Phillips, in other words, abolitionist agitation was an end in itself, a duty—and not just because it could help to make public opinion more sympathetic to slaves. The role of the agitator was essential to keep democracy from degenerating into a government of despots, a society of selfish materialists, a tyranny of the majority—or all of the above. The ocean of unchained democracy could not be dammed, he knew, just as Tocqueville and Mill did. But if left alone, the ocean could grow becalmed and stagnant on its own. The only way to prevent that fate was through individuality, education, "eternal vigilance," and, above all, agitation.

Mill had a similar view, which is one reason why he was an early admirer of the Garrisonians. Mill shared their opposition to slavery and their support for women's rights, but he also admired their commitment to fearless and free discussion. In 1850, for example, Mill wrote excitedly to Harriet Taylor about a recent report he had read in the New York *Tribune* about a Massachusetts convention on women's rights, which had been attended by "the chief slavery abolitionists Garrison, Wendell Phillips, the negro Douglas &c." Mill effused that "I never remember any public meetings or agitation comparable to it in the proportion which good sense bears to nonsense."[67]

Even more than explaining Mill's interest in Phillips, however, Phillips's ideas about agitation help explain his solidarity with Garrison. Phillips's Harvard-educated and high-born peers always found his loyalty to the AASS difficult to understand, especially since many Garrisonians embraced unorthodox religious views and doctrines like "non-resistance" that Phillips himself rejected. Yet Phillips's support for Garrison is understandable in view of his conviction that "ever-restless" agitation and discussion were needed to educate popular thought and avoid the dangers of democracy. According to Phillips, antislavery agitation was more than a means; it was "the normal state of the nation," "an essential part of the machinery of the state," and "a necessity of each age." To Phillips, Garrisonians, of all abolitionist factions, best upheld this ideal of constant agitation.[68]

To be sure, some reformers believed that Garrisonians were still not committed enough to "free speech," and some had a point. Frederick Douglass, an ally of the Garrisonians throughout the 1840s, later came to see their opposition to his founding of his own newspaper, the *North Star,* as an attempt to limit his speech. Nathaniel P. Rogers later left the society because he believed the apparatus of reform meetings constrained discussion. Garrisonians were also sometimes intolerant of highly disruptive New England agitators like Abigail Folsom—an obscure prison reformer who, because of her frequent unwelcome interruptions of abolitionist meetings, was dubbed "that *Flea of conventions*" and ultimately consigned to an insane asylum. Still, Garrisonians were certainly more tolerant of agitators like Folsom than clerical abolitionists or the organizers of the Liberty Party; as Edmund Quincy explained to Webb in a letter about Folsom, the "tediousness" of outbursts like hers was "the price we have to pay for free discussion."[69]

To Phillips, Garrisonians' willingness to let women speak publicly, as well their refusal to keep abolitionists from discussing unpopular views about non-resistance, the inspiration of Scripture, and a host of other topics, showed they were willing to pay the price of agitation. Phillips therefore praised Garrisonian agitators not just for what they said or why they said it, but also because they kept the ocean "ever-restless." As Phillips concluded in his 1852 "Public Opinion" address, "never, to our latest posterity, can we afford to do without prophets, like Garrison, to stir up the monotony of wealth, and reawake the people to the great ideas that are constantly fading out of their minds,—to trouble the waters, that there may be health in their flow."[70]

Given Phillips's concerns about the dangers of democracy, this was high praise indeed. But it was also more. In speeches like "Public Opinion," Phillips not only explained Garrisonians to others but also explained to Garrisonians why their agitation was so important. In his hand, "distrust" of public opinion, which Garrisonians learned from their experiences, became "the safety of Republics," and agitators viewed by others as divisive and fanatical became guardians and teachers of American Democracy who protected "public opinion" from its own inertia, imperfections, and dangers. "Agitation by somebody there must be," or else "the indolent inactivity of the masses" and selfishness of human nature would allow "the Government to drift toward despotism," just as Tocqueville feared.[71]

THE PROBLEM OF NATIONALISM

ot all Garrisonians drew so directly from Tocqueville, but others echoed Phillips's ideas about democracy. Certainly Garrison agreed that "there is nothing like agitation," and that "we have too little, instead of too much dissent among us." "If we had not innumerable facts to prove the general corruption of the times," said the *Liberator* in 1846, "the fear of free speech and free inquiry would prove it; for where the mind and tongue are fettered, either by imperial edicts, by statutory enactments, by the terrors of summary punishment, [or] by popular sentiment . . . it indicates an evil state of society."[1]

Garrison's experiences—his jailing for libel in Baltimore, his mobbing in Boston, his silencing at the "World's Convention"—also gave him plenty of reasons of his own to deplore majoritarian opposition to new ideas. Yet in the 1830s and 1840s, Garrison and several close allies developed some slightly different ideas about the dangers of governments. While Phillips's reflections were informed by *Democracy in America* and resembled the ideas of European liberals like Mill, Garrisonians like Chapman, Quincy, and Wright were guided more by the home-grown doctrine of "non-resistance."

"Non-resistance" was a movement led by Garrison and composed primarily of disaffected members of the American Peace Society who decided, in the mid-1830s, that most Christian pacifists did not reject violence completely enough. Garrison supported the Peace Society even before becoming an abolitionist, drawing on the deeply held evangelical beliefs of his mother and the preaching he heard in his youth. After 1830, Garrison gradually lost his respect for northern denominations and clergymen who tried to stop his agitation on women's rights and rebuked him for "abusive" language about slaveholders. But Garrison never lost the central religious faith that animated him in the temperance and peace movements of the late 1820s: God wanted servants like him to remove the sins of the people, because everyone who came into the world without "do[ing] something to repair its moral desolation . . . defeats one great purpose of his creation." If Phillips's favorite text to preach from was Tocqueville, Lloyd Garrison preferred the Bible.[2]

Like other members of the Peace Society, founded in 1828, Garrison believed aggressive war was one of the moral desolations contrary to the gospel of Christ. But after the harrowing reign of terror of 1834 and 1835, he ultimately came to believe that Christianity forbade any act of violence or coercion, even in self-defense. From that premise, he also soon concluded that it was sinful to vote or participate in government at all, since "all history shows that [governments] cannot be maintained, except by naval and military power." To follow a crucified Jesus, according to non-resistants, meant withdrawal from any human institution that used, condoned or threatened violence. "We cannot love our enemies," noted Garrison, "and kill them."[3]

Most abolitionists repudiated these doctrines, and only a minority joined Garrison in forming the New England Non-Resistance Society in 1838. But non-resistants drew on some ideas that many abolitionists held in common. "I believe in passing from death unto life—in being born of God—in becoming a new creature in Christ Jesus—in being crucified to the world—in present, perfect, and perpetual deliverance from sin," Garrison wrote in 1838, echoing common assumptions among antebellum reformers. But just as abolitionists did not think the sin of slavery should be abolished gradually, it made little sense to Garrison to delay one's repentance from the sins of murder, bloodshed, war, and participation in governments that did all these things. In that sense, as the movement's best historian has noted, non-resistance was partly the application of immediatism to the problem of violence.[4]

The doctrine of non-resistance also drew strength, however, from the theological ideas of John Humphrey Noyes, whom Garrison met the year before founding the Non-Resistance Society. In contrast to orthodox evangelical ministers, Noyes preached that Christians could live as though the kingdom of God and the personal sanctification it promised were already arriving on earth as in heaven. His "perfectionist" teachings told Christians to "come out" and be separate from any organizations whose authority was limited to the world, including governments and corrupt religious institutions, and live solely in obedience to the kingdom of God.[5]

Garrison agreed with only some of Noyes's ideas, but his utopian "come-outerism" offered non-resistants a compelling rationale for separating themselves from institutions tainted by support for slavery and violence, including northern churches, political parties, and the Peace Society. Noyes's revelatory interpretations of biblical texts also encouraged Garrisonian non-resistants to believe that Christ's rule was destined to overthrow all human evils, and taught them to identify any moral progress that occurred without physical force as a clear sign of God's kingdom already breaking in on the world. "The will of God, the beneficent Creator of the human family, cannot always be frustrated," Garrison said, and events like British West Indian emancipation showed that, in spite of all the wrong still in the world, "the stream of sympathy still rolls on—its impetus is increasing."[6]

Phillips never became a non-resistant, but that did not always place him at odds with Garrison. For Phillips, non-resistance was a healthy example of independent thinking, and he had reasons of his own for believing abolitionists should stay out of government. Non-resistants saw Phillips's belief in the power of non-violent agitation as compatible with their views. But the differences between their ways of thinking would become more apparent over time, and in the beginning they were best illustrated by the fact that while Phillips was musing on the dangers of public opinion, non-resistants focused much of their thinking on the problems caused by nations and nationalism.

"OUR COUNTRY IS THE WORLD"

Garrison had criticized the evils of narrow love for a nation from the beginning of his abolitionist career. "We are a vain people, and our love of praise is inordinate," he warned in his 1829 Park Street Church address. "We imagine, and are annually taught to believe, that . . . [the] ocean may gather up its forces for a second deluge, and overtop the tallest mountains; but our ark will float securely when the world is drowned." These reflections did not make Garrison conclude that patriotism was always dangerous, but when he reflected on his own previous blindness to slavery, he could not help but see national vanity as a "fatal delusion . . . which, unless the mercy of God interpose, seals the doom of our country."[7]

That belief was one reason why Garrison so often cited the cosmopolitan motto on the *Liberator*'s masthead. In 1833, Garrison began his first major speech to an English audience by declaring that he had "long since sacrificed all my national, complexional and local prejudices upon the altar of Christian love, and breaking down the narrow boundaries of a selfish patriotism, inscribed upon my banner this motto:—*My country is the world, my countrymen are all mankind.*" Both

Garrison and the early immediatists who joined him made that motto central to their arguments against slavery, colonizationism, and even racial prejudice. Since God made "of one blood all nations of men," as one of the abolitionists' favorite passages of Scripture said, even prejudices based on color reflected a kind of love for one nation that was narrower than the love embodied in the gospel.[8]

Garrisonian beliefs about the dangers of national vanity were even more deeply held, however, after the mobs of 1834 and 1835. In those years, foreign interference was one of the most frequent charges leveled at Garrisonians, despite Thompson's rejoinder that he came "as a citizen of the world." And thereafter many Anglophobic anti-abolitionists continued to argue that "the equal lover of 'the entire human race,' such as Mr. Garrison and his associates, is in effect a traitor to his country." For Garrisonians, these arguments underscored the evils that could flow from "the narrow prejudice of clan, dignified by the name of national pride."[9]

Clannish national vanity was not the only reason for the backlash against Thompson, but it did offer Garrisonians what they sorely needed: a ready explanation for their sudden setbacks in 1835. Prior to 1837, Garrisonians believed their movement had been going from strength to strength, thanks to God's help. Looking back on the first few years of the *Liberator* in 1836, Garrison was impressed with "how mighty . . . the growth of our cause [has been] during that brief period!" Not "since the days of Luther, [had] the world witnessed so rapid a transformation in public sentiment," which was evident in the "seven flourishing State Societies" spawned by the AASS and the "flood of our publications sweeping through the land." All of this, Garrison said, was the accomplishment of God, who had merely used abolitionists "as an instrument." But if the progress of abolitionism was the work of God, Garrisonians also needed an explanation of their continued persecution that did not fault him; the sin of national vanity offered one good answer.[10]

In marked contrast to the arguments Phillips and Tocqueville would later make about the tendency of public opinion towards stagnation, however, Garrison's 1836 survey of his movement's progress did not see anything inherent in "public sentiment" that might depress its energies; God stood behind the abolitionists' efforts, and he did not sleep. In 1831, "the land [was] slumbering in the lap of moral death," but God had awakened the nation, answering the prayers and validating the work of abolitionists. "The work is his—the cause is his—and his shall be the victory," Garrison concluded. What threatened the immediate spread of the movement, therefore, were not the innate selfishness of human nature or the natural apathy of public opinion itself, as Phillips believed, but the conservatism and sinfulness of institutions, like the church, the party system, and the government, that had tried to settle an ocean already agitated by the hand of God.[11]

The radical theology of John Humphrey Noyes, whom Garrison first met in the spring of 1837, added nations themselves to the institutions now standing in God's way. By that time Noyes, a former student at Yale Divinity School, had come to believe that Christian perfection was possible in the present life, and he had become a wandering minister who tried to convince other Christians to withdraw from all human institutions and establish new communities governed only by the law of God. He quickly identified in Garrison a potential convert to these ideas, and he hoped to use Garrison's convictions about the sinfulness of slavery to lead him to a broader truth: that all human control of other human beings was every bit as sinful.[12]

In March, Noyes wrote Garrison a long letter describing the "government of the United States" as a "swaggering libertine" that whipped slaves, dispossessed Indians, trampled on the Bible, and had now "declared war" on abolitionists themselves: "on one side" of this national picture "stand the despots of Europe, laughing and mocking at the boasted liberty of their neighbor; on the other stands the Devil, saying 'Esto perpetua.'" Yet Noyes also offered Garrison a powerful antidote to this grim vision: all governments, nations, and human institutions, he said, were temporary. God had slated all of them for abolition, just as the "Jewish dispensation" had given way to Christianity. To hasten their end, Christians had only to live as though they were already ended, and to "nominate Jesus Christ for the Presidency, not only of the United States, but of the world."[13]

Garrison was not prepared to go as far as Noyes, who also considered marriage and sexual monogamy as institutions that perfect Christians could regard as ended by the new dispensation. But Noyes's ideas did help crystallize one explanation for the "reign of terror" that Garrison and his allies already favored: northerners refused to listen to abolitionists because they sinfully clung to their pride in the United States, an entity subordinate to God's kingdom. Blind allegiance to one institution destined to end—the nation—was keeping Americans from abolishing slavery, another institution that stood under judgment.

Noyes's solution—come out and be separate—also appealed to Garrison as a way to reimagine his persecution. Instead of having to deal with being rejected by Americans, churches, and anti-abolitionist politicians, Garrisonians could reject them, claiming the moral high ground in a context where safe political ground was rapidly disappearing. If God's "kingdom is to be established upon the earth," Garrison mused to Henry Clarke Wright shortly after receiving Noyes's letter, then Christians should resolve "to be crucified unto the world" and its temporary institutions right away.[14]

The founding of the Non-Resistance Society the following year kept Garrison's mind turning in this direction. In the Declaration of Sentiments he wrote for the group, Garrison announced that, because they were "bound by the laws of a kingdom which is not of this world," Christians were obliged to "love the land of our nativity only as we love all other lands." "Our country is the world" was the watchword of non-resistance as well as antislavery, and it allowed "no appeal to patriotism, to revenge any national insult or injury."[15]

In 1839 Garrison went farther by claiming that "there is no patriotism in non-resistance," because patriotism belonged "to the kingdoms of this world." Echoing Noyes, he declared that "patriotism is Anti-Christ," and over the next few years, he established a regular non-resistance column in the *Liberator* that often denounced "national organizations" as artificial and antithetical to God's ultimate vision for the world. Many of these essays were by Wright, who became the Non-Resistance Society's general agent and who wrote, in one typical essay, that "nations are little better than demons"—both tried to usurp the dominion of God and both were doomed to destruction.[16]

Yet Noyes's most lasting legacy, for Garrison, was his vivid reminder that the kingdom of heaven was one day guaranteed to triumph over the kingdoms of the world. In 1837, that future-oriented vision not only reassured Garrison at a moment when abolitionists seemed beset by troubles, but also empowered him to believe that, if Christians renounced violence now, their efforts would not be in vain. "I believe that Jesus Christ is to conquer this rebellious world," Garrison said, "as completely as the Spirit of Evil has now possession of it." But "if I belong to his kingdom," he continued, "what have I to do with the kingdoms of this world?" Strong though Satan seemed at present, "his empire of darkness shall be destroyed, and upon its ruins be erected the kingdom of heaven," in which Jesus would "assuredly 'reign from sea to sea, and from the river to the ends of the earth.'"[17]

These thoughts especially encouraged Garrison and other non-resistants to see the "World's Convention" in 1840 not just as an abolitionist conference, but as an anticipation of the kingdom of God in which all the world's people would gather regardless of nationality. Garrison sailed for London in the summer of 1840 with his bags stuffed with non-resistance literature and his mind swirling with the visions that Noyes had sketched of Christ's eventual rule. One day, all human beings would be "reconciled together," he wrote from his ship. They would "mingle together like the kindred drops of the ocean," and "their country shall no longer be hemmed in by geographical boundaries" or national borders. "These blissful events must happen, it seems to me, or the Son of God has come into the world in vain. My faith is perfect in his ability to overcome the evil that is in the world."[18]

Indeed, Garrison told Maria Weston Chapman, a fellow non-resistant, that he looked forward to a convention that would one day "have for its object the recognition and approval of Jesus, the Messiah, as the only King and Ruler on earth—the establishment of his kingdom to the subversion of all others." But "whatever may be said or done at the World's Convention," Garrison mused just before his arrival, "the mere fact that the nations, by their representatives, are about to meet and embrace each other in love . . . is indescribably joyous to my soul." He believed the convention would set a precedent for the final coming of God's kingdom, in which everyone would speak the same language and "all national barriers, castes, and boundaries" would be abolished by "the reconciliation of the world to God."[19]

In the end, of course, abolitionists could not even reconcile with each other in London. But their divisions only convinced non-resistants that their opponents were still more obedient to national custom than to God. Meanwhile, Garrisonian delegates managed their disappointment with the meeting by investing even greater significance in their new friendship networks, which became the true harbingers of God's kingdom. Abby Kimber, for instance, told Pease in May 1841 that she had anticipated that she would form new "acquaintances and friendships" during her journey to London, but the idea "that we should so cordially adopt Garrison's motto—Our Country is the World &c—was more than I had thought." She had so enjoyed the company of Pease and others "that I cannot recognise a 'foreigner' among you." William Bassett, a Massachusetts non-resistant who attended the convention, likewise told Pease that "we feel nearer than ever united to the kindred spirits on your side of the water," which reminded them that the ocean "interposes no barrier to a communion of spirit" to those already translated into the Spirit's kingdom.[20]

For the remainder of their lives, Garrisonians would continue to surround their transatlantic friendships with this sort of imagery, indicating that they never saw Noyes's call to be separate as a mere "coming out"—it was also a "going in" to new relationships and communities not governed by geography or nationality. Garrisonians held up simple acts like mailing boxes for antislavery fairs or exchanging letters and newspapers with transatlantic friends as ways to bring the kingdom of God more quickly to its consummation. It was "by such co-operation," Garrison reminded his colleagues, "that the great idea of human brotherhood becomes a living reality, and national animosities are doomed to an ignominious death."[21]

In their longing for selfless cooperation and brotherhood, Garrisonian non-resistants were in some ways trying to solve problems similar to those identified by Tocqueville as "individualism" and by Phillips as "selfishness." Modern society seemed in various ways to be decreasing concern for neighbors and the interests of others; non-resistants, like other thinkers, believed that trend had to be arrested. But like Noyes, Garrison and Wright also believed that they were not working alone to make human brotherhood a "living reality." God had made all nations one family already under the rule of Christ; the job of Christians, they thought, was to align themselves more fully with that truth—especially by refusing to let their love be bounded by national and geographical lines.

THE ANTI-NATIONAL TOUR OF HENRY CLARKE WRIGHT

Few non-resistants were more excited by such language than Henry Clarke Wright, Garrison's close friend and the general agent of the Non-Resistance Society. Wright did not attend the "World's Convention," but he rapidly assimilated his friends' experiences there into his thinking in 1841. For the previous two years, Wright had been musing about the evils of nations in his *Liberator* columns, gradually building to the conclusion that all people were bearers of "human rights." But after the dispiriting results of the London conference, Wright struck upon the new idea of calling for "*A World's Convention to consider the subject of Human Rights,*" to be held in Boston—a convention that would more clearly anticipate the eventual triumph of Christ's kingdom.[22]

Wright's writings about his "World's Convention on Human Rights" drew on familiar non-resistance ideas: a circular about the meeting declared that "human love is not bounded by latitude & longitude" and pointed yet again to the

Liberator's motto. Yet Wright's specific plans were new. Wright envisioned not just one convention, but the organization of a permanent standing tribunal on "human rights" to which any oppressed person or group could report human rights abuses. "We would collect facts respecting the outrages done to humanity, by individuals & nations, in all parts of the earth" and recognize as delegates all persons regardless of nationality, he explained. Non-resistants like Garrison, Chapman, and Nathaniel P. Rogers quickly endorsed the plan.[23]

Unfortunately for his hopes, however, Wright's idea never materialized, except as the butt of more anti-abolitionist jokes. Even some abolitionists outside the Non-Resistance Society questioned the plan. Richard Davis Webb, for one, wondered whether a true "world's convention" was even possible. "Can you imagine Esquimaux & New Hollanders, Caucasians and Negroes, Tartars and Sardinians all holding solemn council together—understanding the same words in the same sense, reasoning from the same premises in the same way & coming to a harmonious conclusion?" Webb asked Phillips. "I cannot." The fact that Wright could imagine such a convention, however, indicates how important the idea of transnational "human rights" was to non-resistants as the 1840s began, and how confident they were of the ultimate harmony of the world under the rule of Christ. Wright was seized, like Garrison and Noyes, by the idea that God's government was already breaking in on the world, and that "National Organizations" were standing in the way of the "*Human Brotherhood*" that would prevail in the kingdom of heaven.[24]

Clearly "*Nations*" were "a fruitful theme" for reflection, as Wright noted in his diary in May 1842, and he continued to muse on that theme during a five-year tour in Europe that began that year. In Europe, Wright lectured on slavery and made the rounds to the Garrisonians' circle of friends. But he traveled officially as the agent of Non-Resistance, and his reports showed his desire to enact its ideals. "I came to this nation as a human being," not as the member of a nation, Wright told the *Liberator* from England, and over the next few years, he returned endlessly in his transatlantic lectures to the evils of slavery, non-resistance, and what he called "nationalism."[25]

At the time Wright used it, the word "nationalism" was itself quite rare. The French term *nationalisme* surfaced in one 1798 text, and German philosopher Johann Herder also referred to *Nationalismus* in the 1790s, but several more decades passed before the term moved into common usage or received sustained analysis in any language. The year 1836, according to one close study, witnessed the publication of the first text to make critical use of the French term "national-isme" after nearly four decades in which the term was virtually unused. So when Wright declared in 1843 that he had "lost sight of the contemptible distinctions of *sectarianism* and *nationalism*" he was something of a linguistic pioneer.[26]

For Wright, however, the word usefully summarized the non-resistants' ideas about nations, which were soon reinforced by several experiences abroad. First, through Garrisonian allies he met many pacifists and free traders in the famous Anti-Corn Law League who told him they were also working to reduce wars and increase international harmony. The league's leader, Richard Cobden, had authored many polemics against "the spirit of national hate," and in one of his earliest essays, Cobden declared that "patriotism or nationality . . . sometimes burns the brightest in the rudest and least reasoning minds." Free trade, he and other Corn Law Leaguers argued, would succeed in "breaking down the barriers that separate nations" by knitting people of different countries together with commerce and communication.[27]

Wright was impressed by these views, which sounded much like his own, and after attending several Corn Law Repeal meetings, Wright told the *Liberator* that the league's "principal lecturers and delegates . . . are from principle thor-ough non-resistants." From them he learned to see trade protectionism as only one more demonstration of "the folly of regulating the intercourse of human beings by nations." Wright was especially impressed when the Garrisonian sym-pathizer and Member of Parliament John Bowring told Wright over dinner in the Anti-Corn Law League's headquarters that, once free trade triumphed, "men will cease all intercourse by Nations, & come to inter-individual intercourse. In fact, men will cease to be known as Nations, cease to wear national badges . . . & come to individual rights & responsibilities." That rhetoric resonated with Wright's own view, as a non-resistant, that because "nations violate inter-*human* law and etiquette," a true reformer "cannot be faithful to man, and to nations." The noblest argument on behalf of repealing the Corn Laws was that by abolish-ing national tariffs, "you blot out nations in a most important sense."[28]

After struggling with poor health for the majority of his first year abroad, Wright decided in 1844 to travel to a famous "water cure" establishment at Grae-fenberg in the Silesian Alps, beginning a trip that occupied eight months and took Wright through Austria, Germany, Prussia, Switzerland, and Belgium. But for Wright, the recuperative trip further reinforced his ideas about free trade and "nationalism." In a letter to the *Liberator* shortly after crossing the English Channel, Wright wished for the abolition of "states, nations, republics, kingdoms, empires," which would finally make way for "the triumph of Christianity and humanity." His frequent hassles with customs and passports officers on his way to Switzerland struck Wright as yet another way in which states tried to reduce human beings to their identities as members of particular nations, contrary to the will of God. "I do not believe man's obligations and duties change with every change of latitude and longitude, climate and country," declared Wright after one of his last encounters with Austrian officials.[29]

The time that Wright spent at the water-cure establishment only confirmed this credo. Wright frequently noticed the establishment's diverse clientele, which made it "a *Hospital* for all nations" with its own "Graefenberg dialect," "Graefenberg character," and a "Graefenberg state of society." Mealtimes brought together patients from "some fifteen nations," he told the *Liberator*, in a "community [that] assume[d] the form of a democracy." In this fellowship, which included "Russians, Poles, Prussians, Austrians, Hungarians, Italians, Danes, and Tyrolese," Wright found proof, contrary to Webb's doubts and in keeping with Garrison's hopes, that the reconciliation of different nations to God and each other was possible. "There is a sympathy," he wrote, "that binds the whole family of man into one brotherhood."[30]

Wright labored to persuade his fellow patients of this gospel as well. "I renounce my nationalism," Wright reported back to the *Liberator*, "and meet them on the high and heaven-erected platform of HUMAN BROTHERHOOD." At breakfast one morning, Wright startled his fellow patients by announcing that "I never wish to be called an *American* again" and only wanted to be known as "a man, a human being." One bystander ventured to ask, "Can't you be a Human Being—& an American?" "Not well," was Wright's reply.[31]

Only a few patients took Wright's statements seriously, but their friendship helped confirm for him that the "characteristics" of various nations could be "merged into a peculiar people." "Individual hearts are here knit together," Wright concluded, united by "a chord of individual love and sympathy reaching around the globe." As the Graefenberg patients said their goodbyes in Wright's "snug little room," he recorded, "we loved one another. Our nationalism was gone. We were only human beings." Having glimpsed this brotherhood promised in God's kingdom, Wright returned to his abolitionist labors the following year more convinced than ever that "the time will come when" all the institutions of society that divided human beings would "be blotted out, and human hearts be allowed to meet around the world in kindly sympathy." Emboldened by that renewed vision of God's rule, Wright continued to express his "*Anti-nationality,*" writing often of his longing to see all national organizations "blotted from existence." And by the time he returned home in 1847, Wright professed not to feel even "one emotion of patriotism" when he heard a distant musical band playing "Yankee Doodle."[32]

By then this sort of language would have been familiar to the readers of the *Liberator,* which published dozens of Wright's letters and journal entries from abroad. A lengthy report from Wright appeared in almost one out of every two issues of the *Liberator* between April 1844 and February 1846, and many of his writings were soon bundled into book form. Garrison exaggerated when he estimated that Wright's European letters had been "read by thousands at home and abroad," but they did receive a wide audience in the United States and Britain. Nearly all of them returned somehow to his ideas that "humanity [is] above citizenship"; that duties to humanity could not be "regulated by the compass and the clock"; and that, when duties to humanity conflicted with national policy, "*patriotism* becomes a sin."[33]

By 1847, some Americans, even outside the non-resistant camp, were more receptive to these anti-national ideas than they might have been in 1842, thanks to the outbreak of the Mexican-American War in 1846. A broad cross-section of northerners opposed this war as an example of proslavery conquest on the part of the Democratic administration of James K. Polk. And many northerners were especially offended that prowar Democrats appealed to patriotism to defend the fighting. One evangelical newspaper, reprinted in the *Liberator,* lamented that "Our Country, Right or Wrong," was "one of the watchwords of Satan."[34]

Yet Wright's tour was especially meaningful as a living testament for his fellow non-resistants, who viewed it, in Garrison's terms, as an "anti-national" and "world-embracing" mission. For non-resistants, Wright's writings from abroad distilled in purest form the potent ideas that Noyes had introduced to Garrison a decade before. His attacks on "national pride" and his "presentation of Christianity in a new, glorious, sublime form" reinforced their felt obligation to help in "rebuilding this dilapidated world," as Garrison described his task in 1846, thereby "hastening that enrapturing period when" God's kingdom finally came and nations "join[ed] in harmony."[35]

THE PERSISTENCE OF PATRIOTISM

Noyes, however, was not impressed by non-resistance. First, his theology held that any form of human control was equally rebellious against God—even if it was non-violent; a few non-resistants influenced by this line of thinking eventually found even the parliamentary procedures and hierarchies of abolitionist organizations to be a violation of the gospel. But because of their roots in the peace movement, most non-resistants saw a clear and significant difference between "moral force" and "physical force." Even on that point, however, Garrisonian non-resistants waffled more than Noyes liked; they continued to hint that violent resistance by the oppressed was distinguishable from violent oppression by the strong.

The more significant problem with Garrison, according to Noyes, was that he continued to place the abolition of slavery above all other reform goals. Garrison never tried to purge abolitionists who were insufficiently "perfect" Christians from antislavery societies; he conceded that some could conscientiously vote, even if he could not; and he even argued that paying taxes and fines were not contrary to non-resistance principles. For Noyes, "perfect" deliverance from sin required total separation from *all* human institutions, a belief that led him to establish the utopian community of Oneida in the late 1840s. But Garrison regarded experiments in utopian communities as a "new species of colonization" and a desertion of the responsibility to mobilize opposition to slavery in the North. He continued to utilize all the tactics of agitation he learned before 1838 to concentrate public opinion against slavery.[36]

In short, as Lewis Perry notes, if Noyes wanted to convert Garrison to his doctrines of total separation from the kingdoms of the world, "he had failed." Although Garrison published non-resistance columns and urged others to adopt his views, in practical terms he reduced Noyes's comprehensive vision to the practice of not voting. Wright had been in Europe for only a year before Noyes concluded that "Garrisonism" was not sufficiently "religious" in character. The "Anti-Slavery Society," declared Noyes, "is like the government of the United States, an ungodly association." He advised all "believers who are mingling themselves with abolitionists, non-resistants, &c. . . . [to] COME OUT FROM AMONG THEM, AND BE YE SEPARATE."[37]

On closer inspection, even the Garrisonians' censures of "nationalism" did not quite rise to Noyes's standards, for even non-resistants sometimes praised their country. Rogers told his British friends after the "World's Convention" that "we are freer & better off infinitely than you are." And even Wright asserted, in the middle of his "anti-national" tour, that "there is more hope for man in America than in Europe," where there were so many "old institutions to crush by their authority and antiquity."[38]

These judgments underscored again that non-resistants considered opposition to violence and bloodshed their most fundamental ideal. Non-resistants did find all governments sinful, since all relied on force; but they also believed some nations were more aggressive, militaristic, violent, and heavily policed than others. Rogers viewed the history of England as one long "continuation of combat & executions," and Wright agreed. The throne of England, he said repeatedly, was "spattered over with the brains and heart's blood of slaughtered millions."[39]

While passing through Austria on his anti-national tour, Wright also constantly noticed ruined fortifications and famous battlefields, reasoning from his encounters with Europe's professional soldiers and "blood-polluted despotisms" that most Europeans lived under the perpetual watch of "swords and bayonets that are pointed at his breast at every turn." He, unlike Noyes, weighed institutions primarily by the amount of blood they shed and the extent of their crimes against what Wright called human rights, and on that basis he sometimes expressed a preference for the United States. In one lengthy essay comparing "Old England" and "New England," Wright found in favor of New England on a host of points from the extent of land tenancy to levels of taxation and military service. In Old England, Wright added, "the idea of God having any thing to do" with what men did "in this world, seems not to be entertained, to any great extent."[40]

When they blasted England and Austria in this way, non-resistants ultimately betrayed how much their prior patriotic assumptions about American institutions persisted; that was never clearer than when most Garrisonians assumed that a true "World's Convention" like the one Wright proposed would have to be held "in a freer land than old England—it must be holden in *New England*." Rogers was convinced that "the waves of moral revolution must start from an agitation *here*." And Garrison echoed in a letter to Pease that, "bad as we are, there is much more freedom of speech and better materials to carry on the work of reform here, than with you in 'the old world.'"[41]

These sorts of distinctions made no sense to Noyes, however, who viewed all institutions and nations as equally depraved in comparison to the true government of God. That Garrison appeared to disagree underscored the limits of Noyes's influence on his thinking. Indeed, in the same 1839 non-resistance speech that described "patriotism as Anti-Christ," Garrison made clear that non-resistants did not disavow love for country altogether. "We love *all* lands too well to serve our own at their expense," Garrison explained, "but do we expect to get rid of the organs of locality and adhesiveness? No! 'be it ever so lowly, there's no place like home!'"[42]

In the end, Garrison's youthful assumptions about his country's unique qualities were simply too well developed by 1837 to be easily undone by Noyes or non-resistance. After returning from the "World's Convention," Garrison confessed that, "though I have been to England, there is no land as dear to me as my own . . . for here I see once more THE PEOPLE." He thanked God "that my field of labor lies in the United States," where society was free of the rank "inequality," the "dukes, and marquises, and earls, and royalty" of England, and he even asserted that "in all things" other than those pertaining to slavery and racial prejudice, "Great Britain falls far in the rear of the United States," which he still considered a "highly favored country." New England in particular he thought was "a century in advance of England on the score of reform." Thus, a few years later, before departing on his third mission to Britain, Garrison reiterated, "I love this country as I love no other land." Borrowing contemporary pseudo-scientific terms used by phrenologists, Garrison insisted again that his "organs of inhabitativeness and adhesiveness are . . . of unusual strength."[43]

Garrison's "adhesiveness" to his country was sometimes so strong that it even led to dispute with fellow abolitionists like Frederick Douglass. At a May 1847 meeting of the AASS in New York City, held to welcome Douglass back from his two-year tour in the British Isles, Garrison apparently gave offense by suggesting that Douglass had returned to the United States out of deep love for his native country. When Douglass rose to speak after Garrison, he declared sharply that "I cannot agree with my friend Mr. Garrison in relation to my love and attachment to this land. I have no love for America, as such; I have no patriotism. I have no country. What country have I?"[44]

In some ways, Douglass's use of those phrases shows the wide-ranging influence of the non-resistants' anti-national rhetoric. Once Douglass joined the movement in the early 1840s, he quickly learned to describe abolitionists as "strangers to nationality" whose "platform is as broad as humanity," and he claimed "the motto of our illustrious pioneer, 'Our country is the world, and all mankind are our countrymen,'" as an inspiration. Yet Douglass often turned that motto toward new ends. For him it expressed the nation's rejection of black

Americans, leaving them no country *but* the world. Thus, when Garrison suggested that Douglass had actually returned to the United States because of the same preferences he himself felt for his country, he missed an important difference between the situation of white non-resistants and the situation of fugitive slaves. This was only one of several misunderstandings that contributed to a deepening tension between Douglass and his white allies over the next few years.[45]

Still, the difference between Douglass and Garrison was slighter than it may appear, for Douglass also constantly alternated between claims that he was a true American and claims that he had no home. Because he rejected both white colonizationism and black emigrationism, notes one recent historian, Douglass's rhetoric often pivoted between cosmopolitanism and patriotism—alienation and adhesiveness—depending on the context. Non-resistants like Wright, Rogers, and Garrison actually did the same thing, which is what so troubled Noyes. In contrast to his attempt to adhere only to a future, heavenly country, theirs was a rooted cosmopolitanism or "cosmopolitan patriotism" that allowed rapid shifts between criticizing their country and expressing attachment to it.[46]

NATIONS WITHOUT NATIONALISM

Although it chagrined Noyes, Garrisonians saw no contradiction in their complex attitude towards their country, partly because of a long-established intellectual tradition that distinguished republican patriotism from patriotism under despotic rulers. Many eighteenth-century thinkers had argued that, when a country possessed republican institutions, love for that country was compatible with love for the world. Previous republican agitators like Thomas Paine thus saw little tension between, say, fighting for American independence and embracing cosmopolitan ideals. As Paine put it in his *Rights of Man,* foreshadowing Garrison's later motto, "my country is the world, and my religion is to do good." He did not view that identity as incompatible with his descriptions of American institutions as superior to Old World monarchies and titled lords.[47]

The notion that love for country and love for the world were compatible was reinforced by eighteenth-century Christian philosophers like Frances Hutcheson who argued that logic and religion both enjoined "universal benevolence" as the ideal for all moral beings. Just as Christ's love for the world was not narrow, love that expanded beyond one's own small community was more virtuous than a selfish love for country. Yet by the same logic, patriotism—love for one's whole country—could sometimes be more virtuous than even *narrower* loves for one's neighborhood or immediate family.[48]

In sum, eighteenth-century thinkers usually drew a distinction between "selfish" and excessive forms of patriotism and the liberal patriotism that could serve as a stepping stone to universal benevolence; these ideas influenced Garrison long before he ever encountered Noyes. His boyhood heroes like Lafayette and Byron saw no incompatibility between patriotism and philanthropy. Likewise, Garrison's first political mentors, the New England Federalists, often argued that the Christian virtue of "liberality" was opposed to "local" and "narrow" prejudices and warned against selfish patriotism. But patriotism could also be liberal, Federalists argued, since by loving their country—their whole country—patriots transcended regions, sects, and parties. In his early career, Garrison echoed such ideas, writing in 1827 that all "PRIVATE PARTIALITIES AND LOCAL INTERESTS MUST BE LEFT BEHIND" by truly "liberal" patriots.[49]

This idea that patriotism could be "liberal" and benevolent or cramped and selfish persisted into the nineteenth century. Indeed, Garrison made ample use of the distinction in his early abolitionist publications like *Thoughts on African Colonization*. Drawing on the moral philosophy he had learned from Federalists, Garrison portrayed colonizationists as deficient in universal benevolence towards people outside their small social circle. Simultaneously, however, the struggle against colonization encouraged immediatists to describe patriotism as morally good. Garrison insisted that free people of color felt deep attachment to the United States, the land of their birth, and that this feeling was natural and right. Echoing the arguments of black abolitionists like William Whipper, who extolled that "national feeling, which as true patriots we are bound to cherish," Garrison argued that the "*amor patriae*" of the free people of color was placed in all human beings "by the all-wise Creator to bind each separate tribe or community together." God had made of one blood all nations of men, but he had also instilled in all an instinctive "love of home, of neighborhood, of country."[50]

Garrison's immediatist allies reinforced these ideas. In 1839 Charles Follen argued explicitly that only "exclusive" patriotism was invidious. For republican Americans, Follen explained, "genuine patriotism is nothing else than philanthropy beginning at home and extending all over the world." That idea was clearly common among Garrisonian abolitionists, who eulogized Follen after his death as "a philanthropist—not a mere patriot," and in 1854, Garrison described abolitionism as both "the noblest patriotism" and "the broadest philanthropy."[51]

Nonetheless, exposure to non-resistance and Noyes did place unique pressure on the idea that "philanthropy" and "patriotism" were compatible, as did the insistence of anti-abolitionists that Garrisonians did not love their country. If Garrisonian non-resistants were forced to choose between their country and the world, Wright's "anti-national" essays made clear which one they felt obliged to pick. Yet they also sought ways to recuperate ideas like those of Paine or Follen for use in their own, different context—ways that might allow them to distinguish between the "nationalism" that both they and Noyes detested and the patriotism that persisted in their thinking.

In making that effort, Garrisonian non-resistants in some ways resembled Noyes less than Giuseppe Mazzini, the Italian revolutionary and exile whom several Garrisonians met at Ashurst's home during their trips to Britain. Wright himself spent a day with Mazzini at Muswell Hill in 1847, shortly before returning to the United States. And by the time of their meeting, the Italian had developed ideas that would have sounded quite familiar to an American non-resistant.[52]

In the first place, Mazzini often expressed religious hopes about the future of humanity that were similar to those of non-resistants. In a letter that Mazzini once sent to abolitionists through Ashurst, he described himself as "endeavouring to relink Earth to Heaven" and "realize the sense of the only prayer which is worth God & Man, 'Let O Father, thy kingdom come.'" That echoed Garrison's belief that "all prayer is comprehended in a single sentence—'THY will be done on earth, as it is done IN HEAVEN.'" But for Mazzini, God's will on earth included national independence for Italy. He began his political career as an agitator against Austrian rule in his own country, and while Garrison was founding the *Liberator* in the early 1830s, Mazzini was founding a nationalist group known as Young Italy, whose activities eventually forced Mazzini to flee into exile.[53]

As an heir to the same eighteenth-century ideals about universal rights and cosmopolitanism that influenced Paine and Follen, Mazzini never saw his quest for nationality as a license to ignore the struggles of other nations. On the contrary, in a Europe where so many different national groups had been lumped under the rule of the Holy Alliance after the Napoleonic Wars, the struggle of any one group for national independence virtually depended on cooperation with other nationalities. After fleeing Italy, Mazzini formed a group called Young Europe, which aimed to coordinate the national struggles of several groups against common enemies like Austria. Members of Young Europe swore an oath declaring their world citizenship and distinguishing their national goals from "selfish" patriotism.[54]

Mazzini arrived in England in 1836 still longing for an Italian nation. But disillusioning experiences before and after his arrival also convinced him that certain forms of "nationalism"—a term he began using only a few years before Wright—were impeding his crusade for Italy's "nationality." Frustrating collaborations with French revolutionary groups convinced him that republicans there were too obsessed with France to help Italy. And Mazzini's failure to win much tangible support for his revolutionary aims in England suggested that too many Englishmen cared only for their own country, too.[55]

In a series of essays written in exile, with the Tocquevillean title "Thoughts upon Democracy in Europe," Mazzini even suggested that the political democratization that had followed the Age of Revolutions contributed to this problem. By stressing the ideals of universal rights, the revolutions had not paid sufficient attention to the "duties" that individuals owed to each other. The few supporters Mazzini did have in England agreed with this diagnosis, and in 1847 they assisted him in forming a Peoples' International League, whose opening declaration lamented that English "Public Opinion" was too often concerned only with English affairs, encouraging Englishmen to adopt a "selfish solitariness . . . [that] sins against that law of moral gravitation which knits communities" together.[56]

Mazzini's similar diagnosis of his lack of support in England often led him to see his task, much like Phillips saw his, as an *"educational problem."* In order to win help for his own nation, he had to move other Europeans away from the "principle of the *Ego,* of *individual right*," and teach them their duties to humanity as a whole. At the same time, however, Mazzini sometimes viewed the spread of cosmopolitan sentiments as an obstacle to his aims as well. Though sometimes blaming excessive patriotism for his plight while in exile, Mazzini also attributed his lack of support partly to the prevalence of *"Cosmopolitans"* who boasted of "no longer believ[ing] in the *nation*" and who saw his own struggle for Italy as a selfish concern.[57]

Caught between what he saw as excessive nationalism on the part of some and insufficient concern for nationality on the part of others, Mazzini spent much of his time in exile musing, like non-resistants, on the relationship between human brotherhood and nations. Ultimately he developed what one recent historian has called an "anti-nationalistic idea of nationality" that resembled the position of non-resistants like Wright. For example, Mazzini drew a distinction between "nationality" and "nationalism," a term that he, like Wright, defined as a negative sort of attachment to nation.[58]

Just as Wright emphasized that duties to human rights superseded duties to nations, Mazzini also grounded his thinking on the principle of the "one common origin" of God's creation. "We have to teach mankind that humanity is one single body that must be governed by a single law," he wrote in his most systematic book, *The Duties of Man*. The nation was not the end of history, he believed, but one chapter in an increasing march towards the "*association*" of all peoples together. As a result, while support for a nation could be compatible with support for humanity, nationalism could never justify violations of God's moral laws or crimes of aggression against other countries.[59]

Such ideas jibed well with Wright's own notions about nations, even if in other ways Mazzini fell short of the non-resistance faith. When they met at Ashurst's house in 1847, Wright pressed Mazzini on his view that "armed revolution" was the only way "to throw off the incubus of aristocratic institutions." Wright also noticed that Mazzini's "hatred of Austria is deep and bitter," which possibly reflected the sort of animosity that Wright and other non-resistants viewed as the root of so much evil.[60]

Still, Garrisonians were mostly supportive of Mazzini's efforts to win sympathy for Italy in England. Ashurst, Garrison's chief correspondent in London, was one of Mazzini's greatest supporters in England, and in 1847 he sent the opening declaration of the new Peoples' International League to the *Liberator*, explaining that he was sure Garrison would "sympathize" with a movement that sought, through the "unity of nations," to advance the "unity of humanity." The league, wrote Ashurst, was "a step towards realizing your motto, 'My country is the world, my countrymen all mankind,'" and a sign "that patriotism, elevated into the love of the whole human race, has now made its distinct and organized advent."[61]

Garrison published these statements, under the headline "Patriotism Enlarging into Human Brotherhood," only weeks before publishing Wright's report of his meeting with Mazzini. Wright was impressed by Mazzini's work for "the political regeneration of Italy," and instead of objecting to his goals, he told the *Liberator* that Mazzini "would make a stirring, active, and influential leader in such a revolution." Likewise, many years later, when Garrison wrote a eulogy for Mazzini, he did not object to the fact that "Mazzini's love of native land was like a fire in his bones," because Mazzini saw his country's freedom only as a "prelude to the deliverance of all Europe" and "mankind." "This great Italian was also cosmopolitan, and would not allow any considerations to detach him from mankind as a unit"—a balancing act that Garrisonian non-resistants also believed they could perform.[62]

THE IMPORTANCE OF BEING COSMOPOLITAN

In the 1840s, Garrisonian non-resistants were torn between feelings of locality and love for country and a longing for a world without borders, governed only by the love of God. They would not have been so torn if they had been more like Noyes or more like Mazzini. If they had followed Noyes more totally, non-resistants would have felt less comfortable with any invocations of national rights or national feeling, and they would not have cared so much about regenerating their home country in particular. On the other hand, however, non-resistants could never be as comfortable with the ideal of nationality as Mazzini, partly because of their specific experiences and different national situation. As citizens of an already independent, republican nation who had often been bludgeoned with charges of "foreign interference," Garrisonians could see even more clearly than Mazzini how easily appeals to "our country" could lead to the dictum, "Our Country, Right or Wrong."

For just that reason, non-resistants urged each other constantly to examine their love for country and ensure that it was not ossifying into selfish nationalism. Indeed, that was one reason why they so valued their transatlantic friendships as ends in themselves, rather than just as means to an end. Mazzini understood his exile and alliances in England as sorrowful, temporary experiences that he hoped would end with his return home. But Garrisonians saw their temporary exiles from the United States or their communications with distant friends as positive goods.

As Maria Weston Chapman put it, non-resistants believed it was important to seek out alliances with reformers "of all countries," not just as a matter of necessity, but in order to make themselves continuously aware of "a sphere of moral action higher than that of national policy." After moving to Paris with her family in 1848, Chapman explained that "Our Country, Right or Wrong" was "apt to be the war-cry of those who have seen no country but their own." That was why she believed temporary exile could be constructive. "It is good to become cosmopolitan early in life," she explained, and "to be able to say with an experimental feeling, 'My Country is the World My Countrymen are All Mankind.'"[63]

Wright likewise viewed his own "anti-national" tour as a way of constantly keeping his ideas about the relative freedom of New England and the United States in perspective. In one 1844 letter from Graefenberg, Wright told the *Liberator* that his European experiences had impressed on him how much the "United States, as a nation, is centuries in advance of any kingdom in Europe," at least in regard to its principles of government. "But the other day," Wright reported, "when I was drawing this contrast between the United States and the despotisms of Europe, I was asked by an Austrian Count—Do you speak this as a white man, or a black? as a slave, or a freeman?" Wright was struck "dumb" and could only resolve anew to "set at nought all geographical lines and national boundaries." Even more than Mazzini, for whom the creation of new national boundaries was a primary goal, non-resistants viewed their travel as a continual goad to come out from the kingdoms of the world and plant themselves on the higher ground of heaven. The importance of being cosmopolitan also pushed them to spectacular criticisms of their country that few Americans at the time could brook; during the Mexican-American War, for example, the *Liberator* confessed to hoping for the defeat of American troops and emphatically rejected the "profligate motto, 'Our country, right or WRONG.'"[64]

The non-resistants' reflections on nationalism ultimately brought them, in other words, to a special emphasis on the good of crossing the ocean and saying "Our Country is the World." They also, like Phillips and Mazzini, believed egoistic selfishness was a major problem in democracy as it was practiced in the present. Non-resistance even led them to solutions much like Phillips, because ever-restless agitation against the nation's sins was imperative to prevent adhesiveness to home from turning into the evils of nationalism. These were ideas that Phillips also could endorse, despite not being a non-resistant himself. He certainly could agree with non-resistants like Maria Weston Chapman that "foolish pride & patriotism . . . [did] more to sustain slavery than any thing else, except the love of power & money." And he was also critical of the right-or-wrong, narrow love for country that was common among antebellum Americans.[65]

In one of his speeches on the eve of the Civil War, for example, Phillips summarized recent news reports about a Milwaukee resident who had tried to cremate the body of his wife, who was "born in Asia," "according to the custom of her forefathers." The man was forced by an angry mob, led by the local sheriff, "to submit to American funeral rites, which his soul abhorred." "This is not my idea of American civilization," said Phillips, who, like Garrisonian non-resistants, believed it part of his task to rid Americans of all such exclusive nationalism.[66]

Yet there were also subtle differences between the currents that carried Phillips and the non-resistants to similar conclusions about the need for constant agitation. The most significant were the two things that non-resistants *did* share with Noyes. First, they were impressed by the thought that the world's future depended ultimately on God's movements even more than their actions or the actions of any government. Setbacks to reform might occur, but in the face of them Garrison believed that with God "success is certain," and that "sooner, or later, in some form or another," the "sacred enterprise" of abolitionism "must triumph." As Wright put it in his circular letter about a "World's Convention" on human rights, non-resistants knew that at present "Humanity is hunted, bought & sold & butchered; & that by the public sentiment of mankind." They agreed that "this public sentiment must be corrected." But they were confident that "it can be. Humanity will not always be despised, enslaved, slaughtered; but disenthralled, regenerated, loved," and crowned "with glory" by a "Common Father." In the meantime, it was the job of reformers to prevent nationalism and other "obstacles, purely of human device," from slowing God's work.[67]

That belief, in turn, gave non-resistants confidence to remain outside of direct participation in government—the second thing they shared with Noyes. Garrison never voted, nor did other non-resistants, because they continued to see governments as sinfully violent and coercive. For the remainder of his career, Noyes's vision of the federal government as a "swaggering libertine" and Wright's descriptions of nations as blood-soaked engines of war served as warnings to Garrison to remain totally independent of formal politics.

In the short term, these beliefs did not interfere with cooperation between Phillips and Garrisonian non-resistants, who remained engaged in the work of renovating American democracy and agreed that agitation was the best way to do so. To Noyes's chagrin, Garrison did not give up on his country or on trying to influence politics. But under the surface was an important difference in worldview. Phillips believed agitation would forever be necessary to keep public opinion healthy and free; "there is no Canaan in politics," he declared. By contrast, for all their disagreements with Noyes, Garrison and other non-resistants were motivated partly by the idea that there was a Canaan coming. Human sentiment could be corrected once the barriers to God's rule in the world were removed. And agitators could believe in a God who "holds the Ocean in the palm of His hand," as Wright put it, and would not rest until all authorities bowed to His.[68]

Garrison's non-voting diverged from Noyes's vision, but his non-resistance would, during the Civil War, matter greatly to his relationship with Phillips. For non-resistants generally did not appreciate what Phillips saw as a major problem of democracy: the inevitable tendency of the "ever-restless ocean" to return to rest. They knew God would act to ensure that Christ's coming into the world had not been in vain, so their task was a temporary and specific one, focused on the removal of human obstacles from out of God's way. If Phillips looked anxiously for signs of agitation ceasing, non-resistants looked hopefully and confidently for signs of God's rule appearing.

6

THE PROBLEM OF ARISTOCRACY

Experience and reflection brought both Garrison and Phillips to stark conclusions about the dangers of democratic government. Both men concluded, for different reasons, that agitation outside of political office was necessary to counteract those dangers. But neither man concluded that some other form of government would be better than democracy. As Phillips put it in 1859, democratic institutions, while "not perfect," were still "the best possible institutions."[1]

Garrison agreed, though his commitment to democratic institutions can be harder to discern, both because of his belief that voting was a sin for him and because of statements made at the very beginning of his immediatist career. In the second issue of the *Liberator*, and again in *Thoughts on African Colonization*, Garrison sometimes distinguished his campaign for emancipation from a campaign for enfranchisement. "Immediate abolition," he argued, "does not mean that the slaves shall immediately exercise the right of suffrage, or be eligible to any office." But these early statements were not Garrison's last word on the subject. In an address delivered to free people of color in 1831, Garrison described state laws disfranchising people of color unconstitutional and urged their overthrow, and in its early volumes the *Liberator* approvingly covered efforts to challenge complexional language in voting laws and make them more "truly democratic."[2]

Garrison's later career also quickly carried him in democratic directions that were radical for his time. The constitutions of the New England Anti-Slavery Society and the American Anti-Slavery Society both called for equal civil and political rights regardless of color. His early and controversial alliances with abolitionist women also led him to declare in 1850 that "I want the women to have the right to vote." When women were granted that right, Garrison explained, "it will be for them to say whether they will exercise it or not," but first he wanted "impartial liberty to prevail." In 1859, while Massachusetts debated whether to withhold the suffrage from naturalized immigrants for two years after they obtained citizenship, Garrison condemned the proposal as "an act of political injustice," even though "we do not go to the polls ourselves."[3]

The idea of enfranchising women, people of color, and immigrants was extremely controversial in the antebellum United States, but in Jacksonian America and the broader Atlantic World, even universal white manhood suffrage remained a radical doctrine. Many people supported limitations on voting rights, using arguments like the ones Tocqueville used in *Democracy in America*. In an 1849 article printed in the *Liberator*, for example, one non-resistant abolitionist, Abraham Brooke, disagreed with a recent column by William Henry Ashurst arguing for universal suffrage, because "majorities" had no special right "to execute their will against the consent of minorities, simply because a greater number favor than oppose the measure." And in a revealing private note from 1841, Alexis de Tocqueville confessed that, despite his "intellectual preference" for democracy, "I am aristocratic by instinct, that is I despise and fear the crowd." Other European liberals favored limiting suffrage according to notions of capacity to vote, and many American Whigs continued to admire England's mixed government, fearing that full democracy might place King Mob in charge of the country.[4]

By contrast, Garrison, Phillips, and most of their allies opposed aristocracy and limited suffrage, both by instinct and intellectual preference. If the essence of aristocracy was the idea that only some people should be allowed to participate in government, Garrisonians were democrats. Despite the objections of some non-resistant readers like Brooke, Garrison published numerous columns by Ashurst advocating the application of "the democratic principle" in Britain and defending efforts by the Chartist movement there to enfranchise all adult men. And Garrison endorsed and embraced Chartists, too. In one letter to Elizabeth Pease, he made his own political instincts clear by arguing that "the extension of the right of suffrage" did not even go far enough. In Britain, he thought, "the watchword should be . . . Down with the throne! Down with the aristocracy!"[5]

These exclamations underscore again Garrison's differences with Noyes, who denied that there was any significant difference between democratic or monarchical human governments. By contrast, Garrison explained, "non-resistants do not deny that some form of government, however arbitrary and despotic, is better than a state of anarchy; that a limited monarchy is infinitely to be preferred to an absolute despotism; and that a republican is far better than a monarchical form of government." That statement of preferences showed how much Garrison's youthful adulation for the republican experiment in the United States survived his encounter with Noyes. As one writer puts it, Garrison saw the coming kingdom of heaven "as the omega point of the progressive liberalization of human governments," but in the meantime democratic republicanism was far better than the alternatives.[6]

Even the non-resistant Wright shared those basic views. Wright always criticized the violence of human government whether it was wielded by the few or the many. But after a conversation "over *Free Suffrage*" with some English reformers in 1847, Wright affirmed that all persons had a right "to a voice in making & administering the government under which he or she lives." And in 1840, Wright recorded in his journal, after a brief survey of European news and a report on the Chartists, that "two great principles" were at work in the world: "Aristocracy & Democracy, *Slavery & Liberty*." Although he once warned that "government in the hands of a majority, may be a most cruel and odious despotism," Wright spoke for most Garrisonians in confessing that he would "a little rather have it in the hands of the many" than in the hands of the few.[7]

Such statements were, in part, a reflection of how much Garrisonians still shared with other post-revolutionary Americans, but their statements of support for republican and democratic institutions were not simply vestigial. Rather, support for democracy was integrally related to Garrisonians' attacks on slavery in the United States, which they believed was the greatest proof of the dangers that aristocracy posed to human rights. While always prioritizing emancipation over enfranchisement, and while always pointing out the dangers of democracy, Garrisonians in the 1840s and 1850s remained fully alive to the problems of aristocracy on both sides of the Atlantic.

DESPOTISM IN AMERICA

Garrisonians who traveled abroad sometimes sounded like the typical American in Europe: they were inclined to shake their heads and wag their fingers at the old institutions of the "Old World." As one Philadelphia abolitionist told Phillips after returning from the "World's Convention," "to every real lover of freedom, a visit to Europe . . . will have the effect to make him a truer democrat than he was before he witnessed the crushing effect of the aristocracy of that country." Phil-

lips himself returned from his brief tour of Europe appalled by its vast dispari-
ties in wealth and power, which he attributed partly to its political institutions.
Wright likewise prayed for the removal of the evils he saw in Britain and Europe,
including "restricted Suffrage—Primogeniture . . . Aristocracy and Royalty."[8]

Yet unlike typical American tourists, abolitionists stressed that the United
States was not yet free of these evils. In its 1849 report, the Massachusetts Anti-
Slavery Society argued that, although Americans prided themselves on having
defeated "the Aristocracy of English Acres" and the principle of "power resting
on the ownership of land," they still tolerated an "Aristocracy of American Flesh
and Blood," an "abominable Oligarchy" whose power rested "on the ownership
of Human Beings." Two years before, in a *Liberator* column comparing "democratic England" with "oligarchic America," Edmund Quincy described England
as "a democracy under the forms of a monarchy," whereas the United States,
because of slavery, possessed "an hereditary aristocracy of the closest and vilest
nature, under the forms of an unlimited democracy." Voting slaveholders did not
comprise much more than 100,000 people, Quincy said, yet their "ownership
of human souls" sometimes gave them a "clear majority" in Congress by virtue
of the Constitution's rules about representation. "There is but *one* power" in the
United States government, he concluded, and "that is THE SLAVE POWER."[9]

By describing slaveholders as aristocrats, Garrisonians joined a long political tradition in northern politics. In 1804, for instance, John Quincy Adams
feared that southerners in the federal government were conspiring "to establish
an impregnable rampart of Slaveholding power, under the false batteries of democracy." The same argument soon became a favorite of northern Federalists
in their battle against Jeffersonian Republicans from the South, and during the
Missouri crisis, New Englanders again warned of the rise of an "aristocratical
order" within the country if slavery were allowed to expand. Slavery should be
checked, argued Connecticut Governor Oliver Wolcott in 1820, to "protect the
people against the masked-batteries of aristocracy."[10]

In the antebellum period, other northern writers built these early charges into
a powerful indictment of the "slaveocracy"—a powerful, landed class accustomed to deference and dictatorial rule at home and intent on using their concentrated political power to dictate to everyone else. In 1840, for example, the
Massachusetts Whig historian Richard Hildreth, perhaps with Tocqueville's title
in mind, published a book on *Despotism in America* which argued that southern
states were "aristocracies of the sternest and most odious kind." Beginning in

1839, a small number of antislavery Democrats also began to apply earlier Jacksonian attacks on the aristocratic abuses of the National Bank and the "Money Power" into a parallel attack on the "Slave Power," a term used first by the dissident Jacksonian and Liberty Party man Thomas Morris, who warned that "the slave power of the South, and the banking power of the North, are now uniting to rule this country."[11]

Though often identified most closely with political abolitionists like Hildreth and Morris, however, the "Slave Power" argument appealed to Garrisonians, too. Phillips praised Hildreth's book as "the profoundest philosophical investigation" ever made into "the influence of slavery on our government." Moreover, he and other Garrisonians traced the protections given to the slaveholding aristocracy directly to the Constitution itself. Phillips's 1845 pamphlet, *The Constitution a Pro-Slavery Compact,* used extracts from the notes of the Constitutional Convention in Philadelphia to show how southerners had won undemocratic protections for the interests of large planters. But the text of the document itself also contained undemocratic provisions—especially the inclusion of the "three-fifths clause" that awarded slaveholders extra political representation. In this clause, Garrisonians saw, "veiled beneath a form of words as deceitful as it is unmeaning in a truly democratic government, . . . a provision for the safety, perpetuity and augmentation of the slaveholding power." And the results, Phillips argued in 1853, were abundantly clear: the three-fifths clause had created a "money power of two thousand millions of dollars, as the prices of slaves now range, held by a small body of able and desperate men" who were elevated into a "political aristocracy by special constitutional provisions," reducing even the free North into a state of "vassalage" to the "Slave Power."[12]

In short, although Garrisonians differed from political abolitionists in blaming the "Slave Power" on a proslavery Constitution, they also believed that Americans were ruled politically by what Garrison called "a slaveholding oligarchy (incomparably more oppressive and dangerous than an hereditary nobility)." Their opposition to slavery and the Slave Power underlined for them why such forms of government were so evil.[13]

Where Garrisonians most differed from other critics of the Slave Power, however, was in their belief that the North was blighted by despotism and aristocratic distinction, too, in the form of legalized color prejudice. That conviction sometimes kept them from aligning themselves with movements with which they otherwise could agree. In particular, small-d democrats like the Garrisonians could not align with the big-D Democratic Party forged in the 1830s by Andrew Jackson and Martin van Buren—both because of its alliance with southern aristocrats and because of its opposition to racial equality and abolitionist agitation in the North.

The dilemma of abolitionist democrats like the Garrisonians was never clearer than in Rhode Island's so-called "Dorr Rebellion" of 1842. Between 1820 and the 1860s, property and residency qualifications for voting rights were steadily disappearing in every state. But in the midst of that wave of democratization (which extended only to white men), Rhode Island had steadfastly resisted change. In 1840, its government was still based on its colonial charter, which disfranchised the state's growing urban working class and concentrated almost all political power in the hands of an elite of wealthy Whig landowners. In the late 1830s, however, working-class reformers and democrats began to rally against the state's charter, and in 1841 their forces coalesced under the leadership of Thomas Dorr, a former Whig turned Democrat, who demanded a more democratic "People's Constitution." Dorr's followers elected him governor under the provisions of this extralegal Constitution, but Rhode Island's Whig-dominated government refused to recognize the results, leading to armed clashes between local militias and Dorrites and the declaration of martial law in the state.[14]

Like other northerners, Garrisonians watched this unfolding drama in Rhode Island with deep interest, but unlike most northerners, they focused their attention on one clause in Dorr's Constitution: a "color clause" limiting votes to whites only. Outraged by this "pandering to a wicked prejudice," Garrisonians sent Douglass and other lecturers into Rhode Island to denounce the Dorrites for making "the rights of a man dependant on the hue of his skin." But, more controversially, Garrisonians also praised a compromise proposal made by the state's Whigs to lower property qualifications for voting without abolishing them completely, reasoning that this proposal at least would restore suffrage to some black men whose voting rights had been totally revoked by an earlier decision in 1822.[15]

Dorrites interpreted the abolitionists' support for such an obvious flanking maneuver by the state's conservatives as a lack of sympathy for their democratic aims. But Garrisonians made clear that their objection to the "People's Constitution" was based solely on its color clause; they had little love for the Whigs' aristocracy, which had opposed abolitionist agitation in the past. Garrison described the state government as hostile to the "rights of man" and the embodiment of "the spirit of ancient despotism." "Every genuine republican must be, and especially every consistent abolitionist, . . . found on the side of Free Suffrage, and against the oppression of the existing Charter government in Rhode-Island," noted the *Liberator* in one article. Another declared that "whenever a constitution shall be presented, based on the truth 'that all men are created free and equal,' the abolitionists of the State will not oppose, but hail it with delight." In the meantime, Garrisonians felt torn between their commitments to democratic suffrage and their commitments to racial equality. Garrison privately confessed that he regarded "the state of things" in Rhode Island as perfectly "horrible." He had "very little sympathy" with the Dorrites who were protesting "against a land holding aristocracy" only to create an aristocracy of the skin. But he had "still less sympathy" with the state's aristocratic rulers.[16]

In the end, the Dorr rebellion presented Garrisonians with a "diabolical" choice that was all too familiar in the antebellum United States: on the one hand, northern Democrats denounced the principle of aristocracy; but on the other hand, they helped elect slaveholders and mobilized voters in opposition to abolitionist agitation and racial equality. Democrats like the Dorrites, in the *Liberator*'s words, were really only "pseudo champions of free suffrage." The choice for Garrisonians was obvious—they could not support a "pseudo" democracy that drew distinctions between the rights of white and black men—but as opponents of aristocracy, they also resented having to make the choice.[17]

"THE CHARTISTS . . . ARE THE ABOLITIONISTS OF THE UNITED STATES"

On the other side of the Atlantic, however, Garrisonians associated with a democratic movement that did not require them to choose between denouncing aristocracy and denouncing racism, giving them more opportunity to assert fully their hatred of both. At the same moment that Dorrites in Rhode Island were calling for a "People's Constitution," workers and parliamentary reformers in Great Britain were advocating a similar "People's Charter"—the document that gave Chartism its name. Chartism was a movement composed primarily of wage workers, but Chartism was also, above all, a movement for democracy. Unlike contemporary and later labor radicals who blamed the impoverishment of wage workers on capitalism itself, Chartists, as a group, blamed economic evils like poverty and low wages primarily on their continued political disempowerment. They sought redress through politics.[18]

In particular, Chartists worked to revive calls for parliamentary reform that had receded after the Reform Act of 1832. Many workers who later became Chartists initially cheered the 1832 Reform, yet even after 1832, the vast majority of British subjects remained disfranchised, and the first Reformed Parliament proved unfriendly to the interests of workers. In the 1830s, Parliament rejected ten-hour-workday legislation, created a stringent new poor-relief system, broke strikes, persecuted unions, and repressed popular dissent in Ireland, leading many workers to conclude that their plight was worse than ever before. They now feared that parliamentary elections would only allow their employers, some of whom had been newly enfranchised in 1832, to conspire with the landed aristocrats who most wanted to keep the masses at bay. Working-class grievances would not be redressed, they believed, until political democracy prevailed.[19]

In attempting to solve these political problems, Chartists looked first to political means. In 1838, working-class radicals in London drew up a "People's Charter" that made only six basic demands, including universal adult male suffrage, annual elections, and other reforms designed to make Parliament more responsive to the people. But over the next ten years, this simple document rallied British workers into a dynamic, national movement with its own Chartist newspapers, its own martyrology revolving around early leaders arrested by the government, and even its own churches.[20]

News of this gathering movement arrived piecemeal in the United States, but Garrisonians knew a great deal about Chartism because some of their closest allies supported it. For example, by the time Garrisonians met Ashurst at the "World's Convention," his family had a long history of supporting parliamentary reform. In 1832, Ashurst displayed a banner on the walls of his house declaring "This House pays no taxes until the Reform Bill becomes law." But Ashurst also quickly adopted the position of "Radicals and Chartists" that the Reform Bill "proved to be any thing but a remedy for the evils it was expected to remove" because it continued to tie suffrage to the ownership of real estate. Although small farmers and middle-class "shop-keepers" had been given the vote in 1832, Ashurst later told the *Liberator,* aristocrats still had a "monopoly of legislation" and "the people have nothing to do with [laws] but to obey them." For that reason, shortly before the "World's Convention" Ashurst joined the National Association of the United Kingdom for Promoting the Political and Social Improvement of the People, a Chartist group formed by the London radical William Lovett, who helped draft the original Charter.[21]

Relationships between Chartists and abolitionists were not always so cordial, however. Many advocates of the Charter argued that it should take precedence over the work of abolitionists now that emancipation had been achieved. And some Chartists contended that the condition of factory workers in Britain was now comparable to—if not worse than—the condition of slaves on American plantations. Some British and European radicals developed critiques of "wage slavery" that were quickly echoed by proslavery writers in the American South to justify their peculiar institutions.[22]

For these reasons and others, not all British abolitionists were so supportive of Chartism, as Garrison discovered when he visited Glasgow after the "World's Convention" and found abolitionists deeply divided over how to deal with the movement. Chartists in the city had recently begun to publish articles comparing "white" and "black" slavery, as well as to disrupt abolitionists' meetings with the aim of forcing discussion of the Charter. But leading members of the Glasgow Emancipation Society (GES), like Dr. Ralph Wardlaw, firmly opposed the Charter and the Chartists' tactics. That made Wardlaw's Chapel a volatile place when Garrison arrived at its doors on July 27. Before he could enter to attend a meeting of the GES, he was confronted at the door by a Chartist with a placard that asked, "Have we no white slaves?"[23]

Garrison took the handbill, which was being "extensively" circulated outside the chapel, and proceeded inside, pondering carefully how to respond. To side with Glasgow's Chartists, Garrison knew, would outrage abolitionist leaders like Wardlaw. But Wardlaw and much of the society's leadership already opposed Garrison's views on non-resistance and women's rights, so there would be little love lost if Garrison commended the handbill. More importantly, however, before leaving London, Garrison had spent time with Ashurst discussing "the oppressive laws by which the poor are bound down and made serfs in England," so he was already inclined to view the Charter sympathetically. By the time Garrison rose to address the meeting, he had therefore made up his mind to express support for Glasgow's workers, establishing a pattern that would continue for the remainder of his career.[24]

Garrison began his speech, unsurprisingly, by criticizing the treatment of women at the World's Convention, but in the process, he also alluded to the treatment of working-class women, giving his first indication of how he felt about the plight of the British poor. In Scotland, Garrison said, he had seen "woman laboring and toiling" in fields and brickyards, with greater burdens placed on her back than he had ever seen "except in the slave States"—a comment that drew "great cheering," most likely from the Chartists in attendance. Then, to the even greater chagrin of his conservative opponents, Garrison proceeded to read aloud the placard he was handed at the door. Garrison made clear that he did not endorse all of its sentiments; there were "no white slaves" in Britain, even if there was widespread "oppression." But Garrison added "that the abolitionists who were not the enemies of oppression, could never, in the nature of things, be the enemies of slavery," a pointed rebuke of Wardlaw and his allies. After asking the audience whether British abolitionists were "sympathising with the people" and hearing a mixture of "No, no, and yes, yes," Garrison declared that he "was sorry if they were not" and could "assure them American abolitionists did."[25]

Garrison's speech did not fully satisfy all the Chartists present, but what Garrison said about "the people" was also much more radical than Wardlaw's supporters would have liked. He had voluntarily inserted Chartists' grievances into an abolitionist meeting—the very thing they most desired. And Garrison also endorsed the Chartists' position that abolitionists should support them. If British abolitionists "wanted to prove themselves the friends of suffering humanity abroad," Garrison said, "they must do so by showing themselves the best friends of suffering humanity at home." In his closing statements, which were greeted with "great cheering" from the Chartist-heavy crowd, Garrison concluded that the whole of British society was in a "bad state" and that "a radical cure was wanted." The people should "take the axe of reform"—a likely reference, in the context of the time, to *parliamentary* reform—"and vigorously lay it at the root of the matter."[26]

Garrison continued to declare his sympathy for the Chartists after returning to Boston, too, even after learning that the same Glasgow Chartists had taken over a meeting of the GES the month after Garrison left town. "We scarcely found an abolitionist in England, who was ready to avow himself a chartist," said Garrison in the *Liberator*. "Why then should not the Chartists complain?" The same issue approvingly printed a speech by John Collins, an early Chartist hero who had been imprisoned for his political views, and while Garrison still refused to equate "slavery" with "oppression," he concluded with a ringing endorsement of the Charter. "The Chartists, in their struggle for emancipation, are the abolitionists of the United States," Garrison wrote, adding that "what they seek, and all that they ask, is most reasonable."[27]

The implications of Garrison's identification of abolitionists with Chartists became even clearer during the ill-fated British fundraising tour of John A. Collins (not to be confused with Chartist John Collins) in 1840 and 1841. When Collins arrived in Glasgow in the spring of 1841, he was quickly shunned, as he had been elsewhere, by local BFASS allies. But in response, Collins and his supporters forged an alliance with local Chartists who were already primed to view Collins favorably, thanks partly to Garrison's visit and the work of Chartist abolitionist Patrick Brewster of Paisley, a staunch supporter of the AASS. In April, Collins and his friends packed a meeting of the GES with Chartists, who helped to purge the society's officers of anti-Garrisonians and then adopted an "Address of the Workingmen of Glasgow" that affirmed their support for Collins's mission. The next day, the new, Garrisonian, leadership of the GES reciprocated by passing a pro-Chartist resolution, declaring that "the people of this country are entitled to those rights of suffrage for which they have been contending these last three years." According to newspaper reports, soon reprinted in the *Liberator*, the meeting then ended with a "series of the usual stereotyped Chartist cheers" for "the Charter, &c. &c." The *Liberator*, for its part, praised the Glasgow "Address" as "admirable in its spirit and conception."[28]

Garrison's praise for Chartists only continued and deepened when he returned to Britain in 1846. On this trip, leading Chartists William Lovett and Henry Vincent were among those Garrison most wanted to meet, and by the time he left he considered both men "cherished friends." Even more than during his 1840 trip, Garrison also sought to identify his movement explicitly with the Chartists. At one antislavery meeting held at the Crown and Anchor Tavern in London, a place with rich symbolic associations as the very site where the "People's Charter" was first drafted, Garrison seized the opportunity to reassure the "working men" in the audience that, in denouncing American slavery, "I do not denounce democracy." He urged workers to "join us," for "we are with you." Frederick Douglass added his own endorsement of the Charter at the same meeting, and Chartists, for their part, endorsed the Garrisonians. Vincent was present on the platform at the Crown and Anchor, and Lovett's memoir later recalled a convivial evening of conversation and socializing spent at the home of a Chartist friend with Garrison, Wright, Thompson, and Douglass.[29]

Of course, one of the primary reasons Garrison endorsed Chartists like Lovett and Vincent was because they were abolitionists, too; unlike Dorrite democrats, they did not reject Douglass or defend racial prejudice. On the contrary, both Lovett and Vincent told Garrisonians that slavery in the United States was injuring their case for suffrage in Britain. In the same year he and Garrison met, Vincent told the *Liberator*, through Wright, that the persistence of the American slave system ("an aristocracy more unchristian and pernicious than any aristocracy in the world") allowed opponents of the Charter to say "*Ah, but in America the people have the power—your own system is in operation there, and why does it not crush these evils?*" Precisely because English radicals like Vincent, Lovett, and Ashurst denounced the Slave Power loudly and clearly, the "People's Charter" gave Garrisonians opportunities to give full-throated expression to their own beliefs about democracy, without the qualifications they were forced to give in the case of a racist Rhode Island democracy. In London, where he addressed a large group of Chartists in 1846, Garrison could declare that "I wish to be identified with you out and out."[30]

He knew there were some on both sides of the Atlantic who looked down on workers as undeserving of political power, Garrison told London Chartists in this, his longest address to members of the movement. But he did not. On the contrary, as a "working man" himself—a reference to his manual labor as a printer—Garrison praised Lovett and Vincent, and just as he had in Glasgow in 1840, he urged all abolitionists to support the Charter's primary aim. "If there are any [here] struggling after an extension of the elective franchise," Garrison said, then he wanted them to know that "I am with them." Four years after the Dorr War, and four years before his similar comments supporting women's suffrage, Garrison made clear to Chartists that he favored impartial liberty at the polls.[31]

GOVERNMENT OF AND FOR THE PEOPLE

Garrison's description of himself as a "working man" won him cheers from his Chartist audience in 1846, but in retrospect it was a questionable claim. Socially he had little in common with Glasgow cotton spinners or English children sent to the coal mines, whose condition was the "nearest approach" to slavery that Irish abolitionist Richard Allen could imagine. Other Garrisonians who followed Garrison in endorsing the Charter, like Phillips and Chapman, had even less claim to the title of "workers," given their independent wealth. Despite Garrison's desire to be identified with Chartists, he and his allies also hobnobbed with many wealthy supporters while abroad, seldom stepping off their platforms to investigate workers' conditions up close.[32]

These facts led some observers at the time to conclude that Garrison's appeals to Chartists were little more than a pose. John B. Estlin, one of Garrison's wealthiest patrons and one of the few Garrisonian abolitionists in England who disliked Chartism, certainly thought so. In a series of letters to Samuel May Jr., Estlin even implied that Garrison's 1846 speeches were typical attempts by a brash American to blast monarchy and aristocracy while in Old England. Garrison did not really understand Chartism, Estlin said; he only embraced it because he thought it would increase "his credit in *America*." In the meantime, by meddling with "all sorts of questions that divide the population of this country" and "*going out of his way*" to fraternize with Chartists, Garrison was unknowingly alienating wealthy, aristocratic abolitionists who could help him.[33]

Estlin was certainly right that, by endorsing the Charter, Garrison only burned more bridges with mainstream abolitionists like Wardlaw; with the notable exception of Joseph Sturge, most members of the BFASS steered clear of Chartists. Moreover, Estlin's idea that Garrison was thinking of audiences at home when he spoke to Chartists may have had some truth. Garrison may have hoped that, by identifying with Chartists abroad, he could silence critics at home, like the Dorrites, who accused abolitionists of spending all their charity on slaves and saving none for impoverished workers.[34]

Yet Estlin's suspicions of Garrison's motives failed to explain fully why he and other American abolitionists viewed the Charter positively, mainly because Estlin had trouble believing that universal suffrage and universal emancipation were "joined & allied, each to the other," as May Jr. tried to explain. Estlin thought Garrison was going out of his way to meddle in British politics, but in his speech to London Chartists in 1846, Garrison stated again, as he often had before, that one of the worst effects of American slavery was the dishonor it cast on republican institutions, retarding the spread of democracy and the rights of "labouring men" around the world.[35]

Estlin also wrongly assumed that Garrisonians had a shallow understanding of the Chartists' positions. In reality, between Garrison's 1840 and 1846 trips to Britain, Garrisonians had actively informed themselves about the movement. By the time Garrison met Lovett, Vincent, and other Chartists in 1846, their views were already quite well known and well regarded among American abolitionists.

Few Garrisonians made a more concerted effort to inform themselves about Chartism than Wendell Phillips, who gave nearly as much attention and praise to the movement as he did to Tocqueville's *Democracy in America*. Sometime shortly after returning home from the "World's Convention," Phillips began compiling a sheaf of sprawling notes on Chartism, but he was most impressed by the arguments he read in *Chartism,* a seminal 1840 book co-authored by Chartists William Lovett and John Collins. Among other things, their paean to "the powers and energies of representative democracy" offered Phillips a lucid account of the movement's origins and aims, which they traced to the deficiencies in the Reform of 1832. Since then, Lovett and Collins explained, the working classes' lack of political power had made it possible for aristocrats and their allies to pass laws "*partial*" to their interests, putting a damper on democratic reform. Now only the Charter could secure "*to all classes of society their just share of political power*" and procure for "our brethren *equality of political rights.*" Phillips absorbed these lessons rapidly, scribbling in his notes that "power" in England had so far "legislated for a class instead of for the people," but that the people had now resolved "to govern themselves." Chartism, he concluded, belonged to the larger struggle to establish government "of the people & for the people."[36]

Impressed by the justice of these demands, Phillips continued to seek information about the Chartists in the 1840s, writing to Pease multiple times in 1842 with questions about the movement. Phillips already had copies of the Charter, he told her, and "your pamphlets & our newspapers throw much light on [the Chartists'] movements," but he desired more details for a speech he was beginning to prepare on the topic. Happy to oblige, Pease passed some of Phillips's inquiries on to Ashurst, who in turn directed them to "three of the leading Chartists," including Lovett himself. Later, Pease sent a "parcel of tracts which Mr Lovett forwarded to my care."[37]

Meanwhile, Pease gave Phillips her own impressions of the Charter, which were surprisingly positive given that she was the daughter of a well-off family of mill owners. Pease admitted that it was considered "*ungenteel*" and "*vulgar*" for a woman of her class to "sympathise with the poor oppressed Chartists." Nonetheless, she told her Garrisonian friends that "I *do most sincerely,*" describing her political views as "*ultra radical.*" The suffrage question, she believed, was "at the very foundation of the prosperity—almost of the existence—of this country." Chartists were justly criticizing "the oppressive domination of the aristocracy" and the Tory Party, and Pease also clearly agreed with Garrison that abolitionists should be Chartists as well; in 1841 she was glad to report, for example, that antislavery journalist William Howitt had recently endorsed the Charter, too.[38]

William Henry Ashurst complemented Pease's letters with his own regular reports about Chartism. Between 1842 and 1854, about one in every five issues of the *Liberator* contained a dispatch from Ashurst under the pseudonym "Edward Search," and these columns returned constantly to Ashurst's belief that Britain was still struggling against "white slavery—the slavery of the unrepresented many." He supported that point with multiple, detailed examples of Parliament's actions since 1832, all of which suggested the continued power of England's landed aristocrats.[39]

With transatlantic informants like these, it should be no surprise that Phillips's finished speech on "Chartism," which he began delivering in late 1842, roundly praised the movement. Phillips described Chartists in glowing terms as the prophetic bearers of an "unquenched torch of civil liberty" ignited by the Puritans. The English working classes, he argued, were not primarily to blame for their poverty and hunger. Instead, the fault lay with an aristocratic government of "legislative landlords" who poured all of the nation's resources into its "military policy," thereby keeping taxes and food prices high for the bulk of the population. Phillips also chastised the American press for the contempt it often showed the Chartists and told Americans that they should feel a "brotherly interest in the cause." "The people, convinced that nothing favorable is to be expected while the Legislature is in the hands of a privileged class, are concentrating their efforts on the question of Universal Suffrage," Phillips explained.[40]

By year's end, Phillips had delivered his speech "several times in different towns" and "excited great attention & interest," and on December 30, he sent a report of the speech from the New York *Tribune* to Pease, asking her to forward copies to Ashurst, "whose letter was a great help to me." Phillips indeed had drawn directly from information provided by his British correspondents; according to the *Tribune,* he praised *Chartism* as a pamphlet with "few equals in any of the Essays which recent political events in England have produced," and he made use of a quotation that Ashurst had cited in a *Liberator* column only a few weeks before. Pease, in turn, happily passed copies of the speech to a Chartist she knew in Darlington, who told her he was "very glad" to read it—as well he might have been. Phillips had not only provided Americans with a portrait of the Chartists as genuine democrats; he also, like Garrison in Glasgow, implied that abolitionists should be Chartists, too.[41]

To be sure, these Garrisonian endorsements of the Charter had some definite limits. First, like Garrison in 1840, Garrisonians consistently rebuked Chartists who conflated American chattel slavery with the oppression of white workers; while in England, Douglass often used his own experiences to deny that wage work was equivalent to enslavement. Second, Garrisonians mostly opposed the so-called "physical force" Chartists who threatened revolution if Parliament did not embrace the Charter.

Still, these views mirrored divisions within the Chartist movement, and they did not keep Garrisonians from supporting the Charter itself, which was "dear to the heart of every genuine republican and christian." Indeed, when Rhode Island abolitionist Thomas Davis traveled to Britain in 1842, he even told the *Liberator* that Feargus O'Connor, typically seen as the leader of "physical force" Chartism, was actually "more 'sinned against than sinning,'" a judgment that Phillips echoed in his lecture. Even Wright—a staunch non-resistant—ultimately concluded that "sword and gun, stone and club Chartists cannot make their principles odious, nor retard their onward course, for God is in them. The principles of the Charter, when understood in their fullest extent, are of God, and must prevail."[42]

Some Garrisonians even proved surprisingly tolerant of Chartists' comparisons between slaves and disfranchised workers. Ashurst's columns sometimes referred to the English poor as "the slave class" in Britain. In another letter published in the *Liberator,* Pease likewise contended that the poor "in our manufacturing districts" were "in reality, though not in name . . . the slaves of the aristocracy." And even American Garrisonians sometimes tiptoed around the "slavery" analogy. Chapman assured Pease, in an 1843 letter, that "I am deeply interested for the common people of England; no less so than for our own slaves—the corresponding class in this country."[43]

Estlin, for his part, viewed such statements as proof that Garrisonians were listening to the wrong people; he singled out Ashurst as an untrustworthy radical in his letters to May. Despite Estlin's warnings, however, Garrisonians listened closely to correspondents who favored the Charter, and their interest in suffrage reform in England continued even beyond the dissolution of the Chartist movement in 1848. In 1849, George Thompson joined forces with a small group of parliamentary reformers and former Chartists who continued to advocate universal suffrage, and his speeches—which called on Parliament to "enfranchise the cottage, as well as the mansion"—were favorably covered in the *Liberator*. Garrison's embrace of Chartists in 1846 was thus not an isolated episode, as Estlin suspected; instead, it showed the Garrisonians' consistent and well-informed approval of what they regarded, in Phillips's terms, as a struggle for government of and for the people.[44]

DEMOCRACY IN AMERICA

The picture of Chartism that Garrisonians received from their British friends was, to be sure, a limited perspective on a diverse and often divided movement. By 1849, many former Chartists were convinced that the grievances of workers could be traced to the wage system itself, rather than to a simple lack of political rights, but the few Garrisonians who entertained such ideas in the 1840s, most notably John A. Collins, found little support from most abolitionists. Garrisonians' lack of real experience as wage workers also sometimes made them insensitive to particular Chartists' complaints. After his first encounter with Chartists in Glasgow in 1840, Garrison received a letter from one worker, Charles M'Ewan, who complained that the abolitionist had made too "fine" a distinction between slavery and oppression; according to M'Ewan, the fact that Garrison spent part of his speech urging workers to adopt temperance and industrious habits showed that he had a tin ear to the real cries of the people.[45]

Still, a tin ear was not a blind eye. Even M'Ewan praised Garrison for reading the Chartist placard in Glasgow and paying attention to the movement. Moreover, when Garrisonians recommended "self-reform" to workers, that did not prove their ignorance of the movement, for Chartist writers like Lovett and Collins also stressed the need for workers to join mutual aid and educational organizations that would prove their ability to govern themselves. Indeed, M'Ewan's letter faulted Garrison mainly for failing to note that working men in Scotland were already in the forefront of the temperance movement. Garrison was happy to concede this point, and in the end, the two men agreed more than they disagreed. In his rejoinder to M'Ewan, Garrison held fast to his original position: even if "slavery" and "oppression" were not identical, he believed abolitionists should oppose both and should support the Chartists.[46]

The fact that Garrisonians understood Chartism primarily as a demand for "political rights," rather than a campaign against the wage system itself, also showed the extent of their information about the movement. Only from the perspective of the post-Chartist period and the 1848 Communist Manifesto does the Garrisonians' emphasis on democratic remedies for economic problems seem like a misunderstanding of working-class radicalism, for Chartists themselves constantly returned to suffrage and parliamentary reform as their most important demands. Most Chartists looked back to Thomas Paine's critiques of aristocrats and monarchs rather than forward to Marx's democratic socialism; as

Lovett and Collins put it, they blamed poverty on "class legislation" more than on class warfare, and emphasized "*political reformation,* as the most certain and direct means of all *moral* as of all *social* reformation."[47]

This picture of Chartism as a movement that placed "political reformation" above "social reformation" was constantly reinforced by the reading material that Garrisonians received from abroad. When Glasgow workingmen presented their "Address" to John A. Collins in 1841, for example, they traced the low wages, poor diet, and poverty of British workers primarily to the evil of "class legislation" and the continued political power of a "debauched aristocracy." Pease, too, echoed many Chartists when she attributed most of Britain's social evils to the "hydra-headed monster" of "class Legislation." Until aristocratic government was "*destroyed* utterly—blood, bones & sinews—like the fabled monster of old, two heads will spring up to fill the place of one."[48]

Of course, reading these polemics against "class legislation" did allow Garrisonians to avoid confronting the possibility of other monsters in their midst; later in life, Phillips would become a noted supporter of the economic rights of labor, but in the 1840s he believed that many of the complaints made by radical American workers about private property and "wage slavery" came from looking too much through "European spectacles." In the United States, he said in 1847, workers had more "ample power to defend themselves" because of the opportunities afforded by suffrage and the market. Except in "a few crowded cities and a few manufacturing towns," the sufferings of laborers did not compare to those of slaves, Phillips believed.[49]

In making these statements, Phillips was mainly trying to refute the concepts of "white slavery" and "wage slavery," which were often used as "party watchwords" to stir up American voters against abolitionists. But Phillips, like most Garrisonians and many Chartists, did still think of aristocracy in political terms, rather than economic ones. That position allowed him and others to believe that New England was immune from some of the evils he had seen in Europe. In his speech on Chartism, for instance, Phillips professed amazement that "the thrones of Europe" were so "startled" by Chartists' demands for universal manhood suffrage, annual elections, and vote by ballot. "An American can only be surprised that they ask so little, and that their catalogue of rights embraces only things so familiar here, that, like the alphabet, they are almost forgotten." Privately, Phillips reinforced this point. While observing the harassment of Chartists in 1842, for example, he wrote to Pease that "I never understood the (unjust) tiger like strength of your *Government* till now. Here light does not follow the day quicker than our Govert. changes at the peoples bidding."[50]

Still, Phillips and other Garrisonians were aware that there were states even in New England where the people's bidding was ignored by elites, as their angst about that year's events in Rhode Island showed. And the public endorsements that Phillips and Garrison gave to Chartists hardly would have endeared them to conservatives like Rhode Island's Whigs. Indeed, when Phillips delivered his speech on Chartism again in Providence in 1844, a "respected correspondent" to the *Liberator* wrote that the lecture was "very slimly attended" by Whigs. The *Liberator*'s informant supposed, probably with good reason, that "the aristocracy" of the state "did not wish to hear anything about the misery of the Chartists." Those few "ladies and gentlemen of property and standing" who did turn out to hear Phillips simply "stared" at him in shock. Though not the radical reformer that some critics of "wage slavery" wanted him to be, Phillips also acknowledged, even in his editorial about the distortions of "European spectacles," that "the imperfections which still cling to our social and political arrangements bear hardest on the laborer."[51]

Garrisonians also generally rejected the idea that anything—whether property, education, or temperate habits—should serve as a prerequisite for being able to vote. Phillips believed that universal education, virtue, and elevation would follow universal suffrage, instead of the other way around—an argument that would later become especially important in debates over black suffrage during Reconstruction. Simply having the right to vote—even if one did not use it—had an educative and elevating effect on the electorate, he often explained, because only those entrusted with power over the government would take genuine interest in government. A right to vote was an essential tool for acquiring the virtues—like disinterestedness and participation in free discussion—that Phillips considered essential to the duties of citizenship: "responsibility teaches as nothing else can."[52]

Educational qualifications for voting made little sense on this view, for the franchise itself was "one instrument—a great instrument—of education, both moral and intellectual." It "sharpens the faculties . . . unfolds the moral nature," and would expedite the extension of education to all. Once wealthy elites saw that the masses had the power to make law, "selfishness" would be enough to compel them to help educate every "poor, ignorant" citizen in the state. Simply on the grounds of "the highest expediency," therefore, it made sense to enfranchise every woman and man first, instead of waiting until each could meet some educational test.[53]

In making these arguments, Phillips again echoed common transatlantic liberal ideas. In 1851, for example, in a speech defending woman suffrage, Phillips cited Tocqueville in support of his claim that "the great school of this people is the jury-box and the ballot-box." Tocqueville had already argued, especially in the first volume of *Democracy,* that Americans had so far mitigated the dangers of individualism and majority tyranny by enabling such widespread participation in the functions of government; Mill agreed in some of his own writings about the power of participation in a democracy to elevate citizens and equip them to govern. But unlike Phillips, both Tocqueville and Mill remained ambivalent about whether the effects of participation were, on balance, good; they also wavered about whether the right to vote was necessary to secure benefits that other forms of civic participation might bring. Phillips, by comparison, was certain that "responsibility" itself—the right to vote—was essential to the "education of the American citizen."[54]

Phillips argued for universal suffrage not only as an instrument of education, however; he also believed it was essential for the protection of all citizens and classes from the abuses of irresponsible power. That reasoning best explains his sympathy for the Chartists struggling against "class legislation," and for Phillips, the disfranchisement of women by men was another perfect example of why anything short of universal suffrage was dangerous. Limited democracy always allowed the class with political power—in this case men—to subject all other classes to taxation, penal codes, and discriminatory laws without giving them any say in the formation of the law. Phillips dismissed the argument that women needed men to take care of them as a transparent case of self-justification; every aristocratic government in history showed that a class invested with exclusive power would find some reason why those without power were inferior. Justice therefore demanded that, "in government, every individual should be endowed, as far as possible, with the means of protecting himself," and "every class should be endowed with the power to protect itself"—principles that struck at the very foundations of contemporary arguments for limiting suffrage.[55]

Such democratic statements perhaps explain why several Chartists who emigrated to the United States gravitated towards Garrisonians once they arrived. As the run of the *Liberator* drew to a close in 1864, one English worker who had been a Chartist wrote to tell Garrison that it had been natural for him to pass from reading Chartist newspapers to reading the *Liberator* when he came to the United States. And his testimony is borne out by the examples of other Chartist exiles like James W. Walker, who became a Garrisonian agent in Ohio and Michigan after being "hunted from England as a Chartist." Ultimately, even Charles M'Ewan, who had criticized Garrison's speech in Glasgow, supported the Garrisonian faction when John A. Collins returned to the city the following year.[56]

John C. Cluer, a Chartist who came to the United States in 1839, was an even more prominent Garrisonian ally. Cluer brought his labor radicalism with him from Scotland and in the 1840s became an active participant in the "ten-hour" workday movement in New England. But unlike many other leaders of this movement, Cluer joined forces with abolitionists. In 1845, he delivered lectures on abolitionism and Chartism in Nantucket that were reported approvingly in the *Liberator*, and in 1848 he and another exile held a public meeting on the Charter in Boston that the *Liberator* praised for the "excellent remarks" made. Finally, in 1852, Cluer appeared at the twentieth-anniversary meeting of the MASS, the first of at least three such appearances at Garrisonian meetings. At these meetings Cluer spoke of the Chartist movement's "strong resemblance to, and in fact its identity in spirit with, the anti-slavery movement of this country," confirming what Garrison himself had argued since 1840.[57]

Cluer, unlike Dorr, was the sort of small-d democrat whom Garrisonians had no trouble inviting to their platforms, especially since he echoed all their claims about the likenesses between the aristocrats he knew and the "Slave Power" in the United States. At one Garrisonian meeting, John C. Cluer pointed out that suffrage laws in South Carolina—one of the last states to embrace universal white manhood suffrage—were more restrictive than in England. Such points reinforced for Garrisonians the primary reason why they supported democracy: the oligarchical rule of slaveholders showed all too well the dangers of aristocracy.[58]

Indeed, their exchanges with Chartists and British reformers impressed the parallels between aristocrats and slaveholders even more deeply on Garrisonians' minds. Ashurst told his American friends that "selfish class legislation is the cause of your slavery and ours." Pease linked "the Slaveocrat spirit" in Westminster to the same spirit in the slaveholding South. And Richard D. Webb noted "that there are many points of resemblance between a Slaveocracy and an Aristocracy, and the influence of both is, in many particulars, identical."[59]

No wonder, given this chorus, that Henry Clarke Wright likewise concluded that "*the Aristocracy of England* resemble the slaveholders of America exceedingly." As Phillips reminded abolitionists in 1861, on the eve of the Civil War, Americans under slavery were not exempt from the problems facing Chartists in Britain; they too faced a hydra-headed monster made up of "the prejudice of race, the omnipotence of money, and the almost irresistible power of aristocracy." For decades, he said, the three-fifths compromise had more or less succeeded in canceling the votes of northerners: "You may take a small town here in New England, with a busy, active population of 2,500, and three or four such men as Governor Aikin of South Carolina, riding leisurely to the polls, and throwing in their visiting-cards for ballots, will blot out the entire influence of that New England town in the Federal Government." This was a Union based not on democracy, Phillips made clear, but on "despotism," "money power," and an "artificial aristocracy."[60]

No other aristocracy had even "half its power," concluded Phillips, and if experience on both sides of the Atlantic was any guide, it would only seek to increase its might. Wary though he and other Garrisonians might be about democracy's own dangers, they had no rosy illusions about government by a landed class. "Power is ever stealing from the many to the few," he noted in his 1852 speech on "Public Opinion," and rule by the few was no refuge from the perils of rule by the many. Both could be despotical if citizens were not eternally vigilant. As agitators, abolitionists therefore always claimed a twofold task: to keep the ocean of democracy restless all the time, and to abolish the aristocracies that hoped, on both sides of the Atlantic, to stem democracy's tide.

THE PROBLEM OF INFLUENCE

By the mid-1840s, Garrisonians agreed with a growing number of antislavery northerners about the dangers posed by the Slave Power. As historian Leonard L. Richards notes, "hostility toward slave oligarchs . . . provided common ground" for a wide range of people—including anti-expansion Whigs, antislavery Jacksonians, and political abolitionists—precisely because "men and women could differ on scores of issues . . . and still lambaste the 'slaveocracy.'"[1]

Garrisonians differed from other opponents of the Slave Power, however, in their steady refusal to vote or run for political office, even as others grew more convinced that slaveocrats could not be beaten any other way. By 1839, political abolitionists like Gerrit Smith, a wealthy New York philanthropist who supported the Liberty Party, were convinced that only a preponderance of "right-voting abolitionists" could exert enough pressure on the major national parties to break the power of slavery in the federal government. But throughout the antebellum period, Garrisonians remained united in their abstention from voting and office.[2]

The Garrisonians' reasons for not voting were actually more diverse than some opponents acknowledged. For some, non-voting was a consequence of non-resistance. Garrison supported the Chartists' aims of what Lovett and Collins called "political reformation," but he did not believe political reformation was a prerequisite for moral reformation. He continued to prioritize moral reform and refused voting as a kind of complicity in the sins that governments committed. But other Garrisonians simply believed they could not vote or take office without endorsing the Constitution's protection of slavery. To these points, others added a fear that power would stifle their freedom of advocacy and rob them of their independence as agitators.

These lines of reasoning were not incompatible, however, and they all led AASS members to limit their tactical range: they printed newspapers without party tickets; they gave speeches, but not in Congress; they vilified politicians but did not vote. Above all, they talked. "Worshipping the tongue," Phillips told his fellow Garrisonians, "let us be willing, at all times, to be known throughout the community as the all-talk party."[3]

Many political abolitionists agreed that defeating the Slave Power required inciting "talk" over slavery; it was the idea of being an "all-talk" party to which they objected. Even after Frederick Douglass became "a Liberty party man" in 1851, he often still cited the Garrisonian argument "that political action is necessary only in the rear of public sentiment." Douglass therefore urged antislavery politicians to "agitate, *agitate*. This is the grand instrumentality, and without this you . . . will come to nothing." But Douglass and his fellow political abolitionists disagreed with Phillips that an aristocracy as powerful as the Slave Power could be defeated with agitation *alone*; they believed slaveholders had to be bested in the arena of politics because the government was what gave them so much protection and power.[4]

The distance between political abolitionists and Garrisonians on that point was slighter than it may appear, however, for one important reason: Garrisonians never believed that refusing to seek political *power* meant giving up on attempts to *influence* what happened inside Congress, political parties, or polling booths. Even in a speech to the Non-Resistance Society, Garrison predicted that "non-resistance" would one day "be felt powerfully at the polls." And in 1839, Garrison made clear that, despite his non-resistance views, "I have always expected, I still expect, to see abolition at the ballot-box, renovating the political action of the country." He and other members of the AASS maintained that a reformation of the "moral vision of the people" would ultimately lead to "political reformation." In short, just as Garrison saw the government of God as the omega point of the progressive liberalization of human governments, he perceived political change as the omega point of progressive moral reformation.[5]

For just that reason, however, Garrison still longed for evidence of his political influence, even as he laid down his right to vote. For Wendell Phillips, meanwhile, the desire for influence may even have been greater. In 1844 Phillips confessed to Elizabeth Pease that "politics is a sore temptation, to me at least," especially as he watched his old Harvard friend Charles Sumner move into Congress as a leader of the anti–Slave Power wing of the Whig Party.[6]

When tempted by politics, Garrisonians reassured themselves that they were at least doing their duty. They reminded each other that agitation was valuable in itself as a way to protect democratic discussion. But like most agitators, Garrisonians wanted more: they constantly searched for arguments and evidence to reassure themselves and others that "ever-restless" agitation could influence current events. They wanted to stir up the waters of public opinion but also longed to ride its waves to political influence.[7]

At the same time, Garrisonians always recognized this desire as a temptation. Garrison remained enough of a non-resistant to fear what the possession of political influence would do to his work for the kingdom of God. That was one reason why he was so ambivalent when his friend George Thompson decided to run for election to the House of Commons in 1847. After Thompson's successful campaign, Garrison confessed that he was "somewhat apprehensive lest [Thompson's new duties] should contract, rather than enlarge, his sphere of usefulness as a popular reformer, and a world-embracing philanthropist." For Phillips, meanwhile, the ghost of politicians like Webster always haunted whatever dreams he had of political office; if he won political influence, would he, too, surrender his independence?[8]

That question created a constant dilemma for agitators: they needed the confirmation of politicians and the people to validate their efforts, but when confirmation came, did that mean the people had changed or that agitators had? Caught between a desire for influence and a fear of where it might lead, Garrisonians spent much of their time in the 1840s thinking about this problem. But transatlantic events and ideas gave them part of their answer. Two massive extra-parliamentary movements in Britain—the Irish campaign for a Repeal of the Union, and the Anti–Corn Law League's campaign for free trade—resolved one horn of the Garrisonians' dilemma by confirming that agitation could influence politics. But these models did not entirely alleviate their fears of what influence could do to agitation.

THE APPEAL OF CORN LAW REPEAL

When wrestling with the problem of political influence, Garrisonians sought reassurance first in the past. Phillips turned, as usual, to Greece: "When Socrates walked the streets of Athens, and, questioning everyday life, struck the altar till the faith of the passer-by faltered, it came close to *action*, and immediately they gave him hemlock, for the city was turned upside down." At other times, Phillips turned to sacred or American history, citing figures like Martin Luther, Peter the Hermit, Oliver Cromwell, the Pilgrims, James Otis, Elijah Lovejoy, or Jesus Christ himself as proof that a single individual or small group, without direct political power, could influence millions.[9]

Yet Garrisonians also took courage from contemporary reform movements in Great Britain that suggested the effectiveness of "pressure from without." In a page in his commonplace book titled "Not Voting," Phillips listed a few of these movements, ending with the observation that "Chartist agitation [was] influential tho' without suffrage." And in an 1853 speech, Phillips linked Garrisonians' hopes to several other transatlantic reforms. "If the leaders of popular movements in Great Britain for the last fifty years have been *losers*," he asked, "I should be curious to know what party . . . have won? . . . If the men who, by popular agitation, outside of Parliament, wrung from a powerful oligarchy Parliamentary Reform, and the Abolition of the Test Acts, of High Post Rates, of Catholic Disability, of Negro Slavery and the Corn Laws, did 'not win anything,' it would be hard to say what winning is."[10]

When looking abroad for victorious models of popular agitation, Garrisonians turned first and most obviously to the British abolitionist movement. Yet it also had weaknesses as a model for "all-talk" agitation. First, politicians within Parliament had been instrumental to emancipation. The Congressional "gag rule" also raised some serious doubts among all abolitionist factions about the efficacy of British methods like petitions in their case. After 1840 many Garrisonians concluded that British abolitionists had never dealt with intense persecution or an anti-abolitionist reign of terror. "Uncorrupted by the presence and unsubdued by the power of slavery," British antislavery "has never been tried in a fiery furnace," argued the *Liberator*. It was *too easy* to be an abolitionist in England.[11]

These wilting estimations of British abolitionism were partly signs of sour grapes over the "World's Convention," but they contained hard truths: antislavery mobilization in England had not been met with the gag rules, mob violence, and almost universal condemnation that greeted calls for immediate abolition in the United States. In the 1830s and 1840s, American abolitionists of all stripes were thus forced to rethink the applicability of the British movement's experience.

One overseas movement that initially struck Garrisonians as a more useful model was the campaign for Catholic emancipation in the 1820s. This grassroots

Irish movement, led by O'Connell, challenged the political disabilities that kept Catholics out of Parliament, especially the requirement that members of Parliament disavow allegiance to the Pope. It culminated in 1829 with a series of extralegal elections that demonstrated massive support in Ireland for O'Connell. And it ended successfully when O'Connell and other Irish Catholics were admitted into the House of Commons. Even this movement was not a perfect model. Still, Garrisonians were impressed that a group proscribed by law and deep-seated prejudice—much like American abolitionists—succeeded in changing politics at the highest levels. As late as 1850, Douglass (who had not yet become a Liberty Man) pointed to the movement when anyone asked "who will alter the laws, if you can elect no one?" In answer, he cited "the admission of Daniel O'Connell to the British Parliament," which "was compelled by public sentiment to admit him."[12]

Garrisonians found an even more important model, however, in the Corn Law Repeal movement, another extra-parliamentary campaign that O'Connell also supported. The Corn Laws were a set of protectionist trade regulations designed to protect England's food supply in times of war, and they had attracted sporadic criticism throughout the early nineteenth century. But it was not until after the abolition of West Indian slavery and the simultaneous onset of economic depression that a small group of commercial men in Manchester, led by Richard Cobden, formed an Anti–Corn Law Association in 1838. That group became the germ of a national organization founded the following year—the Anti–Corn Law League (ACLL), which spent seven years mounting a sophisticated pressure campaign for repeal.[13]

Garrisonians watched the league closely, not least because they had close allies in it. John Bowring gave the speech in 1838 that prompted the formation of the Manchester Anti–Corn Law Association, and in 1841, the British India Society merged with the ACLL, which hired George Thompson for the next five years as one of its most prominent lecturers. Pease answered multiple requests from friends like Phillips to send them copies of anti–Corn Law publications, and in 1841 and 1842, the *Liberator* reprinted many items by or about Thompson from ACLL journals.[14]

These reports did raise some reservations, however. The first was the controversial support of some ACLL leaders for an end to the sugar duties that protected the free-labor economies of the British Caribbean. Some Garrisonians agreed with leaders of the BFASS that lifting the sugar duties would encourage slave-grown produce. Garrisonians were also disturbed by the willingness of

ACLL leaders to correspond with proslavery southern free traders. This last issue led Haughton to publicly cancel his ACLL membership, a move that American friends applauded.[15]

Even so, most Garrisonians endorsed the specific aims of the Anti–Corn Law League and praised its methods. Some Garrisonians also favored absolute free trade and repeal of the sugar duties, and on the narrower question of whether Corn Laws should be repealed, Garrisonians were nearly unanimous on both sides of the water. Moreover, from the beginning, American Garrisonians were even more interested in the means used by the ACLL than in their agenda, and their transatlantic networks kept them well informed about those.[16]

Indeed, Garrisonians were connected directly to the family of ACLL leader John Bright, who frequented a water-cure establishment where Pease was a regular. Bright's sister was a member of a Garrisonian antislavery circle in Scotland, and his brother also corresponded with Garrisonians, some of whom had personal encounters with leaguers even in the United States. Garrison, for example, met Joseph Adshead, a Manchester leaguer, in Boston and sent a letter to Pease through him. Traveling Garrisonians also supplemented written reports about Corn Law Repeal with firsthand observation. Remond attended Thompson's first ACLL lecture in the Corn Exchange, and after arriving in England in 1843, Henry Clarke Wright also attended league meetings and even addressed a large free-trade banquet in Manchester. Later that year he happened to meet Cobden in the Manchester train station, and when Douglass and the Massachusetts Garrisonian James N. Buffum arrived in Britain two years later, they too attended ACLL meetings and reported back on what they saw.[17]

What they saw was a movement whose methods of agitation seemed much like their own—meetings, speeches, publications, *talk*. Writing to the *Liberator* in December 1845, Buffum said that a recent free-trade meeting in Manchester "reminded me of one of our New-England Conventions." And Thompson encouraged this perception by attributing the growth of the ACLL to the very thing that Garrisonians worshipped—the tongue. The league's secret of success, he declared in 1844, was that "the pulpit, the exchange, the market-place, the crowded hall, the farmers' dining room, the ladies' drawing room, the county meeting, the open field, the highways and byways of the country—all have been made the scenes and theatres of an animated and instructive discussion" about the Corn Laws.[18]

Thompson was not the only one who made such claims. Contemporaries across the political spectrum also described the ACLL as an organization with unprecedented skills in propaganda. Accounts of the league's rooms in Manchester, for example, described a sprawling multi-story building that served as a public reading room, a headquarters for league lecturers, a printing office, and a bustling distribution center responsible, in one year alone, for dispatching approximately nine million tracts and printed items, weighing approximately one hundred tons, into the public sphere. Talk was what leaguers seemed to do best.[19]

Some ACLL orators also had a flair for dramatic and provocative public demonstrations that resembled Garrison's controversial tactics. In 1842, for example, the Rev. James W. Massie, an abolitionist who knew some Garrisonians and later attended the 1867 Public Breakfast for Garrison, was actively working as an advocate of Corn Law Repeal, and on March 22, in a widely reported speech, Massie produced a copy of the latest Corn Bill and torched it in a nearby gas light. Whether Garrison knew of Massie's speech by the time he burned the Constitution twelve years later is unknown, though it seems likely that he did, given Massie's connections to abolitionists. More important, however, was the Garrisonians' general awareness that Corn Law Repealers often combined published propaganda with public spectacles like Massie's or like their occasional exhibitions of two loaves of bread, one taxed and one untaxed, before curious crowds.[20]

These tactics did not always mirror Garrisonian activities directly, but sometimes the parallels were too close to miss. Take, for example, the parallels between Garrisonians' annual antislavery fairs and two massive Free Trade "bazaars" organized by ACLL women in Manchester in 1842 and in London in 1845. These Free Trade bazaars sold the same sorts of merchandise as the Garrisonians' Boston fairs—like luxury items, curios from famous reformers, and printed literature. A gift book by Harriet Martineau, *Dawn Island,* was sold at the Covent Garden bazaar, much like the *Liberty Bell* (to which Martineau also contributed) was sold at the Boston fair, and portraits of and speeches by ACLL orators were also offered for sale by fair organizers in the United States—including one by Massie.[21]

Such resemblances may not have been coincidental; many British women who actively supported the Boston and Philadelphia antislavery fairs, like Eliza Wigham, Pease, and Martineau, were also involved in supporting the Anti–Corn Law League. Pease, Wigham, and abolitionist Mary Brady were all listed as secretaries on the national organizing committee for the 1845 Covent Garden bazaar, and since leading men in the ACLL—like Thompson—were familiar with the antislavery fairs, they may have served as partial models for the English bazaars.[22]

Even more likely, however, is that the Free Trade bazaars encouraged American abolitionists. Sometimes the encouragement was direct, as when British abolitionists sent American friends surplus items from a Corn Law bazaar, including some boxes packed by "Mrs. Cobden" and Massie's wife. Even more significant, however, was the indirect encouragement given by the popularity of the free-trade bazaars. The 1845 Covent Garden bazaar was so successful that it served as a prototype for the Great Exhibition of commercial goods that took place in London in 1851, and it was credited by many observers for having played a crucial role in the eventual repeal of the Corn Laws in 1846.[23]

The British example may even have inspired the rechristening of the Boston women's antislavery "fair" as the "national anti-slavery bazaar" in 1842. In December 1841, Pease reported in a letter to Anne Warren Weston about British women's efforts to put together "a national bazaar" for Corn Law Repeal, and the first direct reference to the Boston fair as a "bazaar" appeared in the *Liberator* the following year. John B. Estlin later explicitly suggested the name change in a letter discussing boxes for the 1844 "fair— 'Bazaar,' we should call it"—and it was during the next year, after the gigantic Covent Garden fair, that abolitionists began titling the Boston fair the "National Anti-Slavery Bazaar."[24]

In short, in the very years when Garrisonians were searching for evidence of agitation's "influence," the ACLL seemed to provide a rough analogue to what they were doing. They learned from close friends that Thompson's Corn Law lectures were drawing thousands of listeners, and as early as May 1844, Ashurst was predicting in his regular dispatches that repeal was inevitable now that "agitation, —without which nothing is done," was being directed by energetic, efficient reformers like Cobden and Bright. Later, Ashurst again reported to the *Liberator* that the ACLL had decisively proved "the power of public opinion."[25]

Garrisonians took these reports to heart and echoed them back, partly for the benefit of their abolitionist opponents who thought agitation alone was insufficient to build a movement against the Slave Power. The Anti–Corn Law movement was a "splendid and majestic demonstration of the reform spirit in England," and whatever faults it had, declared the *Liberator* in 1846, its rapid ascendancy seemed "without a parallel in the history of Reform. . . . [I]t is only a very few years since that movement which now overspreads throne, parliament and the people was 'no bigger than a man's hand.'" Perhaps Garrisonian agitation, despite similarly humble beginnings, could also overtake the American slaveocracy.[26]

THE APPEAL OF IRISH REPEAL

Another encouraging British movement that Garrisonians followed closely also seemed to be overspreading the country in the early 1840s: "Irish Repeal." Led by O'Connell, this movement advocated the repeal of the Union of 1800 that disbanded Ireland's national legislature and placed Ireland under British Parliamentary rule. Irish nationalists had long blamed their Union with England for numerous evils. But it was not until the 1840s that O'Connell applied the popular tactics he used in the Catholic emancipation movement to a campaign for repeal. In 1842, O'Connell organized the Loyal National Repeal Association (LNRA) and declared 1843 as the "Repeal Year." That year, Irish repealers held several huge public demonstrations, known as "monster meetings," that could attract hundreds of thousands at a time.[27]

Garrisonians followed these developments closely, using newspapers and letters sent by Hibernian abolitionists. James Haughton, for example, frequently attended LNRA meetings and knew its leaders well. These informants did not shy away from criticizing O'Connell's missteps, however, any more than they spared Cobden when he flirted with proslavery Americans. Webb in particular filled his letters with tirades about repealers' machinations and his fear that all Protestants would be expelled from Ireland. In Webb's view, the monster meetings of 1843 tried to inspire fears of Irish rebellion, and his reports painted a negative picture of O'Connell as a superstitious Catholic, a drinker, and a bad landlord to boot. In one letter Webb put the difference between himself and Haughton bluntly: "He is a repealer and believes in O'Connell. I am not and I don't."[28]

Webb's criticisms raised many of the familiar warnings that already made Garrisonians worry about political influence. He depicted O'Connell as "a politician" above all and "void of principle." He thought most Irish repealers joined the movement for reasons that were fundamentally selfish and nationalistic; few actually understood what "Repeal" even meant. And he complained that O'Connell—instead of encouraging the people to consider the higher ideals that might justify home rule—simply "flattered" the multitudes. "He promises them all sorts of things and readily chimes in with all their prejudices," Webb told Phillips. "No wonder they like him."[29]

Such complaints actually revealed Webb's own prejudices more than anything else, however. Despite the faults he found in O'Connell, American abolitionists were captivated by the Irish repealers' example of popular mobilization and sometimes compared their own tactics to O'Connell's. Indeed, O'Connell's movement provided Garrison with a partial inspiration for a new campaign that he launched in 1842: a campaign for the repeal of the American Union.

The Garrisonians' campaign for the "Dissolution of the American Union" so defined them after 1842 that it is easy to forget they had not always used this slogan. Garrison and his followers had always denounced the Constitution and the Union for making northern states complicit in supporting slavery. But it was not until 1842 that Garrison unfurled a new motto in the *Liberator*—No Union with Slaveholders. Soon he was joined by a vocal abolitionist minority who agreed, as Henry Clarke Wright put it, that "we ought to have laid before the slaveholders, long ago, this alternative. *You must abolish slavery, or we shall dissolve the Union.*" Two years later, when the AASS adopted "No Union with Slaveholders" as its own motto, all Garrisonians, Phillips included, became disunionists.[30]

Disunionism reinforced Garrisonians' decision to remain outside of Congress, but the idea for it actually originated with an event in Congress. On January 24, 1842, former president John Quincy Adams took the floor of the House and began to read an antislavery petition in defiance of the "gag rule," just as he had often done since the rule's inception. But this petition, sent from forty-six citizens of Haverhill, Massachusetts, was unprecedented. Instead of asking only for abolition, it asked Congress to "adopt measures peaceably to dissolve the Union of these States."[31]

These explosive lines, not surprisingly, outraged representatives from the South. George Hopkins suggested burning the document, while Virginian Henry A. Wise advocated the censure of "any member presenting such a petition." House business stalled for two weeks before the offending petition was refused. But the intervening debate gave southerners repeated opportunities to explain why they viewed disunion as disastrous to their interests, and during that time, Garrisonians were listening. Southerners like Wise saw the petition as more proof of a British scheme to bring the country to ruin. But Joseph Underwood of Kentucky sounded a more ominous warning: if "the bonds of this Union" broke, he said, the Ohio River and Mason and Dixon Line would suddenly beckon as foreign borders for fugitive slaves, and "slavery was done in Kentucky, Maryland, and a large portion of Virginia." "The dissolution of the Union," Underwood concluded, "was the dissolution of slavery."[32]

That statement immediately caught the eye of Garrison, who printed excerpts from the debates in Congress throughout February and March. At a February meeting of the Essex County Anti-Slavery Society, Garrison submitted his own resolutions for the "dissolution of the Union," echoing Underwood's claim that this would dissolve slavery. And on March 11, he excerpted Underwood's speech in the *Liberator*, highlighting its "precious confessions" that ending the Union would end slavery. The AASS took two years to adopt the same view, but Garrison's career as a disunionist had begun.[33]

The fact that the Essex resolutions were the first time Garrison ever called for disunion suggests that the Haverhill petition and Underwood's speech were crucial triggers. In May, he cited Underwood's argument as proof that disunion meant abolition, and years later, in 1849, the *Liberator* reminded readers to "let the Southern confession on the floor of Congress never be forgotten:—'The dissolution of the Union is the abolition of slavery!' To this issue must the people of the North be constantly kept." Even on the eve of the Civil War—in 1857, in 1860, and again in 1861—Garrisonians continued to invoke the Haverhill petition and Underwood's comments to defend disunionism.[34]

Garrison's transatlantic correspondence also emphasized the Haverhill debates as catalysts for disunionism. A month after the petition, he told one Irish friend that "a crisis is [n]ear at hand, which, though it may possibly end in a dissolution of the American Union, will inevitably result in the downfall of our nefarious slave system." And to Webb, Garrison reported that the "tremendous excitement in Congress, arising from the presentation of a petition for the peaceable dissolution of the American Union" was "driving the slaveholding representatives to the wall." For Garrison, the lesson was clear: nothing more combustible could be lobbed into Congress than a demand for the Union's "dissolution"—even if it came from only forty-six people.[35]

Garrison's critics learned a more familiar lesson, however: Garrison had succumbed to yet another destructive fantasy. Many blamed "disunionism" on the continuing influence of Noyes's perfectionist theology, an idea Garrison sometimes encouraged by framing disunionism as a way for northerners to "come out" and "be separate" from slavery. But despite the perception that disunionism was just another fruit of non-resistance, the model Garrison actually invoked was not Noyes but O'Connell.

In April 1842, for example, when Garrison began campaigning to make disunion "the grand rallying point" of the AASS, he called for "the REPEAL OF THE UNION," the motto O'Connell was then popularizing in Ireland. In his personal correspondence Garrison made the allusion to O'Connell's movement even more explicit, explaining in one letter that "I avow myself to be both an Irish Repealer and an American Repealer." In another, he claimed to support "the repeal of the union between England and Ireland . . . on the same ground, and for the same reason" that he supported "the repeal of the union between the North and the South." Thereafter, references to disunion as "the banner of 'Repeal'" periodically resurfaced in Garrisonian discourse, and "repeal" was even used by opponents of the measure.[36]

Correspondence with British Garrisonians, especially in Ireland, reinforced this language. Writing from Ireland, Richard Allen said he enjoyed Garrison's "heart-burning articles on the repeal of the American Union." Webb praised the *Liberator* for "the course thou art taking in advocating the Repeal of the Union," having already told Phillips two months earlier that "I am with Garrison for the Repeal of the Union." Subsequently, in a letter to Pease, Phillips called disunionism "*our* Repeal," and two years later, when the AASS officially endorsed disunionism, Quincy told Webb "that we have a repeal question as well as you."[37]

Such wordplay was partly fun among friends, but Ireland stayed on the minds of Garrisonians as they took up their own "repeal question" over the next year. First, they received constant reminders from correspondents about O'Connell's progress. As Wright told Phillips in September 1843, "O'Connell the Lion of Ireland & Cobden the Lion of England—are shaking both Islands, & the Government knows not how to deal with them." Allen also hinted at the implications in his letters to the *Liberator* from Ireland. "A mighty movement is in this land," he said, and "O'Connell's popularity, his power, his influence over the people seems but beginning—the gatherings of the masses are, I believe, immense beyond precedent." Would not Garrison's own calls for "the repeal of the American Union" also be "a powerful engine with which to agitate the public mind"?[38]

An unforeseen coincidence also encouraged comparisons between Garrison's Repeal and O'Connell's. Throughout the latter half of 1841, Irish abolitionists had been working hard to collect signatures for a massive antislavery address that O'Connell had promised to sign at the "World's Convention," hoping that a strong appeal from the Liberator himself might persuade Irish American immigrants in the United States to align with abolitionists. They could not have known, however, that Charles Lenox Remond would arrive in Boston with the completed address at almost the same moment that Congress erupted in debates about disunion. When Garrisonians unveiled the address at a dramatic meeting in Faneuil Hall in January 1842, it was only four days after the reading of the Haverhill petition in the House.[39]

Because Garrisonians were absorbed, simultaneously, with publicizing the Irish Address and developing their own "repeal," drawing analogies between their movement and O'Connell's followed almost as a matter of course, especially once Irish Americans began loudly denouncing the Irish Address. There was considerable support for O'Connell's repeal movement among Americans in 1842, but most American repealers rejected his abolitionism, and after the publication of the Irish Address, immigrants in Boston and elsewhere immediately began blasting O'Connell's attempt at foreign interference. But this led Garrisonians quite naturally to retort that their own movement for "disunion" was no different from the American campaign for Irish Repeal. In an 1843 editorial in the *Liberator*, Quincy argued that American repealers' tactics of agitation were "precisely analogous" to abolitionists' own "line of policy," making it hypocritical for them to denounce the abolitionists or O'Connell.[40]

Quincy did not stop, however, at noting the hypocrisy of Irish American repealers; he also hinted at why Garrisonians admired O'Connell in the first place. "It is true of the anti-slavery reform, as of the Repeal movement, and of all other Reforms," Quincy concluded, "that AGITATION is the breath of its nostrils," and O'Connell was clearly a master of agitation. Every report from abroad—including one in the same issue as Quincy's editorial—showed that O'Connell's repealers were "going steadily on with their great work of agitation," using peaceful methods to rouse the whole country.[41]

Those reports offered hope to Garrisonians, even in the midst of their setbacks with the Irish Address, that their new repeal campaign could have similar effects. In another 1843 editorial, Maria Weston Chapman pointed to the tremendous "progress of the Repeal movement," which had convulsed not only Ireland but "Parliament itself," as a justification for the Garrisonians' decision to remain outside of Congress. "O'Connell in parliament is merely an M.P.," she said: "O'Connell out of parliament may be the saviour" of Britain.[42]

Ultimately, this was the appeal of Irish Repeal to Garrisonians: like Corn Law Repeal, it seemed to be a practical demonstration of the power of agitation to rouse an entire people and unsettle politics from without. Perhaps, Chapman said, those who were still unable to see the "beauty" of Garrisonian non-resistance and disunionism as a "principle" could "now see its expediency." And two years later, an AASS pamphlet on disunionism made the same point with a rhetorical question. To those who would "ask what can be done, if you abandon the ballot-box," Garrisonians could respond: "What has Daniel O'Connell done for Irish repeal?"[43]

THE TRIUMPH OF THE LEAGUE

Irish Repeal was still an imperfect model, however. First, O'Connell himself disappointed Garrisonians by often appearing to placate anti-abolitionist repealers in the United States. When O'Connell intimated in 1842 that he would accept donations from the American South, Garrisonians on both sides of the Atlantic grew "red hot" with outrage. The next year, Garrisonians were again dismayed when O'Connell reportedly denied his acquaintance with Garrison. In both cases, direct ties to O'Connell enabled Garrisonians to state their grievances to him directly, and in both episodes, O'Connell regained abolitionists' trust with several key speeches that reiterated his abhorrence of slavery and blasted anti-abolitionists. But the episodes gave troubling credence to Webb's warnings about O'Connell the politician.[44]

The more serious problem with Irish Repeal as a model was that by 1844 English authorities had largely defeated it. In October 1843 soldiers forcibly suppressed the last scheduled "monster meeting" of the "Repeal Year" in Clontarf. Soon after, O'Connell was arrested, tried, and convicted of conspiracy by a jury stacked with Protestants, and by the summer of 1844, he was imprisoned in Dublin. Even after the government reversed O'Connell's conviction, the LNRA had been damaged beyond repair, both by internal disagreements and by a few English concessions on Irish reform designed, in one historian's words, to "kill repeal by kindness." Worn down by his struggle, a disappointed O'Connell died in 1847.[45]

O'Connell's fall won him unanimous sympathy from Garrisonians, even those who criticized him most severely before. Webb and Wright both went to see the Irish Lion in his confinement, and even Webb sympathized with his plight. While he was still "neither Catholic, O'Connellite, Repealer, or even a voting politician," he told Quincy, he could not help feeling "a little bitterness" towards "John Bull" for this latest round of "repression" and bullying. Other Garrisonians, too, expressed outrage over English treatment of "poor O'Connell" and cheered his release from prison.[46]

Still, O'Connell's gagging posed a problem for Garrisonians trying to show that their own calls for repealing the Union could work. The problem was compounded, too, by the similar fates of other extra-parliamentary movements that Garrisonians admired. In the same decade, the government arrested Chartist leaders, and in 1848 the government moved swiftly to make sure that revolutions in Europe did not spread to Britain. Chartist rallies were disrupted with displays of force, several Irish nationalist leaders were arrested and expelled, and habeas corpus was suspended in Ireland.[47]

Yet Garrisonians could still look to the ACLL for encouragement, because in 1846, the same government that worked to defeat O'Connell finally repealed the Corn Laws, led by Robert Peel. Triumphant leaguers immediately declared that their pressure had won the victory, and Peel—for political reasons of his own—encouraged the idea by crediting his decision to the work of the ACLL. Buoyed by their success, a raft of leaguers swept into Parliament, including George Thompson, who was elected to the House of Commons in 1847 because of his Corn Law work.[48]

Garrisonians in the United States also rejoiced over these developments. "Three thousand cheers for the League," exclaimed Phillips in a letter to Pease, after learning of its victory. "How I clap my hands at their success & wish I could have heard & seen Cobden [and] Bright." A number of Garrisonians already in England did witness the league's victory firsthand, and they were soon joined by Garrison. In 1846 several Corn Law repealers even hosted Garrison in their homes.[49]

Not surprisingly, these encounters greatly reinforced Garrisonians' optimism about their own methods. Douglass, who at the time remained a Garrisonian disunionist, concluded that Corn Law Repeal was a case in which "Democratic freedom" had "triumphed" over aristocrats and class legislation, and once he returned home he told abolitionists that the extra-parliamentary efforts of "Cobden, Bright, Thompson and others," including O'Connell, were "examples filled with encouragement" for Garrisonians. They "had triumphed by means of the spreading of . . . tracts, and lectures, and newspapers; until a great moral public sentiment was formed," Douglass explained in Massachusetts. "So it must be in the Anti-Slavery cause in this country." To another audience in Pennsylvania, Douglass reiterated that, "as the Anti-Corn-Law League did, so can we do . . . nor have we cause to fear that we shall be less successful."[50]

In the same speech, Douglass also alluded to a new abolitionist organization that Garrisonian supporters formed in London in August 1846: the Anti-Slavery League. This organization, intended as an alternative to the BFASS, was only one of many such "leagues" whose names were inspired by Cobden's group, including Mazzini's Peoples' International League the following year. But the founders of the Anti-Slavery League worked especially hard to claim Cobden's mantle. Thompson was elected as the first president, and Bowring and Jacob Bright sat on the executive council together with Chartist abolitionists William Lovett and

Henry Vincent. At the first meeting, Thompson noted that the new Anti-Slavery League, "though small at present, was not smaller than another 'League,' which had, however, nobly done its work." The allusion immediately elicited cheers from the audience, demonstrating how Corn Law Repeal could bolster abolitionist hopes.[51]

Few Garrisonians drew more hope from the triumph of the ACLL than Phillips, who told Pease in 1850 that "I envy you the neighborhood . . . of Cobden— that is a man I much long to see." He admired Cobden partly because he supported the idea that free trade would undermine slavery, a hope that had inspired some "new organization" abolitionists to pursue direct alliances with the ACLL. But Phillips's admiration of Cobden primarily signified his desire for proof that the course Garrisonians had chosen could work.[52]

As someone who admitted the temptation of politics, this was proof that Phillips sorely needed. In his 1852 speech on "Public Opinion," he confessed that even "the best of us are conscious of being, at times, somewhat awed by the colossal institutions about us, which seem to be opposing our progress." Abolitionists committed to moral suasion, he noted, sometimes would "sigh for something tangible; some power that they can feel, and see its operation."[53]

But the Anti–Corn Law League and Irish Repeal helped to give him that tangible reassurance, even before Cobden's final triumph. "While the old world echoes the voice of O'Connell—while England trembles before Cobden and the masses," he told Garrisonians in 1845, "the South feels that the spirit of the age is against her." Recurring to his favorite metaphor for agitation, Phillips recalled that "the earthquake of Lisbon sent thirty-six huge waves across the vast Atlantic, to break in thunder on the shores of Antigua." That ever-restless ocean offered "a type of the moral thunders, before which our Bastile shall yet go down."[54]

"A POLITICAL QUESTION"

In retrospect, it is possible to see that Garrisonian interpretations of Corn Law repeal were highly selective, even misleading. In reality, political leaders had been slowly implementing a rationalization of the Corn Laws long before Cobden. Moreover, the ACLL ultimately won as much by quiet electioneering tactics designed to put supporters in Parliament as by moral suasion. Yet the Garrisonians' correspondents implied that, "as soon as . . . the public mind" turned against the Corn Laws, aristocratic power "melted before it."[55]

Such accounts did not so much influence Garrisonians to adopt new conclusions as they confirmed prior beliefs. Yet Garrisonians were not alone in seeing Corn Law Repeal as proof of the power of "public opinion." Many contemporaries on both sides of the Atlantic described the Anti–Corn Law League, in the words of one recent historian, "as the archetype of agitation aimed at convincing public opinion." Cobden himself promoted that impression, calling "the influence of public opinion," especially "as exercised through the Press," the "distinguishing feature in modern civilization." In the 1840s, these sorts of statements would have been pervasive in the British newspapers that Phillips loved to read; they help explain his confidence, by 1852, that, "in such an age as ours, the so-called statesman has far less influence than the many little men who, at various points, are silently maturing a regeneration of public opinion."[56]

More important than the accuracy of Garrisonians' interpretations of Corn Law Repeal, however, was what they signified: a deep desire for proof that "talk" could work to effect political change. For although political abolitionists after 1840 continued to criticize the AASS for remaining aloof from the polls, Garrisonians still earnestly wished for political influence. Indeed, even Garrison's embrace of "repeal" as a term for disunionism was partly a gambit with political overtones, especially at a time when President John Tyler's son and many Democratic politicians were seeking to establish themselves as allies of O'Connell and thus appeal to Irish American voters. Garrison's own efforts to establish himself as a friend of repeal were, in their own way, attempts to appeal to Irish American voters, too.

After all, as Garrison noted in March 1842, "the Irish population among us is nearly all 'democratic,'" because "leading democratic journals" and politicians were all "in favor of Irish Repeal." Garrison hoped O'Connell's addresses would repeal this "'union,' most unnatural and horrible," between freedom-loving Irishmen and proslavery "Demagogues," and that was one reason why Garrisonians made a point, throughout the Repeal Year, to advertise their connections to actual repealers in Ireland. As late as October 1843, the Pennsylvania Anti-Slavery Society even kept its public reading room stocked with Irish newspapers sent by Hibernian abolitionists, believing, as James Miller McKim put it, that evidence of "sympathy & correspondence between us & the Dublin Repealers" would "increase the hold which we are of late beginning to have on the confidence of the Irish population."[57]

Chimerical as these efforts may seem in retrospect, they show that, even as Garrisonians withdrew from the polls in the 1840s, they still hoped to affect what went on inside them—a fact that Lydia Maria Child noticed and criticized at the time. Child confessed that mobilizing the Irish "by the use of O'Connell's name, strikes me as work that peculiarly belongs to the Third Party." Its most likely outcome, she predicted, would be to "drive them to the polls," a goal that seemed out of character for Garrison. The more accurate interpretation was that Garrison hoped to drive the Irish out of the polls and away from alliance with the Democrats. But Child's basic instinct—that Garrison was still trying to affect what went on at the ballot box—was basically sound.[58]

Indeed, some disunionist Garrisonians even thought of creative ways to enter the polls in the early 1840s. In the 1844 elections, for example, disunionists in New Hampshire invented write-in candidates like "John C. Repeal" and "Martin Van Repeal" and printed special ballots for abolitionists to cast. Later, in 1846, Stephen S. Foster again urged Ohio abolitionists in 1846 to "throw as many ballots as the election at the time permits, giving them for 'John Repeal,' 'Thomas Repeal,' etc." And in defense of Foster's plan, the *National Anti-Slavery Standard* noted the influence it had on politicians in New Hampshire: "at the next session of the Legislature, a law was passed, expressly intended to do away with the purpose of such voting."[59]

These were, to be sure, very indirect ways to affect the polls, because Garrisonians continued to have a problem with political influence: they desired it, but they knew its dangers. Even the examples of Cobden and O'Connell had shown what might happen if agitators flew too close to political power: Cobden flirted with proslavery free traders like John C. Calhoun, and O'Connell feigned ignorance of William Lloyd Garrison. As Phillips told Webb after one of O'Connell's vacillations, "I tell the third party men it proves how little trust can be reposed in the *best* politicians in the *best* circumstances, & yet they can't dream of having 1/100th the part of their timber half as sound as Dan[ie]l."[60]

Concerns about what could happen even to the "best politicians" explain why calls for "No Union with Slaveholders" ultimately attracted Garrisonians. Disunionism was, as one historian put it, "antipolitics with a strong political message . . . a method of translating moral outrage into political force" while still retaining a posture of moral independence. But Garrisonians would not have been satisfied with moral independence unless they thought it could create political force. Garrison urged northerners to "come out" and be separate from the Union just as he had separated from politics, but all the while he printed speeches from Congress, held up Underwood's confessions, and watched to see how his agitation drove political slaveholders to the wall.[61]

Indeed, even disunionism betrayed Garrison's continued hope for tangible political influence. The "Disunion Pledge" that Garrison published in the *Liberator* claimed that disunion would "clear our skirts from innocent blood," but at the same time asserted that disunion was "the most consistent, feasible means of abolishing slavery." From the beginning Garrison and his allies also framed "No Union with Slaveholders" as a conditional ultimatum for the "*Dissolution of the Union, or the Abolition of Slavery,*" whichever "alternative" came first. Garrison's first editorial on the subject promised to demand disunion "until it be accomplished, or slavery cease to pollute our soil," and other abolitionists followed suit. One paper still allied with Garrison in 1842 claimed not to advocate an "unconditional repeal of the Union, but if slavery is to be perpetuated in this free republic . . . we should go for repeal. But our hope is yet, that slavery will be overcome without so great a sacrifice as such a repeal would be."[62]

Such extenuating "buts" and "ifs" were typical of early disunionism, and suggested a savvy plan for winning political influence that was reminiscent of O'Connell's own intentional vagueness about repeal. Sometimes O'Connell seemed to be making a non-negotiable demand for an independent legislative body in Ireland like the one that had existed in Dublin before the Union of 1800. But at many other moments O'Connell implied that he never viewed the total dissolution of the Union as the only favorable outcome of his movement. Rather, he wanted to use repeal as an ultimatum to win concessions from Parliament. "If we get the justice we require," O'Connell once admitted, "then our Repeal association is at an end." At least one Garrisonian abroad, Elizabeth Pease, interpreted Garrison's disunionism as a similar ultimatum: she believed "LIBERTY or REPEAL" should become the "rallying cry" of abolitionists in America "as it is the watchword of Freedom in Ireland."[63]

Garrison certainly did not dispel confusion on this point, and sometimes lent credence to the idea that "disunionism" was an agitational tool, a "watchword" intended more to affect politics than to clear innocent skirts of blood. Indeed, while in England in 1846, Garrison explained at one breakfast that southerners "knew right well that the dissolution of the Union was the dissolution of slavery," again borrowing the language Underwood used in the Haverhill debates of 1842. But "he did not think," Garrison said, in seldom noticed remarks reprinted in the *Liberator*, "that it would be necessary to dissolve the Union. The Southern States, when they found the abolitionists determined, and that they had no choice but emancipation or dissolution, would say the time had come for the abolition of slavery, and let their slaves go free."[64]

An 1845 *Disunion* pamphlet issued by the AASS delineated the strategy in much the same way. It called on northerners to "circulate a declaration of DIS-UNION FROM SLAVEHOLDERS, throughout the country. Hold mass meetings—assemble in conventions." Disunionists were "no anarchical movement," it explained. Rather, they had four aims: "first, to create discussion and agitation throughout the North"; "secondly, to convulse the South like an earthquake, and convince her that her only alternative is, to abolish slavery, or be abandoned by that power on which she now relies for safety"; "thirdly, to attack the slave power in its most vulnerable point"; and "fourthly, to exalt the moral sense" of northerners. Actually dissolving the Union was conspicuously absent from that list.[65]

These later descriptions of disunion may explain why, even in 1842, some Garrisonians questioned whether the new doctrine was too connected to politics for true non-resistants. From the other side of the ocean, Allen noted that at first glance disunionism looked like "politics." Certainly Noyes thought so; he advised true Christian perfectionists to come out of the anti-slavery societies, even Garrisonian ones, in 1843. But Elizabeth Neall also reported to Pease in June 1842 that "the Dissolution Question is creating quite a stir among us. Garrison is accused of inconsistency . . . because it is a Political Question."[66]

Garrison would never have admitted openly that this was so, but these rumblings of disagreement highlighted an undeniable truth: leading Garrisonian disunionists did not relinquish the hope of political influence. That was why they watched the movements of Cobden and O'Connell so closely, and why they constantly monitored politics at home to see whether and to what extent they were still able to shake Congress. In 1842, for example, Garrisonians supported the reelection to Congress of Joshua Giddings, an antislavery Ohio Whig who was expelled from the House for supporting the reading of antislavery petitions.[67]

Disunionists were also encouraged by the reaction among northern Whigs two years later when secret negotiations by the White House for the annexation of Texas became public knowledge. In January 1845, Garrison was loudly applauded when he appeared as a delegate to a large anti-Texas convention held in Faneuil Hall, which was organized and attended mainly by Whigs like Sumner. The disunion resolution that Garrison submitted at the meeting was tabled, but the respectful attention that antislavery politicians like Sumner paid to Garrison gratified him and other disunionists. Garrisonians were especially thrilled when Massachusetts Whig Henry Wilson—who read the *Liberator* faithfully and began appearing at their meetings, too—echoed Garrison on the floor of the state legislature, declaring that he preferred "liberty without union" over "union without liberty." In the same year, both the Massachusetts and Ohio state legislatures warned Washington that their states would defy Texas annexation, in essence declaring that they would view the Union as dissolved if the state were admitted.[68]

Such episodes suggested to disunionists that their "pressure from without" was beginning to have an influence within the halls of power. In 1845, for example, Phillips told Pease that the Texas convention showed a "relish" for "*strong talk*," and the following year he noted that northerners who very recently "would have whispered Disunion with white lips now love to talk about it." Phillips predicted that politicians "will talk as we were once laughed at for talking." British correspondents, in turn, described such episodes as "a sure indication of the public mind moving in the right direction"—the very thing American Garrisonians most wanted to hear.[69]

Garrison, too, was impressed by the direction in which things seemed to be moving after he returned to England in 1846, fresh from his firsthand view of the Anti–Corn Law movement. On a western tour with Douglass, he found Liberty Party men in Ohio to be more cordial than those in the East, and he could not conceal his excitement that Giddings, "who [had] nobly battled for freedom" in Congress, "alluded to me in very handsome terms, as also to Douglass." Around the same time, Garrisonian newspapers began regularly publishing speeches sent to them by politicians like Giddings, Sumner, Wilson, and John P. Hale of New Hampshire, a favorite of Boston-area Garrisonians. Indeed, in 1845, the board of the MASS, feeling "*very* anxious," in Garrison's words, "to do something that should secure John P. Hale's election," dispatched lecturers into New Hampshire during his campaign. Early the next year, Anne Warren Weston reported to Pease that Hale, "who has behaved so well in New Hampshire politics," gave a well-received speech at the annual bazaar in Boston.[70]

That Garrisonians would praise politicians for behaving well, even while denouncing politics and calling for disunion, should not be surprising, however. Garrison, Phillips, and other leading members of the AASS had always made clear that they hoped for a political reformation, and the close eye they kept on extra-parliamentary movements in England and Ireland trained them to look for signs that their influence was beginning to be felt. In 1847, Phillips rejoiced over the "influx of new blood into Parliament" caused by Corn Law Repeal, predicting "great times" ahead from the election of Anti-Slavery League members like Thompson and Henry Vincent. Hale, Wilson, Giddings, and others suggested a similar influx into Congress in the wake of Garrison's new demands for repeal.[71]

Nonetheless, despite gathering signs that their agitation was winning them influence, at least with some politicians, Garrisonians still publicly recoiled from becoming politicians themselves. In his 1845 pamphlet on why abolitionists should still not vote, Phillips argued that the time for such actions was not yet: "when the public mind is thoroughly revolutionized, and ready for the change, when the billow has reached its height and begins to crest into foam," Phillips said, "then such a measure may bring matters to a crisis." To illustrate his point, Phillips turned once again to O'Connell's example, this time stressing his career as an agitator over his political successes. In response to those who noted that O'Connell ran for election to Parliament even before Catholic Emancipation took effect, Phillips replied that the analogy would only work "if we stood in the same circumstances as the Catholics did in 1828." But O'Connell's election culminated a long extra-parliamentary campaign that had prepared public opinion for it. "Let us first go through, in patience, as O'Connell did, our twenty years of agitation," Phillips concluded.[72]

As that statement shows, O'Connell and the transatlantic reforms of the 1840s offered Garrisonians like Phillips reassurance that their attempts to stir the waters of public opinion would eventually bring matters to a crisis. But the two repeal movements were less helpful in answering how to gauge when—if ever—it was time to end agitation and enter politics, just as O'Connell, Cobden, and even Thompson had done. Aquatic metaphors worked well for showing the importance of agitation, but what did it mean for "the billow" to reach its height and "crest into foam"? And what would Garrisonians do once it did? Even as late as 1860, Phillips continued to point to the triumphs of Cobden and O'Connell as an argument for why Garrisonians should remain fiercely independent of Congress even if public opinion changed: "Cobden and O'Connell, out of the House of Commons, were giants; in it, dwarfs."[73]

That view showed that the British extra-parliamentary movements of the 1840s did not resolve all the questions Garrisonians had about influence. They showed that agitation could one day make them giants, but also made them worry about being dwarfed by the effort. For the time being, this was a problem that could remain unresolved, since Garrisonians were still looking for the first signs that they had influence on politics at all. But in the years to come, as abolitionists gradually came to perceive that they had the ability to affect politics directly, the problem of influence first raised in the 1840s would rear its head again.

III

EVENTS

TRANSATLANTIC REVOLUTIONS
AND REVERSALS, 1848–1854

F or all their heady talk of Christian perfection"—one historian has noted— Garrison and "his disciples were liberal nineteenth-century reformers" who "were not so very different from others of their kind—Richard Cobden, John Bright, and Daniel O'Connell." But most Americans at the time could only hear "talk of Christian perfection" when they listened to Garrison and his allies. Even though Noyes himself criticized the AASS and the Non-Resistance Society as insufficiently "religious," and even though leading orators like Phillips never embraced non-resistance, many abolitionists continued to identify disunionism with non-resistance, and non-resistance with a total abjuration of politics.[1]

Garrison's style of agitation did not exactly discourage confusion on these points. In 1854, at the Fourth of July meeting of abolitionists in Framingham, Massachusetts, Garrison famously burned a copy of the Constitution "to ashes on the spot," before leading his audience in a responsive chant: "And let all the people say, *Amen.*" This extraordinary gesture, so reminiscent of Martin Luther's burning of papal bulls, could not help but strike political abolitionists as further evidence of Garrison's fanatical come-outer zeal. Moncure D. Conway, a Unitarian from Virginia who delivered his first antislavery speech at the same meeting, remembered concluding on that very day that Garrison was the leader of "a religion," not a political movement.[2]

But Conway's judgments failed to explain the vast range of political subjects that Garrisonians had considered over the previous twelve years. Chartism, the Dorr Rebellion, the Free Soil Party, Giddings's censure, Texas annexation, Wilson's speeches, Irish Repeal, the Anti–Corn Law League, the Haverhill petition— all found a place in the pages of the *Liberator*. Indeed, in the very same issue that reported his burning of the Constitution, Garrison covered the entire front page of the *Liberator* with transcripts of the latest debates in Congress. Inside were comments on a speech by Charles Sumner, items about the Fugitive Slave Law, and a letter from an English friend about European events.

This was nothing new. As early as 1844, the non-resistant Nathaniel P. Rogers complained that "Garrison holds politics a mortal sin, yet he fills his paper with the doings of politicians." Shortly thereafter Rogers even left the AASS, convinced that Garrison had lowered his standard from the moral high ground of non-resistance and perfectionism. In the early 1840s Rogers was appalled by the attention Garrison paid to politicians like O'Connell and Giddings, and he singled out disunionism, the very thing most outsiders viewed as proof of Garrison's zealotry, as proof of how far the AASS had fallen from its task of declaring all politics unclean. "Garrison is advocating the dissolution of our political Union," Rogers wrote in an anguished series of letters to Webb, shortly before retiring in disgust. But such an act was "a thing our politicians alone can do" and would ultimately require "the act of suffrage at the polls." Garrisonians were therefore becoming "purblind with politics," Rogers said. "They do not throw political dust, but they kick it up and love to be in it. They do not hold office or vote, but they love to hover about the polls . . . and about the state houses, where they can enjoy the turmoil of legislation."[3]

Rogers died prematurely not long after these lines, but had he lived to see Garrison burn the Constitution, the event would only have confirmed his suspicions. The years between 1844 and 1854 also would have given him new evidence to support his charges that his friends were "purblind with politics," for in these years Garrisonians continued to watch political events closely—searching the news for signs of their influence, debating whether it was time to take a more active role in politics, and oscillating between fears and hopes for the future of democracy in their country and elsewhere. Political events and the "turmoil of legislation," both at home and abroad, would remain near the forefront of their thinking, even at Framingham, proving Rogers more correct about Garrison than Conway.

Both Rogers and Conway erred, however, in assuming that Garrison's religious views and his interest in political events stood in conflict. For Garrison, the belief that the kingdom of Christ would one day relink earth and heaven, and that abolitionists were instruments in God's hands, made him all the more eager to search the present for signs of the future. Like Noyes, Garrison was confident that God would triumph in the world, but when and how would "depend, perhaps, upon ourselves, in some measure." As "coworkers with God," abolitionists could labor and look for the world's regeneration, being sure all along that it was coming.[4]

Garrison found a similar perspective contained in "Verses, Suggested by the Present Crisis," a famous contemporary poem by abolitionist and Garrisonian ally James Russell Lowell. As A. J. Aiséirithe notes, Garrisonians during the Civil War later made repeated references to this poem's final verse, which declared that "new occasions teach new duties," to justify their increased optimism about Republican politicians in the 1860s. Yet Garrison, who always remained a zealous reader and writer of verse, embraced the poem long before the war began, publishing it in 1845 and quoting it at length in an 1847 editorial. Even then, it captured Garrison's own keen interest in political events and present crises while simultaneously reconciling that interest with confidence in God's movements:

> Careless seems the great Avenger; history's pages but record
> One death-grapple in the darkness 'twixt old systems and the Word;
> Truth forever on the scaffold, Wrong forever on the throne,—
> Yet that scaffold sways the future, and, behind the dim unknown,
> Standeth God within the shadow, keeping watch above his own.

Believing that God was yet keeping watch over events, Garrison saw nothing wrong with watching events, too, scanning the shadows for signs of God. Indeed, his hope that darkness would not always prevail *needed* the nourishment of evidence that truth was beginning to sway the future.[5]

As the 1840s came to a close, Garrisonians also believed they actually could see such evidence in the events of the world. As democratic revolutions roiled the European continent and new antislavery champions appeared in Congress, the shadows seemed to be lifting and the scaffold seemed to be swaying. Some Garrisonians even began to argue that new occasions made possible a new posture towards politicians. By 1854, a wave of counter-revolution in Europe and compromise in the United States convinced Garrisonians that wrong was back on the throne, but they never stopped keeping watch over the news or mulling the duties of the moment in light of political events.

PROGRESS AT LAST

Six years before Framingham, in the spring and summer of 1848, Garrisonians' hopes for the future received a noticeable boost from a series of revolutions in

Europe. After a series of uprisings in Italy in January 1848, revolutionaries in Paris dethroned their king and reestablished the French republic in February, and soon thereafter, revolution spread to Austria, the German states, and back to Italy. This dramatic sequence of events electrified the Atlantic World and posed a powerful challenge to absolutists like the Habsburg dynasty in central Europe. Over the next few years, the Hungarian politician Louis Kossuth led an armed revolution of Magyar nationalists against Austrian rule, while reformers across the continent demanded constitutions and parliamentary rule. To many Europeans, anything seemed possible in this "springtime of peoples."[6]

In the United States, reactions to the revolutions were more mixed. Initially the uprisings struck many Americans, as most European revolutions did, as evidence of the continuing influence of the American Revolution. But by the time the dust cleared in Europe, many—perhaps even most—Americans saw the revolutions as too radical or as violent threats to social order.[7]

Garrisonians, however, were enthusiastic about the "social earthquake" that was "rocking Europe" and followed events there closely, not least because some, like Wright, had been overseas so recently. Others were actually in Europe as the earthquake began. The wealthy Garrisonian Charles B. Hovey and the daughter of abolitionist Francis Jackson embarked on a European tour in 1848. And Maria Weston Chapman moved with her daughters and two sisters to Paris only a few weeks after the "Bloody June Days" of 1848, which resulted in violent clashes between the new Provisional Government and radical workers. From her salon in Paris, where she remained until 1855, Chapman closely observed events on the continent, hosted British and American abolitionists who came to France, and eventually met French republican leaders like Alexis de Tocqueville, Victor Hugo, long-time abolitionist Victor Schoelcher, and Alphonse de Lamartine, who thanked her for a copy of the *Liberty Bell* and invited her for a social visit.[8]

British Garrisonians also converged on Paris as the revolutions broke. By the time Chapman arrived, Anne Knight—an English Quaker feminist who supported Garrisonians at the 1840 "World's Convention"—was already there and cooperated directly with French feminist Jeanne Deroin to urge the provisional government to recognize women's rights. Meanwhile, William Henry Ashurst and one of his daughters, Eliza, arrived in Paris during the Bloody June Days and had to be escorted under guard through several barricades to reach their hotel. Eliza reported on these events to her longtime Philadelphia correspondent Elizabeth Neall, whom she wrote several more times about encounters with revolutionary leaders like Lamartine. While in Paris, Ashurst and Knight also associated with Chapman, who wrote favorably about Deroin's feminism in the *Liberator*.[9]

These contacts not only made Garrisonians especially interested in the latest news from Europe; they also gave them unusual feelings of connection to what they read. When Mazzini rushed to Rome in 1848 to join the revolutions, Ashurst salted his dispatches to the *Liberator* with coded references to the "Italian friend of mine, whom you met at my house when in England." Soon *Liberator* readers also learned about the movements of Ashurst's youngest daughter, Emilie, who acted as a secret courier of money and information to Italy and once crossed the Alps in the middle of the winter, "on foot part of the way," to bring Mazzini aid.[10]

Even apart from their acquaintances, however, Garrisonians had ample reason to watch the revolutions closely, especially because of their implications for slavery. After French abolitionists were suddenly vaulted into positions of power by the February revolution, the new republic abolished slavery in the French West Indies, an act soon followed by an edict of emancipation in the Danish West Indies. These acts gave abolitionists in the AASS renewed "assurance of success" in their own efforts, and the English secretary of the Anti-Slavery League rejoiced that so many cracks were appearing in the edifice of global oppression. "The slaveholders and their partisans may daub over the apertures with untempered mortar, but the heat of public opinion will, to their mortification, make it crack again in a thousand places."[11]

Yet while slave emancipation was the most obvious reason why Garrisonians sympathized with the revolutions, their beliefs about democracy also gave them cause for rejoicing. Wright had hoped, before leaving Europe, that "the people" would soon throw off their oppressors, and now he and others were glad to see the Continent's old institutions treated "as things of no value." Lucretia Mott noted that abolitionists had long criticized "the oppression existing in other lands" and saw the "struggle for liberty in the old world, the anti-slavery movement in France, the Chartist movement in England, and the repeal movement of Ireland" as linked movements. Wendell Phillips likewise suggested that, because all the oppression in the world was linked, "an Hungarian triumph" over the Russian czar would benefit slaves in South Carolina, just as the repression of abolitionism in the United States "adds darkness to the dungeon where German patriots lie entombed." Returning to one of his favorite metaphors, Phillips declared that "the cause of reform, too, is one,—'distinct like the billows, but one like the sea.'"[12]

Among Garrisonians, there were very few exceptions to these positive re-actions to Europe's unrest. John B. Estlin admitted he was skeptical that the French could maintain a republic any better in 1848 than they had in 1789, and other Garrisonians lamented the violence of the uprisings. But most of the Garrisonians' circle nonetheless felt hopeful about the people's spring. "Does it not make your heart throb to think that however Calhoun may lord it in the West, good times are coming for the downtrodden people of Europe?" Webb asked in his April 1849 column in the *National Anti-Slavery Standard*, which rejoiced in the prospects of Germany's "emancipation" if it could wrest a new constitution from Austria. Likewise, when Ashurst asked, in one of his 1848 dispatches to the *Liberator*, "Can progress be arrested?" his answer was a confident "No."[13]

In short, many abolitionists on both sides of the Atlantic believed that "a *world era*" of progress had begun. Theodore Parker, a Transcendentalist min-ister who was beginning to appear at Garrisonian meetings by the end of the 1840s, declared before the AASS that the "signs of the times" were good, and African American abolitionists also praised the revolutions. Unfortunately, how-ever, signs of hope abroad were accompanied by reasons for discouragement at home. In 1848, the Mexican American War was ending, provoking new debates about slavery's future in the vast territories the United States had acquired from Mexico. And many ardent expansionists in the Democratic Party were pushing for the expansion of slavery into the Mexican cession, while simultaneously cel-ebrating the spread of European revolution.[14]

Some expansionists even styled themselves as "Young America" in imitation of Mazzini's "Young Europe," all the while hoping that 1848 would create new opportunities for territorial conquest. In June 1848, for example, the *Standard's* weekly "Proslavery" column reprinted an article from the New Orleans *Delta*, which declared that, with the European powers "compelled to keep all their attention fixed, and all their resources concentrated in resisting the alarming encroachments of the popular will at home," the United States might be able to acquire "distant colonies" like Jamaica, Cuba, and the Yucatan. Energetic action might even create an American empire "like unto that of old Rome."[15]

These statements provided abolitionists with rich new material for the mo-bilization of shame, just as previous revolutions had proved useful to Garrison at the founding of the *Liberator*. Quincy pointed out, for example, that by gobbling up one-third of Mexico's territory, Americans were behaving no differently from Austrians or Russians. And when expansionists like Democratic presidential candidate Lewis Cass claimed to sympathize with liberty in Europe, abolitionists highlighted their hypocrisy, pointing in particular to a bold escape attempt by slaves in Washington, D.C., that unfolded on the very same day as local ceremonies held to congratulate the French republic.[16]

Events like these made the European revolutions a rhetorical gold mine for the mobilization of shame, and in 1848 and 1849 Garrisonians had their own gold rush. The United States was "a Despotism in the mask of a Republic," said one resolution adopted in Massachusetts, a Russia masquerading as a France. France's consistency in abolishing slavery, thundered Douglass in Rochester, "puts our own country to the blush." In 1849 Quincy went so far as to say that it was "unfair" to Austria and Russia "to put them into the same category with ourselves." Meanwhile, British correspondents echoed back the same points. Even Estlin, despite his skepticism about events in France, could not resist noting to Samuel May that French abolition would be a "bitter pill to some of your Southern Aristocrats!"[17]

Yet underneath this rhetoric were also signs of a new buoyancy in abolitionists' hopes. First, their platforms and publications were becoming crowded with a host of new sympathizers who had previously held aloof from Garrisonian organizations, like Parker and Thomas Wentworth Higginson—both of whom echoed the Garrisonian line on French abolition and the Revolutions of 1848. The Garrisonian Sydney Howard Gay also secured Lowell, the renowned poet, as a coeditor of the *National Anti-Slavery Standard,* where he helped broadcast the Garrisonians' belief that "tyranny is of one complexion all the world over" to a wider audience.[18]

Even more encouraging, however, was the growing caucus of antislavery politicians in Congress, which became increasingly assertive during the Mexican American War and the republican revolution in France. Most antislavery Congressmen, like Giddings, Hale, Charles Francis Adams, and Horace Mann, continued to distinguish themselves from abolitionists, and vice-versa. But they heartily joined Garrisonians in tweaking southern congressmen about their support for European freedom; they sent public letters to Garrisonian committees; and they provided copies of their speeches to the *Standard,* now made more respectable by Lowell's presence. Although Garrisonians still considered themselves "called" by "a divine voice" to refrain from participating in the "methods of action" that politicians like these used, many still rejoiced in their successes. The *Standard* was quick to "congratulate the Anti-Slavery party of the country" whenever conservative congressmen were replaced by new members, like Salmon P. Chase of Ohio, who identified more openly with abolitionists.[19]

Outside of Congress, too, encouraging new alignments were afoot. In June 1848, antislavery Whigs like Sumner joined with former Liberty Party men to organize a "People's Convention" in Worcester, Massachusetts, which attracted five thousand people and elected delegates to the founding convention of the Free Soil Party that August. Claiming the mantles of the Declaration of Independence and "the spirit of the age," the assembled delegates concluded their official address by referencing events in Europe: "Every steam-ship that now crosses the Atlantic is an Anti-Slavery packet, and comes here freighted with intelligence which serves to advance the cause of freedom. Every revolution in Europe reacts upon America." These lines closely followed Garrisonians' interpretations of events, and the *Liberator* printed the address of the People's Convention under the headline, "The Cause of Liberty Advancing."[20]

Garrisonians were still of two minds about political developments, however. While they suggested a growing influence for abolitionists, they also raised with new force the question of what that influence might do to their independence as agitators. Henry Clarke Wright, for one, urged Garrisonians to repudiate the Free Soil Party as totally as they had the Liberty Men in 1839 and 1840, especially after the new party nominated the former Democrat Martin van Buren as its first presidential candidate. Chapman was glad of Zachary Taylor's victory in the 1848 presidential race, largely because "the longer the new free soil party can be kept out of the presidential seat, the purer they will be kept, & the more surely will their political agitation produce a moral effect. Success would be their moral extinction." Officially, the main Garrisonian organizations continued to deride the "voting mania" and blast Free Soilers who "trimmed" their principles to fit the people's prejudices.[21]

Even for those wary of celebrating Free Soilers, however, there were new reasons to be hopeful about liberty's advance. One of the most important was the increasing number of fugitive slaves crowding Garrisonian platforms as the decade closed. In 1848 the enslaved couple William and Ellen Craft successfully fled from Georgia to Boston in a dramatic escape that involved Ellen's disguising herself as a man and pretending to be the owner of her husband. The Crafts toured extensively in New England with William Wells Brown, who published his own narrative of slavery and escape in 1848 before departing for a three-year sojourn in Europe, armed with letters of introduction to the Garrisonians' "European branch."[22]

The Crafts also appeared on platforms with Henry "Box" Brown, an enslaved Virginian who in 1849 managed to have himself mailed in a crate to the Pennsylvania Anti-Slavery Society. After finding him still alive in his box, several Garrisonians, including James Miller McKim, Edward Davis, and the Motts, assisted him in moving farther north to Boston. There, he and his "box" proved a dramatic addition to Garrisonian platforms, and in a preface to the published narrative of Brown's escape, abolitionists capitalized on the event's timing. "Nothing that was done on the barricades of Paris exceeded" Brown's courage, they declared.[23]

These new allies boosted Garrisonians' hopes even more than speeches in Congress by Giddings or Mann. As Garrison noted in a letter to Pease, after May 1849 antislavery meetings at which the Crafts and "Box" Brown had appeared, abolitionist meetings had "never had so many runaway slaves." Garrisonians had enough new opportunities for agitation to avoid temporarily the question of their relationship to politicians.[24]

But for many Garrisonians, the signs of the times in politics were too encouraging to ignore entirely. The *Standard* praised the formation of the Free Soil Party as a watershed moment, and even announced that, "were we voters, we should esteem it a privilege, to cast a vote" for the Free Soilers' presidential ticket. At the very least, abolitionists regarded the Free Soil movement as evidence that public opinion was moving in the right directions. Indeed, when some Boston friends objected that Chapman decided to leave for Paris, even she brushed away such objections by noting that "the Non-extension Movement makes our position a far more comfortable one."[25]

Not all Garrisonians joined in Chapman's optimism. Still, most Garrisonian publications, speeches, and letters about the Free Soilers showed a different, more hopeful tone than they had ever used about the Liberty Party. Webb confessed that an antislavery speech by Giddings in the summer of 1848 had done his heart more good than "any speech I have read for many a year." Meanwhile, other British Garrisonians told American friends that the mere fact that slavery had become a major question in a presidential election, as it was in 1848, was an indisputable sign of the "advancing *power* of *opinion*, which Abolitionists are doing so much to spread & strengthen."[26]

Garrison and Phillips both added their own amens to such optimistic readings of Free Soil, despite being mostly sidelined in 1848 by personal tragedy or sickness—Garrison mourned the death of two children between April 1848 and April 1849, and Phillips suffered a nearly fatal case of dysentery near the end of the presidential race. Phillips considered the Free Soil movement "the unavoidable result of our principles and agitation, and hail[ed] it so far as its formation gives proof of the wider spread of a degree of antislavery feeling in the community." Responding in December 1848 to the party's growing strength, Garrison similarly told Samuel May Jr. that "I am for hailing it as a cheering sign of the times, and an unmistakable proof of the progress we have made, under God, in changing public sentiment." He advised abolitionists to criticize the Free Soilers' shortcomings but to concentrate their criticisms "on the two old parties," the Democrats and the Whigs.[27]

Phillips and Garrison were inclined to look more favorably on Free Soilers than they had been with Liberty Men, for two important reasons. First, their relationships with Liberty Party politicians were, from the beginning, weighed down with other issues like women's roles in the abolitionist movement and the schismatic debates in the AASS over whether abolitionists were duty-bound to vote. More importantly, Garrisonians regarded the Liberty Party as a movement designed to curtail and constrain agitation in the wake of the "reign of terror." So when Free Soil politicians, by contrast, seemed to take up radical talking points like disunionism and put them into circulation, Garrisonians looked more favorably on their efforts.[28]

Meanwhile, Garrison and Phillips treated those political abolitionists who seemed desirous of less agitation with the same scorn as ever. In 1842, for example, when local political abolitionists in Massachusetts mounted a campaign to capitalize on the Latimer rescue and elect Liberty Party candidates, Garrisonians objected to the candidacy of men like Nathaniel Colver, who had participated in the exclusion of women from the "World's Convention," on the grounds that a man who would "put gags into the mouths of anti-slavery women" could not be trusted in office. Garrison pressed the attack on Colver by noting that, when Garrisonians had recently mounted a separate meeting to rally public outrage about Latimer's case, Colver used his pulpit to criticize the Garrisonians for holding their meeting in Faneuil Hall on a Sabbath day. Later figures like Giddings, Hale, and Sumner were more appealing than Colver, because they did not urge Garrisonians to stop talking but instead read the *Liberator*, attended Garrisonian meetings, engaged them in discussion, and, in short, welcomed their agitation even when they disagreed.[29]

For just that reason, however, Free Soilers raised temptations to politics that Colver never could, especially since the signs of the times on both sides of the Atlantic suggested so much progress. In 1849 May Jr. told Webb that "we feel confident that the Antislavery movement has got such headway, that no power on earth can stop it. . . . I never felt more assured, than I do now, of the downfall of Slavery, and that at no very distant day." But if abolitionists really were on the cusp of victory, was it time to grasp the reins of politics at last?[30]

PROGRESS ARRESTED

Events temporarily allowed Garrisonians to avoid answering that difficult question, because by 1850, developments on both sides of the Atlantic showed them all how easily progress *could* be arrested, demoralizing abolitionists before their fledgling hopes of political influence had really taken flight. The first blow to abolitionist hopes came with the election of the ambitious Louis Napoleon as president of France in late 1848, followed by Napoleon's rapid marginalization of republican leaders. The next spring, to the further shock of republicans across Europe, and to the "disgust" of Garrisonians, Napoleon sent French troops to Italy, helping to end Mazzini's brief Roman republic.[31]

Meanwhile, by the end of 1849, Hungary's bid for independence had collapsed when Kossuth was defeated by Austria with the help of Russian armies led by the fearsome General Ludwig Haynau. Kossuth was soon forced into Turkish exile even as Mazzini made his melancholy way back to England. A new nadir came in December 1851, when Louis Napoleon abruptly dissolved the French National Assembly, preparing the way for his assumption of the title of French emperor. "One feels as if the night of tyranny & darkness were settling down again upon the Continent," Webb concluded.[32]

For Garrisonians, events in France were especially troubling, given that Napoleon's coup proceeded through democratic means. Napoleon himself was no democrat; in April 1848, while living as an exile in London, he volunteered to help break up Chartist demonstrations. But he ultimately won the French presidency through popular election, despite the warnings of Alexis de Tocqueville and others that Napoleon would use the office to make himself king—or worse.[33]

Chapman and her family sent similar warnings from Paris. Up to the end of November, she remained confident that the people would elect the republican general Eugène Cavaignac to the presidency. But the Chapman family also confessed a sense of foreboding when they saw the "crowds of admirers & spectators" who followed Napoleon's carriage through the streets. Even more ominous was the "quiet" that they observed, the lack of popular discussion about the dangers Napoleon posed. While "the higher & privileged classes" were "discussing great principles," Caroline Weston told Samuel May Jr., many of "the Peasantry" simply shouted "Vive l'empereur" whenever they heard Bonaparte's name and showed little knowledge about the questions at issue in the election.[34]

Chapman herself had initially been confident that the French Republic's new institutions—its "free speech—freedom of assemblage—a free press," would "[prevent] explosion, however appearances may threaten." She believed, much like Phillips often argued, that the people would be elevated by the "*grave* responsibility" of "self-government." Still, the results of the election and the subsequent behavior of Napoleon raised Tocqueville's troubling questions about whether the bare machinery of self-government could create sufficient discussion and disinterestedness to prevent a despot from ascending to power by popular acclamation.[35]

Indeed, it was no wonder that Phillips began to cite Tocqueville and insist on the importance of "ever-restless" agitation most often after 1849, especially since, while Louis Napoleon was quietly voted to power in France, nominal democrats in the United States also seemed ready to submit to the Slave Power. In 1850, Congress resolved the still heated question of slavery in the Mexican territories with a set of compromise measures that included a strengthened Fugitive Slave Law. Yet numerous northern politicians and their constituents blindly applauded the decision with the same aplomb that French peasants showed when tossing their hats for Napoleon.

The Fugitive Slave Law struck Garrisonians as the ultimate proof of the way that the American Union served the interests of the Slave Power. It also immediately threatened the freedom of new fixtures on antislavery platforms like "Box" Brown and the Crafts, whose former owners dispatched agents to the North to recapture and silence them. By the end of 1850, both the Crafts and Brown were forced for their own safety to follow William Wells Brown across the Atlantic, joining Mazzini and Kossuth in the streams of defeated, persecuted exiles now converging again on London.[36]

Meanwhile, back in the United States, the response of the major parties to the compromise measures of 1850 showed that third-party antislavery efforts were still far from controlling "public opinion." Even northern congressmen who had denounced Texas annexation supported the 1850 Compromise, fearing sectional crisis. Leaders of both major parties also declared the compromise a "final" settlement and suggested that all agitation on the subject of slavery could henceforth cease. In this dark hour, even the supposedly improving North had confirmed Lowell's worries in an 1848 editorial that asked, "Shall We Ever be Republican?" "People talk a great deal of the tyranny of Public Opinion," Lowell told readers of the *Standard* in that essay. But "it is not this we groan under, but rather the public *want of Opinion.*" Northern politicians, "instead of trying to form and direct public sentiment," seemed simply to "pamper" it, he said, echoing the fears of Phillips and Tocqueville that democracy would produce quiescence and conformism in the end.[37]

The epitome of these problems, for most Garrisonians as for Phillips, was Daniel Webster, who became the archetypical example of a northern man with southern principles after declaring his support for the Fugitive Slave Law on March 7, 1850. Nothing more clearly confirmed Webster's apostasy, Garrisonians believed, than the fact that he was busily taunting European despots at the very same moment. By 1850 Webster was serving as President Millard Fillmore's secretary of state, and his hated Seventh of March speech was followed later that year by a strongly worded, nationalistic letter to the Austrian ambassador that expressed sympathy for Kossuth's uprising in Hungary and defended America as a model republic, while avoiding the subject of slavery.[38]

These actions only deepened Webster's infamy among Garrisonians. Phillips noted his hypocrisy explicitly in a blistering oration that quoted liberally from Webster's own declarations that Kossuth's defeat would outrage world opinion and bring just retribution on his oppressors. "Put the name of Douglass, Brown, or Ellen Crafts in place of Kossuth," suggested Phillips in his rejoinder, "and we commend this fine sentiment to Mr. Webster's mature consideration." Charles C. Burleigh noted the same paradox: "If Kossuth comes here, we will welcome him; but if Ellen Crafts comes, we will send her back. If Mazzini comes, we will bestow on him the hospitality of the country; but if Henry Box Brown . . . should come, we will nail him into a worse box than he was ever in before"—a line that elicited cries of "Shame, shame!" from his audience.[39]

Fortunately not all northerners seemed blind to the Slave Power's growing strength. Free Soil Congressmen, for example, made many of the same arguments against the Fugitive Slave Law as abolitionists. Hale even introduced a petition in Congress calling for the peaceful dissolution of the Union, to the delight of Garrisonians. Even more encouraging was the creation of a host of vigilance committees dedicated to resistance of the Fugitive Slave Law. The Boston committee, which numbered Phillips among its early supporters, won a signal victory in 1851 when it succeeded in helping a Boston man named "Shadrach" evade capture by slave catchers. Later in the year, armed abolitionists successfully defended "Jerry" from federal marshals in Syracuse, New York.[40]

But victories by the Slave Power cast a pall over these successes. Henry Long of New York and Thomas Sims of Boston were captured and sent south under federal auspices. Then, in September 1851, the attempt of Maryland slaveholder Edward Gorsuch to capture some fugitive slaves in Pennsylvania led to a fierce gun battle in Christiana. Gorsuch was killed, but over two dozen locals were charged with treason for resisting the Fugitive Slave Law. Although the accused were acquitted, the incident showed how resistant federal law remained to antislavery public opinion. As one item in the *Liberator* put it, the United States seemed to be "adopt[ing] the treason code of their Imperial Majesties of Russia and Austria," making it "quite as reputable to shoot and choke the abolitionists, as it has been for the Europeans to amuse themselves in a like manner with Poles and Hungarians."[41]

The very fact that those who resisted the Fugitive Slave Law had to work in secret struck abolitionists as proof of distressing similarities between European despots and northern doughfaces like Webster. Writing to Pease of his work in helping to free Shadrach Minkins, Phillips noted that "the long evening sessions—debates about secret escapes—plans to evade where we can't resist—the door watched that no spy may enter—the whispering consultations of the morning . . . all remind me of those foreign scenes which have hitherto been known to us, transatlantic republicans, only in books." Garrison also concluded in 1850 that, while "there is nothing in Italy, nothing in Austria, nothing in Russia, more ferocious or more terrible in its opposition to the spirit of liberty, than exists in the slaveholding States," northerners too were now "living under a despotism, a most appalling despotism."[42]

These impressions were strengthened in 1850 and 1851 by two nearly simultaneous visitations by Europeans to the United States: one by their old friend George Thompson and one by the exiled Hungarian leader Louis Kossuth. Thompson, now a member of Parliament, returned to the United States for a fundraising lecture tour at the end of 1850, and many of his speeches called attention to the inconsistencies in American rebukes of European despotism. But at a large reception meeting for Thompson in Faneuil Hall, a rowdy mob—stirred up, according to abolitionists, "by the cotton aristocracy" of Boston and Webster's pro-Compromise Whigs—verged on a violent riot and prevented

Thompson and Phillips from speaking while city officials and the police silently looked on. Thompson was also greeted with a fresh round of anti-abolitionist Anglophobia in the press. Though more restrained than the mobs of the earlier reign of terror, this outrage was still "cause [for] humiliation to every true American heart," said the *Pennsylvania Freeman*, adding that "it could not be more dishonorable" to the nation if Americans were to show the same inhospitable welcome to a more famous visitor like Lamartine, Garibaldi, and Kossuth.[43]

Unbeknownst to the *Freeman*, Kossuth actually would arrive in America the following year, but the contrast between Kossuth's reception and Thompson's was striking. Kossuth arrived in the United States on a naval steamer as the honored guest of the president and was invited to address Congress. There, he won the praise of members of both major parties (including Webster), before touring the nation in a series of triumphal receptions unlike anything since Lafayette's visit in 1824. He was whisked from one lavish banquet to another, and by December 12, just one week after his arrival, diarist George Templeton Strong noted that "Magyar-mania [was] epidemic" in New York. The mania became pandemic as Kossuth continued his speaking tour to New England and the Midwest, where a young Abraham Lincoln was among his admirers. Almost everywhere he went, journalists praised Kossuth's eloquent compliments about the American Revolution while entrepreneurs sold Kossuth hats to his many admirers.[44]

Initially abolitionists were also excited by Kossuth's visit. First, they hoped that the spectacle of a "fugitive Kossuth" being welcomed by Fugitive Slave Law supporters would mobilize new feelings of patriotic shame. They frequently reminded audiences of "the exiled Hungarians of our Austria" who were now increasingly threatened with removal to the South. The Fugitive Slave Law, if applied to Hungary, would "legislate into existence a nation of Haynaus, and authorize them to whip Magyar women," argued Garrisonians, while "the escape of Jerry from the United States government at Syracuse is an event as much to be rejoiced at as the escape of Kossuth from Austrian despotism."[45]

Garrisonians also initially hoped the great Hungarian might use his international celebrity to endorse their criticisms of the Fugitive Slave Law, just like other European luminaries such as Follen, O'Connell, and Lafayette. After all, the Garrisonians' British allies had contacted Kossuth when he stopped briefly in England en route to New York. Webb and Haughton both sent letters to Kossuth through mutual acquaintances, and Webb passed a copy of Theodore Dwight Weld's *American Slavery As It Is*, along with facts about the Fugitive Slave Law, to

Kossuth, using Ashurst as an intermediary. By November 1851, Ashurst assured Webb that "all you could wish has been done to possess Kossuth with right and just views on the subject of American Slavery."[46]

Such reports gave Garrisonians an exaggerated sense of how much access their friends actually had to Kossuth, but they also encouraged their perception that leaders of European revolutions were on their side. Indeed, Kossuth's party brought letters of introduction from England to Lucretia and James Mott, who met him and invited him to dinner. (He declined.) But while Garrisonians clung to a slender hope that Kossuth might lend them aid, that hope, too, would soon be arrested.[47]

TRANSATLANTIC AFFINITIES

Kossuth began disappointing abolitionists almost as soon as he arrived in New York. First, he announced he would "not meddle with any domestic concerns," and then he proceeded, at nearly every stop, to pay florid compliments to the "free nation of America." In a speech in December, Phillips lamented that Kossuth was courting the approval of slave catchers while failing to make "a hint, even, at any blot on our national escutcheon."[48]

But Phillips's speech became only the first salvo in a relentless campaign by Garrisonians to rain fire on Kossuth's parades. For the next several months, they constantly harangued the Hungarian, comparing his actions with Thompson's, Lafayette's, and O'Connell's, and peppering him with analogies between fugitive slaves and Magyars, on the one hand, and Webster and Haynau on the other. In February, Garrison compiled many of these analogies into a blistering 112-page pamphlet written as an open letter to Kossuth. Rebuking his "flattery" of Americans, Garrison warned the Hungarian that he had made a Faustian bargain with proslavery Americans, for a nation that would not allow its North to interfere with its South and had executed the "heroic . . . NATHANIEL TURNER" was unlikely to "rally in behalf of Hungary, or to arraign the Autocrat of Russia for his tyranny."[49]

Garrison's prediction that Kossuth would fail to win American aid was accurate enough; the South turned a cold shoulder from the beginning, and even his strongest supporters in the Democratic Party seldom advocated more than a quiet retirement for Kossuth on a western farm. While visiting Faneuil Hall, Kossuth summarized his position by complaining that he was "charged from one side with being in the hands of abolitionists, and from the other side with being in the hands of the slaveholders." But while some antislavery northerners were moved by such appeals, Garrisonians never stopped upbraiding him.[50]

One reason they refused to let Kossuth off the hook was that he appeared to use the same argument against foreign interference Garrisonians had been battling for twenty years, even as he asked at the same time for American interference in Hungary. No previous potential "moral Lafayette"—not Follen, not Thompson, not even O'Connell—had declined any comment on slavery at all. No wonder, then, that the most frequent argument Garrisonians leveled against Kossuth was that he was behaving like a man whose only country was Hungary—the antithesis of the cosmopolitan patriots they aspired to be. Garrison's book on Kossuth concluded that he was "a Hungarian for Hungarians, and nothing for mankind," but in the final analysis, "local patriotism, courageous and self-sacrificing to the last extremity, is no anomaly in human history. To prove that it is neither selfish nor exclusive, a world-wide test must be applied to it." Phillips agreed that Kossuth "loves Hungary so much that his charity stops at the banks of the Danube," and Wright added that Kossuth was "daily addressing multitudes, not on human freedom, but on Nationalism."[51]

Yet as hard as the Garrisonians were on Kossuth, their real targets were his hosts. After all, compromisers like Webster had also offered a narrow concern for national union to excuse compromise with slavery. In the name of patriotism, the architects of the Fugitive Slave Law concluded that northerners' love had to stop at the Ohio or the Mason-Dixon Line, just as Kossuth's love stopped at the Danube. But "is a certain course of conduct glorious on the banks of the Danube, and infamous on the banks of the Hudson?" asked a contributor to the *Liberator*. In asking such questions, Garrisonians had northern politicians in their sights as much as Kossuth.[52]

Perhaps even more importantly, Kossuth's tour, when combined with the reversals to revolutions in Europe, underscored how susceptible to despotism American democracy remained, even after two decades of agitation. Edmund Quincy noted that the Slave Power had always pressured its guests to seal their lips on slavery, making Kossuth only "the most signal, as he is the latest, example of the application of this national test." His failure to win more than honorary toasts proved that "the governing influences of this country have no sympathy with the oppressed classes anywhere. Their secret yearnings are towards Austria and Russia and not towards Hungary." What Kossuth's visit best revealed, in Garrison's words, was "how absolute is the sway of the slave power over this whole nation."[53]

For abolitionists, unfortunately, things would get worse before they got better, on both sides of the Atlantic. In 1853, Napoleon declared himself emperor, and Russia launched an expansionist war against the Ottoman Empire. Meanwhile, the Democratic Party returned to the White House in the form of Mexican-American War veteran Franklin Pierce, while Hale, the Non-Extension candidate and a favorite of Garrisonians, received fewer votes than Free Soilers had won in 1848. Pierce also made clear he expected all agitation on the issue of slavery to cease, leading Garrison to conclude that Pierce—a native of New Hampshire, just like Hale—became president by "crawl[ing] on his belly, like a serpent, in homage to the Slave Power." Pierce's administration—with a cabinet that included Jefferson Davis as secretary of war and the inveterate anti-abolitionist Caleb Cushing as attorney general—stepped up enforcement of the Fugitive Slave Law, while simultaneously demanding the release of Martin Koszta, a Hungarian exile being held by the Austrian government, merely because he had spent some time in the United States.[54]

By 1854, Garrisonians saw distressing similarities between Napoleon in France and Pierce in Washington. "Affinities will ever seek to blend together—the near with the remote," Garrison thundered in 1853. If anti-abolitionists from the United States were "located in Russia," he added, "they would pay servile homage to the Czar; in Austria, they would take sides against Hungary; in Italy, they would anathematize Mazzini and his brave compatriots; [and] in France, they would pay court to Louis Napoleon, and exult in the banishment of the leading 'agitators.'" Garrisonians had made such shocking analogies before, for rhetorical purposes. But now, rather than suggesting only that American and European despots were comparable, Garrisonians believed they could point to direct connections and cooperation between them.[55]

The primary reason was the encouragement that Pierce's administration appeared to give to proslavery expansionists in the South. Many slaveholders had been dreaming of a Caribbean American empire for years, and instead of dispelling those visions, Pierce made clear in his inaugural address that he favored further territorial expansion. Garrisonians were therefore convinced, as the *Liberator* put it, that Pierce's election had been aided "by thousands who were satisfied that with Pierce for President, there would be no fear of any check to their filibustering schemes."[56]

The adventurous, armed groups of men known as "filibusterers" had hatched several schemes for the southward expansion of the United States even before 1852, including two attempts to invade and conquer Cuba. But after 1852, as the *Liberator* feared, filibusterers only became bolder. In 1853, proslavery swashbuckler William Walker and his men invaded Mexico and declared a new state called Baja California, a prelude to Walker's later invasion and conquest of Nicaragua. Meanwhile, the Pierce administration's appointment of known supporters of filibustering, like John L. O'Sullivan, John T. Pickett, and Pierre Soulé, to key diplomatic posts in Portugal, Mexico, and Madrid seemed to indicate that what proslavery expansionists could not accomplish by piracy they would seek to accomplish by other means. Weeks into Pierce's tenure as president, Phillips was already predicting that soon "the stars and stripes will float over the capital of Mexico" and of Cuba as well. Those predictions gained more plausibility following the Pierce administration's campaign to purchase Cuba from Spain, which gathered steam in 1853 and 1854.[57]

For abolitionists, that movement alone suggested an affinity between Pierce's policy and Russia's simultaneous, unprovoked assault on the Ottoman Empire in a war that would eventually draw England into the Crimea. Pierce claimed to be pursuing Cuba legitimately. But to abolitionists, the timing of the Cuba campaign suggested that he wanted to exploit European unrest to gain new territory. Because Britain was staunchly opposed to American annexation of the island, they argued, the government had timed its bid for Cuba to coincide with the very moment when England was distracted by fighting against Russia.[58]

During his Fourth of July speech in 1853, for example, Garrison read some revealing excerpts directly from the Washington *Union*, widely understood to be the Pierce administration's mouthpiece, which said explicitly that, if the United States tried to obtain Cuba from Spain in order to prevent slave emancipation, its chief opposition would come from England and France. That made it "sound policy and true diplomacy" to encourage conflict between these nations and Russia, a nation the *Union* praised for having never made an issue of American slavery. "And this is what we are doing for the freedom of the world?" asked an incredulous Garrison. "Nicholas of Russia is our chosen ally, our special friend."[59]

The very next year, the administration requested an appropriation of $10 million from Congress to seek the purchase of Cuba, around the same time that rumors were circulating of a friendly understanding between Russia and the United States about the Crimean War. "I send you a little slip, showing that measures are in train for a treaty of amity, or something of the sort, between the *United States & Russia!*" exclaimed Samuel May Jr. in a July 21, 1854, letter to Webb. "Russia will keep England & France busy, while the U. States rifle Spain of Cuba. This is evidently the meaning. In return this slaveholding Govt. will help the Czar in some way,—perhaps by a loan of money!" Nine days later May added that such an alliance was now "highly probable—nothing more natural." "Russian Czarism & American slaveholding are one in spirit," he concluded, "and we have the European war to thank for developing the fact so that all may see it."[60]

If the government's rumored overtures to Russia—Kossuth's arch-nemesis—left any doubt that Democrats' professed sympathy for European republicanism was a cover for aggression, the behavior of Pierce's diplomatic corps dispelled those doubts entirely for abolitionists. After Pierre Soulé, an unabashed supporter of filibustering, was appointed as minister to Spain in 1853, he alienated himself from the Court at Madrid and even fought a duel with the French minister to Spain. After that, Soulé collaborated with anti-monarchical revolutionaries in an apparent attempt to frighten Spain into ceding Cuba to the United States.[61]

Meanwhile, Pierce's London consul, George N. Sanders, and English minister, James Buchanan, seemed equally willing to hold American support for republicanism hostage to the Slave Power's interests. Sanders hosted Mazzini, Kossuth, and other European exiles at an 1854 dinner in his home, with the intention of discussing the provision of material aid to their causes. But in July—the very time the Cuba campaign was coming to a climax—he reacted angrily to a published letter by Mazzini that denounced slavery and endorsed an upcoming antislavery celebration of the First of August at Manchester. An outraged Sanders convinced Kossuth to publish a clarifying letter disavowing any attention by European republicans to meddle with American slavery. Then, in October 1854, after meeting with the American ministers to England and France in Ostend, Belgium, Soulé issued a manifesto that implicitly threatened war if Spain would not cede Cuba.[62]

Abolitionists saw the Sanders-Mazzini affair and the Ostend Manifesto as further proof that slavery overruled everything else in the United States, whose affinities with European despotism now seemed clearer than ever. With those affinities now seeming to blend into outright alliance, the only word that seemed appropriate to describe the Union was "despotism"—a description conveniently reinforced in 1854 by the release of a second edition of Hildreth's *Despotism in America,* which the *Liberator* now praised more than ever as a "masterly work"

that seemed to describe the signs of the times. To Garrisonians and their transatlantic allies, American laws were no longer even partial models for the world,
but "links in the chain . . . of oppression and misrule" that included "aristocratic
domination" in Britain and "Cossack Despotism on the Continent of Europe."[63]

FRAMINGHAM REFRAMED

Less than ten years after the encouraging stirrings of freedom in Europe and the
United States, the Pierce administration brought Garrisonians to new depths of
disgust and shame about American slavery. "We shall have Cuba in a year or two,
Mexico in five," Phillips grimly predicted to Pease in August 1854, "and I should
not wonder if efforts were made to revive the slave trade . . . The future seems
to unfold a vast slave Empire united with Brazil & darkening the whole West."
Considering the evidence that "the *Govt.* has fallen into the hands of the slave
power completely," he continued, it seemed increasingly obvious that "so far as
national politics are concerned we are beaten."[64]

But if "the sky was never so dark," as Phillips believed, there was a perverse
upside for Garrisonians; they now, more than ever, seemed on the outskirts of
power and did not have to worry about what to do once political influence was
secured. Had the Free Soil Party built on its early gains, Garrisonians might have
had to confront more directly the conflicting feelings they had about its rise.
But now, apparently beaten in national politics, Garrisonians could fully embrace their role as restless agitators charged with awakening the nation's moral
conscience. And agitation, as Garrison showed at Framingham in 1854, was still
what Garrisonians did best.[65]

In view of the foregoing, it should not be difficult to understand why July 4,
1854—the date when Garrison burned the U.S. Constitution—found Garrisonians in a foul mood about the nation's future. A month earlier, a band of southern
filibusters led by Mississippi slaveholder and former governor John Quitman
began openly preparing to invade Cuba. Only weeks before, the fugitive slave
Anthony Burns had been returned from Boston to Virginia under the guard of
federal troops sent by Pierce. Congress had just passed the Kansas-Nebraska Act,
raising the specter of slavery's expansion into federal territories where it was
once prohibited. On every side—in the South, in Washington, D.C., and even
in Boston—the power of slavery seemed to be rising. So when Massachusetts
Garrisonians gathered in a grove in Framingham to hold their annual Fourth of

July meeting, organizers hung the American flag upside down and "draped [it] in black."[66]

Recent events were also on Garrison's mind as he reached the peroration of his opening speech at the meeting. "The forms of a republic are yet left to us," Garrison cried, "but corruption is general, and mal-administration the order of the day." Surveying the recent "astounding plans" for the expansion for slavery, "openly avowed" by diplomats and filibusterers alike, Garrison lamented that "Cuba, Hayti, Mexico, South America, Brazil, the Sandwich Islands, &c. &c. all are designed for ultimate absorption by the Slave Power, which scorns the moral sentiment of the world, and defies the retribution of Heaven." He would therefore "proceed to perform an action which would be the testimony . . . of the estimation in which he held the pro-slavery laws and deeds of the nation." Producing a copy of the Fugitive Slave Law and two recent judicial decisions in the Anthony Burns case, Garrison incinerated each of them in front of the audience. Then, for his final act, he held up the U.S. Constitution, "branded it . . . 'a covenant with death, and an agreement with hell,'" and torched it, too, exclaiming, "So perish all compromises with tyranny!"[67]

From the crowd, Moncure Conway interpreted these events, like most other observers then and since, as a sort of mock "Judgment Day," with Garrison "the adamantine judge parting to the right and left the leaders of the people, constitutionalists, free-soilers, and abolitionists." The description of the Constitution as an "agreement with hell" had "a Calvinistic accent," he later recalled, and at first glance, Conway was not wrong to see Framingham in this light. As smoke swirled around him in this isolated grove, Garrison seemed to be retreating from politics into a prophetic role, far away from the temptations to political influence. He seemed to identify now with a long succession of "inspired axe-bearers, —John the Baptizer, Luther, Wesley," religious heroes all, rather than with Free Soilers and politicans.[68]

In reality, however, Framingham was the latest in a long succession of episodes in which Garrison had introduced some tactical innovation in response to a particular political event. Indeed, just as Garrison's calls for disunion were inspired by congressional debates over the Haverhill debates, Garrison's speech at Framingham followed recent debates in the Senate that he had been reading closely. On June 26, the Senate had just debated a petition from Boston calling for the repeal of the Fugitive Slave Law, prompting a discussion in which Charles Sumner, a senator since 1851, declared that the Constitution did not oblige him to assist in the return of fugitive slaves. Sumner also added that "if the Union could not exist without . . . the Fugitive Slave Law, then the Union ought not to exist." These statements delighted disunionists, especially since they then sparked a revealing and useful exchange between Sumner and Senator John Pettit, Democrat from Indiana. Pettit not only accused Sumner of breaking his vow as a congressman to protect the Constitution; he also provocatively introduced the nation's other founding document into the Senate debates. After quoting "that part of the Declaration of Independence which says that 'all men are created equal,'" Pettit argued "for half an hour" that, "if these words were used in the sense placed upon them by the abolitionists, they were a self-evident lie."[69]

A few weeks later, Garrison reprinted these debates on the front page of the same *Liberator* that contained his Framingham speech. That placement forced readers to consider the two events side by side, but so did Garrison's speech itself. It began, after all, with a ringing endorsement of the Declaration of Independence as "the most radical political instrument in the world," whose "practical enforcement will be the redemption of the world." And it concluded, moments before Garrison began setting papers on fire, by noting that "on the floor of the American Senate, the Declaration of Independence has been scouted as a tissue of lies and absurdities!!!" By next burning the Fugitive Slave Law and the Constitution, Garrison reversed, in dramatic fashion, the order of priority in which Pettit had placed these three documents.[70]

Thus, just as the Haverhill petition had prompted a useful admission from Joseph Underwood of Kentucky in 1842, the Sumner-Petit duel inspired Garrison to see Framingham as another opportunity to agitate Congress from without. That made his burning of the Constitution more like Massie's burning of the Corn Law Bill than Luther's burning of a papal bull. Most of all, however, it showed that Garrisonians continued to kick up political dust—quoting the *Union*, following the movements of diplomats, and listening in on congressional debates.

Framingham also showed, no less clearly, that Garrison continued to follow transatlantic events in Europe closely and to worry about the effects of American slavery on democrats abroad. Before burning the Constitution and mentioning Pettit's speech, Garrison even gave his audience a lengthy survey of recent events in Europe: France was now ruled with "perfidious and high-handed usurpation" by Emperor Louis Napoleon; Pope Pius IX again ruled Rome, temporally and spiritually; Austria remained a haven of "bloody despotism"; and the "iron autocracy" of Czar Nicholas still gripped Russia. "No people are visible," Garrison concluded. "I do not see a man, erect and indomitable, from the Seine to the Black Sea, from Paris to Constantinople. I see tyrants who rule, and the masses who submit." Garrison admitted the possibility that there was yet another revolutionary "volcano beneath the surface, silently at work." But it was hard to deny that "the bayonet" ruled Europe once more and that, "at present . . . the extinction of the people [is] complete."[71]

Garrison did not, however, blame "the people" of Europe for their fate. "Talk not of the unfitness of any people, or of any country, to be free!" he exclaimed. The real reason for the dismal state of democracy in Europe, Garrison told his audience, was the state of democracy in the United States. European counterrevolution since 1848 was the climax to the long, tragic "story of American influence upon the liberties of the world." That story had begun promisingly in 1776 with the Declaration of Independence, Garrison said, whose principles should have subverted monarchy, hereditary aristocracy, and absolutism wherever they existed. But since 1776, even Americans' faith in the Declaration's promise of equality had steadily deteriorated. "We have proved recreant to our own faith," Garrison cried, "false to our own standard, treacherous to the trust committed to our hands."[72]

These lines, though often obscured by the fire that followed, showed Garrison's continued hope that republican and democratic institutions would spread around the world. They also betrayed his abiding belief that the United States should have been a model republic. Indeed, in many ways Garrison's Framingham speech reprised the themes of his "Dangers of the Nation" speech at Park Street Church many years before. Both addresses shared the aim of making his audience blush, and in both cases, Garrison assumed that Americans still had much to boast about. Garrison told the crowd at Framingham that Americans had "abundant reason for exultation, gratitude, thanksgiving" for the Declaration of Independence, and after an hour of "refreshment and social recreation" following Garrison's speech, abolitionists reconvened by singing a hymn to the "patriot dead" of Bunker Hill.[73]

After Garrisonians left the Framingham grove, they also continued their familiar efforts to arrest the growth of the Slave Power and save the nation from its shame, using many of the same tactics—like the mobilization of shame through Atlantic crossings—that had always defined their movement. In fact, there was a noticeable surge in transatlantic abolitionist activity between 1852 and 1854, as Sarah Pugh, Abby Kimber, Daniel Neall, James Miller McKim, Samuel J. May,

Edward M. Davis, William Henry Ashurst, and Parker Pillsbury all crossed the Atlantic, some for the second time. British Garrisonians also began publishing a new journal in London, the *Anti-Slavery Advocate,* edited by Webb, while a new ally, Quaker philanthropist Wilson Armistead, published two large compendiums of antislavery tracts in 1853. Frederick W. Chesson, a young liberal journalist who would marry George Thompson's daughter Amelia in 1855, also soon joined with other Manchester abolitionists to start a new antislavery organization in London aligned mainly with the Garrisonians.[74]

One result of this flurry of activity was to stimulate abolitionist infighting, particularly between Pillsbury and the BFASS. But their motives, as before, were shaped by a desire to surround the United States with international opprobrium at a moment that seemed especially urgent and opportune. The moment was opportune because African American exiles like the Crafts and "Box" Brown had attracted widespread attention with their British lectures on American slavery and their attempts to embarrass Americans at the Great Exhibition of 1851, where they promenaded with white friends in the famous Crystal Palace erected in London for the show. William Wells Brown's appearance with Maria Weston Chapman at a peace conference in Paris in 1849 also provided new material for mobilizing shame when two Americans who had scorned Brown on his transatlantic steamship had to approach him, hats in hand, to ask for introductions to Richard Cobden and Tocqueville's wife. Young new activists like Chesson seemed ready to capitalize on efforts like those of the Crafts, and the pump had also been primed, abolitionists thought, by the international success of *Uncle Tom's Cabin,* whose author Harriet Beecher Stowe toured Britain in 1853 and 1854 to wide notice and acclaim, also visiting the Chapman salon while in France.[75]

But the mid-1850s also seemed like an urgent moment for renewed transatlantic agitation. At a time when American expansionists were talking openly of Britain's inability to save Cuba, all while proslavery diplomats were casting themselves as friends of republican exiles, there were new and pressing imperatives to publicize British antislavery sentiment. That was one reason why Garrison devoted nearly the entire issue of the *Liberator* on September 1, 1854, to a large First of August celebration in Manchester, England, at which Pillsbury, Chesson, Thompson, William Wells Brown, and many others spoke. This meeting, like most of those at which Pillsbury appeared, managed to reopen some familiar factional squabbles. But more significant were the speeches themselves, many of which placed the event within a broad geopolitical context.[76]

Pillsbury, for example, talked about recent discussions in the United States about reopening the African slave trade and seizing Cuba, "peaceably, if they can; but forcibly, if they must." Alluding to the Crimean War, Pillsbury also warned his British audience that "our government is taking advantage of your just now being very busy with your eastern affairs, to prosecute and consummate this measure." Another speaker read the scandalous correspondence between Kossuth, Sanders, and Mazzini. Finally, a long series of resolutions was passed denouncing the attempts of the American Slave Power to take Cuba and urging the English public to issue loud protests against the act.[77]

Afterwards, sympathetic newspaper commentary about the meeting stressed how urgent it was to show that the British people, their eastern affairs notwith-standing, remained united in opposition to the slave trade and in favor of univer-sal emancipation. The Manchester *Examiner and Times,* for example, pointed out how much "the anti-slavery party in America need to be encouraged by the ex-pression of English sympathy and approval." Conversely, American abolitionists used *Liberty Bell* articles by European exiles and letters from overseas friends to emphasize that, as one London correspondent wrote, Americans were "becom-ing a taunt, a proverb and a bye word in the mouths of our Tories here, when-ever we Democrats open our mouths in favor of Republicanism." Garrisonians also made ample use of visits from Thompson and Ashurst, who came to visit his Garrisonian friends in 1853, two years before his death. At an 1853 First of August meeting, Garrison read aloud a letter that Ashurst brought with him from Mazzini, who gave direct endorsements of Garrison and Mott: "Will you shake hands with them for me and tell them how much I do sympathize with their aims and efforts?"[78]

In sum, in the early 1850s Garrisonians worked hard to show that, Sanders and Soulé notwithstanding, European liberals still stood with them, and still believed "the abolition of [America's] slave system" was injuring "the swooning liberties of Europe." Indeed, the very same issue of the *Liberator* that reported on Garrison's actions at Framingham also printed a letter from English suffrag-ist and Garrisonian ally Joseph Barker that developed yet again the connections between aristocratic rule in Europe and slavery in the United States. And the no-tion that democrats abroad depended on American abolitionists was only further reinforced by the presence at Framingham of John C. Cluer, the Chartist exile who had recently been jailed for participating in a famous attempt by abolition-ists to rush the Boston Court House and rescue Anthony Burns. Cluer spoke to the crowd almost immediately after Garrison's burning of the Constitution, thereby reinforcing Garrison's own depiction of abolitionism as part of a global struggle against despotism.[79]

In short, even as Garrisonians' hopes for victory darkened after 1849, they continued to seek ways to agitate public opinion, both at home and abroad. Even at Framingham, their ultimate goal remained the creation of an agitation that would respond to and affect what went on in Congress. Indeed, these goals combined in a telling message Garrison sent to Sumner the day after his June 26, 1854, debate with John Pettit in Congress: "If you have some enemies on this side of the Atlantic," Garrison's note began, "you have many friends in the old world. Your enemies here are among the vilest of the vile; your friends there are among the best and noblest of mankind." He then provided Sumner an introduction to one such friend who was visiting the United States and wished to meet Sumner—abolitionist Robert Smith of Glasgow, quite possibly the same R. Smith who served for many years as secretary of the Anti-Slavery League.[80]

These statements and actions showed how closely Garrisonians continued to follow political events in Congress and in Europe. Indeed, a bright chain connected the Garrison of 1854 to the Lloyd of 1824 who had closely watched the course of transatlantic revolutions in Greece, South America, and France. In Lloyd's continued concern for the global influence of the Declaration, in his continued expressions of shame for the effect that slavery was having on the republic, and in his attention to the revolutions of 1848, there was more than a little of the young man who had admired Lafayette and Lord Byron and imagined himself as part of a transatlantic league of reformers battling the Holy Alliance.

The difference was that, in the thirty years since, Garrison had become a member of transatlantic reform networks in truth and not in imagination only. That reality deepened his belief that he and like-minded agitators in the United States had to do something about slavery if they wanted to do something about the staggering oppression elsewhere in the world. Over his actions at Framingham hung the anguished question he had asked at a meeting on the previous Fourth of July: "What are we doing for the cause of the oppressed millions of Europe?" As long as Pierce was in power, Burns was in Virginia, Mazzini was in exile, and Kossuth was gagged by American slavery, the answer seemed painfully obvious: not nearly enough.[81]

THE CIVIL WAR AND THE RUPTURING OF
TRANSATLANTIC ABOLITIONISM, 1854–1863

A t Framingham, Garrisonians still believed their primary role was to agitate, but the temptation to politics did not go away. Neither did their questions about how to measure or deal with political influence. Even in the dark days of the Pierce administration, there were some antislavery men in Congress who raised those questions anew. Phillips "rejoice[d] beyond measure" when Gerrit Smith, a onetime foe, was elected to Congress in 1852, hailing it as "a striking sign of the times." Likewise, when Hale chastised proslavery southerners during Congressional debates over welcoming Kossuth, Garrisonians noted his efforts approvingly. In 1853, Phillips even declared that "our opinions differ very little from those of our Free Soil friends, or of intelligent men generally, when you really get at them."[1]

By 1854 there were even some striking similarities between Garrisonians' speeches and those of an antislavery politician whose name they did not yet know: Abraham Lincoln. In 1854, while Garrison was burning the Constitution in Framingham, Lincoln was in Illinois, fuming over the passage of the Kansas-Nebraska Act and helping to build a new Republican Party determined to revoke it. But Lincoln was also, like Garrison, keeping an eye on events in Europe. In an October speech in Peoria, he expressed special concern that American slavery was injuring the cause of democracy abroad: "Already the liberal party throughout the world, express the apprehension 'that the one retrograde institution in America, is undermining the principles of progress, and fatally violating the noblest political system the world ever saw.'"

Those lines were actually a quotation that Lincoln took from an 1854 editorial in the liberal *London Daily News,* a newspaper that was generally friendly to "popular government" and the republican experiment in the United States. "We have ever been among the heartiest well-wishers of the Americans," the *Daily News* had said only a few weeks before Lincoln spoke. But liberal Englishmen now feared, on behalf of "the Liberal Party throughout Europe," that "the one retrograde institution in America is undermining the principle of progress, and fatally vitiating the noblest political system that the world ever saw." As proof, the paper pointed especially to the conduct of proslavery American diplomats like Pierre Soulé and George Sanders, whose behavior was "a symptom of peril which all true Americans should take heed to without the loss of a moment."[2]

Lincoln, like Garrison, did "take heed" of what Sanders and Soulé were doing. His Peoria speech focused primarily on the Kansas-Nebraska Act, but the European escapades of the Pierce administration and their effect on "the liberal party throughout the world" provided an ominous backdrop for the whole address, which concluded by reminding Americans of their responsibility to model republicanism for the world. The expansionist ambitions of the Democratic Party, Lincoln warned, were soiling "our republican robe" and "trail[ing] it in the dust," while northern congressmen like John Pettit were "call[ing] the Declaration of Independence 'a self-evident lie'"—a nadir that Garrison had also cited only a few months before at Framingham.[3]

Garrisonians did not notice Lincoln's Peoria speech, but its themes were indicative of a new era in antislavery politics; in the Republican Party, Garrisonians would find increasing evidence of what seemed like sympathy with their own views, causing them to hope their agitation was finally influencing politics. In 1856, James Miller McKim told Webb that the "the Republicans now acknowledge that we have the correct philosophy: that is that the first thing to be done is to enlighten & convert the people." Many disunionists, he reported, had even decided to "make no especial opposition" to Republicans in that year's presidential contest and would instead "wish well to the Republican candidate as the best man, and will speak & act accordingly." Indeed, only two years after he had burned the Constitution, Garrison came close to making a public presidential endorsement, declaring "that if there were no moral barrier to our voting, and we had a million votes to bestow, we should cast them all for the Republican candidate."[4]

These statements showed how far Garrison remained from Noyes and Rogers, and they deeply troubled some other Garrisonians who feared Garrison was deserting the non-resistant faith. Abby Kelley—one of Garrison's allies of longest standing—insisted in 1858 that "our business is, to cry unclean, unclean" and "to put the brand of Cain" on all politicians, instead of "bestowing compliments on the good points in their characters" as Phillips had recently done with Charles Sumner, who was now a Republican. Her warnings foreshadowed an impending crisis in the abolitionists' ranks over the proper attitude of Garrisonians towards politicians.[5]

For the time being, Garrisonians averted that crisis, because they agreed that most politicians still deserved censure. In the same 1853 speech that praised "our Free Soil friends," Phillips blasted Hale—the politician most deserving of "the respect and confidence of the antislavery public"—for supporting calls for a monument to Henry Clay. Other Free Soilers had also applauded the eulogies to the apostate Webster upon his recent death. Garrisonians, by contrast, "could not shape our lips to ask any man to do [Webster] honor. . . . Haynau on the Danube is no more hateful to us than Haynau on the Potomac." After 1854, Garrisonians likewise criticized timid Republican leaders like William Henry Seward and Lincoln—whom Phillips famously dubbed "the Slavehound of Illinois"—and they continued to demand "No Union with Slaveholders."[6]

These continuities temporarily allowed Garrisonians to maintain their unity, but events would soon put unprecedented pressure on their networks at home and abroad. The election of Lincoln as president in 1860, followed by the secession of South Carolina and the outbreak of war, dramatically exposed the implications and unresolved questions of their earlier discussions on public opinion, political influence, democracy, and national allegiance, in ways that sometimes surprised longtime friends. Thirty years after Garrison's first Atlantic crossing, and less than ten years after Framingham, Garrisonians on both sides of the Atlantic suddenly seized arguments that were worn from frequent use and began to turn them on each other.

THE DEATH OF DISUNIONISM

The abolitionists' war within the war did not begin until shots were fired at Fort Sumter; before then, while southern states were slowly seceding in reaction to Lincoln's election, Garrisonians remained united in their calls for "No Union with Slaveholders." The reasons were twofold. First, in early 1861 many Garrisonians still believed that the southern secession movement might not actually succeed. After all, Garrisonians' arguments about the Slave Power had always rested on the premise that slaveholders needed the Union and would cling to its compromises for as long as possible. On January 20, 1861—at a moment when only three other states had joined South Carolina—Phillips reached all the way back to the debates over the Haverhill petition to remind abolitionists that "many years ago, on the floor of Congress, Kentucky and Tennessee both confessed that 'the dissolution of the Union was the dissolution of slavery.'" Both Phillips and the *Liberator* also pointed to more recent examples of southerners who confessed that slavery depended on the Union.[7]

These confessions made some Garrisonians believe that secessionists were only trying to bluff northerners into another humiliating compromise. The real aim of the fledgling confederacy, Phillips suspected, was to stand on its own just "long enough for the North to ask for annexation on their terms"; southerners knew, or would realize quickly, that they could not save slavery without the North. That was why, at least during the secession winter, it was imperative for northerners to preach disunion. Better to indicate a willingness to let them go, argued Chapman, than to "stoop so *much* lower beneath the Slaveholding lash."[8]

In January 1861, Phillips also sensed that many Republican leaders *were* tempted to compromise with the seceding states. Though President-Elect Lincoln kept his plans close to his chest, leading Republican William Henry Seward declared publicly that some resolution to the crisis had to be found to prevent the rise of "an European, an uncompromising hostility to slavery." That timid response to secession outdid "the servile silence of the 7th of March, 1850," Phillips thundered, and raised the danger that the evils of Webster's compromise might be repeated. At this pivotal juncture, it was crucial for Garrisonians to steel the nerves and courage of the North. "While [the South] holds out her hand for Seward's offer," Phillips said, "she keeps her eye fixed" on the people of the North "to see what we think." Let them therefore "laugh" the Confederacy to "scorn."[9]

By doing so, Phillips added, disunionism could still speed emancipation. If the North would only "announce frankly that we welcome the black race to liberty, won in battle, as cordially as we have done Kossuth," then before long southerners would be forced to make "just concession" to the slaves. Compromise, on the other hand, would do more than imperil the freedom of slaves, who were poised to seize the opportunities afforded them by disunion. It would also damage the cause of millions of Europeans reeling from the counterrevolutions of 1848 and 1849, whose eyes were still "fixed on us as the great example of self-government." Whether they were bluffing or not, secessionists had challenged the results of a democratic election. So if the North acquiesced, despots everywhere would have good reason to gloat that democracy had failed. If the North caved to the Slave Power's demands, Phillips asked, "How, then, shall Kossuth answer, when Austria laughs him to scorn? . . . How, then, shall Garibaldi dare look in the face of Napoleon?" Until circumstances changed, abolitionists would still preach disunion even if "it were only to honor self-government, to prove that it educates men."[10]

Each of these early arguments made the case for continuing to preach disunionism even after secession. But they also laid the groundwork for some Garrisonians to join the Union cause once the war came. First, Phillips clearly defined disunionism as a way to resist compromise on slavery, thereby distinguishing it from a southern secession designed to perpetuate bondage. Moreover, he and others based the logic of disunionism on the assumption that the South as a whole could not really last on its own and might not even try. If that was the case, it made sense to abolish northern timidity and show the South that the North would not cave. But if secession gathered momentum, and eventually resulted in war, the tactical assumptions underlying Garrisonian disunionism for twenty years—that the South considered disunion to mean emancipation—would also no longer apply.

These considerations help explain the Garrisonians' immediate reaction to the fall of Fort Sumter. Now Garrison suddenly effused that "all our sympathies and wishes must be with the government," and within a week, Phillips ascended a Boston platform decked with flags to declare that "I think the South is all wrong, and the administration is all right." Having urged disunion only a few months before, Phillips declared that "to-day Abolitionist is merged in citizen,— in American." Garrison agreed: "it is no time for minute criticism of Lincoln, Republicanism, or even the other parties, now that they are fusing for a death-grapple with the Southern slave oligarchy." The echo of Lowell's poem about the "death-grapple" betwixt old systems and the Word suggested Garrison's sense that God was swaying the future, and in May he published the first of several wartime columns by Charles K. Whipple arguing that Lowell had been right: "New Occasions Teach New Duties."[11]

Yet to other members of the AASS, like Kelley, her husband Stephen Foster, and Parker Pillsbury, these statements were shocking departures. They were even more bewildering to transatlantic Garrisonians, who had difficulty understanding what made Garrison and Phillips abandon disunionism so quickly. Before the Battle of Bull Run had even been fought, confused allies began writing

Garrisonians of their "deep regret" and thwarted "anticipations," and curious letters soon gave way to censorious ones accusing Phillips and others of letting their standards "droop." Meanwhile, American Garrisonians responded with rebukes of their own. James Miller McKim, who now supported the administration, wrote testily to Webb that "I am not convinced of my error."[12]

Neither side was convinced of its error, because both positions in this internal debate made some sense from within the Garrisonians' camp. First, given the history of non-resistance in their ranks, some abolitionists were understandably perplexed by the sudden war fever among their friends; a few long-time Garrisonians had even donned uniforms before one year had passed. To non-resistants who supported the war, however, this particular reversal felt less abrupt than it appeared. Non-resistants like Garrison and Wright always held that, if violence were ever justified, it was in the case of a slave rebellion, and in the decade before the war, many Garrisonians had already warmed to the idea that force directed at slavery or used in defense of democratic principles was sometimes legitimate. Some had wished success to armed revolution by Mazzini and Garibaldi in Italy; others sympathized with the 1857 revolt against British rule in India.[13]

The following year, in May 1858, Garrison even publicly approved of a meeting of radical European exiles that had convened to protest the execution of Felice Orsini, an Italian nationalist who became internationally famous after attempting to assassinate Louis Napoleon. Justifying his sympathy for Orsini on the grounds that "MY COUNTRY IS THE WORLD; MY COUNTRYMEN ARE ALL MANKIND," Garrison explained that he did not consider Orsini an "assassin" but "a brave man, true to his convictions of duty." While he believed in "the inviolability of human life," he saw a wide difference between Orsini and a "wholesale murderer" like Louis Napoleon, "who deserved to be beheaded, rather than Orsini." Garrison saw the same wide difference between Confederates and Americans in 1861.[14]

In short, ambivalent non-resistants had been making subtle accommodations to violence for several years. Besides, as Garrison noted in defense of the AASS on May 10, 1861, "the number of avowed non-resistants in their ranks is, and always has been, extremely small." Only those who conflated non-resistance with total Christian perfectionism were truly confounded by Garrison's seeming change of heart; he had always, to Noyes's chagrin, deemed some evils to be in more urgent need of remedy than others, and in this case, he could subordinate his peace views to the potential good that might come for slaves. In 1861, he had already begun to think about how armed conflict might speed the jubilee through "a movement for the abolition of slavery under the war power."[15]

What still seemed inexplicable to his transatlantic friends, however, was why the outbreak of war caused Garrisonians to abandon disunionism: had not they always said that disunion could free the slaves, too, and peacefully? Haughton confessed in May 1861 that he had expected Garrison simply to let the southern states go, believing that secession was "the realization of that event so long demanded by *your* section of the American abolitionists." He and others could not understand why the outbreak of war had changed Garrison's policy. A related complaint was made by critics like Kelley and Webb who chastised Garrisonians for suddenly lowering the lances so recently aimed at the Republicans. Were they not abandoning the ever-restless agitation needed to keep a democracy pure?[16]

Phillips and Garrison could appreciate those concerns; they had, after all, helped articulate the premises behind them. But their responses to critics also made sense: disunionism before the war had been based tactically on the assumption that southerners would rather abolish slavery themselves than see the Union repealed, and that was no longer the case. As Garrison often said when explaining why he no longer preached against the Union as a "covenant with death and an agreement with hell," he had never expected to live to see "death" and "hell" secede.[17]

Moreover, Phillips, Garrison, and their allies explained, the goal of disunionism had always been partly to influence politics and "public opinion" in the North, too. As Phillips explained a few years into the war, "our effort to break the Union was only a means to an end. Our object was the abolition of slavery," but they hoped to do so by maturing "a public opinion throughout the North adverse to slavery." Before the war, disunionism had been a tool "to convert the Nation, and create a strong anti-slavery public opinion." The difference between now and then, Phillips believed, was that war had decisively and favorably transformed northern public opinion, making it possible for agitators to adjust their positions.[18]

THE WHEEL OF PUBLIC OPINION

Phillips's wartime interpretation of disunionism was, of course, a selective one; alternative interpretations of what disunionism meant were plausible even on Garrisonians' own terms. But his explanation went to the heart of what he and most other Garrisonians had always believed: "creat[ing] a strong anti-slavery public opinion" was the first and most vital step to any reformation that might follow. Those Garrisonians who supported the war effort in 1861 defended their course most often on the grounds that a stronger public opinion now prevailed in the North than ever before.

Because Unionists like Phillips and Garrison were so convinced that Fort Sumter had revolutionized public opinion, they were even unconcerned that not all Republicans yet saw abolition as a war aim. Phillips conceded that there was a class of people "whose only idea in this controversy is sovereignty and the flag," but "the PEOPLE" were now moving quickly to join "their Abolition neighbors," and were determined "to strangle" the Slave Power "aristocracy." Indeed, Garrison was so impressed by the state of northern public opinion that in September, the AASS even decided against holding "a national Anti-Slavery Convention, in relation to the war," concluding that it would be best "to merge ourselves, as far as we can without a compromise of principle, in the onward sweeping current of Northern sentiment."[19]

British Garrisonians were not convinced, however, that the current was sweeping in the right direction. From their side of the water, it looked as though the North was rushing to war without any thought of the slave. "As far as its professions go," Webb told one of the Weston sisters in July, "the war on the part of the north is only an armed attempt to punish traitors and to restore the Union to its former dimensions." Eliza Wigham likewise believed the war fever in the North was sparked by "heat & novelty & imagined patriotism" instead of high principle. Could their friends not see that northern sentiment was moving on without them?[20]

At issue in these disagreements about the state of northern public opinion was the larger question of what public opinion was and how it could be measured at all. Unfortunately, however, Garrisonians' definitions of "public opinion" had always been remarkably vague given the power and importance they attributed to it. In 1857, for example, McKim confidently told Webb that, while abolitionists were still "labouring at the crank of public opinion," they believed "the wheel is turning with an increasing momentum." Yet such metaphors obscured an underlying lack of consensus about how to gauge the rate at which public opinion turned. The war finally made that basic dilemma unavoidable: how could Garrisonians measure the character of "public opinion" and the effects of their "agitation" upon it?[21]

Until the 1860s, the Garrisonian movement had not foundered on that problem because they agreed that the state of antebellum American "public opinion"
remained bad. Moreover, Phillips had always urged agitators to keep the ocean
"ever-restless," leaving unanswered the question of how abolitionists would know
when the tide was turning in their favor. But now that some Garrisonians did
believe that "public opinion" was shifting, and in the right direction, they needed
standards by which to evaluate such claims, and found that they had none.

Some prowar Garrisonians pointed to political events to validate their claims
about public opinion. Even before Fort Sumter, when the Democratic Party split
into northern and southern proslavery wings at its nominating convention, abolitionists rejoiced that their years of antislavery pressure on northern "doughfaces" were finally having an effect. In light of such events, an ebullient May
asked Webb how he could be as "despondent" as before. "Do you not discern
some proof of the action of A[nti] S[lavery] ideas on the national mind?" Later,
despite their reservations about Lincoln's caliber, most Garrisonians were also
delighted by the Republican victory in November; it indicated "that, by their
persistent and unflinching agitation of the question of Slavery for the last 25
years," the AASS had "created antislavery voters by the thousands." Other electoral results seemed to be even more encouraging, like the election of radical
Free Soiler John Andrew to the governorship of Massachusetts and Elijah Lovejoy's brother Owen to Congress.[22]

Most importantly, many Garrisonians believed the election of 1860 had
brought agitation and discussion about slavery in the country to a high tide. "The
late canvass was worth a dozen Lincolns," Phillips concluded. "The agitation was
a yeomanly service to liberty. It educated the people." Indeed, although "Lincoln
is in *place*," Phillips added, it was really "Garrison in *power*." Lincoln was like
the chocolate grinders who could sometimes be seen cranking their machines
in the streets of Naples and New York: "he seems to turn the wheel, but in truth
the wheel turns him."[23]

Yet Phillips's recourse to metaphor dodged the essential question again: how
would Garrisonians really know when Garrison was in power? Cobden's power
had been clear to abolitionists once the Corn Laws were repealed; O'Connell's
was revealed when the Catholic Relief Act was passed. But how would Garrisonians know when their agitations had become the "public opinion" of the North
instead of the views of a trampled "minority"? Surely the results of an election
were not perfect, because Lincoln had run explicitly on a platform disavowing

any abolitionist intentions. In his "Under the Flag" speech a few months later, Phillips also explicitly distinguished between the views of "the PEOPLE" and their political leaders. So how could agitators know that what really stood behind the election results was a more determined and "educated" people than before?

Phillips had actually considered that question in 1844, but only long enough to dismiss it. The issue came up in a reply by Phillips to political abolitionists who had claimed that, if all were non-voters, like the Garrisonians, there would be no way of determining the public mind on an issue. Phillips replied that "the difficulties thought to lie in the way of finding where and when a majority exists, move me very little. Should the case ever occur, there will be no practical difficulty. But if there were, it is no matter of mine" in the present.[24]

By neglecting to take up the problem of how to measure popular opinion apart from electoral results, however, antebellum Garrisonians had simply tolerated a kaleidoscope of ways to view "public opinion." In 1839, for example, the AASS annual report argued that the number of antislavery organizations in the country was one way of gauging "the progress of our cause," though it was not the most "exact index." An even "more correct index" was the number of antislavery publications and subscriptions to them. Yet the report also cited still another indicator: "the yielding of the ordinary newspaper press to become the channel of Anti-Slavery discussion." In a haphazard fashion typical of many contemporary writings on how to measure agitation's effects, this single report had pointed to three very different ways to "index" public opinion. That diversity of views later made it possible for wartime Garrisonians to disagree in their readings of events. If one index of opinion returned an unfavorable result, turning the kaleidoscope slightly could cause the signs of the times to fall into a more pleasing pattern.[25]

In early 1861, for example, Garrisonians knew that the circulation of their own publications was relatively small. But some were more impressed by the many national newspapers now disseminating abolitionist arguments and reporting on their movements. At a January 1861 MASS meeting, Phillips ignored the jeers from some rowdy boys in the gallery and simply pointed to the scribbling reporters now crowded around the dais. "Friends of the slave, look here! These pencils . . . will do more to create opinion than a hundred thousand mobs. While I speak to these pencils, I speak to a million of men." Now that editors knew abolitionist speeches would "sell their papers," Phillips added, "we have got the press of the country in our hands."[26]

That began to seem literally true a year later, when the young Garrisonian Theodore Tilton became acting editor for the influential New York *Independent,* a post he assumed officially in 1863. More impressively, in March 1862, Sydney Howard Gay, the longtime Garrisonian and fourteen-year editor of the *National Anti-Slavery Standard,* ascended to the position of managing editor of Horace Greeley's Republican organ, the New York *Tribune,* a paper whose daily circulation was possibly the largest in the nation.[27]

In the meantime, prowar Garrisonians also cited other indices of improving opinion in the North, like the seemingly changed mood of the audiences at abolitionist meetings after Fort Sumter. In December 1861, Phillips addressed an overflow crowd of respectful listeners at New York City's famous Cooper Union Institute. Garrison's own address at Cooper Union the next week on "The Abolitionists, and their Relations to the War," was also well received and widely reprinted. By some estimates Phillips received about two hundred invitations to speak in the winter of 1861 and 1862 on abolitionist subjects.[28]

For Garrisonians this openness to the discussion of their ideas was striking. "Every public meeting in Athens was opened with a curse on any one who should not speak what he really thought," Phillips noted in April 1861. Public meetings in America now seemed to be opening the same way, at least for abolitionists. The fact that abolitionists were now able to speak what they really thought—without the threat of "mobs," and in highly public forums—was itself an indication that the North was moving closer to his Athenian ideal. Finally, "we are strong enough to tolerate dissent," Phillips rejoiced. Equally encouraging was the fact that the Lincoln administration seemed to welcome and invite public discussion on the issues involved in the crisis. Phillips argued that even Lincoln's decision to postpone calling a special session of Congress "till July 4th plainly invites discussion,—evidently contemplates the ripening of public opinion in the interval."[29]

Once the first year of the war passed, Garrisonians believed they could look back on even more startling proofs of a ripened "public opinion." One particularly striking sign was the reception that greeted Phillips's popular new lecture on Toussaint L'Ouverture, the hero of the Haitian Revolution, which he delivered to a packed audience at the Smithsonian Institution in Washington, D.C., in March 1862 and repeated dozens of times in the months that followed. Thousands of copies of the oration were reprinted by a wide swath of abolitionist and non-abolitionist newspapers, including the *Tribune,* which also printed Phillips's speech as a prepackaged supplement designed to be distributed as a tract.[30]

Such developments were the primary reason why Garrisonians "see everywhere signs & proofs of a very remarkable change in the public mind on the subject of Slavery," as May Jr. told Webb in the same month Phillips gave his Smithsonian lecture. At the 1862 meeting of the MASS, Garrison likewise reflected on how much had changed since mobs disrupted the society's meeting just one year before. "Although, as a people, we do not yet come up to the high standard of duty in striking directly at the slave system for its extirpation as the root and source of all our woe," Garrison admitted, "nevertheless, the sentiment of the North is deepening daily in the right direction." Phillips, for his part, had been convinced of this even in February 1861, when he asserted that Seward and other pro-compromising Republicans were misreading the feeling of the North: "I believe you might have polled the North, and had a response, three to one: 'Let the Union go to pieces, rather than yield one inch.' I know no sublimer hour in history."[31]

The problem, of course, was that it was impossible for Phillips or any other abolitionist to actually poll the North on such specific questions, leaving room for honest disagreement. On the one hand, Garrisonians like Phillips thought the secession winter had "matured a public opinion definite, decisive, and ready to keep step to the music of the government march." The North was finally being transformed by "peaceful, moral, intellectual agitation" of the abolitionist campaign, as "year after year, event by event, has indicated the rising education of the people,—the readiness for a higher moral life." To explain why he now stood "Under the Flag," Phillips said that "the only mistake that I have made, was in supposing Massachusetts wholly choked with cotton-dust and cankered with gold."[32]

But many British Garrisonians focused on other indices of opinion and were not so easily persuaded. After all, at the annual meeting of the MASS in the Tremont Temple in January 1861, a rowdy mob of young men took over the galleries and threw seat cushions down on the heads of the assembled abolitionists, causing such a disturbance that Garrisonians were unable to finish any speeches until the mayor arrived and reluctantly ordered the gallery cleared. Support for Lincoln, meanwhile, could just as easily be interpreted as nationalistic support for the Union. "As yet there is no right anti-slavery feeling in the North as a mass," Eliza Wigham told May Jr. in June 1861. "I think dear Garrison's prophetic spirit has led him to believe that what he sees *will* come out of the present excitement *has already* come."[33]

Those who agreed with Garrison, on the other hand, could only see positive signs in the state of northern public opinion after Fort Sumter. "We never expected anything but *temporary* disunion," McKim explained to Webb, but now the war promised an alternative means of forcing abolition. "We knew that collision would come, then abolition, and then we supposed re-union. But we are having all these together." Samuel May Jr. also declared that *"never before* [had] the North been so united!" And by November, he was even surer that there were obvious signs of "the Nation's progress towards a high and just antislavery position. . . . [N]ever, since I became an Abolitionist, have I seen such hopeful times as these for the Anti Slavery cause—never, when the fields were so white to the harvest,—never a time when the minds & hearts of the people were so receptive of light touching Slavery, its character, nature, & fruits."[34]

THE SPECTER OF NATIONALISM

Who was right? Were the fields white for harvest in 1861? Was the wheel of public opinion turning with increasing momentum? Or were Americans only marching to the drumbeat of war, concerned for Union but not for emancipation, as British abolitionists suspected? The question was—and is—nearly impossible to answer. Historians still debate what northerners were fighting for in 1861, pointing to various sources of public opinion and disagreeing about how to create a statistically significant sample of documents to determine the state of popular thought. For agitators in search of influence, however, the question was more than academic. They believed the proper course of action depended in part on being able to read the signs of the time. Yet they could not agree on how events should be read.[35]

This confusion was partly because northern opinion in 1861 really was a jumble, leaving it open to interpretation. Reading election returns and the northern papers yielded different conclusions depending on the reader, much as an inkblot test reveals more about the viewer than about the blot itself. If Garrisonians reached different opinions about the North in 1861, it only showed that they brought specific inclinations, goals, and previous experiences to the question.

Garrison, for example, read public opinion partly through the eyes of faith, as Wigham's reference to his "prophetic spirit" suggested. Since the 1830s Garrison had believed that God would ultimately vindicate the abolitionists' cause and overthrow slavery. Now he believed that the great Avenger was moving in the people's midst. "It is for the abolitionists to 'stand still, and see the salvation of God,'" Garrison said in April 1861, citing a passage from Exodus that other

Garrisonians also used to interpret events around them. Republicans were now "instruments in the hands of God to carry forward and help achieve the great object of emancipation, for which we have so long been striving." Garrison did concede, in May, that the war was "technically" being waged to "restore the old state of things," and that "comparatively few" of the soldiers rushing to enlist wanted to emancipate slaves. But "God, 'who is above all, and greater than all,' and who '—moves in a mysterious way, His wonders to perform,'" would make use of them to do his righteous work. Seeing the movements of Providence in the movements of public opinion, Garrison believed that what God would ultimately do was as good as done already, so long as agitators continued to mark sinful backsliding and keep opposite forces at bay.[36]

Many Garrisonians also read public opinion through the prism of their deeply rooted belief in the importance of the United States to the success of democracy around the world. Phillips argued in December 1861 that, if Americans lost the struggle for Union they would fail the nation's mission, citing Tocqueville's depiction of the United States as "the normal school of the nations, set by God to try the experiment of popular education and popular government . . . and hasten the world's progress." Such comments showed that Phillips and many other abolitionists still believed their country was crucial to "the world's progress." Indeed, the more that American Garrisonians had learned about European aristocrats and monarchs from Chartists, continental exiles, and British friends, the more convinced they had become that the world needed the United States to survive.[37]

According to British abolitionists, however, this belief was clouding Americans' judgment of public opinion in 1861, for they had learned a different lesson from antebellum exchanges with American reformers. Every time Garrisonian lecturers or writers argued that their slavery was worse than "white slavery" in Britain, or that the Slave Power was more entrenched than any European aristocracy, or that the emancipating acts of Britain and France put them ahead of the United States, they had concluded that the United States was no longer the "school of the nations"—if it ever had been. As a result, some British allies could only see the Garrisonians' sudden Unionism as evidence of the same mere patriotism that abolitionists had always criticized in Kossuth and others.

Prowar Garrisonians, however, did not see a concern for the vindication of American democracy as mere patriotism; instead they described it as a contest with great implications for democrats abroad. If the war was *only* about slavery, Garrisonians might have been inclined to agree that northern public opinion was insufficiently advanced; but many abolitionists also perceived the war as "the commencement of the great struggle between the disguised aristocracy and the democracy of America. . . . It resembles closely that struggle between aristocrat and democrat which began in France in 1789, and continues still." To let the South leave by force of arms might force southerners to free their slaves eventually for the sake of self-preservation. But it would also allow the forces of aristocracy to win.[38]

After all, as the examples of England and France showed, slave emancipation in a country was no guarantee that democratic institutions would follow, especially in a post–1848 world where despots and aristocrats seemed more secure than ever. Phillips therefore concluded that "our object now" was "to show the world, if it be indeed so, that democratic institutions are strong enough for such an hour as this." In fact, in a foreshadowing of Lincoln's more famous statement, a year later, that the war for Union was a war to save the last, best hope on earth, Phillips declared that he no longer viewed the war "simply and exclusively as an Abolitionist." He was a "proud" American citizen who believed his country had a "responsibility" to vindicate, "if not the only, then the grandest system of pure self-government" left in the world.[39]

One abolitionist who agreed with that view was "Charles Follen" of Brookline, Massachusetts, who wrote to the *Liberator* in April 1861 that "our duty" was to fight a "war of institutions"—a war "not for our homes alone," but for the "civilization of the nineteenth century" and "democratic institutions with all their rights." "Charles Follen" may have been a pseudonym, or it may have been the abbreviated signature of the German professor's son Charles Christopher Follen, an abolitionist and architect who became a Union supporter at the outbreak of war. Either way, the name of one of the first foreigners Garrisonians had enlisted as a "moral Lafayette" may well have reminded veteran agitators of what they had long believed: ridding the nation of the shame of slavery was necessary partly to show the sustainability of "democratic institutions" in their country, in Follen's homeland, and around the world. By bringing into final conflict "the principles of democracy and the doctrines of absolutism," as Garrison put it the following month, perhaps the war would prove that the first Follen's hopes had not been entirely misplaced when he fled from Europe to the United States.[40]

To be sure, Garrisonians had not forgotten all the potential dangers of democratic institutions. They agreed, as Phillips put it, that "if I am to love my country, it must be lovable." But their desire to see democracy vindicated encouraged them to look for signs that these dangers were receding. Indeed, even in the years immediately before the war they had begun to find their country more lovable, though understanding why requires remembering what made it unlovable in the first place.[41]

Chattel slavery, of course, had always been the major reason why Garrisonians could not wholeheartedly champion American democracy. But they also named other problems that slavery had revealed: mass conformity, individualistic materialism, hostility to independent thought and free discussion. The early 1850s had seemed like a nadir to Phillips partly because those evils seemed more powerful than ever before, yet beginning in 1859, Phillips's speeches revealed a growing optimism about American democracy—an optimism that brimmed after the famous raid on Harpers Ferry by abolitionist John Brown, who was executed by the state of Virginia on December 2, 1859.

The Garrisonians' relationship to Brown has typically been construed as antagonistic because of Brown's rejection of non-resistance in favor of violent means. But Phillips and McKim—who were not non-resistants—played prominent roles in Brown's burial in North Elba, New York. And all Garrisonians joined in the general northern outrage over Brown's execution, even those who still questioned his means. Non-resistants often compared the martyr of Harpers Ferry to European revolutionaries like Garibaldi, whom Wright called both "the Italian John Brown" and "the Italian Nat Turner." Garrisonians also used their transatlantic networks to generate and publicize international opinion about his life and death; American correspondents provided Webb with information for a British biography and made sure to publish foreign writings about Brown's martyrdom.[42]

For Phillips, however, Brown was more than a martyr. He represented proof that Tocqueville's dystopian vision of the American future—one of mass conformity and total moral stagnation—had not yet arrived. The fact that Brown took "twenty-two men" from ordinary walks of life and found them "ready to die for an idea," instead of being content simply to make money and serve themselves, showed, Phillips thought, that democratic institutions were safer than he, and Tocqueville, had feared. "One brave act of an old Puritan soul, that did not stop to ask what the majority thought," suggested that "an insurrection of thought" was possible even under majoritarian rule, and even in "a generation poisoned with printing ink or cotton dust."[43]

In short, Brown ultimately made Phillips as confident in the march of northern public opinion as Garrison was in God's ultimate triumph. Harpers Ferry showed, Phillips contended, that "in God's world there are no majorities" that could not be overcome by "one, on God's side." The reaction of the North to Brown's attempt also showed that one truly independent thinker could rapidly create improved public opinion. "You meet with the evidence of it everywhere," Phillips claimed in 1859. "When the first news from Harper's Ferry came to Massachusetts, if you were riding in the cars, if you were walking in the streets, if you met a Democrat or a Whig or a Republican . . . the first outbreak of every man's words was, 'What a pity he did not succeed!'" Such chatter "indicated the unconscious leavening of a sympathy with the attempt."[44]

Most significantly for the debates that soon erupted among Garrisonians after Fort Sumter, Brown encouraged Phillips to see a full loaf even in a little leaven. "Why, this is a decent country to live in now," Phillips told a Boston audience a month before Brown's hanging. That line led to "laughter and cheers," but Phillips was serious and pressed the point: "I should feel some pride, if I was in Europe now, in confessing that I was an American," for Brown had "redeemed the long infamy of sixty years of subservience" and revealed Americans' true "national character." As proof, Phillips pointed not just to Brown's own individual independence, but to the sudden buzz of discussion his raid had sparked across the North. The "braving of public thought" had been going on for years, thanks to abolitionist agitation, but it had finally "bloomed" thanks to Brown's raid: "It has changed the whole face of the sentiment in these Northern states." His execution was "nothing but education,—nothing but the first step to something better."

Already prepared to see "something better" in the North after Harpers Ferry, it is not surprising that Phillips found it in the reaction to Fort Sumter. For thirty years, he said, northerners had wallowed in "conciliation and compromise," but now, like Brown himself, the North "offers its wealth and blood in glad atonement for the selfishness of seventy years. The result is as sure as the throne of God." From where they were standing, Garrison and Phillips both thought they were seeing the salvation of God.[45]

British Garrisonians, however, thought they were seeing something else: the specter of nationalism. One British pacifist who had previous aligned with the "old organization" actually wrote to Garrison's son that "the North has no more right to control the South than Austria has to control Hungary, Russia Poland, or England, Ireland," and implied that abolitionists were acting as narrow "Americans or New Englanders" instead of *Universal Men.* Few Garrisonians went as far towards justifying secession, but many British abolitionists did seem to take the position of Harriet Martineau, who wrote condescending editorials to the *National Anti-Slavery Standard* criticizing the United States for not explicitly making emancipation a war aim and for raising its tariffs, both policies which belied the nation's "republican professions" and suggested that Americans were acting according to national prejudice more than principle.[46]

Garrisonians in the United States, however, regarded such quibbling over tariffs as indicative of deeply flawed priorities on the part of England. Indeed, American abolitionists were shocked in general by the British government's tepid response to the outbreak of the civil war. Their impressions of Britain had always fluctuated greatly since the "World's Convention," of course. Nonetheless, transatlantic experiences had encouraged them to expect that the antislavery "mother country" would lend at least some aid and encouragement to the northern cause. Instead, Britain adopted an official posture of neutrality that sometimes seemed to tilt towards recognition of the Confederacy. Samuel May Jr. told Webb he could scarcely believe that Britain's daily journals spoke so "coldly, derisively, or adversely of our Government's war against the slaveholding Rebellion." And he and other Garrisonians were even more shocked when abolitionists they considered friends seemed to excuse Britain's posture and note all the ways the North was in the wrong. When Webb appeared to make the same mistake, McKim ventured to suggest that nationality was clouding his vision: "you are an abolitionist but a *British* abolitionist."[47]

These exchanges opened a long-running war of words between transatlantic friends. When his friends attacked Martineau and England, Webb accused his American correspondents of falling prey to "national hatreds" and a "quarrelsome antipathy." Meanwhile, American complaints about British policy increased in the fall, when the capture of Confederate agents James Mason and John Slidell onboard a British ship sparked the first of a series of tense panics about the threat of a transatlantic war. British saber-rattling in the *Trent* affair surprised antislavery Unionists; "the last news staggers us," McKim told Webb at the beginning of December. But Webb and other British Garrisonians were staggered, instead, by the way their correspondents uniformly defended the American position in the case. Americans seemed to have descended into a "white heat of anti British enthusiasm," Webb charged.[48]

Such accusations cut deep. After all, accusing friends of being over-national was to make the same charge both sides had used to blast Kossuth during his American tour. "You speak of me as 'so intensely national,'" May Jr. later complained to Webb, "and thereby give an added proof that (as I see myself) you do not understand me aright, or see our national struggle in its true light. It is on *far* higher ground than 'nationality,' or anything of the sort that I uphold my country now, & that I condemn . . . 'pro-slavery England.'" McKim suspected that the war had simply revealed a basic difference between Americans and the British: "I fancy that if you were, in political principles, more of a democrat your views & ours would more nearly accord," he told Webb. Conversely, however, Webb continued to express surprise when even Quincy seemed to find fault with everything the British were doing while defending the Republican Party's protectionist policies, despite his earlier support for Corn Law Repeal and free trade.[49]

What these quarrels ultimately revealed was how much national feeling had survived despite all the abolitionists' invocations of "Our Country is the World" over the last thirty years. Indeed, to some extent, transatlantic cooperation had reinforced those feelings more than Garrisonians realized at the time. On the one hand, British reformers had done such a good job detailing the horrors of "class legislation," the repression of movements like Irish Repeal, the conservatism even of most English abolitionists—that the litany helped convince Garrisonians in the United States of their different situation. Quincy told Webb as early as 1843 that he was convinced "we have nothing at all answering to your aristocracy. . . . Imagine that if you could only abolish all hereditary rank," disestablish the church, and "reduce the landed gentry to five hundred acres a piece, and you would have much such a sort of society as we have."[50]

Meanwhile, British Garrisonians had spent years reading their friends' denunciations of the Mexican-American War, the despotism of the Slave Power, the horrors of slave plantations, and the violence of anti-abolitionist mobs—an American litany that convinced them of their *own* better situation. "We have no class like that fearful aristocracy, the American slaveholders," Webb told the *National Anti-Slavery Standard* in 1846: "We have a recognized aristocracy it is true, distinguished by foolish titles from the rest of their fellow-men. . . . But their power for evil, and the evil they are the means of, are as nothing compared with the authority, and the tyranny of your aristocracy of untitled, irresponsible Southern slave-drivers." The next year, Webb admitted some parallels between the British conquest of India and the Mexican American War, but concluded that "the world has never seen a greater libel on the sacred names of religion and liberty, than this odious war."[51]

American abolitionists gladly printed such transatlantic judgments at the time because they were useful in mobilizing shame. But the transatlantic quarrels of 1861 and 1862 revealed how differently each side had been reading the evidence all along. In October 1861, May cited Webb's own letters over the years as evidence for his judgments that the British were too conservative, "as you have always declared." McKim told Webb "I am not unaware of England's virtues or of our faults," as he wrote in August 1861. "It has been our business and our policy to set forth both, and in the broadest possible contrast." But now McKim believed that "our mission in this respect has ceased" and could not understand why Webb kept condemning Americans while letting England off the hook. Webb, for his part, defended himself by pointing out what his American friends had always declared: that the aristocratic evils remaining in Europe were the fault of their slavery's influence on the world.[52]

Such letters suggest that the misunderstandings between transatlantic friends at the beginning of the 1860s were partly of their own making. But in the end, those misunderstandings simply made plain how deeply rooted pride in country was on both sides of the ocean. Following West Indian emancipation, most British abolitionists—even among the Garrisonians' allies—were inclined to believe that their empire had accrued the world's largest balance of "moral capital." While many still believed radical reform of British institutions was necessary, their pride was reinforced every time abolitionists and black Americans praised the British Lion and contrasted monarchical liberty with democratic slavery.[53]

American abolitionists, meanwhile, revealed their deepest longings after the war began. "This country *compared with our ideal,* is desperately wicked & deserves as she is receiving God's penal judgments," McKim retorted in one letter to Webb, "but this country, relatively, in virtue, intelligence, magnanimity, is without a peer on the face of the earth." In 1862, Maria Weston Chapman likewise confessed her "own earnest wishes" that "America might be *one* from the Northern to the Southern Arctic by means of Freedom: & that Europe might be so magnetically drawn to the happiness & goodness of a hemisphere so free." "So I began life," Chapman told her sister, and so had Garrison, Phillips, and other Americans. The intervening years had never entirely erased their wishes that the Old World would learn from the example of the New.[54]

In the same letter, Chapman clarified that she still remained "against all that is selfish in Nationality." Phillips also maintained, in his first pro-Union speech, that "I do not acknowledge the motto, in its full significance, 'Our country, right or wrong,'" which was "knavish" when it "trespass[ed] on the domain of morals." Yet the debates between American and British Garrisonians in 1861 and 1862 ultimately brought to the surface latent ideas about democracy and the United

States that shaped the perspectives of both sides. Confronted by the same evidence regarding northern public opinion, those perspectives led to vastly different interpretations of the facts, leading Garrisonians for the first time to doubt the cosmopolitan sympathies of their longtime friends.[55]

Most of the Garrisonians' transatlantic friendships would ultimately survive, however, because they were held together by two strong bonds. The first was a long history of intimate exchanges, correspondence, and visits that were difficult to erase. When Webb's wife died in 1862, Phillips assured him that "no mere difference of opinion will ever divide us" and asked him to "keep a warm place in your heart for us." Webb and May Jr. would later have a happy reunion in Leicester when Webb finally visited the United States in 1868.[56]

Transatlantic abolitionists remained bound together, secondly, by their unwavering belief that slavery was the cause of the Civil War and that emancipation would be its only acceptable outcome. To propagate those views, Garrisonians on both sides of the Atlantic continued to work together publicly much as they always had. Key allies from the 1850s, like Frederick W. Chesson and George Thompson, continued to actively disseminate abolitionists' views about the war in Britain and helped found the London Emancipation Society to hold the Garrisonian line against Confederate sympathizers abroad. Garrisonians continued to use their transatlantic networks much as they had before the war—to pressure those in the United States who remained unconvinced that emancipation should be the war's major aim.

Garrisonians also continued to point to events abroad, like the abolition of slavery by the Bey of Tunis or the emancipation of Russian serfs, to embarrass Americans into more resolute action. And just as Garrisonians had circulated antislavery testimonies from the "liberal party" of the world on the eve of Lincoln's election, during the war they continued to use their transatlantic networks to solicit testimonials from European reformers like Nicholas Tourgeneff, Victor Hugo, and Henry Vincent, who declared that the war would vindicate republicanism to conservatives abroad. After the Emancipation Proclamation of 1863, when a new wave of European liberals flocked to the side of the Union, Garrisonians made sure their names were regularly mentioned in movement publications, both to ensure that northern resolve remained firm and to demonstrate that the cause of the Union was the world's cause, too.[57]

Even prowar Garrisonians continued these activities partly because, despite their general optimism in 1861, they realized the danger that the government might not respond to the popular will. In the fall of 1861, all abolitionists were outraged when Lincoln revoked a military order by the antislavery General John Fremont to emancipate all the slaves in a portion of the loyal border state of Missouri. After that revocation, Garrison exclaimed that Lincoln was "a man of very small calibre," and abolitionists were again disappointed when Lincoln revoked a similar order by General David Hunter in Union-occupied islands off the coast of South Carolina. Garrison believed that veto would "increase the disgust and uneasiness felt in Europe at our shilly-shallying course."[58]

That comment showed that their British friends' doubts had made some impression on Garrisonians. Still, Garrisonians had never found a way, in the heat of 1861 and 1862, to settle on a way to measure the quality of "public opinion," especially when the stakes were so high. As their transatlantic relationships became increasingly strained, Garrisonians had no standard of judgment to turn to besides images of fields white with harvest, wheels turning, waters rising to the top of a dam, sentiment being leavened and ripened. Apart from polls, there was no good way to settle the disagreements that were keeping British and American friends poles apart.

Sharp words therefore continued to fly across the ocean throughout the war, as when Abby Kimber told Webb that "it gives me grief to find thee playing into the hands of the enemy!" McKim simply let his correspondence to Dublin drop for some time, and when he resumed writing to Webb in March 1864, he confessed that "I have not always been in the mood to write to you. Indeed, to be frank with you, until lately I have not been in the mood at all. The pleasure of correspondence between friends depends upon correspondence of views." In turn, Webb confessed to Anne Warren Weston that it took him ten days "to pluck up courage to answer" a critical letter she had written—"a strange expression for me to use when talking of writing to you with whom I have so much enjoyed all chances of communication." Even stranger and more painful, however, would be the new fractures that came in 1864.[59]

RECONSTRUCTION AND THE RUPTURING
OF GARRISONIAN ABOLITIONISM, 1863–1865

Tensions between American and British Garrisonians eased slightly when Lincoln issued the Emancipation Proclamation in 1863 and Congress passed the Thirteenth Amendment abolishing slavery in 1865. After 1863, prominent European liberals in Britain and France also swelled the ranks of the Union's transatlantic allies. In an open letter published in England and re-published in the *Liberator*, John Stuart Mill now identified "the prospects of the human race" with the Union cause. And in January 1865, the London Emancipation Society, led by Thompson's son-in-law Chesson, presented a congratulatory address to Lincoln through the American minister in London, with signatures by French abolitionist Victor Schoelcher, English freethinker and labor radical George Holyoake, and Karl Blind, one of the European exiles in the Ashursts' extended circle.[1]

But as transatlantic relationships slowly healed, new tensions arose within the AASS, caused primarily by Lincoln's actions on slavery prior to 1863 and his halting steps since then on the question of black suffrage. The president's revocation of military orders of emancipation by Fremont and Hunter, and his proposals for colonization and gradual emancipation, made a growing number of Garrisonians more sympathetic to the arguments of the vocal abolitionist minority, led by Pillsbury and the Fosters, who had always excoriated Lincoln as criminally conservative. As early as April 1862, Phillips submitted resolutions at an antislavery meeting holding Lincoln "culpable" for the perpetuation of slavery. By July he was calling Lincoln "a second-rate man" and intimating that he preferred Fremont for president.[2]

Finally, in 1864, a deep rift opened within the American Anti-Slavery Society over whether to support Lincoln's reelection, eventually rupturing the friendship between Garrison and Phillips and grieving their British allies. As in the case of earlier ruptures with British friends, however, the debate over Lincoln emerged from shared premises that rested near the center of Garrisonian thinking. Phillips and Garrison both took seriously, as they always had, the need to watch events carefully and consider how best to influence politicians. And as A. J. Aiséirithe notes in the most recent study of the Garrisonians' wartime disagreements, "one of the ironies of the multivalent dispute between Garrison and Phillips is that they ended up not so very apart."[3]

Indeed, Phillips and Garrison remained united in their fundamental commitments to make democracy work, to keep American society agitated, and to abolish slavery. The rupture between them, as they conceded in candid moments, was primarily about means rather than ends. Nonetheless, the disagreements made apparent the slightly different inclinations that had guided each man's thinking about the problem of democracy for decades, leading Garrison towards non-resistance and Phillips towards Tocqueville. And their rupture also illuminated questions that had never seemed so pressing before, including the question of how to measure public opinion and whether elected officials should lead or be led by its movements.

ARGUING OVER LINCOLN

The rupture between Phillips and Garrison appeared slowly, because in 1861 and 1862 both men agreed on several points. Northern public opinion was moving in the direction of emancipation. When the government did begin to use emancipation as an instrument of war in 1862, Phillips and Garrison also remained united on the need to ensure that military policies were liberating in fact as well as in theory. For example, after Major General Nathaniel P. Banks was installed in Union-occupied New Orleans in December 1862 as commander of the Gulf, abolitionists united in denouncing the early labor policies he instituted, which resulted in most former slaves in Louisiana being required by Union military forces to work, for fixed wages, on or near their former plantations.[4]

The trouble between Phillips and Garrison did not really begin until 1864, when Phillips, over Garrison's objections, began to support a campaign to nominate Fremont and unseat Lincoln. Phillips opposed Lincoln's reelection primarily because he doubted Lincoln would extend suffrage to black southerners, which would be the only way for freedpeople to protect their interests against aristocratic former masters. "The North has democratic institutions, and their essence is this—no class is safe which has not the means to protect itself. . . . [A]nd hence we have given the ballot, which is the Gibraltar of self-defence, to every class." Phillips wanted a president who agreed with this crucial feature of American "nationality," but Lincoln's actions in 1863 destroyed Phillips's belief that he was the man for the job.[5]

Lincoln's worst misstep, in Phillips's eyes, came in December 1863, when the White House issued an Amnesty Proclamation and a promise that, as soon as 10 percent of a state's antebellum voting population swore a loyalty oath, the state could organize a government. To Phillips, such a narrow basis for reconstructing conquered states was an open invitation to southern aristocrats to reassert their power, stall or prevent emancipation, and crush the rights of freedpeople. "The question is, whether we shall have, in the future, democratic institutions or an aristocracy," Phillips stated in June 1864. "Mr. Lincoln thinks we can get along for a while yet with aristocratic institutions, as we have done." Phillips, by contrast, believed that, since emancipation, the South's "aristocracy" was "the essential distinction" between it and the North; only by obliterating the power of the planter class and enfranchising freedpeople could the war be brought to a victorious end.[6]

Garrison, however, argued that it was imperative for abolitionists to support Lincoln's reelection in 1864. The differences between them first became apparent at the January 1864 meeting of the MASS, when anti-Lincoln resolutions were narrowly passed over Garrison's objections. At the AASS meeting in May, Garrison's resolutions supporting the president prevailed instead, indicating, as Garrison put it, that "breakers are ahead."[7]

Still, the disagreements between Garrison and Phillips were, at first glance, relatively small. There was no difference of principle between the two men on the evils of planter aristocracy, or on the importance of black suffrage. Garrison agreed with Phillips that "the democratic principle, that the people have a right to choose their own rulers, is involved in this struggle" and had "world-wide" implications. Indeed, that was one reason he supported Lincoln in 1864. Since secessionists had left the Union upon Lincoln's election "by a constitutional majority of the people" in 1860, removing him would give the rebels what they wanted. If he were a voter, Garrison said, he would vote for Lincoln "until I had made him the confessed President of the United States" in a conquered South as well as in the North.[8]

This did not mean that Garrison believed Lincoln was beyond reproach. He agreed with Phillips that the Amnesty Proclamation and 10-percent plan for Reconstruction were condemnable. A close look at the evidence also shows that the two abolitionist leaders did not disagree about suffrage for freedpeople. Both believed complexional distinctions should be struck from suffrage laws throughout the Union, and the demand for equal civil and political rights without regard to color had been enshrined in the main Garrisonian constitutions for three decades. Even Phillips conceded in February 1865 that the differences between him and Garrison had never been "of principle, but of measures."[9]

Those differences over measures stemmed, in turn, from differences over how to measure the state of northern public opinion in 1864. On the one hand, Garrison believed that Lincoln, while not progressing as far as abolitionists wished, had moved as quickly as the public opinion of the country would allow. Phillips took a different view of public opinion that led to a dimmer view of Lincoln.

As their reactions to Fort Sumter showed, both men initially believed that the wheel of northern opinion was rapidly turning in their direction. But in 1863 and 1864, Garrison was more impressed than Phillips by the growing strength of "Copperhead" Democrats—a movement of antiwar northerners who were campaigning to elect George McClellan as president. The "Copperheads" promised they would end the war at once and intimated that even slavery would be open to negotiation in peace talks, and by the time that Garrison and Phillips clashed in 1864, Garrison was convinced that this "seditious element" constituted "nearly a majority" of the northern public. He was also sure that a conspiratorial agreement between "the leading rebels and the leading copperheads" had been behind the draft riots that resulted in terroristic killings of black New Yorkers in July 1863, riots which only confirmed for him that "the whole North is volcanic."[10]

Many northerners feared that Copperhead programs for ending the war were gaining ground in the first half of 1864, causing worry that battlefield defeats might jeopardize Lincoln's reelection. But it was, and is, difficult to tell just how "nearly a majority" Copperheads were. As the movement's best historian notes, "it is impossible to quantify the strength of the Copperheads," given that "public opinion polls did not exist in the nineteenth century." That ambiguity allowed Garrison free rein to imagine the extent of the threat, and in his mind—always alert to anti-abolitionist rumblings—the danger was huge. In October 1863, Garrison privately admitted his fear that "with so formidable a division in the political and moral sentiment of the North," even the Emancipation Proclamation might still be contested through Republican defections to pro-peace Democrats or through "political intrigue" once the war ended.[11]

This perception of the divided state of public opinion was the most important reason why Garrison defended Lincoln's reelection. Indeed, it colored his view of Lincoln's entire record on emancipation in 1862 and 1863. In his first confrontation with Phillips in February 1864, Garrison declared that "in proportion as [Lincoln] has fallen in the estimation of the disloyal portion of the North, he has risen in my own." Indeed, in view of the steadily growing peace sentiment in the North, Garrison believed that the advances made by the Union under Lincoln's tenure were nothing short of remarkable—including abolition of the Fugitive Slave Law, abolition in the territories and the District of Columbia, recognition of Haiti and Liberia, and the Emancipation Proclamation, which also enabled the enlistment of thousands of black soldiers.[12]

This record of dramatic change proved Lincoln's receptivity to more advanced positions in the future, Garrison thought. So did the reception that abolitionists like Garrison, Phillips, and Douglass had received in Washington, D.C. One month before the divisive 1864 meeting of the AASS, George Thompson, who had returned to the United States, was even escorted by Lincoln himself to Congress, where the once maligned "foreign emissary" gave a speech. Garrison concluded "that the progress of the Anti-Slavery cause, since the rebellion broke out, in view of the fearfully divided state of public sentiment, of the feeling toward the negro race throughout the North, almost verging upon bloody civil war at our doors, has been wonderful."[13]

These defenses of Lincoln's record showed that the president had earned a grudging respect from Garrison. But his primary aim in defending Lincoln was to stop Phillips's campaign for Fremont, which Garrison thought would be disastrous given the strength of Copperhead sentiment for McClellan. Garrison never stated his pragmatic approach to the 1864 election more clearly than in the very first public dispute with Phillips in February. "In my judgment the re-election of Abraham Lincoln to the Presidency . . . would be the safest and wisest course, in the present state of our national affairs," he said, explaining that "no other candidate would probably carry so strong a vote in opposition to copperhead democracy." Floating other candidates risked splitting Republican votes or inviting a compromise between Lincoln's challenger and the Peace Democrats.[14]

Phillips, by contrast, believed the threat of Copperhead victory was greatly exaggerated in 1864, protesting to Samuel May Jr. that he would "cut off both hands before unnecessarily doing anything to elect McC[lellan]." He acknowledged that there were still treasonous Democrats who longed to see peace and compromise return to the Capitol. But in Phillips's view, this party was not strong enough to sustain itself. It only survived because Lincoln's Amnesty policy and Ten-Percent Plan had given them scraps of hope that the Union might be reconstructed with minimal social disruption. Such conservative policies were unsatisfactory to the mass of "the people," however, who now represented "the largest portion in the Government. . . . [O]nly their agents reside at Washington."[15]

Phillips was inclined to see the emancipation orders of Fremont and Hunter in 1861 and 1862 as more indicative of northern public opinion. While Garrison was impressed by Lincoln's rapid movement since 1861, Phillips was more impressed by how rapidly public opinion had matured. The North, he conceded, was not yet where abolitionists desired it to be, just as Garrison conceded that Lincoln had more progress to make. But by 1864 Phillips was beginning to argue that the North was ready to follow the abolitionists completely—if only their elected representatives would more actively lead and shape public opinion.

ARGUING OVER PUBLIC OPINION

Nothing better indicates how widely Phillips and Garrison differed on the state of "public opinion" than the fact that Phillips began, in the middle of the war, to return to some of his antebellum musings about the nature of democracy. In the 1850s, while reading Tocqueville, Phillips had seen the mediocrity of leaders like Webster as a sign of the general moral stagnation that majority rule always threatened to produce. His case against Lincoln was slightly different, however, because now he believed that the North—far from being stagnant—was alive and ready to be agitated further. To articulate fully his frustration with Lincoln, Phillips turned in 1861 and 1862 to a closer examination of what he called the "machinery" of representative democracy. In the process he revealed yet another important intellectual debt to John Stuart Mill.

In his recently published book *Considerations on Representative Government* (1861), Mill built on his earlier reviews of Tocqueville's *Democracy in America* to offer a theory of representative political institutions that could guard simultaneously against two evils: first, the evil of aristocratic class legislation, and second, the potential tyranny of the majority. But what most attracted Phillips's interest was Mill's observation that modern representative institutions, which assumed that a numerical majority of the people should rule, often resulted in giving power to one minority of voters, while leaving all other minorities without any representative at all.

According to Mill, this was especially true in countries, like England and the United States, that elected representatives by small territorial districts. In closely contested districts, political parties had to select a candidate who could win them the most votes. But the result was the selection of candidates with whom the minorities within each party often disagreed vigorously. Meanwhile, minorities outside either party had no hope of competing in a local election, even if a large number of like-minded citizens lived elsewhere in the country.

"Democracy, thus constituted," Mill argued, "does not even attain its ostensible object, that of giving the powers of government in all cases to the numerical majority. . . . [I]t gives them to a majority of the majority; who may be, and often are, but a minority of the whole." It also resulted in the election of the smallest minded representatives—those whose vulgar opinions or local power allowed them to win over the group of electors that held sway in their particular district. The "*élite* of the country" who possessed "the intellectual qualifications desirable in the representatives" were thereby virtually barred from the legislature.[16]

To solve the problem, Mill endorsed a new solution that had been proposed by British reformer Thomas Hare several years before, known as "proportional" or "personal" representation. Under Hare's plan, to be elected to Parliament a representative would have to win a specified quota of votes, determined by dividing the total number of voters by the total number of seats in the House of Commons. If a candidate anywhere received more votes than the quota required, his surplus votes would be transferred to other candidates still under the quota, as directed by a list of preferences specified by each voter. But if a voter could find no candidate in his district that represented his own views, he could cast his vote for any candidate anywhere in the country, using newspapers and modern communications networks to learn about their views. According to Hare's own defenses of his plan, any man of ability could make his views widely known and, under a proportional representative scheme, collect votes.[17]

Mill agreed: Hare's scheme made it possible for every voter to cast a vote for a member of the House who personally represented at least some of his views.

As an added benefit, "hundreds of able men of independent thought, who would have no chance whatever of being chosen by the majority of any existing [district]," but who "have by their writings, or their exertions in some field of public usefulness, made themselves known and approved by a few persons in almost every district," could be elected, thereby raising "the intellectual standard" of the body. Without giving unequal advantage to such intellectual elites, since each representative would be elected by the same quota, "modern democracy" could still "have its occasional Pericles," and an "instructed minority" could check or correct "the instincts of a democratic [numerical] majority." Proportional representation would also provide "a *point d'appui,* for individual resistance to the tendencies of the ruling power; a protection, a rallying point, for opinions and interests which the ascendant public opinion views with disfavour."[18]

Phillips's thoughts turned to this scheme in the summer of 1862, when he was increasingly depressed by Lincoln's policies. In an address delivered before the Twenty-eighth Congregational Society at the Music Hall in Boston, Phillips began by posing the question of why the abolitionists had not had more influence on the administration, even though their influence on national newspapers like the New York *Tribune,* in pulpits across the North, and even on Lincoln's cabinet and generals, seemed to be growing. The answer was that Lincoln was "listen[ing] to Congress"—"the official voice of the people" in a democracy—even though Congress was not always truly representative of "the present mind of all the people."[19]

Phillips then told his listeners he would "try to unfold to you, in half an hour, what Stuart Mill has been urging in England for twenty years—the rights of minorities; and to show you that, I think, here lies the obstacle to the success of the North in this struggle." What followed was a point-by-point reconstruction of Mill's argument in favor of proportional representation. Each step of Mill's critique was there—the anachronism of voting by "locality" in a country where the *Tribune* reached tens of thousands outside New York; the ability of one small minority in a district to elect its stooge; the resultant lack of representation for other minorities; the election of "the most selfish and the most timid" men "whose intellects are of the lowest type"; the refusal of congressmen to be bold out of fear their local constituencies would not reelect them. The dismal thesis Phillips placed above all these points was this: "not only has the great Southern Oligarchy hitherto smothered the tendency toward Democracy in the Northern States, which it now threatens to annihilate, but we have never had a Democracy even here."[20]

Under "Stuart Mill's plan" of proportional and personal representation, Phillips continued, Radical Republicans would gain immediately. "If Massachusetts does not like Charles Sumner, a million of men the Union over may send him into the Senate." He also couldn't help noting that, if "Stuart Mill's method had governed here" thirty years before, abolitionists would have been able, long ago, to elect a Parker or a Garrison directly to Congress, where they could have formed "that base of resistance, that *point d'appui*"—a phrase Phillips borrowed from Mill without quoting him—"which is always needed in a Democracy to sustain an unpopular reform." "We need not say with De Tocqueville, 'Every Government is always just as rascally as the people will allow,'" Phillips said, returning to the writer whose reflections had also inspired Mill, "but we may ask what sort of a Government have we a right to expect when the authoritative voice of the people reaches it only through such channels as I have described."[21]

Phillips's views on these subjects evidently impressed Mill himself. A few years later, Moncure Conway—who was then in England—wrote to Phillips that he had recently "passed half a day" and dined with Mill, who "made many inquiries about you, and was much gratified when I told him how you believed in his works & still more when I told him how you had spoken in favour of the 'Representation of Minorities.'" Mill asked Conway to obtain Phillips's speeches on the subject, and when he did in 1865, he told Conway that "I cannot thank you enough. . . . I was not aware that [Phillips] was so thorough an adherent of not only representation of minorities, but what is much more, personal representation." Mill credited Hare with the idea, deflecting Phillips's praise, but he added that "it is hardly possible to state the merits of the principle more forcibly . . . than Mr. Phillips has done." Mill was also "much gratified by receiving so strong a confirmation, from such authority, of my opinion concerning Tocqueville, which I shall now hold with increased confidence."[22]

More importantly, however, Mill's views contributed directly to Phillips's criticisms of Lincoln. First, Mill's analysis of the "machinery" of representation enabled him to understand why the rapid improvement of public opinion in the North was not yet reflected in the actions of Congress or the president. Now he could finally understand why agitators like himself "have not had . . . all the influence, all the direct power, upon the nation's character and course that belonged to us, that we ought to have attained."[23]

Moreover, the idea of proportional representation allowed Phillips to imagine a system in which political leaders themselves could be agitators. Before the war, of course, Phillips had usually seen politicians and agitators as opposed, because he assumed that seeking election always encouraged a compromise of principle. Only an extra-parliamentary agitator could truly educate the people in disinterestedness. Mill, however, helped Phillips see compromise not as a universal feature of politicians, but as a mere artifact of the way elections were conducted according to "a cut and squared surface of population." That machinery made it virtually impossible for a true independent thinker or agitator ever to be elected. But a slight tweaking of the machinery could change everything! If Mill's system had been in operation since 1845, then "instead of an outside pressure, instead of a Congress to-day that represents men of no opinion," perhaps Americans could have had a Congress with "the utter and outside Garrisonianism" being represented on the floor of Congress, whose "deliberations" could then have been "educating the people to be ready for just such a crisis as this."[24]

Reflecting on Mill's *Considerations* in the first years of the war actually made Phillips somewhat more forgiving of Lincoln at first. The president "stands hesitating to-day" not because he was dishonest, Phillips said. "I believe he honestly wishes that this convulsion shall result in the destruction of the slave system." Lincoln was "not a genius" and "not a leader" of public opinion, but that was not entirely his fault, since Mill's analysis made it "doubtful whether, under Democratic institutions, a leader ever can be President."[25]

Yet once Mill had enabled Phillips to imagine a possible world in which politicians could be teachers of American democracy, just as agitators had always been, his judgments of Lincoln would never be the same. Now Phillips criticized Lincoln because he did not seek to lead public opinion, he merely followed its dictates. In 1862, Phillips credited Lincoln with at least doing that much: "he holds out his hands to the millions and says, 'Support me!'" But Lincoln never moved boldly in a new direction without first being sure he would have support: that was his problem. "I hold a statesman to be one who is ready to do all the people allow. He is one who drags public sentiment up to its utmost possible efficiency," Phillips said in July 1861. "I hold a politician to be one who does all the people demand. He yields, he does not lead." Even then Phillips was beginning to think that the Lincoln administration was made up of politicians, not statesmen. "It stands looking to the North and the West, and saying, 'What shall I do?' . . . The administration propose nothing. They merely cry with the people, 'The stars and stripes!'"[26]

These reflections led Phillips to conclude that Lincoln was squandering an opportunity that no American president had ever been presented with before.

A crisis had struck the nation—uniting the entire North, revolutionizing public opinion, preparing it to do whatever its leaders asked. In response, Lincoln was spouting nationalistic bromides and drifting, allowing Congress to tell him what the people wanted instead of telling the people what they should want.

These conclusions involved disputable judgments, however, both about Lincoln and about public opinion. They assumed public opinion really was ready to be led, when this was precisely the point on which Garrison, impressed by the power of Copperhead sedition in the North, disagreed. "Grant that there are many sad things to look in the face" about Lincoln, Garrison said in May 1864, but "looking at the question broadly, comprehensively, and philosophically, I think the people will ask another question—whether they themselves have been one hair's breadth in advance of Abraham Lincoln? . . . Whether they are not conscious that he has not only been fully up with [them], but, on the whole, a little beyond them?" In the metaphor Garrison then gave to answer his own questions, he summarized how far pessimism about northern public opinion drove his positions on Lincoln throughout 1864: "As the stream cannot rise higher than the fountain, so the President of the United States, amenable to public sentiment, could not, if he wished to do it, far transcend public sentiment in any direction."[27]

Yet the recourse to metaphor showed again the difficulty of defining and measuring public opinion: how was it possible to know how high the "stream" of public sentiment was rising and where it was flowing? Garrison himself admitted in February 1864 that the question only admitted subjective answers. When Garrison declared that "without approving all Mr. Lincoln's acts . . . he was inclined to regard him as a fair representative of the popular sentiment, and perhaps to have advanced, on the whole, as fast and as far as the people were ready to endorse him," he was surprised by the shouts of "No, no!" from the MASS audience. "Well, that is a matter of opinion," Garrison rejoined. "Every one must decide for himself."[28]

Phillips would soon be forced to exactly the same admission. At the New England Anti-Slavery Convention in June 1864, Phillips conceded that there was now much unsoundness in northern public opinion, but contended that this had not been so in 1861 and 1862. According to Phillips, public sentiment had been more united, radical, and malleable then, raising the question "whose fault is it? My friend Garrison says, 'The people's; Mr. Lincoln has done as well as he could . . . and has always led rather than lagged behind public opinion.'" Phillips disagreed but admitted that "it is a matter of opinion whether he has or not. One can fortify his judgment with facts, and another can—but in the end, it is a matter of judgment."[29]

Garrison immediately rose and insisted that "to declare that, in 1861 and '62, there was a universal sentiment in favor of abolition, radical abolition, the abolitionism of Wendell Phillips, and that the people were all ready for it, is preposterous. Can my friend believe it for a moment?" When Phillips reportedly answered, "Certainly," Garrison denied that public opinion had been in favor of emancipation at that juncture, contending instead that "from that hour, the Copperhead element began to work, and has been working ever since." Garrison also quoted from Phillips's own speeches earlier in the war, in which his adversary had depicted Lincoln as ready to follow the lead of public opinion. But he missed the criticism hidden in those statements: what Garrison saw as a virtue, that Lincoln was going only as far as the people demanded, Phillips now saw as a deficiency in statesmanship.[30]

Still, both men rested their arguments partly on judgments about what the public was demanding or what the public would allow, and their exchanges showed how subjective these judgments remained. Phillips tried to defend his conclusions by pointing to two of the most familiar gauges that Garrisonians used to measure public opinion. First, he cited newspapers, which were nothing more than "Vanes—weathercocks" of public opinion. In 1861, he argued, "the press, from the Mississippi to the Bay of Massachusetts, from the lakes down to Maryland, with the single exception of the Boston *Courier* (and the exception makes the unanimity all the more remarkable,) when Fremont issued his proclamation, said, enthusiastically, 'Amen!' . . . There was not a print, from the New York *Herald* to the worst print in New York, that did not endorse it." And Phillips also pointed to a second "weathercock" to justify his claims about opinion at the beginning of the war—the attitudes of crowds at public assemblies.[31]

But at this crucial juncture, with the unity of the abolitionist movement hanging in the balance, it was telling that Phillips could turn to no more final tribunal than these. The difficulty of relying on public assemblies for proof of the public's wishes was dramatically demonstrated in the very same meeting, when Samuel May Jr. noted that the tier of the galleries that most frequently applauded Phillips's denunciation were "not Abolitionists" and probably were not Republicans either. When May charged Phillips with implying that "the President is carrying on this war to elect himself," thereby heaping on Lincoln "the worst denunciation he can heap upon him," May's own words were greeted by "Great applause and throwing up of hats in the extreme seats." But Phillips claimed that May's applause came from "the outskirts of the audience—the chance spectator; not from the body of the house" where abolitionists sat. The exchange showed how difficult it was to use public assemblies as proof of what the popular demand was.[32]

At the same convention, Phillips conceded that even newspapers were not decisive enough to settle all disagreement about the nature of public opinion. After citing the press's views in 1861, Phillips added that "there is no use in my standing here and undertaking to give you the grounds of my opinion, for I should have to go over the entire record. Mr. Garrison reads the facts contrary-wise. I cannot find fault with him; he reads them just as honestly that way as I do the other. I do not doubt it." A shared faith in the power of public opinion had carried Garrisonians as a group throughout the antebellum period and into active support for the Union war effort. But by 1864, their opinions about opinion were as open to contest as any other battlefield of the Civil War.[33]

ARGUING ABOUT SUFFRAGE

The persistent difficulty of measuring "public opinion"—except with metaphors like "streams," "wheels," "currents" and "vanes"—was one underappreciated reason why Garrison and Phillips could not agree about Lincoln. But their disagreements were also clearly more than technical or semantic. The reason they flummoxed Garrisonians at the time was because they also arose from substantive and usually familiar ideas.

On the one hand, the strikingly new way of thinking about democratic "machinery" that Phillips had gleaned from Mill enabled him to hold Lincoln to a new standard of statesmanship and encouraged him to embrace Fremont. But Garrison foresaw a real danger in this: while Phillips dreamed of a new electoral system in which a man of genius like Fremont could be elected by virtue of newspaper publicity across state lines, he risked forgetting the way candidates were actually elected in the present. If candidates really were selected according to the lowest common denominator in a district, as Mill suggested, then politicians like Lincoln had to think about not going too far beyond what the public demanded, and the Republicans also needed to be aware that much of the public was demanding a sham peace that might threaten the legal basis of wartime emancipation.

Yet the differences in the way that Phillips and Garrison regarded the state of public opinion also revealed some long-standing differences between the two men. Phillips's reading of Mill was only the latest example of his interest in European liberal thinkers like Tocqueville, and these thinkers—while believing in the importance of extra-parliamentary agitation—had never been averse to thinking of politicians as potential agitators, too. Tocqueville had served as an abolitionist legislator under the July Monarchy, and Mill entered the House of Commons in 1865. Attracted by their ideas and examples, Phillips inclined towards the possibility that agitators could work from inside, as well as outside, politics.

Garrison, on the other hand, remained a non-resistant. His religious and moral principles made it harder for him either to contemplate entering government himself or to expect that a politician would be the leader of opinion. Paradoxically, his defense of Lincoln betrayed a continued reluctance to put political reformation before moral reform. Garrison's idea that the president could only go as far as public opinion asked instead continued to privilege extra-parliamentary agitators like himself—God's true coworkers—as the real drivers of political change. Agitators could still afford to concentrate on moral reform because the ultimate victory of God's kingdom was beyond doubt.

These long-standing ideas explain some of the differences in inclination that led Phillips and Garrison to read events so differently in 1864, but the distinctions should not be exaggerated. Although both men changed somewhat during the war, in many ways they remained fundamentally the same. On the one hand, while he remained a non-resistant, Garrison was becoming a presumptive spokesman for the administration, and he was gratified to be cheered to the rafters when he spoke at the Baltimore convention that re-nominated the president. Yet, to the chagrin of reformers like Rogers and Noyes, Garrison had always held together his non-resistant faith with a keen interest in politics. Just as earlier political developments like the Free Soil Party had encouraged Garrison to make subtle adjustments in his rhetoric, he closely read political events during the war and calibrated his own tactics accordingly. "I am solicitous to maintain, uncompromisingly, all the principles I have advocated for the last thirty years," Garrison wrote in January 1865, but "I am equally anxious to be entirely just to all men and all parties, in connection with the new order of things."[34]

Conversely, Phillips, as always, remained reluctant to give up his role as an independent agitator, since he had always feared that even a giant like Cobden or O'Connell could be dwarfed by politics. Even as he spoke of Mill's new scheme and began to call on Lincoln to lead public opinion, Phillips also sometimes said, "I do not look to the Government. I have no confidence in official leading. I think the people lead." For that reason he continued to believe abolitionists' main duty was to "ripen, manifest, aggregate public sentiment as swiftly as possible," from outside of Congress.[35]

Phillips also continued to be surrounded by friends who urged him to stay at his primary task of agitating the ocean of democracy. His wife, who had served for decades as his muse and sounding board, expressed deep unease in 1862 with Phillips's new closeness to politicians and with his decision to meet with Lincoln, which she feared would compromise his autonomy as a radical. In the midst of supporting Fremont's campaign, Phillips also tried to maintain to former allies like Samuel May Jr. that "I still remain reformer & not politician." As historian A. J. Aiséirithe notes, Phillips reconciled his support for the Fremont campaign with his commitments as an agitator by describing it less as an exercise in electioneering and more as a way for "radical reformers" to influence "the political process."[36]

Clearly, then, despite their open disagreements about Fremont and Lincoln, neither abolitionist entirely abandoned the common ground on which they had long stood together. Even Garrison's trust that God would use him properly and accomplish his goals was echoed by Phillips, who declared in May 1864 that "I believe in God and Democracy." Phillips trusted that "the inevitable gravitation of all time is toward universal suffrage and universal democracy." He had "not a doubt of it, God reigns."[37]

Still, wartime events did bring to the surface, as never before, disagreements between Garrison and Phillips about what role elected leaders or politicians might play in God's work, and the consequences may best be seen by the way each responded to events in Union-occupied Louisiana after 1863. Both men agreed that what the Lincoln administration had done in Louisiana immediately after the Amnesty Proclamation, including its support for Nathaniel P. Banks's slavery-like labor system there, deserved censure. They also agreed that freedpeople should have the right to vote. But in the spring and summer of 1864, Garrison offered a highly qualified defense of Banks's course that reflected his views on the relationship between politicians and public opinion.

Garrison knew that Louisiana's new state constitution, drafted under Banks's supervision in the summer of 1864, did not directly enfranchise any black voters, despite the petitions of New Orleans's elite free black community that he do so. But Garrison argued, first, that Banks's measures were designed to be temporary: he left open the possibility that the state's legislature could extend suffrage. Banks had also been bound by orders from the president, who, in turn, was constrained by the Constitution, which reserved the power to grant suffrage for the states.[38]

Given that fact, Garrison and others said, it would have been inconsistent for Lincoln to demand equal voting rights from the South as a condition for readmission into the Union, especially when only five northern states then extended votes equally to black and white men. More importantly, it would have been impolitic. In reconstructing states, Garrison said, Lincoln could not "safely and advantageously . . . enforce a rule, *ab initio,* touching the ballot, which abolishes complexional distinctions; any more than he could safely or advantageously decree that all women (whose title is equally good) should enjoy the electoral right, and help form the State." Lincoln had to "be judged by the circumstances and necessities of his position."[39]

In the summer of 1864, Garrison elaborated on those "circumstances and necessities" in a highly controversial open letter to Francis W. Newman, a British supporter of the Union who had criticized Lincoln's emancipation policy and demanded that Lincoln enfranchise black Louisianans as part of the state's reconstruction. Garrison responded with a question:

> By what political precedent or administrative policy, in any country, could [Lincoln] have been justified if he had attempted to do this? When was it ever known that liberation from bondage was accompanied by a recognition of political equality? Chattels personal may be instantly translated from the auction block into freemen; but when were they ever taken at the same time to the ballot-box, and invested with all political rights and immunities? According to the laws of development and progress, it is not practicable. To denounce or complain of President Lincoln for not disregarding public sentiment, and not flying in the face of these laws, is hardly just.[40]

Phillips's allies seized on this passage as proof that Garrison's support for Lincoln was weakening his support for the slaves. Perhaps, they implied, he was beginning to doubt that people of color were developed enough to have the franchise, or was beginning to think that freedom was the simple removal of "chattels personal" from "the auction block." But a careful read shows that Garrison's argument was not an appeal to morality, and still less to ideas about racial development, but instead an appeal based on "political precedent," "administrative policy," and questions about what was "practicable." The context suggests that the "laws of development and progress" to which Garrison referred were not statements about racial capacity, but general statements about the way that societies progressed and developed—by first changing "public sentiment" and then changing policy.

The crux of Garrison's argument was that Lincoln could not disregard public sentiment and put the cart of political reformation before the horse of moral reformation. Yet Phillips was convinced that Lincoln should be a statesman willing to lead public opinion. Indeed, Lincoln should have used raw military power, if necessary, to enfranchise black voters in Louisiana in 1864. "Now . . . while the thunderbolt is grasped in the President's hand, while his omnipotence is unquestioned, while the progress in opinion is marvellous [sic] . . . why give up the priceless opportunities of the hour?" Phillips asked pointedly in February 1864. Why not push the progress in opinion farther?[41]

When Garrison and his supporters objected that Banks had to follow the orders of the president, Phillips retorted that even Banks "could have given the negro the ballot, had he chosen." Suffrage was so vital, and the southern aristocracy was so powerful, that this was no time to be sticklers for what public sentiment or the Constitution would allow. "The only sound basis for the reconstruction of this nation is black citizenship," Phillips had maintained since June 1864. "Mr. Lincoln resists and opposes it. To do this work, I want . . . Fremont."[42]

Banks actually did exert his power as military commander of the Gulf to push Louisiana's 1864 state Constitutional Convention farther in the direction of black suffrage than it otherwise would have been willing to go. But instead of using the force of military power to mandate black suffrage, Banks left it to the newly formed state legislature to decide whether to enfranchise black voters, partly because, as a military commander, his first priority in Louisiana was holding the Union Army's fragile grasp on the southern portion of the state. As one historian notes, "New Orleans was not located in the Hudson River Valley or on Cape Cod Bay; it was a pocket of Union control enclosed by hundreds of miles of enemy territory," which meant that any policy that risked alienating the loyalist population also endangered Union occupation itself. What Phillips seemed to demand from Banks—a military order of black enfranchisement—most assuredly would have alienated virtually every white Unionist in the state.[43]

Garrison's argument that Lincoln could not safely disregard public sentiment turned partly on his awareness of these hostile conditions. In an editorial published on January 13, 1865, Garrison asked why Phillips did not demand that

Banks use his military power to enfranchise black women as well, knowing that the answer was obvious: woman suffrage would have been so radical as to torpedo all hopes of expanding the suffrage. But "perhaps the same motive—the danger of creating a reactionary feeling, and so imperilling the safety of New Orleans itself—may have led Gen. Banks to follow the State usage, in providing only for white voters." In view of those conditions, it was marvelous that Banks even allowed the state constitutional convention to empower the new legislature to enfranchise black voters at some later date, thereby creating in Louisiana "a better Constitution for the colored citizen than that of Connecticut, New York, New Jersey, Pennsylvania, or any Western State," which continued to limit citizenship explicitly to "white" residents.[44]

This interpretation of Banks showed that Garrison, as before, continued to be pessimistic about northern public opinion, too. Phillips's argument that Lincoln should have enfranchised freed Louisianans using the "thunderbolt" of war or a militarily imposed state constitution would have placed black suffrage on the same footing as the Emancipation Proclamation—a measure justified by military necessity that would have to be replaced by a constitutional amendment in order to have any permanence. Garrison was relatively confident that emancipation could be permanently legalized by constitutional amendment after the war, so long as Lincoln defeated Copperheads in 1864, because northern states were closer to uniting on that issue than on black suffrage, and because the war itself would destroy the institution beyond the hope of revival. But it was not at all certain that black suffrage imposed on the South by military power would survive the end of the war, given how unpopular equal suffrage remained even in the North.

Indeed, "if the freed blacks were admitted to the polls by Presidential fiat" in the same way they had been freed, Garrison explained to Francis Newman, he did not "see any permanent advantage likely to be secured by it; for, submitted to as a necessity at the outset, as soon as the State was organized and left to manage its own affairs," whites would immediately exclude black voters from the polls again. "Coercion would gain nothing." Meanwhile, by using coercion hastily, with his reelection in jeopardy, Lincoln stood to lose everything. "When to transcend public sentiment so far as to outrage and defy it, is to imperil the existence of the government itself—may not something be charitably allowed for anxious doubt, cautious procedure, and deliberate action?" Garrison asked.[45]

In short, in his defense of Banks no less than his defense of Lincoln, Garrison always reminded Phillips of how divided northern public opinion remained on the question of black citizenship. It would be perilous to press that controversial issue during a campaign in which Copperheads were already making gains, particularly in western states where suffrage laws were the most racially discriminatory. It would also ask Lincoln to go far beyond public opinion. In a revealing question from his letter to Newman in July 1864, Garrison asked, "Is it creditable in England for a man to take office, and then do as he pleases, without regard to the conditions imposed upon him?"[46]

Such arguments sounded like special pleading to anti-Lincoln Garrisonians, however; they resembled earlier Liberty Party arguments about why controversial issues like women's rights should be detached from the abolitionist movement. Garrison's appeal to the conditions imposed on politicians and generals also could not persuade Phillips, given his developing, Millian view that statesmen and military commanders should seize their opportunities to challenge and direct public opinion. Indeed, in a telling admission in July 1865, Phillips "estimated that 'two thirds of the North are willing that he [the black man] should vote,' but . . . that 'the opposition is *very strong*' among 'men in high places.'" He reiterated that view in 1866 by declaring that "the country is ready for its duty. It only needs leaders."[47]

These statements showed once again how differing estimates of northern public opinion affected Garrisonians' calculations during the war, but they also underscored the now apparent distance between Phillips and Garrison in particular. Garrison, both on familiar grounds as a non-resistant and on practical grounds specific to 1864, continued to believe that moral reformation should lead political change. Meanwhile, Phillips was increasingly doubtful that extra-parliamentary agitation alone—which he had always championed in the past—could secure the ballot for freedpeople in the South. Yet neither Garrison nor Phillips abandoned the long-standing practice that had always distinguished both of them from doctrinaire non-resistants and come-outers: they continued to hover around polls and political debates, studying closely the drift of political events and attempting to discern their own influence upon them.

ARGUING ABOUT EDUCATION

It is also important to stress that Garrison and Phillips did not really disagree over the importance of the ballot. As Garrison considered the questions surrounding Louisiana's reconstruction on January 13, 1865, he observed that it was not "difficult to decide, *per se*, what absolute justice demands in this case." For him, it was simply more difficult to determine "the possibilities of statesmanship in a comparatively chaotic state of society." For that reason, once the "chaotic" state of 1864 had begun to stabilize, Garrison and his allies also called for a constitutional amendment to remove complexional distinctions from state voting laws. After the 1864 election, with the threat of Copperhead Democrats averted, and especially after congressional passage of the Thirteenth Amendment abolishing slavery on January 31, 1865, Garrison and his allies began calling publicly for what they always supported in principle.[48]

For example, a few days before the passage of the Thirteenth Amendment, at the annual meeting of the MASS, Henry Clarke Wright accurately noted that, "if the question before this Society were, 'Shall the right of suffrage be extended at once to the freedmen?' I do not believe there is a solitary individual in the Society who would raise his voice against it." At the same meeting, Garrison proposed a resolution "that Congress should lose no time in submitting to the people an amendment to the Constitution, making the electoral law uniform in all the States, without regard to complexional distinctions."[49]

Believing that moral reformation was essential to secure this political reformation, Wright and Garrison urged abolitionists to be vigilant in denouncing the injustice of northern state disfranchisement laws; they hoped to use the debates over Reconstruction in the South to prepare northern voters for black suffrage in *every* state. But Garrison also now agreed with Phillips that in the "chaotic state of things" in the South, "military rule must be dominant, leaving such scope for local civil action as opportunity may present." Once the Thirteenth Amendment had been finally ratified at the end of 1865, Garrison urged the North not to withdraw militarily from the South so long as black southerners were without the vital protection of the ballot.[50]

In short, in May 1865, Garrison and Phillips agreed, as Garrison put it, that the nation had to give "the ballot to those who have been so long disfranchised." Garrison added that "there is no difference among Abolitionists . . . in regard to this matter." Even so, the rupture between Garrison and Phillips did not heal after Lincoln's reelection, partly because of personality, private traumas, and the personal rancor of the previous year. Both men's domestic affairs had played a role in their debates over Lincoln and may also have kept wounds fresh. A few days after Christmas in 1863, for example, Garrison's wife suffered a debilitating stroke that left her virtually paralyzed. The distressing medical treatments that followed may have simultaneously made him eager for fewer public duties, anxious about the loss of financial security that antislavery infighting always threatened, and more sensitive to the perception that his friends were abandoning him at a moment of personal trial. Conversely, Phillips's own invalid wife continued to press him not to retreat from his positions.[51]

The extent of friction in 1864 had also diminished the possibility of reconciliation between the Phillips and Garrison camps, despite their many points of principled agreement. Garrison was deeply sensitive to attacks from former friends and was on high alert for any sign that Foster and Pillsbury, who had long ago lost his trust for other reasons, were behind Phillips's turnabout. A transatlantic debacle involving Moncure Conway, who embarrassed Garrison in 1863 when he publicly represented himself as a quasi-official spokesman of American abolitionists in England, may also have made Garrison more vigilant against signs of a challenge to his leadership as president of the AASS, especially when Conway joined in the aspersions cast at Lincoln in 1864.[52]

The air was further poisoned by sarcastic tones and sharp words, as when Phillips facetiously told Garrison's ilk to "applaud" Lincoln and "lay him up in lavender, with Washington, for aught I care," or haughtily declared that "only a brain thrice sodden" would trust Banks's reports about conditions in Louisiana. Invective on both sides made Phillips and company feel that they were being accused of treason for daring to question Lincoln, while Garrison's side felt their critics were making them out to be sycophants, despite their record of criticizing Lincoln's missteps.[53]

Debates over Lincoln and Louisiana also gave way to further arguments, particularly over abolitionists' responsibilities to the Freedmen's Aid movement, an effort that began during the war to supply material goods like clothing to freedpeople and to organize new schools for their education. As early as 1862, some Garrisonians had begun to argue that abolitionists should shift their efforts almost entirely to aid for freedpeople. Even before the Emancipation Proclamation, James Miller McKim submitted his resignation as corresponding secretary of the PASS so he could devote himself fulltime to organizing material relief and education for freed slaves in Union-occupied territories like the Sea Islands of South Carolina. Against the advice of their friends, other Garrisonians, including Maria Weston Chapman and her sisters, soon followed McKim's lead, sharpening divisions about whether abolitionists should merge themselves in other organizations.[54]

In 1862 most Garrisonians, including both Phillips and Garrison, regarded these moves as premature. But several steps taken by Garrison in 1863 and 1864 made Phillips's allies believe that Garrison was preparing to retreat from the fray as McKim and Chapman had done. First, in December 1863 Garrison organized a celebratory meeting to mark the thirtieth anniversary of the American Anti-Slavery Society and the effects of the Emancipation Proclamation. Critics like Phillips, the Fosters, and Frederick Douglass saw the meeting as evidence of the same eagerness to retire from the abolitionist cause that McKim and Chapman had shown. The following year, Phillips and his allies also reacted negatively when Garrison praised some of the efforts at education and uplift that Banks had implemented in Louisiana, especially when the *Liberator* began publishing letters from McKim urging "Abolitionists" to become "Elevationists" and focus on "the school-house" and black education in the South as the primary levers of reform.[55]

In reality, Garrison's reasons for holding the celebration of the Emancipation Proclamation in December 1863 stemmed less from a desire to end the movement than from his continued worries about the poor state of northern public opinion in the year leading up to Lincoln's reelection. At a time when Democrats were holding out the possibility of rolling back emancipation to voters who were anxious for peace, Garrison wanted abolitionists to emphasize the finality of emancipation and the impossibility of reconstructing slavery from the ruins of the war. At the thirtieth-anniversary celebration for the AASS, where letter after letter was read from abolitionist veterans and new allies, the roll call was actually a public performance more than a self-satisfied commemoration. One by one, the letter writers and speakers emphasized that attempts to resurrect slavery were chimerical, amounting to a collective rebuke of Copperheads who implied that could be done.[56]

Garrison's critics, however, saw the celebration of emancipation, coupled with Garrison's praise for the schoolhouses Banks had built in Louisiana, as a sign that he was prepared to prioritize freedmen's aid over suffrage. Their fears were only heightened when Garrison began arguing, in early 1865, that the antislavery societies should disband at the end of the year, once the Thirteenth Amendment had been ratified. That proposal reopened the war of words between Garrison and Phillips, who maintained that dissolution was still premature so long as the Thirteenth Amendment was not yet enforced throughout the states.[57]

Those who were most opposed to Garrison's proposal about dissolving the AASS and the MASS argued that even people freed by the Thirteenth Amendment would continue to be slaves until they had other hallmarks of freedom like land of their own and the right to vote. As Frederick Douglass put it in May 1865, "slavery is not abolished until the black man has the ballot." Garrison believed, however, that such an expansive definition of slavery violated the long abolitionist tradition of drawing a sharp contrast between "slavery" and other forms of oppression, dating all the way back to their praise of Britain in the 1830s for having abolished *slavery*, even while it retained various other evils. As Wright put it, "we have been careful for the last thirty-five years—and I speak from my personal knowledge—in all our publications, and in all our addresses, to draw a distinction between slavery and other forms of oppression."[58]

In reality, Garrisonians had sometimes broken or come near to breaking their own rules of usage, as in some of their writings on Chartism. Partisans on both sides of the 1865 debate could point to past examples proving their case. Douglass, for example, noted that in 1842 abolitionists had directed agents into Rhode Island to protest the exclusion of black voters from the Dorr Constitution, without fearing that such agitation violated their mission as anti-*slavery* reformers. At that same time, however, Garrisonians, including Douglass himself, had also contested the arguments of reformers in Rhode Island and elsewhere that disfranchised white workers were wage slaves or white slaves.[59]

Still, Garrison believed his critics were unfairly accusing him of neglecting the rights of freedpeople simply by declaring that the *titular* goal of anti-slavery societies was ceasing. Garrison did argue in the pages of the *Liberator* that the work of bringing education and aid to freedpeople should be ongoing, since "the leading and most efficient means of renovating any country or section of a country is the instruction of the people" in literacy, labor, and the like. In the South such instruction would raise the "black and white" population alike "to a fit position in the republic." But for Garrison these calls for education were not arguments against enfranchisement. Even as he urged the educational "renovation of the South," he also made clear that he still supported suffrage and even the distribution of land to former slaves in forty-acre lots by the application of the Confiscation Act and the Homestead Act. "Cognate to the obligation on the part of the government and the liberal mind of the North to secure popular instruction to the people of the South of all colors and conditions is the still more imperative duty to provide a way by which they may become possessed of land," so as to destroy "the old landed aristocracy" of the planter class.[60]

All of these programs of renovation, according to Garrison, were "cognate" to the others; no single one was the precondition of another. Agitation should continue even after anti-slavery organizations, as specifically anti-slavery groups, were ended. As Garrison noted in February 1866, "All that I assume—all that those who agree with me assume—is that, slavery being constitutionally abolished and prohibited, the work of agitating for its overthrow is ended. There is no need of any more anti-slavery journals, anti-slavery lectures, anti-slavery speeches. . . . But the work of educating, elevating, protecting, and vindicating the emancipated millions, in regard to all possible rights and immunities, is not done; *it is only just begun*."[61]

On this point, as on most others during the war, Garrison and Phillips actually were not far apart on the main principles at stake. Phillips, after all, had always argued that education was an essential part of a democracy, and he had no objection to freedmen's aid per se. His Athenian ideal of a democratic society always stressed the importance of information, literacy, and moral elevation through movements like temperance. That was why Garrisonians deeply involved in freedmen's aid work were offended by his suggestion that their benevolent work was unconnected to the creation of a regenerated democracy in the South. The relief efforts were not just "an *old clo'* movement," complained McKim after some derisive comments by Phillips about his and Garrison's talk of elevationism. "It is a reconstruction movement. It is to reorganize Southern society and that on a basis of impartial liberty. It is to remodel public opinion in regard to the black man by fitting him for & putting him into his place" as a full member of that society. May Jr. agreed that aid work was not "'cheap soup & primers,' as W.P. called it, but a combined, concentrated effort of . . . the Nation to lift up the emancipated man, and secure for him all his rights."[62]

Phillips could agree in principle with these ideas that emancipation and education were "cognate" efforts. But in 1865, it was his turn to point to the dangerous state of public opinion on these issues. In particular, Phillips worried that there were too many northerners and Europeans willing to entertain the idea of educational qualifications for voting. Indeed, even his transatlantic interlocutor John Stuart Mill argued, after reading some of Phillips's speeches, that he still believed an educational qualification for voting was best in a democracy, for "without the aid of reading," it would be difficult for citizens to gain "intelligence of public affairs, or the power of judging of public men, save perhaps in exceptional cases."[63]

Conway told Phillips he shared some of Mill's doubts about the wisdom of universal suffrage without any educational qualification. "Your fidelity to the *vox populi* when it so invariably turns up the Pierces, Buchanans, Lincolns, Johnsons—and never in any case a real head & leader for mankind—proves you the model idealist of this age," Conway told Phillips. "I cannot go with you." Conway even wished there had been some sort of "educational test" allowing the Union "to disfranchise every scoundrelly Copperhead, every *wild* Irishman" during the war.[64]

Both Mill and Conway clarified that they did not advocate an educational test for the enfranchisement of freed slaves; universal manhood suffrage in the South was too essential at the present crisis. But arguments like theirs worried Phillips, especially when they were echoed by a few Garrisonians. In January 1865, Theodore Tilton—one of the Garrisonians who had assumed a key journalistic post in New York—hinted at his possible support for a literacy test for voting, so long as it did not make a distinction on the basis of color. And Banks also implied that his efforts in Louisiana were designed to "*prepare*" freed people for political rights.[65]

Phillips rejected this line of thinking entirely, and devoted many of his speeches in 1865 to a central theme: "If there is anything patent on the whole history of our thirty years' struggle, it is that the negro no more needs to be *prepared* for liberty than the white man." Phillips even rejected "the whole theory of the limitation of the suffrage on the ground of information" and expressed surprise "that so masterly a mind as Stuart Mill should proclaim that a man must read before he votes." Even without literacy, Phillips said, "the black knows enough to vote."[66]

Phillips's reasons for that belief were familiar and twofold. First, as he had in the 1850s, Phillips defined education more broadly than literacy; it included disinterestedness, sympathy for the rights of others, and similar virtues. On those definitions, Phillips believed that "the masses of men have their faculties educated by work, not by reading," and that by this standard, "the only class ready for suffrage in the South is the negro," because "the only class that, as a class, has had the manipulation and development of the practical college of the masses, *work*, is the black man." He held that it was "infinitely better, if you have but one," to have "the education of work" to equip voters rather than "book learning." Secondly, Phillips argued, as he had in the 1850s, that support for public education would only come if universal suffrage were granted first. The ballot would secure the schoolhouse, he argued, instead of the other way around. "Wealth sees the ballot in the hands of poverty, and knows that its gold and its roof depend upon the use made of the ballot, and wealth hurries to put intelligence on the one side and religion on the other of the baby footsteps that will one day find their way to the ballot. That is the essence of democratic institutions."[67]

Most Garrisonians shared these views. Garrison did not suggest that education and uplift should come before enfranchisement, any more than his recommendations of temperance to Chartists had implied a lack of support for their political rights. But in a context where liberal thinkers like Mill were providing intellectual cover for voting qualifications, Phillips believed that too much talk about the importance of uplifting freed people from ignorance and degradation might undermine calls for suffrage. As he put it at the annual meeting of the MASS in January 1865, Phillips intended to "use the hours, the precious, golden, momentous hours" left in the war "to educate the nation, if possible," up to the conviction that black suffrage was essential to the nation. "I want every lip on this platform, on both sides, to fill the air with its protest, to waken the public to aid us, and bring the nation to its feet in alert vigilance." His concern was that Garrison was not being alert and vigilant enough to the gathering threat of partial suffrage posed by northern liberal opinion, just as Garrison had feared Phillips was not alert enough to the dangers of Copperhead Democrats.[68]

Indeed, Garrison and Phillips virtually switched places in their reading of northern public sentiment after Lincoln's election. Previously pessimistic about public opinion, Garrison now thought abolitionists could merge with the rest of the nation since the defeat of the Copperheads showed that most took abolitionist positions. While arguing in January 1865 that most abolitionists should stand with the Republicans, he saw this as proof of how far public opinion had moved towards the abolitionists, who finally stood "in the majority." As if to prove his point, he spent the last volume of the *Liberator* reprinting statements from people far outside the abolitionist movement who expressed support for suffrage. Few phrases better summarized his postwar position than one headline he used in July 1865: "Be of Good Cheer."[69]

Phillips, however, was no longer cheery. A decade earlier he had warned of how easily "Despotism, like a shrouding mist, steals over the mirror of Freedom." Now he was worried again by the prospect of relaxed vigilance about the dangers of democracy and aristocracy alike. Phillips had always believed that American democracy could never do "without prophets, like Garrison," to keep the ocean of democracy ever restless. Now that his beau ideal of an agitator seemed ready to retire from the role, Phillips became more convinced than ever that he would have to stir the waters himself. But as Phillips himself would soon acknowledge, his renewed determination to agitate grew as much from what he had learned from and alongside Garrison in the decades before the war as it did from the events of the war itself.[70]

EPILOGUE

On April 7, 1865, one week before Abraham Lincoln's assassination and Garrison's visit to Fort Sumter, the *Liberator* published an excerpt from an essay by Mary Grew, one of the delegates excluded from the World's Convention of 1840. Grew depicted the closing of the war as a moment of congratulation for abolitionists, whose long faith in agitation had finally been vindicated by "the regenerated public opinion of the Northern States." But their victory was also a matter of hope for the world, which had seen countless "up-heaved kingdoms and overturned thrones" and "destroyed nations" in recent years. "There has been nothing new in our contest but its form," Grew declared. "It is the old battle between Democracy and Aristocracy, waged in every land." The defeat of the Slave Power had thus been a victory for democracy itself, as well as for the emancipated slaves.[1]

Similar statements appeared frequently in the *Liberator* during 1865, its final year. The paper's pseudonymous New York correspondent "Maladie du Pays" (who was really Wendell Phillips Garrison) remarked in August that the North's victory was bound to advance the cause of parliamentary reform in England, which had not made much progress "towards the democratic model in regulating the franchise" for the last fifty years. Garrison's son, an editor at the new liberal magazine *The Nation*, attributed the sluggishness of parliamentary reform in England to the previous lack of a "striking and irrefragable proof of the security of our American system." Now, however, the "liberal party across the water" could cite the American example to aid their case for universal manhood suffrage, which seemed to be making some headway. The younger Garrison cited John Stuart Mill's recent election to the House of Commons as a sign that Americans would at last aid the liberal party throughout the world instead of being a source of apprehension to it.[2]

In their joint celebrations of northern victory and liberal reform in Britain, Grew and Garrison continued what earlier Garrisonians started. By linking the career of the nation with the progress of transatlantic reform, Wendell Phillips Garrison, in the beginning of his career at *The Nation*, revealed a worldview not unlike that of his father at the *Newburyport Herald* nearly fifty years before. Perhaps it is also telling that both *The Nation* and *The Atlantic Monthly* were founded within a decade of each other—in both cases with the help of reformers who had ties to Garrisonians. They had always seen commitments to the nation and the Atlantic as complementary instead of antithetical.

William Lloyd Garrison himself continued to insist on that point. At a "Grand Jubilee Meeting" in February 1865 celebrating the Thirteenth Amendment, Garrison invoked the memory of "Professor Follen . . . the friend and champion of impartial freedom in Europe and America" while also rejoicing in "the nation, rising in the majesty of its moral power and political sovereignty." Garrison believed that, with the American example now purified of its major stain, "the despotisms of Europe must be made to tremble to their foundations, and their down-trodden millions summoned to assert their rights." Indeed, with "our country thus redeemed," Garrison believed it was now "qualified to lead and save" the world, which—as the unchanging masthead of the *Liberator* proclaimed—he still regarded as his country too. Two years later at an international conference on slavery in Paris, Garrison reiterated such points. His speech began in a cosmopolitan vein, hoping for the creation of a universal language that would increase global harmony. Yet it went on to describe the victory of the Union as "closely related to the cause of freedom throughout the world."[3]

Phillips echoed such statements, despite his quarrels with Garrison over the extent to which the war had secured abolitionists' goals. In February 1866 he declared that the United States had already accomplished half of its great mission to the world: "we have tried the force and the courage of democratic institutions" and proved to Europe that "republican institutions" could survive civil convulsion. Now all that remained was to show the Old World that "democracy is as competent to govern as to fight." As such lines showed, Phillips continued to enlist himself in an ongoing debate with European observers of democracy like Tocqueville, whom Phillips invoked in this same speech as "that most illustrious of all historical annalists, that profoundest of all statesmen."[4]

As in the past, the *Liberator* could also cite numerous transatlantic reformers, democrats, republicans, and revolutionaries who echoed the idea that the United

States should lead a worldwide democratic movement. After the war ended, European exiles and reformers like Mazzini, Kossuth, and Victor Hugo lined up to declare, as Mazzini put it, that "your triumph is our triumph; the triumph of all, I hope, who are struggling for the advent of a republican era." In reality, however, this round of congratulations muted continued differences among self-described "democrats" or "republicans" throughout the Atlantic World. For there was not yet agreement among all "liberal" reformers that unconditional universal suffrage was required for liberal government.[5]

On the one hand, European supporters of the Union strongly supported the extension of the ballot to freedpeople during Reconstruction. In October 1865, for example, Moncure Conway wrote Mazzini in London to ask for his opinion on black suffrage. "Can you have any doubt about it?" Mazzini replied. "Does liberty exist without the vote?" Mazzini thought not and echoed Phillips's arguments that "the vote [was] the first step towards education," because "the consciousness of a function to be accomplished prepare[d] man for progress." Yet Conway's own doubts about universal suffrage, expressed around the same time in his letter to Phillips, showed the lack of consensus on these points. Mill's complicated views on suffrage also evinced a continued concern about "capacity" for voting that was shared by most liberal reformers who advocated franchise reform in Europe—and by some from the United States as well. The editor of *The Nation*, E. L. Godkin, argued for all sorts of limitations on the franchise, from age and length of residence to literacy and employment.[6]

In some ways, these proposals were unintentional bequeathals by the abolitionists to the generation of liberals who succeeded them. Neither Garrison nor Phillips had endorsed limitations on the franchise, but they had spent decades pointing out the ways that democracy in America had sheltered despotism and slavery. Samuel J. May grasped the horns of this dilemma in 1865, when he told John B. Estlin that Americans needed not only to "put the colored men in all the States, especially in the rebellious states, upon the same level politically with the white men," but also needed to "do the best we can to educate them all. Education, universal education, intellectual and especially *moral culture* is now our only protection against the mischief that may arise from universal suffrage." Wright similarly mused, that same summer, "that unless the ballot was put into the hands of the intelligence and virtue of the country, of whatever color or sex, the Republic was doomed to certain destruction." In speaking of themselves as educators or longing for a system more like Hare's, in which the occasional Pericles or Phillips might be able to instruct the unintelligent and immoral, Garrisonians like Phillips also left open the question of how to ensure the compatibility of democracy and justice.[7]

In the immediate aftermath of the war, however, such questions were often obscured by a general mood of celebration among many abolitionists—especially those allied with Garrison in his debates with Phillips. In early 1865, Garrison regarded his invitation to Fort Sumter by Secretary of War Edwin Stanton as a signal proof "that slavery is annihilated beyond any hope of resurrection," and he basked in the "deference" he was now shown by "the unerring representatives of public opinion." To James Russell Lowell he confessed that he was astonished by "the change in popular sentiment," which amounts to "a revolution" in his "beloved native land." And he was equally gratified by the toasts he received from Mill, Bright, and other British liberals at the public breakfast in his honor thrown in London in 1867.[8]

The public breakfast was a fitting testament to the continued strength and wide-ranging interests of the transatlantic networks that Garrisonian abolitionists had built over the last several decades. The man most responsible for the meeting was Frederick W. Chesson, whose career as an abolitionist had been spurred by an Atlantic crossing of his own when, during a trip to the United States with his stepfather in 1850, he had attended an antislavery meeting held by African Americans in New York. After Chesson returned to England, he met Thompson, who was by then well known not just as an abolitionist but as a member of the House of Commons. Their connection grew much stronger in 1855, when Chesson married Thompson's daughter Amelia and began editing a reform newspaper, *The Empire*, that Thompson had founded.[9]

Chesson and Thompson used this short-lived paper partly to publicize American antislavery news and defend the Garrisonians, but like Thompson, Chesson also plunged into other reform movements. Thompson often took his young protégé to the London Reform Club, a watering hole for radicals, reformers, and assorted politicians beginning to coalesce around the banner of the "Liberal" party. When Thompson's newspaper folded in 1856, these connections led to Chesson's hiring as a full-time journalist for the London *Morning Star*, a paper founded by Cobden and Bright to serve as a semi-official organ for a growing caucus of liberal politicians. In his office at the *Star* over the following decade, Chesson had frequent opportunities to talk with Bright and like-minded reformers in Parliament, including Mill; later, upon Cobden's death, Chesson was the man summoned by Cobden's widow to compile a biography of her husband.[10]

Chesson's connections to England's leading liberal politicians only deepened after 1865, when he co-founded the Jamaica Committee, organized to protest the handling of the infamous Morant Bay Rebellion by the island's racist governor Edward Eyre. On the Jamaica Committee, Chesson worked closely alongside liberal MPs like Bright, Peter Alfred Taylor (who was also a close friend of the Ashurst family), and John Stuart Mill, who became the committee's leading spokesman in 1866. The next year Chesson used these wide-ranging connections to secure both Bright and Mill as speakers at the breakfast for Garrison, who was also roundly praised in the British liberal press for having encouraged "the friends of humanity all over the world." For the man who had once dreamed of joining Lafayette and Byron, nothing could have been more gratifying to hear.[11]

Wendell Phillips, however, was one friend of humanity who did not join in Garrison's celebration of the nation or the international celebrations of Garrison. The strife between him and his old friend was ongoing as Garrison crossed the Atlantic for the penultimate time. The final meeting of the AASS in which Garrison participated was in 1865, when he had submitted a resolution calling for the society's dissolution. His motion failed beneath the force of Phillips's argument that the society could only disband when "the liberty of the negro" had been placed "beyond peril." Rather than remain in an organization whose support he had clearly lost, Garrison promptly resigned as president, leaving the society in Phillips's hands.[12]

Garrison's reasons for leaving his post were complex and ranged from family obligations and fatigue to faith. Having always seen the AASS in part as an instrument in God's hands, Garrison found it ridiculous to think that God would not continue his work beyond the life of the society he had helped to found. "I am not for counseling inaction, nor relaxing in vigilance, because assured that God will, at some time or other, accomplish his great designs," Garrison told a New York audience the year after Phillips took over the AASS. "But I know in whom I have believed, and as He has not failed in the past, so He may be safely trusted in the future."[13]

That belief may have contributed to Garrison's willingness to step away from the society he had defended against mob and threat for so long. Most of all, however, after spending his adult life in an extended lover's quarrel with the country he grew up admiring, Garrison probably longed for some sign of personal vindication for all his efforts. Since he still could not reconcile himself to running for election or voting, he could not seek such vindication in obtaining office, as Mill or his friend George Thompson had done. The Thirteenth Amendment and

retirement offered him alternative ways to mark the victory and political influence he had so long desired.[14]

The desire for vindication goes a long way towards explaining Garrison's resignation, but the same desire was stirring in Phillips. Indeed, their mutual desire
to enjoy some modicum of victory highlights the dilemma of all agitators in a
democratic society. Working to influence public opinion is only worth the effort
if success ultimately comes, but the acclaim of the public, once it does come, can
immediately raise an agitator's concern that his or her independence has now
been lost. For agitators, the endgame is always the problem.

In retrospect, Garrison did not manage this problem as gracefully or nobly
as his colleagues would have liked. But Phillips ultimately wrestled with the
same problem. In the same meeting that witnessed Garrison's resignation, Phillips defined the society's new final objective as a constitutional amendment that
would disallow "any distinction in civil privileges among those born on [Ameri-
can] soil, of parents permanently resident there, on account of race, color or
descent." But Phillips knew even this was not the extent of his democratic ideals. He hoped "in time to be as bold as Stuart Mill, and add to that clause 'sex,'"
but he believed "this hour belongs to the negro"—a statement not so different
from Garrison's arguments that in 1864 the hour had belonged to emancipation
instead of enfranchisement. And only five years later, after the Fifteenth Amendment guaranteeing universal manhood suffrage regardless of color was passed,
Phillips followed Garrison in calling for the dissolution of the society, despite the
objections of some members that there was still more to be done for freedpeople.
As A. J. Aiséirithe and other historians have noted, "the election controversy [in
1864] made it seem as though there were a difference of opinion" between Garrison and Phillips on the requirements for ending the AASS, yet "by the time the
Society [was] disbanded in 1870, the line of difference [seemed] a lot less clear."[15]

Events after 1870 proved that the rights of black Americans in the North and
South had not yet been removed "beyond peril." That was why Phillips and Garrison both remained restless, even after both had decided that it was time for
the AASS to disband. Despite their initial hopes that Lincoln's successor, Andrew
Johnson, might be a president more willing to lead, the opposite had proved to
be true. Johnson's resistance to radical Republicans brought new danger to the
cause of equal civil rights in the South and eventually led to a movement for his
impeachment. In 1867, Phillips compared Johnson to Louis Napoleon—raising
the specter of yet another despot in democrat's clothing. And in 1870, as the

AASS dissolved, Phillips confessed that "I am no longer proud, as I once was, of the flag or of the name of an American." He continued to be active in reform movements for the rest of his life.[16]

Meanwhile, Garrison also continued until his death to send regular dispatches to the major newspapers of the North blasting Johnson's Reconstruction policies and, later, President Ulysses S. Grant's imperial adventures in Santo Domingo. He also worried about the sort of liberalism that Godkin was preaching at *The Nation*. Indeed, looking back on the celebrations of the "jubilee" at the end of the Civil War, Garrison wondered whether all the self-congratulation had once again blinded Americans to their imperfections. On the year of the nation's centennial, Garrison urged his son to remember that "this nation has been the guiltiest of all the nations of the earth since its independence," and was still flouting God's will. Agitators to the end, neither Garrison nor Phillips would find a final rest.[17]

Unable to bring his own career as an agitator to an end, Phillips also returned to eulogizing Garrison upon the editor's death in 1879, his perspective on their quarrels now seasoned by his own tortured decision to disband the AASS. Phillips now believed that Garrison's career was important to remember "on both sides of the ocean," primarily for "the grand lesson" it taught, which was that the weaknesses of democracy Phillips and Tocqueville had always identified were not fatal in the end. Garrison had "sounded the depths of the weakness, he proved the ultimate strength of republican institutions; he gave us to know the perils that confront us; he taught us to rally the strength that lies hid."[18]

That hidden strength, Phillips and Garrison had always believed, could only be rallied by "that *agitation* which alone, in our day, reforms States," and it was to this aspect of Garrison's life that Phillips drew the most attention. Phillips regarded Garrison's agitation as greater even than that of O'Connell, who "leaned back on three millions of Irishmen, all on fire with sympathy," or that of Cobden, who was "held up by the whole manufacturing interest of Great Britain." Those British reformers' agitation was, Phillips still believed, "marvellous." "As you gaze upon it in its successive stages and analyze it, you are astonished at what they invented for tools." But Garrison had started with hardly any sympathy on his side, amidst "apathy, indifference, ignorance, icebergs" instead of a restless ocean. Yet "he [had] made every single home, press, pulpit, and senate-chamber a debating society"; had influenced "guides of public sentiment" like Sumner and Brown; and had shown the possibility of independence in a democracy. "To the day of his death he was as ready as in his boyhood to confront and defy a mad majority. . . . He showed nothing either of the intellectual sluggishness or the timidity of age."[19]

In all these lines, Phillips echoed John Stuart Mill's own toasts to Garrison twelve years earlier at the Public Breakfast. Indeed, Mill's praise suggests that he, like Phillips, saw Garrison primarily as a consoling answer to the worries about democratic institutions that Tocqueville had pointed out. "The whole intellect of the [United States] has been set thinking about the fundamental questions of society and government" thanks to Garrison and the war, Mill said, and as a result "that great nation is saved, probably for a long time to come, from the most formidable danger of a completely settled state of society and opinion— intellectual and moral stagnation."[20]

Both Phillips and Mill saw the "lesson" of Garrison's career primarily as a demonstration of the need for a democracy to remain unsettled. Unable to comfort themselves with some sense of final vindication, agitators could at least feel vindicated that their dissent kept democratic institutions safe. Indeed, Phillips's reading of Tocqueville's warnings in the early 1850s continued to influence his speeches during Reconstruction and beyond. He continued to defend democracy, praising O'Connell in 1875 for having "anticipated Lincoln's wisdom, and framed his movements 'for the people, of the people, and by the people.'" Yet Phillips still saw it as "a singular fact, that the freer a nation becomes, the more utterly democratic the form of its institutions," the more necessary "outside agitation" and the "pressure of public opinion" became. "The general judgment is, that the freest possible government produces the freest possible men and women,—the most individual, the least servile to the judgment of others," Phillips explained. "But a moment's reflection will show any man that this is an unreasonable expectation," especially in the United States, where most people remained "a mass of cowards. More than any other people, we are afraid of each other."[21]

Phillips sounded the same Tocquevillean warnings about stagnation and conformity in the crowning speech of his life, "The Scholar in a Republic," which he delivered as the Phi Beta Kappa address at Harvard in 1881. Here Phillips once again described American history as the greatest chapter of world history—the exemplar of the great idea of popular government. Yet once again Phillips also preached the necessity of "education" for keeping the United States democratic, by which he meant "not book-learning," but the education provided by discussion, agitation, and independent thought.[22]

By those definitions, Phillips said, "the Frémont campaign of 1856 taught Americans more than a hundred colleges; and John Brown's pulpit at Harper's Ferry was equal to any ten thousand ordinary chairs." "Free speech" was "God's normal school for educating men, throwing upon them the grave responsibility of deciding great questions, and so lifting them to a higher level of intellectual and moral life"—a nearly direct quotation from Phillips's 1859 speech on Harpers Ferry. Phillips again invoked Athens as his model for American democracy, again endorsed universal suffrage as a source of education through responsibility, and again pointed to "Cobden and John Bright, Garrison and O'Connell," as the "master-spirits" of "agitation," which was all the more needful "the more utterly democratic" a nation became. In a final jab at the Harvard-bred conservatism he had rejected for almost fifty years, Phillips pointed to the Russian nihilists as the latest in a line of agitators whose freedom of speech should be protected.[23]

In 1881 Phillips also concluded with the same image he had used to make these points in 1852: he urged his young scholars to "recognize that we are afloat on the current of Niagara, eternal vigilance the condition of our safety," and that "we are irrevocably pledged to the world not to go back to bolts and bars,—could not if we would, and would not if we could. . . . If the Alps, piled in cold and silence, be the emblem of despotism, we joyfully take the ever-restless ocean for ours,—only pure because never still."[24]

Phillips, Garrison, and their allies left that image of the ever-restless ocean to a new generation of "critical Americans" and transatlantic liberals who, as Leslie Butler has shown, saw the Civil War not as a demonstration of democracy's failure but as a proof of its viability and a summons to perfect free institutions for the sake of the world. Garrisonians also left behind the problems of political influence and public opinion that ultimately troubled and divided them. But their idea of free and constant agitation as essential to democracy proved to be one of their most important legacies. In her own autobiography published in 1898, Elizabeth Cady Stanton remembered sitting under a tree with Susan B. Anthony in 1881, pondering Phillips's Phi Beta Kappa address. She also excerpted it at length, ending with his passage about "the ever restless ocean."[25]

Garrisonians also passed to the generation of reformers that came after them a sense of the importance of crossing actual oceans, literally or figuratively, just as Phillips and Stanton had done many years before when they both attended the World's Convention of 1840. Despite being occupied with his continuing anti-slavery work, Phillips lectured in support of Cretan revolutionaries in 1867. And the last speech he ever gave, a tribute to Harriet Martineau delivered on December 26, 1883, about one month before he died, began by declaring that "in moral questions there are no nations," for "when a moral issue is stirred, then there is no American, no German. We are all men and women."[26]

Even before then, despite their conflicts with British abolitionists during the war, American Garrisonians had worked to remind each other that their country was still the world. Many revived their correspondence with apologetic letters that reaffirmed friendship. They also renewed those friendships with brief yet poignant meetings, like the ones that took place with the postwar visits of Webb, Mary Estlin, and the former Chartist and Anti-Slavery League officer Henry Vincent to the United States. Well into the early 1870s, members of the Garrisonians' transatlantic band like Webb, Estlin, Quincy, May Jr., McKim, Mott, Chapman, and others continued to write to each other discussing the latest news about the Irish Fenians, woman suffrage, the Franco-Prussian War, labor and civil service reform, the Liberal Republican uprising led by Godkin and *The Nation,* and the parliamentary and suffrage reforms being pursued by Mill, who later worked directly with Webb.[27]

In continuing their ties even after the war, these Garrisonians testified to the importance of their transatlantic relationships and to the supra-national ideals to which they had aspired. They were, to be sure, not the only reformers or Americans who had come to see the struggles of their time in a transatlantic context. In 1910, the Progressive reformer Jane Addams remembered an impressive scene from her childhood when, in 1872, she found her Republican father, John H. Addams, weeping over a newspaper reporting Mazzini's death. When Addams expressed confusion over her father's emotional response to someone who was not an American, he tried to give her "a sense of the genuine relationship which may exist between men who share large hopes and like desires, even though they differ in nationality." Addams remembered leaving the encounter "heartily ashamed of my meager notion of patriotism, and I came out of the room exhilarated with the consciousness that impersonal and international relations are actual facts and not mere phrases."[28]

As Addams's recollections show, Garrison and his allies were not the only Americans who demonstrated how "international relations" could become personal and deeply felt. Yet the ocean-spanning agitators of the American Anti-Slavery Society deserve a great deal of the credit for the fact that reformers like Addams and Garrison's children, who joined her in later reforms like the Anti-

Imperialist League, kept alive their guiding beliefs: that cosmopolitan feeling was important, that agitation was necessary, and that both things could be the deepest signs of love for one's country.

Alfred Webb, for example, the son of Garrison's Dublin friend, later became both an important Irish nationalist and an internationalist who was elected honorary president of the Indian National Congress in 1894. In that capacity he gave an address which explained that he had been "nurtured in the conflict against American slavery" and had learned to say, "in the words of William Lloyd Garrison, the founder of that movement, 'My country is the world; my countrymen are all mankind.'" Five years later, in 1899, William Lloyd Garrison Jr. also revived his father's motto—"Our country is the world, our countrymen are all mankind"—as a pledge suitable for use by the Anti-Imperialist League, an organization he helped to create the year before. Raised under the influence of his father and of Wendell Phillips, Garrison Jr. clearly believed, as they had, that agitation could not end when particular leagues or injustices did. The problem of democracy demanded that new groups would always follow in the wake of the Anti–Corn Law League and the Anti-Slavery League, striving to keep the ever-restless ocean from becoming still.[29]

NOTES

ABBREVIATIONS

AWW	Anne Warren Weston
BAA	*British and American Abolitionists: An Episode in Transatlantic Understanding,* ed. Clare Taylor. Edinburgh: Edinburgh University Press, 1974.
BPL	Boston Public Library, Anti-Slavery Collection, Rare Books and Manuscripts Division
CWJSM	Robson, John M. *The Collected Works of John Stuart Mill.* 33 vols. Toronto: University of Toronto Press, 1963–91.
EPN	Elizabeth Pease (Nichol)
EQ	Edmund Quincy
Garrison and Garrison, *Garrison*	Garrison, Wendell Phillips, and Francis Jackson Garrison. *William Lloyd Garrison, 1805–1879: The Story of His Life Told by His Children.* 4 vols. New York: Century Co., 1885–89.
GUE	*The Genius of Universal Emancipation, a Monthly Periodical Work, containing Original Essays, Documents, and Facts Relative to the Subject of African Slavery,* ed. Benjamin Lundy. Washington, D.C., 1821–39.
GT	George Thompson
HCW-BPL	Henry Clarke Wright. Journals and commonplace books. 47 vols. 1834–1867. BPL, Ms.qAm.1859. Volume numbers refer to accession record.
HCW-HL	Henry Clarke Wright. Journals and commonplace books. 42 vols. HL, MS Am 514–515. Volume numbers refer to Wright's own numbering.
HEG	Helen E. Garrison
HL	Houghton Library, Harvard University
JBE	John B. Estlin
JMM	James Miller McKim

LWLG	*The Letters of William Lloyd Garrison,* edited by Walter M. Merrill and Louis Ruchames. 6 vols. Cambridge, Mass.: Harvard University Press, 1971–81.
MWC	Maria Weston Chapman
NASS	*National Anti-Slavery Standard* (New York)
NPR	Nathaniel P. Rogers
RDW	Richard D. Webb
REAS	Raymond English Antislavery Collection, John Rylands Library, Manchester, U.K.
RHAP	Temperley, Howard R., ed. *The Rhodes House Anti-Slavery Papers: Material Relating to America from the Anti-Slavery Collection in Rhodes House, Oxford; mainly 1839–1868* (East Ardsley, Wakefield, Yorkshire, U.K.: Micro Methods Limited, 1963)
SLL	Phillips, Wendell. *Speeches, Lectures, and Letters.* Boston: Lee and Shephard, 1870.
SLL: Second Series	Phillips, Wendell. *Speeches, Lectures and Letters; Second Series.* Boston: Lee and Shepard, 1894.
SMJr	Samuel May Jr.
WLG	William Lloyd Garrison
WP	Wendell Phillips

INTRODUCTION

1. Henry Mayer, *All on Fire: William Lloyd Garrison and the Abolition of Slavery* (New York: St. Martin's Griffin, 1998), 577–85.

2. Garrison and Thompson told the story about the ten-dollar bill to Frederick W. Chesson. See the entry for June 10, 1867, in Frederick Chesson Diary, May 1867–April 1868, REAS, 11/15. For Garrison's deprecating comment about the American flag, see "Independence Day: Anti-Slavery Celebration at Framingham," *Liberator,* July 20, 1860.

3. See *Proceedings at the Public Breakfast Held in Honour of William Lloyd Garrison, of Boston, Massachusetts, in St. James's Hall, London, on Saturday, June 29th, 1867* (London: William Tweedie, 1868); Richard J. M. Blackett, "'And There Shall Be No More Sea': William Lloyd Garrison and the Transatlantic Abolitionist Movement," in *William Lloyd Garrison at Two Hundred: History, Legacy, and Memory,* ed. James Brewer Stewart (New Haven, Conn.: Yale University Press, 2008), 36–37. On Mill's importance to transatlantic liberals, see Leslie Butler, *Critical Americans: Victorian Intellectuals and Transatlantic Liberal Reform* (Chapel Hill: University of North Carolina Press, 2007), 109–20. Previous studies of transatlantic abolitionism which have informed this work include David Turley, *The Culture of English Antislavery, 1780–1860* (London: Routledge, 1991); Frank Thistlethwaite, *The Anglo-American Connection in the Early Nineteenth Century* (Philadelphia: University of Pennsylvania Press, 1959); Betty Fladeland, *Men and Brothers: Anglo-American Antislavery Cooperation* (Ur-

bana: University of Illinois Press, 1972); Howard Temperley, *British Antislavery, 1833–1870* (London: Longman, 1972); Clare Taylor, ed., *British and American Abolitionists: An Episode in Transatlantic Understanding* (Edinburgh: Edinburgh University Press, 1974); R. J. M. Blackett, *Building an Antislavery Wall: Black Americans in the Atlantic Abolitionist Movement, 1830–1860* (Baton Rouge: Louisiana State University Press, 1983). A focus on the transatlantic dimensions of abolitionism informed and shaped the magisterial works of David Brion Davis, including *The Problem of Slavery in the Age of Revolution* (Ithaca, N.Y.: Cornell University Press, 1975), and *Slavery and Human Progress* (New York: Oxford University Press, 1984).

4. John Stuart Mill to Moncure Daniel Conway, October 23, 1865, *CWJSM* 16:1106. See also Mill to Harriet Taylor, October 29, 1850, *CWJSM* 14:49–50; Mill to John Robertson, October 2, 1838, *CWJSM* 13:389; Mill to Harriet Taylor, March 31, 1849, *CWJSM* 14:21–23; *Oxford Dictionary of National Biography,* online ed., s.v. "Nichol, John Pringle (1804–1859)." One of Mill's close friends was the astronomer John P. Nichol, who in 1853 married Elizabeth Pease, one of Garrison's closest friends since the late 1830s.

5. Entry for June 20 in Frederick Chesson Diary, May 1867–April 1868, REAS; WLG to HEG, August 12, 1867, *LWLG* 5:527. Mill also told John Elliot Cairnes that "it would have given you great pleasure had you been at the Garrison breakfast, and heard, especially Bright, and Garrison himself" (Mill to John Elliot Cairnes, June 30, 1867, *CWJSM* 16:1284). In 1868 Mill would also contribute to a National Testimonial fund for Garrison; see WLG to National Testimonial Committee, 12 March 1868, *LWLG* 6:42. The year after that Garrison would regret that Mill was not reelected. See WLG to Mary Estlin, January 1, 1869, *LWLG* 6:97; WLG to SMJr, July 23, 1869, *LWLG* 6:126.

6. *Special Report of the Anti-Slavery Conference, Held in Paris . . . on the Twenty-Sixth and Twenty-Seventh August, 1867* (London: British and Foreign Anti-Slavery Society, 1867); WLG to HEG, June 7, 1867, *LWLG* 5:499–501; entries for June 20 and June 23 in Frederick Chesson Diary, May 1867–April 1868, REAS; WLG, introduction to *Joseph Mazzini: His Life, Writings, and Political Principles,* ed. Emilie Ashurst Venturi (New York: Hurd and Houghton, 1872), viii.

7. Venturi, ed., *Joseph Mazzini,* xi, vii. See also WLG to William Lloyd Garrison, Jr., August 14, 1867, BPL, Ms.A.1.1.7.52.

8. On these changes, see recent syntheses by Seymour Drescher, *Abolition: A History of Slavery and Antislavery* (Cambridge, U.K.: Cambridge University Press, 2009), esp. ix–x; David Brion Davis, *Inhuman Bondage: The Rise and Fall of Slavery in the New World* (New York: Oxford University Press, 2006); Robin Blackburn, *The American Crucible: Slavery, Emancipation and Human Rights* (London: Verso, 2011).

9. On British national identity and antislavery after emancipation, see Richard Huzzey, *Freedom Burning: Anti-Slavery and Empire in Victorian Britain* (Ithaca, N.Y.: Cornell University Press, 2012).

10. See Edward Bartlett Rugemer, *The Problem of Emancipation: The Caribbean Roots of the American Civil War* (Baton Rouge: Louisiana State University Press, 2008); Seymour Drescher, *The Mighty Experiment: Free Labor versus Slavery in British Emancipation* (New York: Oxford University Press, 2002); Carl Paulus, "The Slaveholding Crisis: The Fear of Insurrection, the Wilmot Proviso, and the Southern Turn against American Exceptionalism," Ph.D. diss., Rice University, 2012.

11. WLG to Harriet Minot, March 19, 1833, *LWLG* 1:215. In November 1861, one of Lincoln's potential timetables for "gradual, federally compensated emancipation" in Delaware would have allowed slavery there to exist until 1893. See George M. Fredrickson, *Big Enough to Be Inconsistent:*

Abraham Lincoln Confronts Slavery and Race (Cambridge, Mass.: Harvard University Press, 2008), 95–96.

12. Mike Rapport, *1848: Year of Revolution* (New York: Basic Books, 2008), 1–41. According to Rapport, after the French Revolution of 1830, "the electorate swelled to include only 170,000 of France's richest men: this was a mere 0.5 per cent of the French population, a sixth of those who enjoyed the vote in Britain after 1832" (p. 3). Timothy Roberts puts the size of the French electorate under Louis Philippe at "the wealthiest 250,000 men out of a population of some 35 million, about twice as large as the U.S. population in 1840." See Timothy Mason Roberts, *Distant Revolutions: 1848 and the Challenge to American Exceptionalism* (Charlottesville, Va.: University of Virginia Press, 2009), 12. On exiles, see Bernard Porter, *The Refugee Question in Mid-Victorian Politics* (Cambridge, U.K.: Cambridge University Press, 1979); Sabine Freitag, ed., *Exiles from European Revolutions: Refugees in Mid-Victorian England* (New York: Berghahn, 1999).

13. K. Theodore Hoppen, *The Mid-Victorian Generation, 1846–1886* (New York: Oxford University Press, 1998), 237–39; James Vernon, *Politics and the People: A Study in English Political Culture, c. 1815–1867* (Cambridge, U.K.: Cambridge University Press, 1993).

14. John Stuart Mill, "De Tocqueville on Democracy in America [I]," *CWJSM* 18:50.

15. Kyle G. Volk, "The Perils of 'Pure Democracy': Minority Rights, Liquor Politics, and Popular Sovereignty in Antebellum America," *Journal of the Early Republic* 29, no. 4 (Summer 2009): 641–79, qtd. on 644. On the contradictions inherent in "democracy" during this period, compare Daniel Walker Howe, *What Hath God Wrought: The Transformation of America, 1815–1848* (New York: Oxford University Press, 2006); Sean Wilentz, *The Rise of American Democracy: Jefferson to Lincoln* (New York: W. W. Norton, 2005); Alexander Keyssar, *The Right to Vote: The Contested History of Democracy in the United States* (New York: Basic Books, 2000).

16. Dwight L. Dumond, ed., *Letters of James Gillespie Birney, 1831–1857* (2 vols., New York: D. Appleton-Century, 1938), vol. 2:733–34, 744–45, qtd. on 733; Daniel Feller, "Rediscovering Jacksonian America," in Melvyn Stokes, ed., *The State of U.S. History* (New York: Berg, 2002), 82. See also Betty Fladeland, *James Gillespie Birney: Slaveholder to Abolitionist* (Ithaca, N.Y.: Cornell University Press, 1955), 215–26; Aileen S. Kraditor, *Means and Ends in American Abolitionism: Garrison and His Critics on Strategy and Tactics, 1834–1850* (1969; rpt. Chicago: Ivan R. Dee, 1989), 149.

17. "Sir Robert Peel at Tamworth," *Liberator,* October 24, 1835; Victor Schoelcher, "American Slavery, and the London Exhibition," *Liberty Bell* 12 (1852): 167.

18. "Another Argument for Sir Robert Peel," *Liberator,* October 24, 1835.

19. Wendell Phillips, "Idols," in *SLL,* 249; "The Republican Scholar of Necessity an Agitator," *Liberator,* August 21, 1857.

20. Amy Gutmann and Dennis Thompson, *Democracy and Disagreement* (Cambridge, Mass.: Harvard University Press, 1996), 28. See also the essays in Seyla Benhabib, ed., *Democracy and Difference: Contesting the Boundaries of the Political* (Princeton, N.J.: Princeton University Press, 1996); Nancy L. Rosenblum, ed., *Liberalism and the Moral Life* (Cambridge, Mass.: Harvard University Press, 1989).

21. Other central concerns in contemporary democratic theory, like the problem of how to reconcile individualism with social feeling and obligation, also date to this period and are mentioned below, but they will occupy less of this book. For a good recent summary of one such strand of democratic theory that stretches back to Tocqueville, see Johann N. Neem, "Taking Modernity's

Wager: Tocqueville, Social Capital, and the American Civil War," *Journal of Interdisciplinary History* 41, no. 4 (Spring 2011): 591–618.

22. WLG to Marcus Gunn, July 27, 1840, *LWLG* 2:672; John W. Blassingame, ed., *The Frederick Douglass Papers, Series One: Speeches, Debates, and Interviews* (New Haven, Conn.: Yale University Press, 1979), vol. 1:212; Wendell Phillips, "A Metropolitan Police," *SLL,* 522; Phillips, "Disunion," in *SLL,* 348.

23. Charles Sumner to Wendell Phillips, February 4, 1845, in *The Selected Letters of Charles Sumner,* ed. Beverly Wilson Palmer (Boston: Northeastern University Press, 199), vol. 1:144.

24. Elizur Wright, Jr., to James G. Birney, 6 February 1844, in Dumond, ed., *Letters of James Gillespie Birney* 2:778.

25. James Oakes, *The Radical and the Republican: Frederick Douglass, Abraham Lincoln, and the Triumph of Antislavery Politics* (New York: W. W. Norton, 2007), 8, 9; Bruce Laurie, *Beyond Garrison: Antislavery and Social Reform* (New York: Cambridge University Press, 2005), 5; Margot Minardi, *Making Slavery History: Abolitionism and the Politics of Memory in Massachusetts* (New York: Oxford University Press, 2010), 92; Peter C. Myers, *Frederick Douglass: Race and the Rebirth of American Liberalism* (Lawrence: University of Kansas Press, 2008), 83; Louis Menand, *The Metaphysical Club: A Story of Ideas in America* (New York: Farrar, Straus and Giroux, 2001), 15. I quote these authors not to criticize their excellent books, which are not primarily or only about Garrisonians anyway, but instead to show how resilient these views remain even in recent historiography. For a good introduction to earlier scholarship, see Betty L. Fladeland, "Revisionists vs. Abolitionists: The Historiographical Cold War of the 1930s and 1940s," *Journal of the Early Republic* 6 (Spring 1986): 1–21.

26. Moncure Daniel Conway, *Autobiography: Memories and Experiences* (Boston: Houghton Mifflin and Co., 1904), vol. 1:185. On uncertainty and flexibility as key concepts for Progressive-era democratic thinkers, see Menand, *The Metaphysical Club;* James T. Kloppenberg, *Uncertain Victory: Social Democracy and Progressivism in European and American Thought, 1870–1920* (New York: Oxford University Press, 1986); and the somewhat discredited but still insightful Morton G. White, *Social Thought in America: The Revolt against Formalism* (Boston: Beacon Press, 1957). On Mill's penchant for resolving contradictions between opposing philosophies, see Nicholas Capaldi, *John Stuart Mill: A Biography* (New York: Cambridge University Press, 2004).

27. The phrase "make democracy safe for the world" is adapted from George Wilson Pierson, *Tocqueville in America* (Baltimore: Johns Hopkins University Press, 1996), 167.

28. On fears of agitation in the early republic, see Mark G. Schmeller, "Imagining Public Opinion in Antebellum America: Fear, Credit, Law, and Honor," Ph.D. diss., University of Chicago, 2001, chap. 5, Joseph Story qtd. on 262. Also see Seth Cotlar's discussion of the early national backlash against participatory democracy and radical agitation in Cotlar, *Tom Paine's America: The Rise and Fall of Transatlantic Radicalism in the Early Republic* (Charlottesville: University of Virginia Press, 2011).

29. Wendell Phillips, "Public Opinion," in *SLL,* 52.

30. Phillips, "Public Opinion," 54. For a sampling of other recent work on the mid-nineteenth-century Atlantic world of reform, see Roberts, *Distant Revolutions;* Angela F. Murphy, *American Slavery, Irish Freedom: Abolition, Immigrant Citizenship, and the Transatlantic Movement for Irish Repeal* (Baton Rouge: Louisiana State University Press, 2010); Amanda Bowie Moniz, "Saving the Lives of Strangers: Humane Societies and the Cosmopolitan Provision of Charitable Aid," *Journal of the Early Republic* 29, no. 4 (2009): 607–40; Mischa Honeck, *We Are the Revolutionists: German-Speaking Immigrants and American Abolitionists after 1848* (Athens: University of Georgia Press, 2011); Kath-

ryn Kish Sklar and James Brewer Stewart, eds., *Women's Rights and Transatlantic Antislavery in the Era of Emancipation* (New Haven, Conn.: Yale University Press, 2007); Bonnie S. Anderson, *Joyous Greetings: The First International Women's Movement, 1830–1860* (New York: Oxford University Press, 2000); Margaret H. McFadden, *Golden Cables of Sympathy: The Transatlantic Sources of Nineteenth-Century Feminism* (Lexington: University Press of Kentucky, 1998); Carl J. Guarneri, *The Utopian Alternative: Fourierism in Nineteenth-Century America* (rpt., Ithaca, N.Y.: Cornell University Press, 1994). For a slightly later period, see Daniel T. Rodgers, *Atlantic Crossings: Social Politics in a Progressive Age* (Cambridge, Mass.: Harvard University Press, 1998); Ian Tyrrell, *Woman's World/Woman's Empire: The Women's Christian Temperance Union in International Perspective, 1880–1930* (Chapel Hill: University of North Carolina Press, 1991); Leila J. Rupp, *Worlds of Women: The Making of an International Women's Movement* (Princeton, N.J.: Princeton University Press, 1997).

31. C. A. Bayly, *The Birth of the Modern World, 1780–1914* (Oxford, U.K.: Blackwell, 2004), 118; SMJr to RDW, March 26, 1871, BPL, Ms.B.1.6.11.9. On the transportation revolution in the United States during this same period, see Howe, *What Hath God Wrought*. For overarching surveys of the persistence of the Atlantic World into the nineteenth century, especially as a zone of cultural and economic exchange, see Donna Gabaccia, "A Long Atlantic in a Wider World," *Atlantic Studies* 1, no. 1 (2004): 1–27; Aaron Spencer Fogleman, "The Transformation of the Atlantic World, 1776–1867," *Atlantic Studies* 6, no. 1 (2009): 5–28; Jürgen Osterhammel and Niels P. Petersson, *Globalization: A Short History* (Princeton, N.J.: Princeton University Press, 2005), 57–80; José C. Moya, "Modernization, Modernity, and the Trans/formation of the Atlantic World in the Nineteenth Century," in *The Atlantic in Global History, 1500–2000*, ed. Jorge Cañizares-Esguerra and Erik R. Seeman (Upper Saddle River, N.J.: Pearson, 2007), 179–98; and Thistlethwaite's still useful *The Anglo-American Connection*. See also the account of nineteenth-century transatlantic connections as one of interplay between the continued "flow" of connections and the "closure" of others in Charles Bright and Michael Geyer, "Where in the World Is America? The History of the United States in the Global Age," in Thomas Bender, ed., *Rethinking American History in a Global Age* (Berkeley: University of California Press, 2002), 76–77. For scholarship relating European politics and the Atlantic economy to early American politics and territorial expansion, see Thomas Bender, *A Nation among Nations: America's Place in World History* (New York: Hill and Wang, 2006), 60–115; François Furstenberg, "The Significance of the Trans-Appalachian Frontier in Atlantic History," *American Historical Review* 113 (June 2008): 647–77; John Craig Hammond, "Slavery, Settlement, and Empire: The Expansion and Growth of Slavery in the Interior of the North American Continent, 1770–1820," *Journal of the Early Republic* 32, no. 2 (Summer 2012): 175–206; Rosemarie Zagarri, "The Significance of the 'Global Turn' for the Early American Republic," *Journal of the Early Republic* 31, no. 1 (Spring 2011): 1–37; Matthew Rainbow Hale, "On their Tiptoes: Political Time and Newspapers during the Advent of the Radicalized French Revolution, circa 1792–1793," *Journal of the Early Republic* 29 (Summer 2009): 191–218; Rachel Hope Cleves, *The Reign of Terror in America: Visions of Violence from Anti-Jacobinism to Antislavery* (New York: Cambridge University Press, 2009). Also see Andre M. Fleche, *The Revolution of 1861: The American Civil War in the Age of Nationalist Conflict* (Chapel Hill: University of North Carolina Press, 2012); and the various works mentioned in two recent forums: "Interchange: Nationalism and Internationalism in the Era of the Civil War," *Journal of American History* 98, no. 2 (2011): 455–89; "AHR Conversation: On Transnational History," *American Historical Review* 111, no. 5 (December 2006).

32. Philip S. Foner, ed., *The Life and Writings of Frederick Douglass*, vol. 1: *Early Years, 1817–1849* (New York: International Publishers, 1950), 323. For the lengths of Garrison's trips, each number represents the number of days for a one-way crossing, rounded up to the nearest whole day, between Boston and Garrison's English port, which was sometimes Liverpool and sometimes London. I have compiled the figures from Wendell Phillips Garrison and Francis Jackson Garrison, *William Lloyd Garrison, 1805–1879: The Story of His Life Told by His Children* (4 vols.; New York: Century Co., 1885–1889); and correspondence in *LWLG*. For more on abolitionists' encounters with steam travel, see my "Saltwater Antislavery: American Abolitionists on the Atlantic Ocean in the Age of Steam," *Atlantic Studies* 8, no. 2 (2011): 141–63.

33. Frederick Douglass, *My Bondage and My Freedom*, ed. John David Smith (1855; New York: Penguin, 2003), 278.

34. See George Armstrong to SMJr, August 14, 1855, and Joseph Mazzini to George Armstrong, in *BAA*, 416–17.

35. Kloppenberg, *Uncertain Victory*, 10.

36. George Thompson, *Addresses; Delivered at Meetings of the Native Community of Calcutta: and on Other Occasions* (Calcutta: Thacker and Co., 1843), 24; Charles Follen, "Speech before the Anti-Slavery Society," in *The Works of Charles Follen, with a Memoir of His Life*, ed. Eliza Lee Follen (Boston: Hilliard, Gray, and Co., 1841), vol. 1:629–30; MWC to EPN, December 25, 1849, Ms.A.1.2.18.88, BPL; HCW-BPL, vol. 47 (1867).

37. For "favorite motto," see Garrison and Garrison, *Garrison* 1:xi. For the memorial cards, see McKim-Garrison Family Papers, New York Public Library, Box 3, MGF 31.

38. Alexis de Tocqueville, *Democracy in America*, trans. Gerald Bevan (London: Penguin, 2003), 277. See also Cotlar, *Tom Paine's America*.

39. Mill qtd. in Maurizio Viroli, *For Love of Country: An Essay on Patriotism and Nationalism* (Oxford: Clarendon Press, 1995), front matter. See also Georgios Varouxakis, *Mill on Nationality* (London: Routledge, 2002).

40. David Hollinger, "Historians and the Discourse of Intellectuals," in *In the American Province: Studies in the History and Historiography of Ideas* (Baltimore: Johns Hopkins University Press, 1985), 130–51, quoted on 132.

41. David W. Blight, "William Lloyd Garrison at Two Hundred: His Radicalism and His Legacy for Our Time," in Stewart, ed., *William Lloyd Garrison at Two Hundred*, 7. Past historiography better recognized the Garrisonians' political aims. See especially James Brewer Stewart, "The Aims and Impact of Garrisonian Abolitionism, 1840–1860," *Civil War History* 15, no. 3 (1969): 197–209; Kraditor, *Means and Ends*; Bertram Wyatt-Brown, "William Lloyd Garrison and Antislavery Unity: A Reappraisal," *Civil War History* 13, no. 1 (1967): 5–24. See also Mark Voss-Hubbard, "The Political Culture of Emancipation: Morality, Politics, and the State in Garrisonian Abolitionism, 1854–1863," *Journal of American Studies* 29, no. 2 (1995): 159–84, which argues that, despite their "doctrinaire" and "antinomian" religious views, Garrisonians "were capable of responding to their circumstances in unpredictable ways," though these unpredictable departures did not happen, according to Voss-Hubbard, until after 1854.

42. Butler, *Critical Americans*, 12. See, for example, Anthony Howe and Simon Morgan, eds., *Rethinking Nineteenth-Century Liberalism: Richard Cobden Bicentenary Essays* (Aldershot, Hampshire, U.K.: Ashgate, 2006); C. A. Bayly and Eugenio F. Biagini, eds., *Giuseppe Mazzini and the Globalisa-*

tion of Democratic Nationalism, 1830–1920 (Oxford, U.K.: Oxford University Press, 2008); Sandra Harbert Petrulionis, *To Set This World Right: The Antislavery Movement in Thoreau's Concord* (Ithaca, N.Y.: Cornell University Press, 2006); Charles Capper and Cristina Giorcelli, eds., *Margaret Fuller: Transatlantic Crossings in a Revolutionary Age* (Madison: University of Wisconsin Press, 2007); Dean Grodzins, *American Heretic: Theodore Parker and Transcendentalism* (Chapel Hill: University of North Carolina Press, 2002); Nadia Urbinati and Alex Zakaras, eds., *J. S. Mill's Political Thought: A Bicentennial Reassessment* (New York: Cambridge University Press, 2007); Stefan Collini, *Public Moralists: Political Thought and Intellectual Life in Britain, 1850–1930* (New York: Oxford University Press, 1991); Butler, *Critical Americans*; Salvo Mastellone, *Mazzini and Marx: Thoughts Upon Democracy in Europe* (Westport, Conn.: Praeger, 2003); Nadia Urbinati, *Mill on Democracy: From the Athenian Polis to Representative Government* (Chicago: University of Chicago Press, 2002).

43. Christopher Leslie Brown has spotlighted the role that concerns about a nation's reputation and "moral capital" played in British reform movements, and Dorothy Ross has argued that broader narratives of the rise of antislavery thought, which focus on the progressive unfolding of liberal or moral sentiment, have obscured the role that nationalism played as a foundation for antislavery critique, particularly in Abraham Lincoln's thinking about emancipation. In this book I will also draw attention to the role that ideas about the "nation" played even in transatlantic Garrisonian abolitionism. See Christopher Leslie Brown, *Moral Capital: Foundations of British Abolitionism* (Chapel Hill: University of North Carolina Press, 2006); Dorothy Ross, "Lincoln and the Ethics of Emancipation: Universalism, Nationalism, Exceptionalism," *Journal of American History* 96, no. 2 (September 2009).

44. Qtd. in Irving H. Bartlett, *Wendell Phillips: Brahmin Radical* (Boston: Beacon Press, 1961), 105; "William Lloyd Garrison," in *SLL: Second Series,* 466. Focusing on these two figures and their closest allies does require leaving to other scholars important questions about the Garrisonians' constitutional theory, the regional diversity of their movement, the limits and radicalism of their explanations of human difference, and even their thinking about the philosophical problem of human bondage itself. Likewise, this book does not attempt to measure their effectiveness in changing public opinion or determine the extent to which Garrisonians contributed directly to the coming of the Civil War, though it does explain how Garrisonians perceived their contributions to the conflict and explores the intellectual sources of those perceptions. Some of the most exciting recent scholarship on the abolitionist movement has considered the question of how abolitionists affected the coming of the Civil War. See, for example, Rugemer, *The Problem of Emancipation*; Elizabeth R. Varon, *Disunion! The Coming of the American Civil War, 1789–1859* (Chapel Hill: University of North Carolina Press, 2008); James Brewer Stewart, "Reconsidering Abolitionists in an Age of Fundamentalist Politics," *Journal of the Early Republic* 26, no. 1 (2006), 1–24; Stanley Harrold, *Subversives: Antislavery Community in Washington, D.C., 1828–1865* (Baton Rouge: Louisiana State University Press, 2003), 253–57. On Garrisonians' contributions to racial theory, see Bruce Dain, *A Hideous Monster of the Mind: American Race Theory in the Early Republic* (Cambridge, Mass.: Harvard University Press, 2002). For good recent works on the regional diversity and rank-and-file members of the abolitionist movement, see Stacey M. Robertson, *Hearts Beating for Liberty: Women Abolitionists in the Old Northwest* (Chapel Hill: University of North Carolina Press, 2010); Julie Roy Jeffrey, *The Great Silent Army of Abolitionism: Ordinary Women in the Antislavery Movement* (Chapel Hill: University of North Carolina Press, 1998).

CHAPTER ONE

1. [William Lloyd Garrison,] *An Address, Delivered before the Members of the Franklin Debating Club, on the Morning of the 5th July, 1824: Being the Forty-Eighth Anniversary of American Independence, by a Member* (Newburyport, Mass.: Herald Office, 1824), 3, 5, 14. For evidence attributing this speech to Garrison, see Mayer, *All On Fire,* 33–34, 639; Garrison and Garrison, *Garrison* 1:56.

2. Garrison and Garrison, *Garrison* 1:45, 96.

3. WLG to the Editor of the Boston *Courier,* [9 July 1829], *LWLG* 1:84; "The Great Crisis!" *Liberator,* December 29, 1832.

4. Garrison and Garrison, *Garrison* 1:127, 130; "The Meeting at Framingham," *Liberator,* July 7, 1854. Two studies that take seriously Garrison's early expressions of patriotism are Ronald G. Walters, *The Antislavery Appeal: American Abolitionism after 1830* (1976; New York: W. W. Norton & Co., 1985), esp. 134–37, and Mayer, *All on Fire.*

5. Garrison and Garrison, *Garrison* 1:127; "The Meeting at Framingham"; "Freedom Triumphant!" *Liberator,* February 10, 1865.

6. Mayer, *All on Fire,* 22–27. On printers' jobs, including the reliance on "exchanges," see Jeffrey L. Pasley, *"The Tyranny of Printers": Newspaper Politics in the Early American Republic* (Charlottesville: University of Virginia Press, 2001), 1–9.

7. Garrison and Garrison, *Garrison* 1:42; James Brewer Stewart, *William Lloyd Garrison and the Challenge of Emancipation* (Arlington Heights, Ill.: Harlan Davidson, 1992), 14–17; Mayer, *All on Fire,* 26–29.

8. Walters, *The Antislavery Appeal,* 134; Marc M. Arkin, "The Federalist Trope: Power and Passion in Abolitionist Rhetoric," *Journal of American History* 88, no. 1 (June 2001): 75–98; John L. Thomas, *The Liberator, William Lloyd Garrison: A Biography* (Boston: Little, Brown & Co., 1963), 27–53; Matthew Mason, "Federalists, Abolitionists, and the Problem of Influence," *American Nineteenth Century History* 10, no. 1 (2009): 1–27; Cleves, *The Reign of Terror in America,* 235–38.

9. Eric Hobsbawm, *The Age of Revolution, 1789–1848* (1962; New York: Vintage, 1996), 109–10; David Sowell, "The Mirror of Public Opinion: Bolívar, Republicanism, and the United States Press, 1821–1831," *Revista de Historia de América* 134 (2004): 165–83; Charles L. Booth, "Let the American Flag Wave in the Aegean: America Responds to the Greek War of Independence (1821–1824)," Ph.D. diss., New York University, 2005; Edward Mead Earle, "American Interest in the Greek Cause, 1821–1827," *The American Historical Review* 33, no. 1 (October 1927): 44–63.

10. "Foreign: The European News," Newburyport *Herald,* February 6, 1821.

11. "From the Liverpool Mercury of April 6," Newburyport *Herald,* May 15, 1821; "Extract from a Letter from an American Gentleman Travelling in Europe, to his Correspondent in Charleston," Newburyport *Herald,* August 21, 1821. See also "La Fayette," December 4, 1821.

12. "Holy Alliance," Newburyport *Herald,* August 17, 1821. From the Newburyport *Herald,* see also "Alarming Proceedings at Manchester," August 16, 1819; "Latest from England," January 19, 1821; "Miscellaneous Items," April 6, 1821; "Latest from Europe," April 3, 1821; "Of Europe," April 10, 1821. On Garrison's early publications, see Mayer, *All on Fire,* 29.

13. For the "South America" series, see Newburyport *Herald,* July 16, 1822; July 19, 1822; July 26, 1822. On the rumors of a Russian war, see "Communication," Newburyport *Herald,* August 6, 1822.

For the "A Glance at Europe" series, see Newburyport *Herald*, April 22, 1823; May 2, 1823; May 16, 1823; WLG to Frances Maria Lloyd Garrison, May 26, 1823, *LWLG* 1:10–14, esp. 11, 13n4.

14. "South America—No. III," Newburyport *Herald*, July 26, 1822; "A Glance at Europe," Newburyport *Herald*, May 16, 1823.

15. "South America—No. I," Newburyport *Herald*, July 16, 1822; "South America—No. III"; "South America—No. II," Newburyport *Herald*, July 19, 1822.

16. "South-America.—No. II"; "South-America.—No. III." On Clay, see James E. Lewis Jr., *The American Union and the Problem of Neighborhood: The United States and the Collapse of the Spanish Empire, 1783–1829* (Baton Rouge: Louisiana State University Press, 1998), qtd. on 158.

17. "A Glance at Europe," Newburyport *Herald*, May 16, 1823. See the communications by "W." in Newburyport *Herald*, July 17, 1821; July 24, 1821.

18. Quotes selected from "A Glance at Europe," May 2, 1823; May 16, 1823.

19. Lewis, *The American Union and the Problem of Neighborhood*, Adams qtd. on 182; Jay Sexton, *The Monroe Doctrine: Empire and Nation in Nineteenth-Century America* (New York: Hill and Wang, 2011), 3–84; Howe, *What Hath God Wrought*, 107–16.

20. [Garrison], *Address*, 3, 5, 6, 8, 9, 13, 14, 16.

21. On "The Shipwreck" and Garrison's poetic aspirations, see Mayer, *All on Fire*, 28–29. On his memorization of "the Ocean," see Garrison and Garrison, *Garrison* 4:332.

22. "Poetry, &c," Newburyport *Herald*, April 29, 1825; Garrison qtd. in Mayer, *All on Fire*, 36; [Garrison], *Address*, 11; "A Glance at Europe," Newburyport *Herald*, May 2, 1823. See also Garrison and Garrison, *Garrison* 1:97.

23. For reports of Byron's escapades in Greece in the *Herald* see the issues for July 1, 1823; March 2, 1824; May 25, 1824; July 5, 1824. On Garrison's interest in Greece, see Garrison and Garrison, *Garrison* 1:63–64. On Howe, see John T. Cumbler, *From Abolition to Rights for All: The Making of a Reform Community in the Nineteenth Century* (Philadelphia: University of Pennsylvania Press, 2008), 39. On Byron's broader appeal to abolitionists and young men on the make, see John Stauffer, *The Black Hearts of Men: Radical Abolitionists and the Transformation of Race* (Cambridge, Mass.: Harvard University Press, 2002); Ethan J. Kytle, "'To Be Free Themselves Must Strike the First Blow': The Romantic Liberalism of Antislavery Intellectuals in the United States, 1845–1865," Ph.D. diss., University of North Carolina–Chapel Hill, 2004, chap. 1; Brian Luskey, *On the Make: Clerks and the Quest for Capital in Nineteenth-Century America* (New York: New York University Press, 2010), 19–20.

24. Garrison and Garrison, *Garrison* 1:57.

25. On Lafeyette's tour, see Fred Somkin, *Unquiet Eagle: Memory and Desire in the Idea of American Freedom, 1815–1860* (Ithaca: Cornell University Press, 1967), 131–74; Robert Pierce Forbes, *The Missouri Compromise and Its Aftermath: Slavery and the Meaning of America* (Chapel Hill: University of North Carolina Press, 2007), 181–84; Lloyd S. Kramer, *Lafayette in Two Worlds: Public Cultures and Personal Identities in an Age of Revolutions* (Chapel Hill: University of North Carolina Press, 1996), 190–95.

26. Lafayette qtd. in Howe, *What Hath God Wrought*, 305.

27. Newburyport *Herald*, September 3, 1824; Garrison and Garrison, *Garrison* 1:57. See also Newburyport *Herald*, August 31, 1824; John Foster, *Sketch of the Tour of General Lafayette, on His Late Visit to the United States, 1824* (Portland: Statesman Office, 1824), 129–32.

28. Quotes selected from "South America—No. III"; "South America—No. I." See also "A Glance at Europe," April 22, 1823; May 2, 1823.

29. "'American Writers,'" Newburyport *Herald*, May 17, 1825.

30. Garrison and Garrison, *Garrison* 1:65, 66. For examples of Garrison's use of "slave" or "enslaved" to refer to political subjection, see [Garrison], *Address*, 7, 9, 13; "South America—No. III," July 26, 1822; "A Glance at Europe," April 22, 1823.

31. See Stewart, *William Lloyd Garrison and the Challenge of Emancipation*, 26–35; Mayer, *All on Fire*, 37–51; Robert H. Abzug, *Cosmos Crumbling: American Reform and the Religious Imagination* (New York: Oxford University Press, 1994), chap. 6.

32. Garrison and Garrison, *Garrison* 1:135.

33. See Mayer, *All on Fire*, 93; Garrison and Garrison, *Garrison* 1:179, 181, 182.

34. See Garrison and Garrison, *Garrison* 1:93–97; "'The National Philanthropist,'" *GUE*, April 12, 1828; Benjamin Lundy, *The Life, Travels, and Opinions of Benjamin Lundy*, comp. Thomas Earle (Philadelphia: William D. Parrish, 1847), 25. On Lundy's career, see Merton L. Dillon, *Benjamin Lundy and the Struggle for Negro Freedom* (Urbana: University of Illinois Press, 1966).

35. "Anniversary of the Declaration of Independence," *GUE*, July 1822; "Portrait of the Holy Alliance," *GUE*, March 25, 1826.

36. "Anniversary of the Declaration of Independence."

37. "Address to the Youth of the U. States: Goodness & Greatness Hostile to Slavery," *GUE*, April 1822.

38. *Annals of Congress*, 15th Cong., 2nd sess., 1211. See also Matthew Mason, *Slavery and Politics in the Early American Republic* (Chapel Hill: University of North Carolina Press, 2006), 191–92; Forbes, *The Missouri Compromise and Its Aftermath*, 35–36, 43–45; Rugemer, *The Problem of Emancipation*, 76–77.

39. François Furstenberg, "Atlantic Slavery, Atlantic Freedom: George Washington, Slavery, and Transatlantic Abolitionist Networks," *William and Mary Quarterly* 68, no. 2 (April 2011): 247–86; Matthew Mason, "Keeping Up Appearances: The International Politics of Slave Trade Abolition in the Nineteenth-Century Atlantic World," *William and Mary Quarterly* 66 (October 2009): 809–32; Matthew Mason, "The Battle of the Slaveholding Liberators: Great Britain, the United States, and Slavery in the Early Nineteenth Century," *William and Mary Quarterly* 59 (July 2002): 665–96; Mason, *Slavery and Politics*, 94–105; Brown, *Moral Capital*, 105–53.

40. "Speech of James Tallmadge Jun.," *GUE*, April 1822; May 1822; June 1822; "Foreign Opinions," *GUE*, September 1821.

41. Lundy qtd. in Davis, *The Problem of Slavery in the Age of Revolution*, 50. Among many examples from the *Genius* illustrative of the points in this paragraph, far too many to cite here, see "Poland" (August 1821); "Colombia" (December 1821); "For the Genius of Universal Emancipation" (March 1822); "Anniversary of the Declaration of Independence" (July 1822); "Mexico" (August 1822); "The 'Mote' and the 'Beam,'" April 10, 1823; "Another Bright Star in the Southern Constellation" (November 1823); "Reason and Truth against Delusion and Error" (February 1824); "Mexican Decree" (December 1824); "General Lafayette" (May 1825); "The Triumph of Philanthropy, or Political Regeneration of America" (May 1825); "To the Editor of the Genius of Universal Emancipation" (April 22, 1826); "For the Genius of Universal Emancipation" (September 15, 1827); "For the

Genius of Universal Emancipation" (July 12, 1828); "Worthy of Imitation" (October 4, 1828); "Correspondence" (May 1830).

42. See Rugemer, *The Problem of Emancipation*, 92–93; Forbes, *The Missouri Compromise and Its Aftermath*, 203–9. For commentary on the Panama Congress in the *GUE*, see "From the N.Y. Daily Advertiser," March 11, 1826; "The First Epistle of Cephas to John," March 25, 1826; "The Second Epistle of Cephas to John," April 1, 1826; "From the Paris Journal des Debats," April 15, 1826; "The Panama Mission," April 15, 1826; "Negro Slavery," May 6, 1826.

43. "For the Genius of Universal Emancipation," *GUE*, September 15, 1827.

44. "For the Genius of Universal Emancipation," *GUE*, February 2, 1828; "Minutes &c. of the American Convention," *GUE*, February 2, 1828; "'Take Notice,'" *GUE*, April 12, 1828; "For the Genius of Universal Emancipation," *GUE*, June 21, 1828; "Views of an English Writer," *GUE*, June 7, 1828. See also "Memorial to Congress," *GUE*, February 2, 1828.

45. "For the Genius of Universal Emancipation," *GUE*, July 12, 1828.

46. "For the Genius of Universal Emancipation," July 12, 1828; WLG to the Editor of the Boston *Courier*, [August 11, 1828,] *LWLG* 1:65; [August 12, 1828,] *LWLG* 1:66; Walter M. Merrill, *Against Wind and Tide: A Biography of Wm. Lloyd Garrison* (Cambridge, Mass.: Harvard University Press, 1963), 23–24; "Fourth of July," *Liberator*, 4 June 1831. In the July 4, 1828, issue of the *Genius*, Lundy reported that he would publish "the communication under the signature 'W.L.'" in the following issue. Lundy professed not to know the writer's identity, but said "we hope to hear from him OFTEN."

47. WLG to Editor of the Boston *Courier*, [July 9, 1829,] *LWLG* 1:84; Garrison and Garrison, *Garrison* 1:127–37, qtd. on 131–32, 137.

48. "Great Britain," *GUE*, October 16, 1829; "Slavery," *GUE*, November 27, 1829; "Washington and Slavery," *GUE*, November 13, 1829. See also "Lafayette," *GUE*, October 30, 1829; "O'Connell and Washington," *GUE*, February 5, 1830.

49. [Garrison,] *Address*, 5. For the concept of the "mobilization of shame," see Sidney Tarrow, *The New Transnational Activism* (New York: Cambridge University Press, 2005), 8; Margaret E. Keck and Kathryn Sikkink, *Activists Beyond Borders: Advocacy Networks in International Politics* (Ithaca, N.Y.: Cornell University Press, 1998), 23.

50. On the importance of black abolitionists to the origins of immediatism, see Richard S. Newman, *The Transformation of American Abolitionism: Fighting Slavery in the Early Republic* (Chapel Hill: University of North Carolina Press, 2002), 86–105.

51. "To the Public," *GUE*, 2 September 1829.

52. Peter P. Hinks, *To Awaken My Afflicted Brethren: David Walker and the Problem of Antebellum Slave Resistance* (University Park: Pennsylvania State University Press, 1997), 112–17; Julie Winch, *A Gentleman of Color: The Life of James Forten* (New York: Oxford University Press, 2002), 239–49.

53. "To the Public," *Liberator*, January 1, 1831.

54. William Lloyd Garrison, *Thoughts on African Colonization, or, An Impartial Exhibition of the Doctrines, Principles and Purposes of the American Colonization Society, together with the Resolutions, Addresses and Remonstrances of the Free People of Color* (Boston: Garrison and Knapp, 1832), part 2, 4, 6; part 1, 134.

55. Garrison, *Thoughts on African Colonization*, part 1, 21; "Marriage Bill," *Liberator*, March 19, 1831; "The Marriage Law," *Liberator*, May 7, 1831; "Thoughts on Color," *Liberator*, August 27, 1831; "The Marriage Question," *Liberator*, November 17, 1832. On race and immediatism, see Paul Good-

man, *Of One Blood: Abolitionism and the Origins of Racial Equality* (Berkeley: University of California Press, 1998).

56. "The Insurrection," *Liberator,* September 3, 1831; "Insurrection in Virginia," *GUE,* September 1831. See also "The Virginia Massacre," *GUE,* December 1831.

57. Peter P. Hinks, ed., *David Walker's Appeal to the Coloured Citizens of the World* (University Park: Pennsylvania State University Press, 2000), 15, 42, 43, 77. See also Winch, *Gentleman of Color,* 4; Julie Winch, "'Onward, Onward, Is Indeed the Watchword': James Forten's Reflections on Revolution and Liberty," in *Prophets of Protest: Reconsidering the History of American Abolitionism,* ed. Timothy Patrick McCarthy and John Stauffer (New York: New Press, 2006), 80–89.

58. Garrison, *Thoughts on African Colonization,* part 1, 142, 146.

59. Hobsbawm, *The Age of Revolution,* 110–31.

60. "To-Day," *Liberator,* January 1, 1831; "Prospectus of the Liberator," *Liberator,* May 28, 1831; Forten qtd. in Winch, *Gentlemen of Color,* 245.

61. Wm. Lloyd Garrison, *An Address, delivered before the Free People of Color, in Philadelphia, New-York, and Other Cities, during the Month of June, 1831* (Boston: Stephen Foster, 1831), 4; "The Liberator and Slavery," *Liberator,* January 7, 1832.

62. "Lafayette," *Liberator,* January 8, 1831; "The Insurrection," *Liberator,* September 3, 1831; "Guilt of New-England," *Liberator,* January 7, 1832. See also "The Slave Trade in the Capital," *Liberator,* January 1, 1831; "Walker's Appeal," *Liberator,* January 8, 1831; Garrison and Garrison, *Garrison* 1:250.

63. "The Insurrection."

64. WLG to the Editor of the London *Patriot,* [August 6, 1833,] *LWLG* 1:251.

65. Garrison and Garrison, *Garrison* 1:127; "Slavery and the Means of its Removal," *Liberator,* April 14, 1832. On the myths surrounding emancipation in Massachusetts, see Minardi, *Making Slavery History,* chap. 1.

66. "The Liberator," *Liberator,* January 22, 1831; "Anti-Slavery Convention," *Liberator,* November 26, 1831; Amos A. Phelps, *Lectures on Slavery and Its Remedy* (Boston: New-England Anti-Slavery Society, 1834), 187; "Prospectus of the Liberator," *Liberator,* May 28, 1831; "The Liberator and Slavery," *Liberator,* January 7, 1832.

67. "The Exile's Departure," in *Poems of John Greenleaf Whittier* (New York: Thomas Y. Crowell, 1902), 329. A few years later, Whittier would also publish, in the *Liberator,* a brief essay on "Byron's Writings." Though troubled by Byron's infidelity, like Garrison himself, Whittier confessed that the great man's poetry had irresistible power. See Whittier, "Byron's Writings," *Liberator,* October 13, 1832, and Byron's "To Miss Chatworth," in *Liberator,* October 3, 1835; Alonzo Lewis, "Byron," *Liberator,* August 27, 1831.

68. Mayer, *All on Fire,* 107.

69. WLG to Messrs. J. Telemachus Hilton, Robert Wood, and J. H. How, August 13, 1831, *LWLG* 1:125.

70. Garrison, *An Address, delivered before the Free People of Color,* 4.

CHAPTER TWO

1. WLG to *The Liberator,* May 23, 1833, *LWLG* 1:228; WLG to HEG, May 28, 1840, *LWLG* 2:630; WLG to Samuel J. May, December 19, 1846, *LWLG* 3:462.

2. WLG to the Board of Managers of the New England Anti-Slavery Society, June 20, 1833, *LWLG* 1:237; and July 1, 1833, *LWLG* 1:243. To see the statement against colonization signed by the abolitionist luminaries mentioned, see "Petition Letter in Opposition to the American Colonization Society," New-York Historical Society, Manuscript Collections Relating to Slavery, cdm15052. contentdm.oclc.org/u?/p15052coll5,25445 (accessed on April 30, 2011).

3. WLG to Harriott Plummer, March 4, 1833, *LWLG* 1:206–7.

4. WLG to the Editor of the *Moral Daily Advertiser,* [May 2, 1833,] *LWLG* 1:226, 227. See Marcus Wood, *Blind Memory: Visual Representations of Slavery in England and America, 1780–1865* (London: Routledge, 2000), 41–68; Marcus Wood, ed., *The Poetry of Slavery: An Anglo-American Anthology, 1764–1865* (New York: Oxford University Press, 2003), 299–304; Leo Costello, "Turner's *The Slave Ship* (1840): Towards a Dialectical History Painting," in *Discourses of Slavery and Abolition: Britain and its Colonies, 1760–1838,* ed. Brycchan Carey, Markman Ellis, and Sara Salih (Houndmills, Basingstoke, Hampshire, U.K.: Palgrave Macmillan, 2004), 209–22; Carl Thompson, *The Suffering Traveller and the Romantic Imagination* (New York: Oxford University Press, 2007).

5. On Paul and Stuart, see Blackett, *Building an Antislavery Wall,* chap. 2; Anthony J. Barker, *Captain Charles Stuart, Anglo-American Abolitionist* (Baton Rouge: Louisiana State University Press, 1986).

6. Donald Yacovone, *Samuel Joseph May and the Dilemmas of the Liberal Persuasion, 1797–1871* (Philadelphia: Temple University Press, 1991), 37–40, May qtd. on 37.

7. See Newman, *Transformation of American Abolitionism;* Goodman, *Of One Blood,* 54–64.

8. "Extracts from the Rev. Mr. May's Sermon on Slavery," *Liberator,* July 2, 1831; "Fourth of July at Attleborough," *Liberator,* July 12, 1834; "Expostulation," in *The Complete Poetical Works of John Greenleaf Whittier* (Boston: Houghton Mifflin, 1894), 267–68, qtd. on 268. See also "Savage and Barbarous Customs of Different Nations," *The Abolitionist* (March 1833), 41; "Revolutionary Movements," *Liberator,* April 30, 1831; "Remarkable Instance of Forgetfulness," *Liberator,* June 11, 1831; "Abominable," *Liberator,* July 16, 1831; "Causes of Slave Insurrections," *Liberator,* September 17, 1831; WLG to Joseph Gales and William W. Seaton, [ca. September 23, 1831,] *LWLG* 1:130–35; "Abstract Enemies to Slavery," *Liberator,* May 11, 1833; "Debate on Colonization," *Liberator,* June 8, 1833; *Proceedings of the New England Anti-Slavery Convention . . .* (Boston: Garrison and Knapp, 1834), 7, 10, 45; "Anti-Slavery Address," *Liberator,* July 4, 1835; *Proceedings of the New England Anti-Slavery Convention . . .* (Boston: Isaac Knapp, 1836), 18.

9. David Lee Child, *The Despotism of Freedom; or the Tyranny and Cruelty of American Republican Slave-Masters, Shown to be the Worst in the World; in a speech, delivered at the first anniversary of the New England Anti-Slavery Society, 1833* (Boston: Young Men's Antislavery Association, 1834), 66; "Annual Meeting of the New England Anti-Slavery Society," *Liberator,* January 26, 1833; Lydia Maria Child, *An Appeal in Favor of that Class of Americans called Africans* (1833; New York: John S. Taylor, 1836), 205. On Child's European experience, see Carolyn L. Karcher, *The First Woman in the Republic: A Cultural Biography of Lydia Maria Child* (Durham, N.C.: Duke University Press, 1994), 48–49.

10. James Brewer Stewart, "The Emergence of Racial Modernity and the Rise of the White North, 1790–1840," *Journal of the Early Republic* 18, no. 2 (Summer 1998): 181–217; W. Caleb McDaniel, "The Fourth and the First: Abolitionist Holidays, Respectability, and Radical Interracial Reform," *American Quarterly* 57, no. 1 (2005): 129–51.

11. WLG to Samuel Fessenden, November 30, 1832, *LWLG* 1:192; Arnold Buffum to WLG, October 18, 1832, *BAA,* 20; WLG to Harriet Minot, March 19, 1833, *LWLG* 1:215; WLG to Samuel J. May, December 4, 1832, *LWLG* 1:193. See also *Credentials of William Lloyd Garrison, Esq. from the Managers*

of the New England Anti-Slavery Society and the Free People of Colour (Boston?: W. Johnston, 1833); Joseph Phillips to WLG, June 6, 1832, *BAA*, 19; WLG to Henry Brougham, August 1, 1832, *LWLG* 1:160–61. For an overview of the British movement, see Drescher, *Abolition*, 205–67.

12. Garrison and Garrison, *Garrison* 1:412; Arthur Tappan qtd. in Bertram Wyatt-Brown, *Lewis Tappan and the Evangelical War Against Slavery* (rpt., Baton Rouge: Louisiana State University Press, 1997), 103. See also Fladeland, *Men and Brothers*, 208–9.

13. *Second Annual Report of the American Anti-Slavery Society . . .* (New York: William S. Dorr, 1835), 26, 32–33; Rugemer, *The Problem of Emancipation*, 222–57; McDaniel, "The Fourth and the First"; Julie Roy Jeffrey, "'No Occurrence in Human History Is More Deserving of Commemoration Than This': Abolitionist Celebrations of Freedom," in McCarthy and Stauffer, eds., *Prophets of Protest*, 200–219.

14. WLG to the Patrons of *The Liberator* and the Friends of Abolition, [October 11, 1833,] *LWLG* 1:264.

15. See WLG to the *Liberator*, May 24, 1833, *LWLG* 1:230–33, esp. 233.

16. See Sam W. Haynes, *Unfinished Revolution: The Early American Republic in a British World* (Charlottesville: University of Virginia Press, 2010), 179–203; Edward B. Rugemer, "The Southern Response to British Abolitionism: The Maturation of Proslavery Apologetics," *Journal of Southern History* 70, no. 2 (May 2004): 221–48.

17. William Lloyd Garrison, comp., *Lectures of George Thompson . . . Also, a Brief History of His Connection with the Anti-Slavery Cause in England* (Boston: Isaac Knapp, 1836), xii; James Cropper to WLG, May 17, 1834, *BAA*, 30. On the dispiriting experiences in France, see Lawrence C. Jennings, *French Anti-Slavery: The Movement for the Abolition of Slavery in France, 1802–1848* (New York: Cambridge University Press, 2006), 1–23.

18. "Lafayette Plan," *GUE*, September 1825. See also "Lafayette Plan," *GUE*, February 18, 1826. On the uniqueness of Thompson's tour, see C. Duncan Rice, *The Scots Abolitionists, 1833–1861* (Baton Rouge: Louisiana State University Press, 1981), 63–68; C. Duncan Rice, "The Anti-Slavery Mission of George Thompson to the United States, 1834–1835," *Journal of American Studies* 2, no. 1 (1968): 13–31, esp. 15–16.

19. "George Thompson, Esq.," *Liberator*, March 22, 1834; George Thompson to WLG, March 27, 1834, *BAA*, 28, 29.

20. Mayer, *All on Fire*, 159; Ronald M. Gifford II, "George Thompson and Trans-Atlantic Antislavery, 1831 –1865," Ph.D. diss., Indiana University, 1999, 98, 107–8; WLG to Helen E. Benson, June 2, 1834, *LWLG* 1:357; WLG to Lewis Tappan, February 29, 1836, *LWLG* 2:52.

21. "George Thompson, Esq." See also Gifford, "George Thompson and Trans-Atlantic Antislavery," 78–79.

22. Edmund Spevack, *Charles Follen's Search for Nationality and Freedom: Germany and America, 1796–1840* (Cambridge, Mass.: Harvard University Press, 1997).

23. Follen quoted in Spevack, *Charles Follen's Search*, 119; WLG to George W. Benson, March 13, 1834, *LWLG* 1:293. See also Debra Gold Hansen, *Strained Sisterhood: Gender and Class in the Boston Female Anti-Slavery Society* (Amherst: University of Massachusetts Press, 1993); Spevack, *Charles Follen's Search*, 206–18.

24. Martineau qtd. in Spevack, *Charles Follen's Search*, 226. See Garrison and Garrison, *Garrison* 1:441; Eliza Lee Follen, *The Life of Charles Follen* (Boston: Thomas H. Webb, 1844), 91–95, 102; WLG to Charles Follen, 18 March 1834, *LWLG* 1:294–95. Follen was a darling of local Transcendentalists.

See Charles Capper, *Margaret Fuller: An American Romantic Life* (New York: Oxford University Press, 1992), 84, 115; Lewis Perry, *Intellectual Life in America: A History* (Chicago: University of Chicago Press, 1989), 212–13.

25. Charles Follen, *Address to the People of the United States on the Subject of Slavery* (Boston: Garrison and Knapp, 1834), 15, 16.

26. "George Thompson, Esq." For Thompson as a "*moral* Lafayette," see WLG to Peleg Sprague, September 5, 1835, *LWLG* 1:513.

27. *Letters and Addresses by George Thompson, During his Mission in the United States, From Oct. 1st, 1834, to Nov. 27, 1835* (Boston: Isaac Knapp, 1837), 78; "Mr. Thompson's Anti-Slavery Lecture at Lowell, Mass.," *Liberator,* October 11, 1834. See also *Letters and Addresses by George Thompson,* 11, 66, 119–20; *Reception of George Thompson in Great Britain, Compiled from Various British Publications* (Boston: Isaac Knapp, 1836), 122.

28. David Grimsted, *American Mobbing, 1828–1861: Toward Civil War* (New York: Oxford University Press, 1998), 4, 36; Leonard L. Richards, *Gentlemen of Property and Standing: Anti-Abolition Mobs in Jacksonian America* (New York: Oxford University Press, 1970), 65–71; WLG to Henry E. Benson, September 12, 1835, *LWLG* 1:525–26.

29. See Mayer, *All on Fire,* 199; Garrison and Garrison, *Garrison* 2:1–72.

30. "Arrival of George Thompson, Esq.," *Liberator,* September 27, 1834; WLG to HEG, July 15, 1834, *LWLG* 1:375; "George Thompson," *Liberator,* October 18, 1834; George Thompson to WLG, 24 September 1834, *BAA,* 33. See also "Extracts from the First Annual Report of the New York State Anti-Slavery Society," *Liberator,* December 17, 1836; WLG to George Benson, September 4, 1835, *LWLG* 1:495.

31. WLG to Peleg Sprague, September 5, 1835, *LWLG* 1:513. For other comparisons between Thompson and Lafayette, see "George Thompson," *Liberator,* August 29, 1835; "George Thompson," *Liberator,* September 12, 1835; *Letters and Addresses by George Thompson,* v–xi; "Extracts from the First Annual Report of the New York State Anti-Slavery Society," *Liberator,* December 17, 1836.

32. Vaux qtd. in Grimsted, *American Mobbing,* 11. See Rugemer, *The Problem of Emancipation.* For Thompson's speeches on St. Domingo, see Garrison, *Letters and Addresses of George Thompson,* 31, 79–83.

33. WLG to HEG, November 7, 1835, *LWLG* 1:549.

34. Lyon G. Tyler, *The Letters and Times of the Tylers* (Richmond, Va.: Whittet & Shepperson, 1884), vol. 1:575–7. For Clay, see Phillip Lapsansky, "Graphic Discord: Abolitionist and Antiabolitionist Images," in Jean Fagan Yellin and John C. Van Horne, eds., *The Abolitionist Sisterhood: Women's Political Culture in Antebellum America* (Ithaca: Cornell University Press, 1994), 227.

35. George Thompson to WLG, 25 November 1835, *BAA,* 51.

36. James D. Richardson, ed., *A Compilation of the Messages and Papers of the Presidents, 1789–1897* (Washington: Government Printing Office, 1896), vol. 3:175; James K. Paulding, *Slavery in the United States* (New York: Harper & Brothers, 1836), 306. See also Garrison's letters to Harrison Gray Otis in *LWLG* 1:496–504, 530–36. On postal campaign and backlash, see Richard R. John, *Spreading the News: The American Postal System from Franklin to Morse* (Cambridge, Mass.: Harvard University Press, 1995), chap. 7; Trish Loughran, *The Republic in Print: Print Culture in the Age of U.S. Nation Building, 1770–1870* (New York: Columbia University Press, 2007), chap. 6.

37. James Brewer Stewart, *Holy Warriors: The Abolitionists and American Slavery,* rev. ed. (New York: Hill and Wang, 1997), 83–85; Daniel Wirls, "'The Only Mode of Avoiding Everlasting Debate':

The Overlooked Senate Gag Rule for Antislavery Petitions," *Journal of the Early Republic* 27, no. 1 (Spring 2007), 115–38; Spevack, *Charles Follen's Search*, 241–44.

38. "Extraordinary Proceedings in Rhode Island—Insult Added to Injury—The Rights of Citizens Invaded," *Liberator*, July 2, 1836; Ira V. Brown, "An Antislavery Agent: C. C. Burleigh in Pennsylvania, 1836–1837," *Pennsylvania Magazine of History and Biography* 105, no. 1 (1981): 77–79. See also Newman, *Transformation of American Abolitionism*, 152–75; Stewart, *Holy Warriors*, 67–68; Grimsted, *American Mobbing*, 33–37.

39. Garrison and Garrison, *Garrison* 2:28.

40. "American Republicanism in Europe," *Liberator*, February 23, 1838. For trips mentioned, see Winch, *Gentleman of Color*, 262–63; WLG to Joseph Sturge, May 7, 1838, HL, bMS, Am 1054 (191); GT to Edward M. Davis, July 10, 1838, HL, bMS, Am 1054 (170); Samuel J. May, *Some Recollections of our Antislavery Conflict* (Boston: Fields, Osgood and Co., 1869), 316–17. See also Temperley, *British Antislavery*, 62–92; Fladeland, *Men and Brothers*, 324–29.

41. On British West Indies trips, see Rugemer, *The Problem of Emancipation*, 165–70; Gale L. Kenny, *Contentious Liberties: American Abolitionists in Post-Emancipation Jamaica, 1834–1866* (Athens: University of Georgia Press, 2010). On the Burleigh, Gunn, and Douglas mission to Haiti, see Brown, "An Antislavery Agent," 84; "Abolition in Hayti," *Liberator*, February 9, 1838; Winch, *Gentleman of Color*, 220; "Speech of Charles C. Burleigh, at a Meeting of the Haytien Abolition Society," Philadelphia *National Enquirer and Constitutional Advocate of Universal Liberty*, February 15, 1838; "Letters from Haiti," *Pennsylvania Freeman*, April 12, 1838. On the Chapmans in Haiti, see MWC, "Haiti," *Liberty Bell* (1842), 164–204; "Letter from Inginac, of Haiti," *Liberator*, July 23, 1841; "Letter from Port-au-Prince," *NASS*, June 26, 1846; John Telemachus Hilton to Chapmans, April 30, 1841, BPL, Ms.A.9.2.15.43; MWC to WLG, January 19, 1841, BPL, Ms.A.1.2.11.33; P. Tredwell to the Chapmans, May 17, 1841, BPL, Ms.A.9.2.15.45; Caroline Weston to Deborah Weston, July 20, 1841, BPL, Ms.A.9.2.3.104, and other related letters in the BPL, especially from William P. Griffin to Chapman. The Haytien Abolition Society appears to have been an organization founded by Anglophone immigrants and missionaries on the island.

42. Fladeland, *Men and Brothers*, 251–52; John F. Quinn, "Expecting the Impossible? Abolitionist Appeals to the Irish in Antebellum America," *New England Quarterly* 82, no. 4 (December 2009): 674–75; Nini Rodgers, "Richard Robert Madden: an Irish Anti-Slavery Activist in the Americas," in *Ireland Abroad: Politics and Professions in the Nineteenth Century*, ed. Oonagh Walsh (Dublin: Four Courts Press, 2002), 119–31.

43. Drescher, *Abolition*, 304, estimates that by 1838 "there were 1,346 local antislavery organizations in the northern states claiming 100,000 members." Other membership estimates range as high as 300,000. See Eric Foner, *The Fiery Trial: Abraham Lincoln and American Slavery* (New York: W. W. Norton, 2010), 21. On Thompson's impact on the people mentioned, see Beth Salerno, *Sister Societies: Women's Antislavery Organizations in Antebellum America* (DeKalb: Northern Illinois University Press, 2005), 29–30; *Memorial of Sarah Pugh: A Tribute of Respect from Her Cousins* (Philadelphia: J. B. Lippincott, 1888), 15; Kathryn Kish Sklar, "'The Throne of My Heart': Religion, Oratory, and Transatlantic Community in Angelina Grimké's Launching of Women's Rights, 1828–1838," in Sklar and Stewart, eds., *Women's Rights and Transatlantic Antislavery*, 222; Jane H. Pease and William Henry Pease, *Bound with Them in Chains: a Biographical History of the Antislavery Movement* (Westport, Conn.: Greenwood Press, 1972), 32; Lewis Perry, *Childhood, Marriage, and Reform: Henry Clarke Wright, 1797–1870* (Chicago: University of Chicago Press, 1980), 19–21; Vincent Sparks, "Abolition

in Silver Slippers: A Biography of Edmund Quincy," Ph.D. diss., Boston College, 1978, chap. 2; James Brewer Stewart, *Wendell Phillips: Liberty's Hero* (rpt., Baton Rouge: Louisiana State University Press, 1998), chap. 4; Cumbler, *From Abolition to Rights for All,* 21.

44. *Life of John C. Calhoun, Presenting a Condensed History of Political Events from 1811 to 1843, Together with a Selection from his Speeches* (New York: Harper and Brothers, 1843), 207; "Abolition Debate in Congress," *Liberator,* March 19, 1836; *Selections from the Letters and Speeches of the Hon. James H. Hammond, of South Carolina* (New York: John F. Trow, 1866), 26.

45. "Speech of Charles C. Burleigh"; Quinn, "Expecting the Impossible?" 672–73; Fladeland, *Men and Brothers,* 241–42.

46. Gifford, "George Thompson and Trans-Atlantic Antislavery," 176–79; Luke E. Harlow, "From Border South to Solid South: Religion, Race, and the Making of Confederate Kentucky, 1830–1880," Ph.D. diss., Rice University, 2009, 52–56.

47. Van Gosse, "'As a Nation, the English are Our Friends': The Emergence of African American Politics in the British Atlantic World, 1772–1861," *American Historical Review* 113, no. 4 (October 2008): 1003–28; Blackett, *Building an Antislavery Wall;* Rugemer, *The Problem of Emancipation;* Gerald Horne, *Negro Comrades of the Crown: African Americans and the British Empire Fight the U.S. Before Emancipation* (New York: New York University, 2012); Benjamin Quarles, *Black Abolitionists* (New York: Oxford University Press, 1969), 116–42.

48. Follen, *Life of Charles Follen,* 247; Harriet Martineau, *Society in America,* (New York: Saunders and Otley, 1837), vol. 2:203–4; "The Martyr Age of the United States," in Harriet Martineau, *Writings on Slavery and the American Civil War,* ed. Deborah A. Logan (DeKalb: Northern Illinois University Press, 2002), 44–80; Deborah A. Logan, "The Redemption of a Heretic: Harriet Martineau and Anglo-American Abolitionism," in Sklar and Stewart, eds., *Women's Rights and Transatlantic Antislavery,* 242–65; Anderson, *Joyous Greetings,* 124–28. For examples of Thompson's speeches on his return, see *Reception of George Thompson;* George Thompson, *An Appeal to the Abolitionists of Great Britain, in Behalf of the Cause of Universal Emancipation* (Edinburgh: William Oliphant and Son, 1837).

49. Clare Midgley, *Women Against Slavery: The British Campaigns, 1780–1870* (London: Routledge, 1992), 128–32; MWC to EPN, December 30, 1837, *BAA,* 63; MWC to EPN, 30 August 1838, *BAA,* 66; Mary Wigham to MWC, 1 April 1839, *BAA,* 69–70; Sarah M. Grimké to EPN, 14 May 1839, *BAA,* 70–71.

50. Dona Brown, "Travel Books," in *A History of the Book in America,* vol. 2: *An Extensive Republic: Print, Culture, and Society in the New Nation, 1790–1840,* ed. Robert A. Gross and Mary Kelley (Chapel Hill: University of North Carolina Press, 2010), 449–58. On an earlier, similar war of words between American and British writers, see Jennifer Clark, "Poisoned Pens: The Anglo-American Relationship and the Paper War," *Symbiosis: A Journal of Anglo-American Literary Relations* 6 (2002): 45–68.

51. Fladeland, *Men and Brothers,* 238–39; "Literary Intelligence: Slavery," *Liberator,* October 10, 1835; Martineau, *Writings on Slavery and the American Civil War,* 3–43.

52. John Hyslop Bell, *British Folks and British India Fifty Years Ago: Joseph Pease and His Contemporaries* (London: John Heywood, 1891), 12–13, 20–21, 68–77; EPN to MWC, July 11, 1839, *BAA,* 72–73; Ann and Wendell Phillips to MWC, July 30, 1839, *BAA,* 77–78; Angelina Grimké Weld to EPN, August 14, 1839; MWC to EPN, August 20, 1839, *BAA,* 81; MWC to EPN, March 16, 1840, BPL,

Ms.A.1.2.9.20; Edward M. Davis to EPN, December 28, 1839, BPL, Ms.A.1.2.8.93; Gerrit Smith to EPN, April 20, 1840, HL, bMS, Am 1906 (621); MWC to EPN, April 21, 1840, BPL, Ms.A.1.2.9.28; William Bassett to EPN, April 25, 1840, BPL, Ms.A.1.2.9.31. See also Elizabeth Kelly Gray, "'Whisper to Him the Word "India"': Trans-Atlantic Critics and American Slavery, 1830–1860," *Journal of the Early Republic* 28, no. 3 (Fall 2008): 379–406.

53. Resolution of the BFASS qtd. in Fladeland, *Men and Brothers*, 260. See also Temperley, *British Antislavery*, 62–84, 184–96; Anne Heloise Abel and Frank Joseph Klingberg, eds., *A Side-light on Anglo-American Relations, 1839–1858* ([Lancaster, Pa.]: Association for the Study of Negro Life and History, 1927), 4–10.

54. *Fourth Annual Report of the Board of Managers of the Massachusetts Anti-Slavery Society* (Boston: Isaac Knapp, 1836), 41.

55. Elisa Tamarkin, *Anglophilia: Deference, Devotion, and Antebellum America* (Chicago: University of Chicago Press, 2008); Kariann Akemi Yokota, *Unbecoming British: How Revolutionary America Became a Postcolonial Nation* (New York: Oxford University Press, 2011); Haynes, *Unfinished Revolution*; Jack P. Greene, "Colonial History and National History: Reflections on a Continuing Problem," *William and Mary Quarterly* 64, no. 2 (April 2007): 235–50; Joseph Eaton, "From Anglophile to Nationalist: Robert Walsh's *An Appeal from the Judgments of Great Britain*," *Pennsylvania Magazine of History & Biography* 132:2 (April 2008): 141–71; Richard Gravil, *Romantic Dialogues: Anglo-American Continuities, 1776–1862* (New York: St. Martin's Press, 2000); Leonard Tennenhouse, *The Importance of Feeling English: American Literature and the British Diaspora, 1750–1850* (Princeton, N.J.: Princeton University Press, 2007); Paul Giles, *Transatlantic Insurrections: British Culture and the Formation of American Literature, 1730–1860* (Philadelphia: University of Pennsylvania Press, 2001); Anthony Mann, "'A Nation First in All the Arts of Civilisation': Boston's Post-Revolutionary Elites View Great Britain," *American Nineteenth-Century History* 2, no. 2 (Summer 2001): 1–34.

56. Cleves, *The Reign of Terror in America*; Richard Carwardine, *Transatlantic Revivalism: Popular Evangelicalism in Britain and America, 1790–1865* (Westport, Conn.: Greenwood Press, 1978); Thistlethwaite, *The Anglo-American Connection*.

57. Sparks, "Abolition in Silver Slippers," chap. 1; Stewart, *Wendell Phillips*, 1–42.

58. Stewart, *Wendell Phillips*, 58–64, Phillips qtd. on 62. See also James Brewer Stewart, "Boston, Abolition, and the Atlantic World, 1820–1861," in *Courage and Conscience: Black and White Abolitionists in Boston*, ed. Donald M. Jacobs (Bloomington: Indiana University Press, 1993), 101–26.

59. WP to EPN, August 12, 1842, BPL, Ms.A.1.2.12.2.77; WP to RDW, August 12, 1842, BPL, Ms.A.1.2.12.2.76; Wendell Phillips, "The Benefits of West India Emancipation," in John A. Collins, *The Anti-Slavery Picknick: A Collection of Speeches, Poems, Dialogues and Songs; Intended for Use in Schools and Anti-Slavery Meetings* (Boston: H. W. Williams, 1842), 23.

60. *Reception of George Thompson*, 67, 44–45; *Letters and Addresses by George Thompson*, 66; David Lee Child, *Oration in Honor of Universal Emancipation in the British Empire, delivered at South Reading, August First, 1834* (Boston: Garrison and Knapp, 1834), 4, 5. See also Rugemer, *The Problem of Emancipation*, 138.

61. Tamarkin, *Anglophilia*, chap. 3; Patrick Rael, *Black Identity and Black Protest in the Antebellum North* (Chapel Hill: University of North Carolina Press, 2002), 227–29.

62. EQ to MWC and Henry G. Chapman, February 25, 1841, BPL, Ms.A.9.2.13.26–28; Child, *Oration*, 35, 36.

63. Robert A. Gross, "Introduction: An Extensive Republic," in *A History of the Book in America*, vol. 2, 1–50; Michael Winship, "The International Trade in Books," in *The History of the Book in America*, vol. 3: *The Industrial Book, 1840–1880*, ed. Scott E. Caspar, Jeffrey D. Groves, Stephen W. Nissenbaum, and Winship (Chapel Hill: University of North Carolina Press, 2007), 148–56; Wayne E. Fuller, *The American Mail: Enlarger of the Common Life* (Chicago: University of Chicago Press, 1972), 210; Richard A. Schwarzlose, "The Foreign Connection: Transatlantic Newspapers in the 1840s," *Journalism History* 10, nos. 3–4 (1983): 44–49.

64. *Fifteenth Annual Report, Presented to the Massachusetts Anti-Slavery Society, by Its Board of Managers, January 27, 1847* (Boston: Andrews & Prentiss, 1847), 55.

65. WP to GT, July 29, 1839, *BAA*, 74–75. Phillips repeated this idea in "Welcome to George Thompson," *SLL: Second Series*, 29.

66. *Fourth Annual Report of the Board of Managers of the Massachusetts Anti-Slavery Society*, 41.

CHAPTER THREE

1. Stewart, *Holy Warriors*, 88–96.

2. Much of the existing scholarship on post-1840 transatlantic abolitionism emphasizes the destructiveness of the American schism. See, for example, Turley, *The Culture of English Antislavery*, 205–6, 217–26; Thistlethwaite, *Anglo-American Connection*, 113–18; Christine Bolt, *The Anti-Slavery Movement and Reconstruction: A Study in Anglo-American Co-Operation, 1833–77* (New York: Oxford University Press, 1969), 24; David Brion Davis, "The Other Revolution," *The New York Review of Books* 47, no. 15 (October 5, 2000), www.nybooks.com/articles/13841. Cf. Temperley, *British Antislavery*, 92; Fladeland, *Men and Brothers*, 301.

3. Quirk Ogee, *Extracts from Humbugiana: or, The World's Convention. A Satire. In Four Parts* (Gotham: Gas, Green & Ginger, 1847), 6; "Parricides of the Republic," *United States Magazine and Democratic Review*, reprinted in *NASS*, July 10, 1851; George Putnam, *God and Our Country: A Discourse Delivered in the First Congregational Church in Roxbury, on Fast Day, April 8, 1847* (Boston: Crosby and Nichols, 1847), 7–13, qtd. on 18.

4. George Bradburn to RDW, March 26, 1845, BPL, Ms.A.1.2.15.32; "Non-Voting Theory: Reply to Messrs. White, Earle, and Bowditch," *Liberator*, October 25, 1844.

5. C. Peter Ripley, ed., *The Black Abolitionist Papers*, vol. 1: *The British Isles, 1830–1865* (Chapel Hill: University of North Carolina Press, 1985), 73; WLG to EQ, August 14, 1846, *LWLG* 3:370.

6. Davis, *Slavery and Human Progress*, 115–16; *Twentieth Annual Report, Presented to the Massachusetts Anti-Slavery Society, by its Board of Managers* (Boston: Prentiss & Sawyer, 1852), 46.

7. Blassingame, ed., *Frederick Douglass Papers* 1:35, 96.

8. "Magnificent Enterprise of Joseph Sturge," *Emancipator*, March 28, 1839; "The World's Convention," *Liberator*, March 20, 1840; Edward M. Davis to EPN, March 30, 1840, BPL, Ms.A.1.2.9.23. For the planning of the convention, see BFASS Minute Books, vol. 1:34, 38, 41, 52, 61–81, 103, *RHAP* (reel 1). For previous accounts of the "World's Convention," see Kathryn Kish Sklar, "'Women Who Speak for an Entire Nation': American and British Women at the World Anti-Slavery Convention, London, 1840," in Yellin and Van Horne, eds., *The Abolitionist Sisterhood*, 301–33; Donald R. Kennon, "'An Apple of Discord': The Woman Question at the World's Anti-Slavery Convention of 1840," *Slavery & Abolition* 5, no. 3 (1984): 244–66; Douglas H. Maynard, "The World's Anti-Slavery Conven-

tion of 1840," *The Mississippi Valley Historical Review* 47, no. 3 (1960): 452–71; Fladeland, *Men and Brothers*, 259–73.

9. Angelina G. Weld to EPN, August 14, 1839, BPL, Ms.A.1.2.8.49; William E. Channing to James G. Birney, April 14, 1840, in Dumond, ed., *Letters of James Gillespie Birney* 1:553; Pennsylvania Anti-Slavery Society Minute Book, 1838–46, 48, in Pennsylvania Abolition Society Papers, Historical Society of Pennsylvania, Ser. 5, Reel 31.

10. Mayer, *All on Fire*, 222–28.

11. Lewis Perry, *Radical Abolitionism: Anarchy and the Government of God in Antislavery Thought* (rpt., Knoxville: University of Tennessee Press, 1995).

12. Aileen S. Kraditor, *Means and Ends*, 39–77; Hansen, *Strained Sisterhood*; Kathryn Kish Sklar, *Women's Rights Emerges Within the Anti-Slavery Movement, 1830–1870: A Short History with Documents* (Boston: Bedford/St. Martin's, 2000).

13. Gamaliel Bailey to James Birney, April 18, 1840, in Dumond, ed., *Letters of James Gillespie Birney* 1:557. See also "The London Conference," *Emancipator*, March 26, 1840; Lewis Tappan to A. A. Phelps, May 19, 1840, BPL, Ms.A.21.11.47; Lewis Tappan to John Scoble, May 5, 1840, in Abel and Klingberg, eds., *Side-light*, 69–70; Joshua Leavitt to James Birney, June 1, 1840, in *Letters of James Gillespie Birney*, 1:581. For the BFASS decisions regarding women delegates, see BFASS Minute Books, vol. 1:206–12, 223–24, RHAP (reel 1); "London Convention—Letter from Mr. Sturge," *Liberator*, May 8, 1840.

14. See *Proceedings of the General Anti-Slavery Convention, Called by the Committee of the British and Foreign Anti-Slavery Society, and Held in London, from Friday, June 12th to Tuesday, June 23rd, 1840* (London: British and Foreign Anti-Slavery Society, 1841). For records of the women's protests of their exclusion, see Frederick B. Tolles, ed., *Slavery and "The Woman Question": Lucretia Mott's Diary of Her Visit to Great Britain to Attend the World's Anti-Slavery Convention of 1840* (Haverford, Pa.: Friends' Historical Association, 1952), 22–28; BFASS Minute Books, vol. 1, 226–28, Rhodes House Antislavery Papers (reel 1); James Mott, *Three Months in Great Britain* (Philadelphia: J. Miller McKim, 1841), 14–18.

15. *Proceedings of the General Anti-Slavery Conference*, 124, 127, 128.

16. WLG to George W. Benson, January 7, 1841, *LWLG* 3:8–9; William Caleb McDaniel, "Our Country Is the World: Radical American Abolitionists Abroad," Ph.D. diss., Johns Hopkins University, 2006, 86–92.

17. WP to EPN, May 15, 1841, BPL, Ms.A.1.2.12.1.18. See also Fladeland, *Men and Brothers*, 281–84; Joseph Sturge, *A Visit to the United States in 1841* (London: Hamilton, Adams, and Co., 1842), 26–27.

18. For even-handed accounts of the schism, see Walters, *The Antislavery Appeal*, chap. 1; Kraditor, *Means and Ends;* Stewart, "The Aims and Impact of Garrisonian Abolitionism, 1840–1860," 197–209; Hugh Davis, *Joshua Leavitt, Evangelical Abolitionist* (Baton Rouge: Louisiana State University Press, 1990), 134–63; Perry, *Radical Abolitionism*.

19. Fladeland, *James Gillespie Birney*, chap. 7; Wyatt-Brown, *Lewis Tappan*, 115–22; Stewart, *Holy Warriors*, 88–94.

20. "Miscellaneous Items," *Liberator*, August 23, 1839; Tappan qtd. in WLG to George W. Benson, September 23, 1837, *LWLG* 2:306. On the Clerical Appeal, see Stewart, *William Lloyd Garrison and the Challenge of Emancipation*, 102–8.

21. See Kraditor, *Means and Ends*, 104–6, 123–24, qtd. on 104.

22. Davis, *Joshua Leavitt*, 158–60.

23. *Proceedings of the General Anti-Slavery Convention*, 16, 25, 26.

24. *Proceedings of the General Anti-Slavery Convention*, 36. A complete survey of the arguments over these issues can be found in McDaniel, "Our Country Is the World," chap. 2.

25. Oliver Johnson to MWC, August 23, 1840, BPL, Ms.A.9.2.14.8; *Sixth Annual Report of the Glasgow Emancipation Society* (Glasgow: Aird & Russell, 1840), 29; William Bassett to EPN, August 31, 1840, BPL, Ms.A.1.2.9.87; "Letter from Wendell Phillips, London, June 1840," *Liberator*, July 24, 1840; "Great Public Meeting of the Glasgow Emancipation Society," *Liberator*, August 28, 1840. See also "To the Abolitionists of New Hampshire," *NASS*, September 10, 1840; NPR to Parker Pillsbury, July 22, 1840, BPL, Ms.A.1.2.9.78; Anne Knight to MWC, August 4, 1840, BPL, Ms.A.9.2.13.49; "Speech of William Lloyd Garrison, at the First Annual Meeting of the British India Society," *Liberator*, September 4, 1840; "News from England," *Liberator*, July 24, 1840; "Arrival of Wm. Lloyd Garrison and N.P. Rogers from England," *Liberator*, August 28, 1840; "The London Convention," *NASS*, July 23, 1840; "The London Convention," *NASS*, October 1, 1840; WLG to Anti-Slavery Friends and Coadjutors, [August 19, 1840,] *LWLG* 2:677; "To John G. Whittier," *Pennsylvania Freeman*, December 3, 1840; NPR to J. H. Tregold, July 9, 1840, Haverford College, Special Manuscripts Collection #806, Box 1.

26. "To the Abolitionists of New Hampshire," *NASS*, September 10, 1840.

27. "Letter from J. G. Whittier," *Pennsylvania Freeman*, November 19, 1840.

28. Sarah Pugh to RDW, Richard Allen, and James Haughton, August 24, 1840, BPL, Ms.A.1.2.9.98; WLG to EPN, September 16, 1841, *LWLG* 3:29. On post-convention tours, see Rice, *Scots Abolitionists*, 89–99; RDW to WLG, 1 August 1840, BPL, Ms.A.1.2.9.88; *BAA*, 72–73, 99–100; Lee Virginia Chambers-Schiller, "The Cab: A Transatlantic Community, Aspects of Nineteenth-Century Reform," Ph.D. diss., University of Michigan, 1977, 69–72. Chambers-Schiller notes that Mott's diary recorded fourteen social visits with Pease (71).

29. *Proceedings of the General Anti-Slavery Convention*, 25; John Bowring to Daniel O'Connell, October 22, 1840, *The Correspondence of Daniel O'Connell*, ed. Maurice O'Connell (8 vols.; Dublin: Blackwater Press, 1972–80), vol. 6:374; Bowring to WLG, November 9, 1840, *BAA*, 122; *Oxford Dictionary of National Biography*, online ed., s.v. "Bowring, Sir John"; Midgley, *Women against Slavery*, 122.

30. Elizabeth A. Ashurst to Elizabeth Neall Gay, January 1, [1841], Sydney Howard Gay Papers, Columbia University; Emilie Ashurst Venturi, *William Henry Ashurst: A Brief Record of His Life* (n.p.: James Morris, 1855); Kathryn Gleadle, *The Early Feminists: Radical Unitarians and the Emergence of the Women's Rights Movements, 1831–1851* (New York: St. Martin's Press, 1995), 1–16, 39–45; entries by Eugene L. Rasor on Elizabeth A. Ashurst, William Henry Ashurst Jr., and William Henry Ashurst Sr. in *Biographical Dictionary of Modern British Radicals*, ed. Joseph O. Baylen and Norbert J. Gossman (Atlantic Highlands, N.J.: Humanities Press, 1979), vol. 2:13–22; Chambers-Schiller, "The Cab," 158–59; Anderson, *Joyous Greetings*, 127.

31. On the Garrisonians' allies in Ireland, see Douglas C. Riach, "Richard Davis Webb and Anti-slavery in Ireland," in *Antislavery Reconsidered: New Perspectives on the Abolitionists*, ed. Lewis Perry and Michael Fellman (Baton Rouge: Louisiana State University Press, 1979), 149–67. Rice, *Scots Abolitionists*, 92–93; Marie-Louise Legg, ed., *Alfred Webb: The Autobiography of a Quaker Nationalist* (Cork, Ireland: Cork University Press, 1999), 24–26; EQ to RDW, May 23, 1846, BPL, Mss. 960, vol. 1, no. 13. On the particularly close relations between the Hibernians and the Garrisonians, see, for example, John A. Collins to WP, June 14, 1841, HL, bMS, Am 1953 (429); "Mr. Collins," *Liberator*,

June 25, 1841; "Letter from James Haughton, of Dublin," *Liberator,* October 14, 1842; RDW to WLG, August 1, 1840, BPL, Ms.A.1.2.9.88; James Haughton to WP, August 13, 1842, HL, bMS Am 1953 (710); Abby Kimber to RDW, 4 November 1840, BPL, Ms.A.1.2.10.31.

32. RDW to WP, July 6, 1840, HL, bMS, Am 1953 (1277/1); "From Our Dublin Correspondent," *NASS,* November 19, 1846.

33. Chambers-Schiller, "The Cab," 83; RDW to JAC, January 7, 1841, BPL, Ms.A.1.2.11.14; Lucretia Mott to RDW, March 17, 1843, BPL, Ms.A.1.2.13.15; Sydney Howard Gay to RDW, July 17, 1844, Gay Papers. See also Chambers-Schiller, "The Cab," 156–83; Blackett, "And There Shall Be No More Sea." For sample correspondence concerning British subscriptions to American antislavery papers, see Charles Lenox Remond to EPN, October 14, 1841, BPL, Ms.A.1.2.12.1.120; WP to RDW, December 1842, BPL, Ms.A.1.2.12.2.113; RDW to Sydney Howard Gay, October 2, 1846, Gay Papers.

34. George Bradburn to RDW, January 1, 1841, BPL, Ms.A.1.2.11.4; RDW to NPR, November 24, 1840, Haverford College Special Collections #806, Box 1. For sample references to the other British papers mentioned here, "The British Friend," *Liberator,* March 24, 1843; RDW to EQ, November 2, 1843, BPL, Mss. 960, vol. 2:7–9; William Henry Ashurst to WLG, February 7, 1847, BPL, Ms.A.1.2.9.11; SHG to RDW, June 6, 1848, Columbia University; SHG to RDW, 17 July 1844, Gay Papers.

35. For an example of information shared "entre nous," see EPN to NPR, September? 22, 1843?, Haverford College, Special Collections #806, Box 1. Clare Midgley has estimated that "some 1,500 letters from American Garrisonians to and from 66 different British and Irish women survive," an estimate that takes into account correspondence involving only European women and, even then, only women in Britain and Ireland. See Midgley, *Women Against Slavery,* 132. Transatlantic letters also make up a significant percentage of the extensive collection of antislavery letters at the BPL, which numbers around 17,000 items. On the affective dimensions of letter exchange, see Chambers-Schiller, "The Cab," 174–83. For examples of "open letter" practices, see SHG to RDW, August 24, 1847, Gay Papers; EQ to RDW, November 27, 1843, BPL, Mss. 960, vol. 1, no. 4; RDW to MWC, September 2, 1844, BPL, Ms.A.1.2.14.51; WP to RDW, December 31, 1841, BPL, Ms.A.1.2.12.1.141; Beverly Wilson Palmer, ed. *Selected Letters of Lucretia Coffin Mott* (Urbana: University of Illinois Press, 2002), 92, 105, 119, 124.

36. Weston qtd. in Chambers-Schiller, "The Cab," 179; EPN to [MWC?], July 17, 1840, BPL, Ms.A.9.2.13.104; MWC to EPN, May 4, 1851, BPL, Ms.A.1.2.20.35. The Quincy-Webb correspondence can be found at the BPL and the Massachusetts Historical Society. See also JAC to RDW, January 28, 1841, BPL, Ms.A.1.2.11.38; Edward M. Davis to WP, July 21, 1842, HL, bMS, Am 1953 (471/1).

37. James Haughton to SMJr, February 2, 1846, BPL, Ms.B.1.6.3.9; Lucretia Mott to RDW and Hannah Webb, April 2, 1841, in Palmer, ed., *Selected Letters,* 93; Abby Kimber to RDW, November 4, 1840, BPL, Ms.A.1.2.10.31. On subscriptions to American antislavery newspapers, see MWC to SHG, September 23, 1847 (mislabeled 1843 in card catalog); RDW to SHG, September 4, 1853; SHG to RDW, July 31, 1847, all in Gay Papers.

38. SHG to RDW, December 10, 1849, Gay Papers; Chambers-Schiller, "The Cab," 168–72; Perry, *Childhood, Marriage, and Reform;* Clare Taylor, *Women of the Anti-Slavery Movement: The Weston Sisters* (New York: St. Martin's Press, 1995).

39. "Letter from Henry C. Wright," *Liberator,* August 27, 1847; Henry Clarke Wright, *Human Life: Illustrated in my Individual Experience as a Child, a Youth, and a Man* (Boston: Bela Marsh,

1849), 391–92. On the Ashursts' friendship with Mazzini, see Denis Mack Smith, *Mazzini* (New Haven, Conn.: Yale University Press, 1994), 45–46; Gleadle, *The Early Feminists*, 39–45; Harry Williams Rudman, *Italian Nationalism and English Letters: Figures of the Risorgimento and Victorian Men of Letters* (London: Allen & Unwin, 1940), 73–74. E. F. Richards, ed., *Mazzini's Letters to an English Family* (3 vols.; London: John Lane, 1920–22); Roland Sarti, *Mazzini: A Life for the Religion of Politics* (Westport, Conn.: Praeger, 1997), 112–13. Mazzini himself singled out the "dear, good, sacred family of Ashurst" when talking about his English friends in his autobiographical writings. See *Life and Writings of Joseph Mazzini* (London: Smith, Elder, & Co., 1866), vol. 3:179–80.

40. For quotes, see *Fifteenth Annual Report, Presented to the Massachusetts Anti-Slavery Society*, 46, 54; WLG to HCW, November 1, 1845, *LWLG* 3:324. On May and the new allies mentioned, see Douglas C. Stange, *British Unitarians against American Slavery, 1833–65* (Rutherford, N.J.: Fairleigh Dickinson University Press, 1984); Midgley, *Women Against Slavery*, 132–35; J. Estlin Carpenter, *The Life and Work of Mary Carpenter* (London: Macmillan & Co., 1879).

41. Isabel Jennings to MWC, April 12, 1843, BPL, Ms.A.9.2.18.28. On African American abolitionists in Europe, see especially Blackett, *Building an Antislavery Wall*; Gosse, "'As a Nation,'" Alan J. Rice and Martin Crawford, eds., *Liberating Sojourn: Frederick Douglass and Transatlantic Reform* (Athens: University of Georgia Press, 1999); Fionnghuala Sweeney and Alan Rice, eds., "African Americans and Transatlantic Abolition 1845–1865," special issue of *Slavery and Abolition* 33, no. 2 (2012).

42. William Wells Brown, *The Travels of William Wells Brown: including Narrative of William Wells Brown, a Fugitive Slave, and The American Fugitive in Europe, Sketches of Places and People Abroad*, ed. Paul Jefferson (New York: M. Weiner Pub., 1991), 222.

43. WLG to EPN, August 31, 1840, *LWLG* 2:682; SMJr to JBE, September 26, 1846, BPL, Ms.B.1.6.2.33; RDW to NPR, June 4, 1842, Haverford College, Special Collections #806, Box 1; WLG to Samuel J. May, December 19, 1846, *BAA*, 304. See also Chambers-Schiller, "The Cab," 242–76; Emma Michell to AWW, November 20, 1853? BPL, Ms.A.9.2.7.26; Harriet Hyman Alonso, *Growing Up Abolitionist: The Story of the Garrison Children* (Amherst: University of Massachusetts Press, 2002); GT to Amelia Thompson, October 19, [1850?], REAS 2/2/25.

44. James G. Birney to Lewis Tappan, July 23, 1840, in Dumond, ed., *Letters of James Gillespie Birney* 2:584; Tappan to John Scoble, November 30, 1846, in Abel and Klingberg, eds., *Side-light*, 212. For pamphlets by Garrisonians on the schism, see, for example, John B. Estlin, *A Brief Notice of American Slavery, and the Abolition Movement* (Bristol, U.K.: R. C. Evans, 1846); *Statements respecting the American Abolitionists, by their Opponents and their Friends . . . by the Bristol and Clifton Ladies' Anti-Slavery Society* (Dublin: Webb and Chapman, 1852); Edmund Quincy, *Examination of the Charges of Mr. John Scoble & Mr. Lewis Tappan against the American Anti-Slavery Society* (Dublin: Webb and Chapman, 1852); Richard D. Webb, *The National Anti-Slavery Societies in England and the United States: Or, Strictures on "A Reply to Certain Charges Brought against the American and Foreign Anti-Slavery Society, etc. etc . . ."* (Dublin, 1852); Eliza Wigham, *The Anti-Slavery Cause in America and its Martyrs* (London: A. W. Bennett, 1863).

45. "Letter from Henry C. Wright," *Liberator*, August 31, 1844. See also WLG to EQ, August 14, 1846, *LWLG* 3:369–74.

46. Estlin, *A Brief Notice of American Slavery*, 15; Haughton and Armstrong qtd. in Stange, *British Unitarians*, 59–66. See also "Frederick Douglass," *Liberator*, December 4, 1846.

47. Blassingame, ed., *Frederick Douglass Papers* 1:81; 2:48. See also 1:76.

48. Blassingame, ed., *Frederick Douglass Papers* 2:11; 1:78; 1:35. See also 1:187.

49. Blackett, *Building an Antislavery Wall*, chap. 1.

50. GT to WLG, March 27, 1834, *BAA*, 28.

51. Fladeland, *Men and Brothers*, 217; "Address to John A. Collins, Esq.," *Liberator*, May 28, 1841; Stange, *British Unitarians*, 59–66; Midgley, *Women Against Slavery*, 132, 149. See also William James to SMJr, November 30, 1843, *BAA*, 208–9. On a similar "National Remonstrance with America" prepared by William Lovett, see Lovett to WLG, March 1, 1847, BPL, Ms.A.1.2.17.18.

52. Rice, *Scots Abolitionists*, 115–50; Blackett, *Building an Antislavery Wall*, 79–117; Perry, *Childhood, Marriage, and Reform*, 45–47; Fladeland, *Men and Brothers*, 296–301; J. F. Maclear, "The Evangelical Alliance and the Antislavery Crusade," *Huntington Library Quarterly* 42, no. 2 (1979): 141–64; C. Duncan Rice, "Controversies over Slavery in Eighteenth-and Nineteenth-Century Scotland," in Perry and Fellman, eds., *Antislavery Reconsidered*, 45–50; Alisdair Pettinger, "Send Back the Money: Douglass and the Free Church of Scotland," in Rice and Crawford, eds., *Liberating Sojourn*, 31–55.

53. On the antislavery fairs, see Lee Chambers-Schiller, "'A Good Work among the People': The Political Culture of the Boston Antislavery Fair," in Yellin and Van Horne, eds., *The Abolitionist Sisterhood*, 249–74; Deborah van Broekhoven, "'Better than a Clay Club': The Organization of Women's Anti-Slavery Fairs, 1835–1860," *Slavery and Abolition* 19 (April 1998): 24–51; Jeffrey, *The Great Silent Army of Abolitionism*, 108–26; Robertson, *Hearts Beating for Liberty*, chap. 4; John L. Brooke, "Cultures of Nationalism, Movements of Reform, and the Composite-Federal Polity: From Revolutionary Settlement to Antebellum Crisis," *Journal of the Early Republic* 29, no. 1 (2009): 28–30.

54. For a few of the many examples of letters concerning fair contributions, see EPN to [MWC], September 1840, BPL, Ms.A.9.2.14.13; WP to RDW, December 31, 1841, BPL, Ms.A.1.2.12.1.141; RDW to MWC, November 16, 1843, BPL, Ms.A.1.2.13.82. For Brown's panorama, see Ripley, ed., *Black Abolitionist Papers* 1:214–15.

55. "The Faneuil Hall Bazaar," *Liberator*, January 23, 1846; "Twelfth National Anti-Slavery Bazaar," *Liberator*, January 23, 1846. See also "Twentieth National Anti-Slavery Bazaar," *Liberator*, 20 January 1854.

56. SMJr to Mary Carpenter, December 29, 1845, *BAA*, 246. See "The Fourteenth National Anti-Slavery Bazaar," *Liberator*, January 14, 1848; "The Twenty-First National Anti-Slavery Bazaar," *Liberator*, January 26, 1855; Chambers-Schiller, "'A Good Work among the People,'" 251n6, 253n11; EPN to [MWC], September 1840; JBE to SMJr, October 29, 1844, *BAA*, 230–31; RDW to MWC, November 16, 1843, BPL, Ms.A.1.2.13.82 (Beaumont book); SMJr to JBE, December 30, 1844, *BAA*, 231. See lists of goods, letters, and advertisements in "National Anti-Slavery Bazaar," *Liberator*, September 5, 1845; "The National Anti-Slavery Bazaar," *Liberator*, December 19, 1845; "National Anti-Slavery Bazaar in Faneuil Hall," *Prisoner's Friend*, December 17, 1845; "Anti-Slavery Bazaar at Faneuil Hall," *Christian Register*, December 19, 1846; *Boston Anti-Slavery Bazaar* (Dublin: Hibernian Ladies' Anti-Slavery Society, 1846).

57. Blassingame, ed., *Frederick Douglass Papers* 1:370; "The Sixteenth National Anti-Slavery Bazaar," January 25, 1850. See also "Boston Anti-Slavery Bazaar," BPL, Ms.A.9.2.25.34. See issues of the *Liberty Bell* available in the American Periodical Series online; Ralph Thompson, "The Liberty Bell and Other Anti-Slavery Gift-Books," *New England Quarterly* 7, no. 1 (March 1934): 159–62. For solicitations of articles for the *Liberty Bell*, see MWC to WP, April 20, 1840, HL, bMS, Am 1953 (394/1); WP to Edward M. Davis, 26 July 1841, HL, bMS, Am 1054 (148–56). Holinski's donation is

noted in "Fourteenth National Anti-Slavery Bazaar." On Browning, see Taylor, *Women of the Anti-Slavery Movement,* 97.

58. "Twelfth National Anti-Slavery Bazaar."

59. Douglass, *My Bondage and My Freedom,* 311; "Thompson's Lectures," *Liberator,* March 20, 1840.

CHAPTER FOUR

1. On Garrisonian mechanisms for maintaining community, see Lawrence J. Friedman, *Gregarious Saints: Self and Community in American Abolitionism, 1830–1870* (New York: Cambridge University Press, 1982), chap. 2; Stewart, *Wendell Phillips,* 127–32. On the difficulty of defining Garrisonians, see Ronald G. Walters, "The Boundaries of Abolitionism," in Perry and Fellman, eds., *Antislavery Reconsidered,* 13–19.

2. Giddings qtd. in Jonathan H. Earle, *Jacksonian Antislavery and the Politics of Free Soil, 1824–1854* (Chapel Hill: University of North Carolina Press, 2004), 183. See also Daniel Walker Howe, *The Political Culture of the American Whigs* (rpt., Chicago: University of Chicago Press, 1984), 173; Corey Brooks, "Building an Antislavery House: Political Abolitionists and the U.S. Congress," Ph.D. diss., University of California–Berkeley, 2010.

3. *Report of the Boston Female Anti-Slavery Society; with a Concise Statement of Events, Previous and Subsequent to the Annual Meeting of 1835* (Boston: By the Society, 1836), 52.

4. Garrison, *Thoughts on African Colonization,* part 1, 146, 150; *Letters and Addresses by George Thompson,* 107. See also Garrison and Garrison, *Garrison* 3:283–84; 1:238, 385.

5. *Letters and Addresses by George Thompson,* 75; Garrison and Garrison, *Garrison* 1:102.

6. Dickens qtd. in Allan Nevins, ed., *America Through British Eyes* (New York: Oxford University Press, 1948), 91.

7. Garrison and Garrison, *Garrison* 1:128.

8. "Free Speech and Free Inquiry," *Liberator,* April 2, 1847.

9. Wendell Phillips, "Public Opinion," in *SLL,* 52; Wendell Phillips, "The Boston Mob," in *SLL,* 213, 225.

10. On Phillips's role as the leading intellectual and orator of the Garrisonian movement, see Stewart, *Wendell Phillips.* For examples of others writing to Phillips with questions about the AASS line, see Edward M. Davis to Wendell Phillips, 21 May 1844, HL, bMS, Am 1953 (471/1); Sydney Howard Gay to Phillips, 23 July 1848, HL, bMS, Am 1953 (593/7); Edmund Quincy to Phillips, 8 January 1846, HL, bMS, Am 1953 (1019/3).

11. This and the following two paragraphs rely on Mona Ozouf, "Public Spirit," in *A Critical Dictionary of the French Revolution,* ed. Francois Furet and Mona Ozouf, trans. Arthur Goldhammer (Cambridge, Mass.: Harvard University Press, 1989), 771–80; J. A. W. Gunn, "Public Opinion," in Terence Ball, James Farr, and Russell L. Hanson, eds., *Political Innovation and Conceptual Change* (Cambridge, U.K.: Cambridge University Press, 1989), 247–65; Mona Ozouf, "'Public Opinion' at the End of the Old Regime," *Journal of Modern History* 60, supp: "Rethinking French Politics in 1788" (September 1988), S1–S21; Keith Michael Baker, "Public Opinion as Political Invention," in *Inventing the French Revolution: Essays on French Political Culture in the Eighteenth Century* (Cambridge, U.K.: Cambridge University Press, 1990), 167–99; J. A. W. Gunn, "Public Spirit to Public Opinion,"

in *Beyond Liberty and Property: The Process of Self-Recognition in 18th Century Political Thought* (Kingston, Ontario, Canada: McGill-Queen's University Press, 1983), 260–315; Colleen A. Sheehan, *James Madison and the Spirit of Republican Self-Government* (Cambridge, U.K.: Cambridge University Press, 2009); Cotlar, *Tom Paine's America*; Mark Schmeller, "The Political Economy of Opinion: Public Credit and Concepts of Public Opinion in the Age of Federalism," *Journal of the Early Republic* 29 (Spring 2009): 35–61; Schmeller, "Imagining Public Opinion in Antebellum America"; Jeffrey L. McNairn, *The Capacity to Judge: Public Opinion and Deliberative Democracy in Upper Canada, 1791–1854* (Toronto: University of Toronto Press, 2000); Paul Beaud, "Common Knowledge on Historical Vicissitudes of the Notion of Public Opinion," *Réseaux* 1, no. 1 (1993): 119–37.

12. See Gunn, "Public Spirit to Public Opinion," 298–99. For radical democratic uses of "public opinion" in the post-revolutionary United States, see Cotlar, *Tom Paine's America*, chap. 5.

13. See Dror Wahrman, *Imagining the Middle Class: the Political Representation of Class in Britain, c. 1780–1840* (New York: Cambridge University Press, 1995), 190–99, 299–303; Boyd Hilton, *A Mad, Bad, and Dangerous People? England, 1783–1846* (New York: Oxford University Press, 2006), 310–11.

14. William Jay, *An Inquiry into the Character and Tendency of the American Colonization, and American Anti-Slavery Societies* (New York: R. G. Williams, 1837), 204; Blassingame, ed., *Frederick Douglass Papers* 1:96; "The Republican Scholar of Necessity an Agitator," *Liberator*, August 21, 1857.

15. Phillips, "Public Opinion," 48, 50, 51.

16. "The Boasted Superiority of the Present Age," in Wendell Phillips, "Student Themes and Dissertations, 1825–1831," Harvard University Archives, HUC 8827.386.70. See also Stewart, *Wendell Phillips*, chap. 1.

17. "Speech of Wendell Phillips," *Liberator*, August 14, 1857; Phillips, "Public Opinion," 40.

18. Phillips, "Public Opinion," 44, 45, 46.

19. Phillips, "A Metropolitan Police," *SLL*, 501, 502.

20. "Non-Voting Theory: Reply to Messrs. White, Earle, and Bowditch"; "Speech of Wendell Phillips," *Liberator*, August 14, 1857.

21. Phillips, "Public Opinion," 40.

22. See Alan S. Kahan, *Alexis de Tocqueville* (New York: Continuum, 2010), 35–57; Kahan, *Aristocratic Liberalism: The Social and Political Thought of Jacob Burckhardt, John Stuart Mill, and Alexis de Tocqueville* (New York: Oxford University Press, 1992).

23. Tocqueville, *Democracy in America*, trans. Henry Reeve (1835; New York: George Adlard, 1838), 180, 182. Unless otherwise noted, quotations from Tocqueville are from the original English translation by Henry Reeve, because Reeve's translation is the one Phillips would have read.

24. Tocqueville, *Democracy in America*, 237, 242.

25. Tocqueville, *Democracy in America*, 240, 241, 242n.

26. Tocqueville, *Democracy in America*, 244, 245.

27. Alexis de Tocqueville, *Democracy in America, Part the Second: The Social Influence of Democracy* (New York: J. & H. G. Langley, 1840), 339, 341; James T. Kloppenberg, "Tocqueville, Mill, and the American Gentry," *The Tocqueville Review/La Revue Tocqueville* 27, no. 2 (2006): 358. See also Alex Zakaras, *Individuality and Mass Democracy: Mill, Emerson, and the Burdens of Citizenship* (New York: Oxford University Press, 2009), 14–17.

28. Tocqueville, *Democracy in America*, 242.

29. Mill qtd. in Kahan, *Aristocratic Liberalism*, 47.

30. Samuel J. May, *Discourse on the life and character of the Rev. Charles Follen, L.L.D.: who per-ished, Jan. 13, 1840, in the conflagration of the Lexington: delivered before the Massachusetts Anti-Slavery Society, in the Marlborough Chapel, Boston* (Boston: Henry L. Devereux, 1840), 11; Thomas Went-worth Higginson, *Wendell Phillips* (Boston: Lee and Shepard, 1884), xiii. For Tocqueville's abolition-ist work, see Jennings, *French Anti-Slavery.*

31. On free black disfranchisement in the antebellum period, see Christopher Malone, *Between Freedom and Bondage: Race, Party, and Voting Rights in the Antebellum North* (New York: Routledge, 2008); Nicholas Wood, "'A Sacrifice on the Altar of Slavery': Doughface Politics and Black Disen-franchisement in Pennsylvania, 1837–1838," *Journal of the Early Republic* 31, no. 1 (Spring 2011): 75–106. For the Philadelphia mob, see Julie Winch, *Philadelphia's Black Elite: Activism, Accommoda-tion, and the Struggle for Autonomy, 1787–1848* (Philadelphia: Temple University Press, 1988), 149–51.

32. "The Philadelphia Mob of Aug. 1st, 1842," *Liberator,* August 19, 1842; "Afflictions of our Col-ored Population," *Liberator,* September 9, 1842. See also "Judicial Mob Law," "Philadelphia Riot," "To the Public," all in *Liberator,* August 26, 1842.

33. See Tocqueville, *Democracy in America,* 243.

34. Phillips, "Mobs and Education," *SLL,* 321.

35. Phillips, "Mobs and Education," 333.

36. Phillips, "Idols," *SLL,* 261. See also Stewart, *Wendell Phillips,* 146–51.

37. "Proceedings of the Massachusetts Anti-Slavery Society, at Its Fifth Annual Meeting," in *Fifth Annual Report of the Board of Managers of the Massachusetts Anti-Slavery Society* (Boston: Isaac Knapp, 1837), xi; Phillips, "The Murder of Lovejoy," in *SLL,* 8.

38. Phillips, "Idols," 248. Phillips's critique echoed Ralph Waldo Emerson's own attack on Web-ster's "sterility of thought" (Len Gougeon and Joel Myerson, eds., *Emerson's Antislavery Writings* [New Haven, Conn.: Yale University Press, 1995], 77).

39. Phillips, "Idols," 248.

40. Phillips, "Idols," 249.

41. Phillips, "Philosophy of the Abolition Movement," *SLL,* 106, 107.

42. Wendell Phillips, "The Pulpit," *SLL: Second Series,* 271; Phillips, "Harper's Ferry," 264, 265, 266.

43. Phillips, "Idols," 249.

44. Phillips, "Harper's Ferry," *SLL,* 265; Wendell Phillips, "The Puritan Principle and John Brown," *SLL: Second Series,* 302.

45. Phillips, "Harper's Ferry," 270.

46. Phillips, "Idols," 250; Phillips, "Public Opinion," 46. On Emerson, see Zakaras, *Individuality and Mass Democracy.*

47. Phillips, "Public Opinion," 54. Phillips repeated this same image five years later in his Phi Beta Kappa address to students at Yale University. See "Republican Scholar of Necessity an Agitator."

48. Phillips, "Puritan Principle and John Brown," 302.

49. Phillips, "Public Opinion," 47; Phillips, "A Metropolitan Police," 498–99.

50. WP to Richard Allen, March 30, 1842, *BAA,* 171–72, qtd. on 172. For a sensitive reading of Phillips's complex views on the Irish, see also Stewart, *Wendell Phillips,* 109–12.

51. Phillips, "Mobs and Education," 333; Phillips, "Idols," 247.

52. Phillips, "Public Opinion," 52; Tocqueville, *Democracy in America: Part the Second,* 105. See also Kahan, *Alexis de Tocqueville,* 45–46.

53. Tocqueville, *Democracy in America: Part the Second,* 136, 141.

54. Phillips, "Public Opinion," 46; Phillips, "Mobs and Education," 333, 338; Phillips, "The Pulpit," 269.

55. Tocqueville, *Democracy in America: Part the Second,* 130, 132. See also Kahan, *Alexis de Tocqueville,* 50–54.

56. Phillips, "Public Opinion," 45; Phillips, "Woman's Rights," *SLL,* 14; "Sims Anniversary," *SLL,* 82. See also Phillips, "Philosophy of the Abolition Movement," 106–7.

57. Phillips, "The Education of the People," *SLL: Second Series,* 314, 316, 327, 329.

58. Phillips, "Idols," 243, 244.

59. Phillips, "The Pulpit," 272. My discussion of Mill in the following paragraphs has been influenced primarily by Urbinati, *Mill on Democracy;* Urbinati and Zakaras, eds., *J. S. Mill's Political Thought;* Butler, *Critical Americans;* Zakaras, *Individuality and Mass Democracy;* Bruce Baum, "Freedom, Power and Public Opinion: J. S. Mill on the Public Sphere," *History of Political Thought* 22, no. 3 (Autumn 2001): 501–24; Bruce Baum, *Rereading Power and Freedom in J. S. Mill* (Toronto: University of Toronto Press, 2000); K. C. O'Rourke, *John Stuart Mill and Freedom of Expression: The Genesis of a Theory* (London: Routledge, 2001).

60. On Mill's notion of individuality as a response to the dangers of conformity, see especially Alex Zakaras, "John Stuart Mill, Individuality, and Participatory Democracy," in *J. S. Mill's Political Thought,* ed. Urbinati and Zakaras, 200–220; and O'Rourke, *John Stuart Mill and Freedom of Expression,* chap. 5. For a summary of Mill's reading of Tocqueville and their importance as "transitional essays" that shaped his later work, see Capaldi, *John Stuart Mill,* 148–56.

61. John Stuart Mill, "On Liberty," in *CWJSM* 18:243.

62. "Nothing in their lives," qtd. in Zakaras, "John Stuart Mill," 210; "patching," qtd. in Capaldi, *John Stuart Mill,* 150.

63. Baum, "Freedom, Power and Public Opinion," 503. On Mill and Athens, see Urbinati, *Mill on Democracy;* Jonathan Riley, "Mill's Neo-Athenian Model of Liberal Democracy," in *J. S. Mill's Political Thought,* ed. Urbinati and Zakaras, 221–49; Eugenio Biagini, "Liberalism and Direct Democracy: John Stuart Mill and the Model of Ancient Athens," in *Citizenship and Community: Liberals, Radicals, and Collective Identities in British Isles, 1865–1931,* ed. Biagini (Cambridge, U.K.: Cambridge University Press, 1996), 21–44.

64. Phillips, "The Education of the People," 312, 313.

65. Phillips, "Harper's Ferry," 267, 268. Anacharsis is also mentioned in Phillips, "The Education of the People," 313.

66. Phillips, "Harper's Ferry," 267.

67. John Stuart Mill to Harriet Taylor, October 29, 1850, *CWJSM* 14:49–50, qtd. on 49.

68. Phillips, "Public Opinion," 53, 54.

69. EQ to RDW, November 27, 1843, BPL, Mss. 960, vol.1:4; EQ to RDW, June 27, 1843, Edmund Quincy Papers, Massachusetts Historical Society, Reel 47. See also EQ to RDW, January 29, 1843, on same reel. The "flea of Conventions" was an epithet for Folsom used by Ralph Waldo Emerson, as Quincy noted, though his letters to Webb show that he clearly shared Emerson's views about her. See Charles E. Morriss III, "'Our Capital Aversion': Abigail Folsom, Madness, and Radical Antislavery Praxis," *Women's Studies in Communication* 24, no. 1 (Spring 2001): 62–89. On Rogers, see Friedman, *Gregarious Saints,* 59–60. On Douglass's breach with Garrisonians, see the still classic article

by Benjamin Quarles, "The Breach between Douglass and Garrison," *Journal of Negro History* 23, no. 2 (April 1938): 144–54.

70. Phillips, "Public Opinion," 53.

71. "The Republican Scholar of Necessity an Agitator."

CHAPTER FIVE

1. Garrison qtd. in Dan McKanan, *Identifying the Image of God: Radical Christians and Nonviolent Power in the Antebellum United States* (New York: Oxford University Press, 2002), 75; "'The Rights of God'—Free Discussion—Freedom of the Press," *Liberator,* January 30, 1846. See also "Free Speech and Free Inquiry," *Liberator,* April 2, 1847.

2. WLG to the Editor of the Newburyport *Herald,* [June 1, 1830], *LWLG* 1:101. For an example of Garrison's penchant for quoting huge blocks of Scripture, see *Letter from Wm. Lloyd Garrison: Read at the Annual Meeting of the Pennsylvania Anti-Slavery Society* ([Philadelphia]: n.p., 1851).

3. William Lloyd Garrison, *Selections from the Writings and Speeches of William Lloyd Garrison* (Boston: R. F. Wallcut, 1852), 94, 282. On the break in the Peace Society, see Valerie Ziegler, *The Advocates of Peace in Antebellum America* (Bloomington: Indiana University Press, 1992), 56–79.

4. WLG to Francis Jackson, June 18, 1838, *LWLG* 2:369. See Perry, *Radical Abolitionism,* for a full discussion of non-resistance.

5. Ronald G. Walters, *American Reformers, 1815–1860,* rev. ed. (New York: Hill and Wang, 1997), 39–60.

6. Garrison, *Selections,* 116, 131.

7. Garrison, *Selections,* 46.

8. *Speeches Delivered at the Anti-Colonization Meeting in Exeter Hall, London, July 13, 1833* (Boston: Garrison & Knapp, 1833), 4.

9. *Letters and Addresses by George Thompson,* 2; Paulding, *Slavery in the United States,* 306; *First Annual Report of the American Anti-Slavery Society* (New York: Dorr & Butterfield, 1834), 52–53.

10. "Our Sixth Volume," *Liberator,* January 2, 1836.

11. "Our Sixth Volume."

12. See Walters, *American Reformers,* 55; Robert David Thomas, *The Man Who Would Be Perfect: John Humphrey Noyes and the Utopian Impulse* (Philadelphia: University of Pennsylvania Press, 1977).

13. Garrison and Garrison, *Garrison* 2:145–46, 147.

14. Garrison and Garrison, *Garrison* 2:149.

15. Garrison and Garrison, *Garrison* 2:230.

16. "Meetings of the Non-Resistance Society," *The Non-Resistant,* June 15, 1839; "National Organizations," *Liberator,* January 4, 1839, January 11, 1839.

17. WLG to Samuel J. May, September 8, 1838, *LWLG* 2:388; WLG to Richard P. Hunt, May 1, 1840, *LWLG* 2:594.

18. WLG to Oliver Johnson, 22 May 1840, *LWLG* 2:626.

19. WLG to MWC, June 3, 1840, *LWLG* 2:632; WLG to Richard P. Hunt, May 1, 1840, *LWLG* 2:595.

20. Abby Kimber to EPN, May 18, 1841? BPL, Ms.A.1.2.9.43; William Bassett to EPN, August 31, 1840, BPL, Ms.A.1.2.9.87.

21. WLG to HWC, March 1, 1843, *LWLG* 3:135. See also Wright's statement that the transatlantic cooperation behind the fair was "the way to make treaties of peace between nations. . . . the hearts of individuals in love" ("Letter from Henry C. Wright," *Liberator,* January 13, 1843).

22. HCW-BPL, vol. 17:212 (May 6, 1841); see also 93, 111, 224–26. "World's Convention," *Liberator,* June 4, 1841; "World's Convention," *Liberator,* August 27, 1841; HCW to WP, August 27, 1841, HL, bMS, Am 1953 (1349/1); "Human Rights Convention for the World," *Liberator,* July 16, 1841.

23. HCW-BPL, vol. 18:1–3 (June 18, 1841). See "Letter from Maria W. Chapman," *Liberator,* November 12, 1841; WLG to EPN, June 1, 1841, *LWLG* 3:25.

24. RDW to WP, October 2, 1841, HL, bMS, Am 1953 (1277/1); HCW-BPL, vol. 18:1. See also John A. Collins to HCW, January 1842, BPL, Ms.A.1.2.12.2.2.

25. HCW-HL, vol. 48:87 (May 15, 1842); "Letter from Henry C. Wright," *Liberator,* November 3, 1843; "Letter from Henry C. Wright," *Liberator,* May 5, 1843.

26. "Letter from Henry C. Wright," *Liberator,* March 3, 1843; emphasis in original. G. de Bertier de Sauvigny, "Liberalism, Nationalism and Socialism: The Birth of Three Words," *The Review of Politics* 32, no. 2 (April 1970): 147–66. See also *Oxford English Dictionary,* s.v. "Nationalism"; Anthony D. Smith, *Nationalism: Theory, Ideology, History* (Cambridge, U.K.: Polity, 2001), 5. Using search results conducted in 2010 in America's Historical Newspapers (Readex) and the American Periodical Series Online (ProQuest), I counted only thirty-three unique instances of the word *nationalism* in American newspapers prior to Wright's use of the term in the *Liberator* in March 1843. Eight of these articles were also reprinted. No more than five or six articles prior to 1843 used *nationalism* in something like Wright's sense of excessive patriotism. America's Historical Newspapers returned only nine instances of the term *nationalism* between 1843 and 1847 when searched in 2010, seven of which were articles written by Wright to the *Liberator* from Europe. A 2010 search for "nationalism" in American Periodical Series Online found two articles in the same period, one of which was an article by Wright. These figures indicate the rarity of the term but should not be interpreted as exact counts, especially given uncertainty over the uneven chronological distribution of newspapers in these databases. See Dael Norwood, "Ex Readex: Not Much?" *Goose Commerce,* April 9, 2011, goosecommerce.wordpress.com/2011/04/09/ex-readex-not-much/.

27. Richard Cobden, *The Political Writings of Richard Cobden,* ed. F. W. Chesson (London: T. F. Unwin, 1903), vol. 1: 5, 178n; John Bright and James E. Thorold Rogers, eds., *Speeches on Questions of Public Policy by Richard Cobden, M.P.* (London: Macmillan, 1870), vol. 1:79. See also J. A. Hobson, *Richard Cobden: The International Man* (1919; rpt., New York: Barnes & Noble, 1968). On the relationship between Cobden's free trade arguments and his anti-war arguments, see Richard Francis Spall Jr., "Free Trade, Foreign Relations, and the Anti-Corn-Law League," *International History Review* 10, no. 3 (August 1988): 405–32; Alexander Tyrrell, "Making the Millennium: The Mid-Nineteenth Century Peace Movement," *Historical Journal* 21, no. 1 (March 1978): 75–95; Martin Ceadel, "Cobden and Peace," in Howe and Morgan, eds., *Rethinking Nineteenth-Century Liberalism,* 189–207.

28. "Letter from Henry C. Wright," *Liberator,* April 7, 1843; "Letters from Henry C. Wright," *Liberator,* July 28, 1843; HWC-BPL, vol. 21:44–45 (June 16, 1843); "Letter from Henry C. Wright," *Liberator,* December 12, 1845. See also "Annual Meeting of the Manchester and Salford Peace Society," *Liberator,* June 9, 1843; "State of Things in England," *Liberator,* March 10, 1843; "Letter from Henry C. Wright," *Liberator,* March 3, 1843; "Letter from Henry C. Wright," *Liberator,* April 14, 1843;

"Letter from Henry C. Wright," *Liberator,* September 1, 1843; "Letter from Henry C. Wright," *Liberator,* May 5, 1843.

29. "Letters from Henry C. Wright, No. II," *Liberator,* April 12, 1844; "Letters from Henry C. Wright," *Liberator,* April 4, 1845.

30. "Letters from Henry C. Wright, No. V," *Liberator,* May 31, 1844; "Letter from Henry C. Wright," *Liberator,* August 31, 1844; "Letter from Henry C. Wright," *Liberator,* August 16, 1844; "Letters from Henry C. Wright, No. III," *Liberator,* October 4, 1844.

31. "Letter from Henry C. Wright," *Liberator,* August 16, 1844; HCW-BPL, vol. 27:80–81 (March 8, 1844).

32. "Letter from Henry C. Wright," *Liberator,* August 31, 1844; "Letters from Henry C. Wright, No. III," *Liberator,* October 4, 1844; "Letters from Henry C. Wright," *Liberator,* October 24, 1845; HCW-BPL, vol. 34:10 (September 8, 1845); HCW-BPL, vol. 32:74 (June 19, 1845); "Box of Correspondence and Manuscripts," HL, bMS, Am 515 (Folder 3, Part 1).

33. "Journal of Henry C. Wright," *Liberator,* February 13, 1846; Henry Clarke Wright, *The Dissolution of the American Union, Demanded by Justice and Humanity, as the Incurable Enemy of Liberty* (Glasgow: David Russell, 1845), 4–6.

34. "Our Country, Right or Wrong," *Liberator,* June 5, 1846, rpt. from the New York *Evangelist.* See also "Peace," *Liberator,* February 6, 1846; "Patriotism," *Liberator,* June 5, 1846; "True Patriotism," *Liberator,* May 7, 1847; "Patriotism," *NASS,* November 26, 1846.

35. "Journal of Henry C. Wright"; WLG to HCW, October 1, 1844, *LWLG* 3:264, 265; WLG to Mary Howitt, September 7, 1846, *LWLG* 3:399. See also "Letters from Henry C. Wright, No. IV," *Liberator,* 11 October 1844.

36. WLG to HCW, December 16, 1843, *LWLG* 3:240. See also WLG to Charles Stearns, February 10, 1840, *LWLG* 2:560–62.

37. Perry, *Radical Abolitionism,* 69; "'Come Out From Among Them,'" *Liberator,* December 15, 1843.

38. NPR to EPN, September 28, 1840, HL, bMS, Am 1906 (616); "Letters from Henry C. Wright," *Liberator,* July 11, 1845.

39. NPR to RDW, March 28, 1841, BPL, Ms.A.1.2.11.126; "Letter from Henry C. Wright," *Liberator,* March 3, 1843.

40. "Letter from Henry C. Wright," *Liberator,* August 16, 1844; "Letters from Henry C. Wright," *Liberator,* April 4, 1845; "Letter from Henry C. Wright," *Liberator,* November 3, 1843. See also WLG to HEG, June 29, 1840, *LWLG* 2:656.

41. "Letter from N. P. Rogers," *NASS,* August 27, 1840; Rogers, "British Abolitionism," *The Liberty Bell* (1842); WLG to EPN, April 4, 1843, 3:148. See also Perry, *Childhood, Marriage, and Reform,* 42.

42. "Meetings of the Non-Resistance Society."

43. "Arrival of Wm. Lloyd Garrison and N. P. Rogers from England," *Liberator,* August 28, 1840; WLG to HCW, August [23,] 1840, *LWLG* 2:680; *Proceedings of a Crowded Meeting of the Colored Population of Boston, Assembled the 15th July, 1846, for the Purpose of Bidding Farewell to William Lloyd Garrison, on His Departure for England* (Dublin: Webb and Chapman, 1846), 6–7.

44. Blassingame, ed., *Frederick Douglass Papers* 2:60; "Annual Meeting of the American Anti-Slavery Society," *Liberator,* May 21, 1847.

45. Blassingame, ed., *Frederick Douglass Papers* 2:71. See also 2:113.

46. Oakes, *The Radical and the Republican*, 28–34. On the notion of rooted cosmopolitanism, see Kwame Anthony Appiah, "Cosmopolitan Patriots," in *Cosmopolitics: Thinking and Feeling Beyond the Nation*, ed. Pheng Cheah and Bruce Robbins (Minneapolis: University of Minnesota Press, 1998), 91–114.

47. Thomas Paine, *Rights of Man* (New York: Penguin, 1984), 228. See Thomas J. Schlereth, *The Cosmopolitan Ideal in Enlightenment Thought: Its Form and Function in the Ideas of Franklin, Hume, and Voltaire, 1694–1790* (Notre Dame, Ind.: University of Notre Dame Press, 1977); Evan Radcliffe, "Revolutionary Writing, Moral Philosophy, and Universal Benevolence in the Eighteenth Century," *Journal of the History of Ideas* 54, no. 2 (April 1993): 221–40; Evan Radcliffe, "Burke, Radical Cosmopolitanism, and the Debates on Patriotism in the 1790s," *Studies in Eighteenth-Century Culture* 28 (1999): 311–39; Viroli, *For Love of Country*.

48. On the impact of these Hutchesonian ideas on abolitionists in particular, see W. Caleb McDaniel, "Philadelphia Abolitionists and Antislavery Cosmopolitanism, 1760–1840," in *Antislavery and Abolition in Philadelphia: Emancipation and the Long Struggle for Racial Justice in the City of Brotherly Love*, ed. Richard Newman and James Mueller (Baton Rouge: Louisiana State University Press, 2011), 149–73.

49. WLG to the Editor of the Boston *Courier*, July 12, 1827, and July 14, 1827, *LWLG* 1:46–51, qtd. on 49. On Federalist ideas about patriotism and cosmopolitanism, see J. M. Opal, "The Labors of Liberality: Christian Benevolence and National Prejudice in the American Founding," *Journal of American History* 94, no. 4 (March 2008): 1082–1107.

50. William Whipper, *Eulogy on William Wilberforce, Esq. Delivered at the Request of the People of Colour of the City of Philadelphia, in the Second African Presbyterian Church, on the Sixth Day of December, 1833* (Philadelphia: William R. Gibbons, [1833?]), 31–33; Garrison, *Thoughts on African Colonization*, 2–4.

51. C.F., "American Patriotism," *Liberator*, November 1, 1839; Samuel J. May, *A Discourse on the Life and Character of the Rev. Charles Follen, L.L.D. . . . Delivered before the Massachusetts Anti-Slavery Society, in the Marlborough Chapel, Boston, April 17, 1840* (Boston: Henry L. Devereux, 1840), 26; William Lloyd Garrison, *No Compromise with Slavery: An Address Delivered in the Broadway Tabernacle, New York, February 14, 1854* (New York: American Anti-Slavery Society, 1854), 4.

52. On Mazzini's life, see Smith, *Mazzini*. My interpretation of Mazzini's ideas of nationalism and nationality draw on Stefano Recchia and Nadia Urbinati, eds., *A Cosmopolitanism of Nations: Giuseppe Mazzini's Writings on Democracy, Nation Building, and International Relations* (Princeton, N.J.: Princeton University Press, 2009); Nadia Urbinati, "The Legacy of Kant: Giuseppe Mazzini's Cosmopolitanism of Nations," in Bayly and Biagini, *Giuseppe Mazzini*, 11–22; Salvo Mastellone, "Mazzini's International League and the Politics of the London Democratic Manifestoes, 1837–1850," in Bayly and Biagini, *Giuseppe Mazzini*, 93–104.

53. Joseph Mazzini to George Armstrong, [1855], *BAA*, 417; WLG to Francis Jackson, June 18, 1833, *LWLG* 2:369.

54. Roland Sarti, "Giuseppe Mazzini and Young Europe," in Bayly and Biagini, *Giuseppe Mazzini*, 275–97; Karma Nabulsi, "Patriotism and Internationalism in the 'Oath of Allegiance' to Young Europe," *European Journal of Political Theory* 5, no. 1 (2006): 61–70; Mazzini, "Toward a Holy Alliance of the Peoples," in Recchia and Urbinati, *A Cosmopolitanism of Nations*, 117–31.

55. Maurizio Isabella, "Mazzini's Internationalism in Context: From the Cosmopolitan Patriotism of the Italian Carbonari to Mazzini's Europe of the Nations," in Bayly and Biagini, *Giuseppe*

Mazzini, 37–58; Maurizio Isabella, "Italian Exiles and British Politics before and after 1848," in Freitag, ed., *Exiles from European Revolutions*, 59–87.

56. "Address of the Council of the Peoples' International League," *Liberator*, June 11, 1847. For Mazzini's democratic thought, see Mastellone, *Mazzini and Marx*. On the Peoples' International League, see Margot C. Finn, *After Chartism: Class and Nation in English Radical Politics, 1848–1874* (New York: Cambridge University Press, 1993), 71–73; Miles Taylor, *The Decline of British Radicalism, 1847–1860* (Oxford, U.K.: Clarendon Press, 1995), 193–97; Maura O'Connor, *The Romance of Italy and the English Political Imagination* (New York: St. Martin's Press, 1998), 72–75.

57. Giuseppe Mazzini, "Thoughts upon Democracy in Europe," in *Life and Writings of Joseph Mazzini*, vol. 6: *Critical and Literary* (London: Smith, Elder & Co., 1891), 109, 114; Recchia and Urbinati, *A Cosmopolitanism of Nations*, 57.

58. Urbinati, "Legacy of Kant," 15.

59. Mazzini quotes from "On the Duties of Man" in Recchia and Urbinati, *A Cosmopolitanism of Nations*, 90, 91. See also Viroli, *For Love of Country*, 150; Urbinati, "The Legacy of Kant," 11–22; Sarti, *Mazzini*; Ian Mcmenamin, "'Self-choosing' and 'right-acting' in the Nationalism of Giuseppe Mazzini," *History of European Ideas* 23, no. 5 (1998): 221–34.

60. There are two versions of Wright's letter describing this meeting. See "Letters from Henry C. Wright," *Liberator*, August 27, 1847; and Wright, *Human Life*, 391–92.

61. "Patriotism Enlarging into Human Brotherhood," *Liberator*, June 25, 1847. See also "A New League," *Liberator*, June 11, 1847.

62. "Letters from Henry C. Wright," *Liberator*, August 27, 1847; WLG, introduction to *Joseph Mazzini*, ed. Venturi, xxi.

63. "Russia and the Russians," *Liberty Bell* (1853), 210; MWC to EPN, December 25, 1849, BPL, Ms.A.1.2.18.88.

64. "Letter from Henry C. Wright," *Liberator*, August 31, 1844; "Twelfth Annual Meeting of the American Anti-Slavery Society," *Liberator*, May 22, 1846. See also "The Mexican News," *Liberator*, October 8, 1847.

65. MWC to EPN, December 25, 1849, BPL.

66. Phillips, "Idols," 244.

67. WLG to George Thompson, August 23, 1839, *LWLG* 2:530; WLG to Joshua T. Everett, April 14, 1840, *LWLG* 2:576; HCW-BPL, vol. 18:2, 3 (June 18, 1841).

68. Phillips, "Public Opinion," 54; HCW-BPL, vol. 17:225 (May 26, 1841).

CHAPTER SIX

1. Phillips, "Harper's Ferry," *SLL*, 267.

2. "Immediate Abolition," *Liberator*, January 7, 1832; "Legislature of Michigan: Report of the Committee on State Affairs," *Liberator*, November 21, 1845. Also see Garrison, *Thoughts on African Colonization*, 80; Garrison and Garrison, *Garrison* 1:256; "A Noble Protest," *Liberator*, March 22, 1834; "Free and Equal," *Liberator*, February 14, 1835.

3. Garrison qtd. in Thomas, *The Liberator*, 372–73; Garrison qtd. in Honeck, *We Are the Revolutionists*, 145. Thomas quotes the same source to argue that Garrison was "something less than an

enthusiastic supporter of the franchise for women," but on what grounds is unclear (372). Cf. Kraditor, *Means and Ends,* 59.

4. "Human Governments," *Liberator,* November 23, 1849; Tocqueville qtd. in Kahan, *Alexis de Tocqueville,* 11. On the slow spread of suffrage in the United States, see Keyssar, *Right to Vote;* Volk, "The Perils of 'Pure Democracy.'" On the wider Atlantic context, see Kahan, *Liberalism in Nineteenth-Century Europe.*

5. "Struggle for Equal Rights in England," *Liberator,* October 14, 1842; WLG to EPN, February 28, 1843, *LWLG* 3:125.

6. Garrison, "The Powers That Be are Ordained of God," *Selections from the Writings and Speeches,* 91–92; McKanan, *Identifying the Image of God,* 85.

7. Henry Clarke Wright Papers, Box of Correspondence and Manuscripts, HL, bMS Am 515 (3/1); HCW-BPL, vol. 17:86–89 (November 25, 1840); "The American Republic a Liar and a Hypocrite," *Liberator,* May 12, 1848.

8. James Mott to Wendell Phillips, August 9, 1841, HL, bMS, Am 1953 (916); "Letter from Henry C. Wright," *Liberator,* February 6, 1846. On Phillips's impressions of Europe, see "Letter from Wendell Phillips, Naples, April 12, 1841," *Liberator,* May 28, 1841; Stewart, *Wendell Phillips,* 78–80.

9. *Seventeenth Annual Report, Presented to the Massachusetts Anti-Slavery Society* (Boston: Andrew & Prentiss, 1849), 71–72; "Democratic England and Oligarchic America," *Liberator,* August 27, 1847.

10. Adams qtd. in David Brion Davis and Steven Mintz, eds., *The Boisterous Sea of Liberty: A Documentary History of America from Discovery through the Civil War* (New York: Oxford University Press, 1998), 299; Wolcott qtd. in Mason, *Slavery and Politics,* 191.

11. Richard Hildreth, *Despotism in America: or, An Inquiry into the Nature and Results of the Slave-Holding System in the United States* (Boston: Whipple and Darrell, 1840), 7–9; Morris quoted in Earle, *Jacksonian Antislavery,* 47. See also Jonathan H. Earle, "Marcus Morton and the Dilemma of Jacksonian Antislavery in Massachusetts, 1817–1849," *The Massachusetts Historical Review* 4 (2002): 60–87; Daniel Feller, "A Brother in Arms: Benjamin Tappan and the Antislavery Democracy," *Journal of American History* 88, no. 1 (June 2001), www.historycooperative.org/journals/jah/88.1/feller .html; Sean Wilentz, "Slavery, Antislavery, and Jacksonian Democracy," in *The Market Revolution in America: Social, Political, and Religious Expressions, 1800–1880,* ed. Melvyn Stokes and Stephen Conway (Charlottesville: University of Virginia Press, 1996), 202–23; Wilentz, *The Rise of American Democracy,* 548–51; Yonatan Eyal, *The Young America Movement and the Transformation of the Democratic Party, 1828–1861* (New York: Cambridge University Press, 2007), 183–201.

12. Wendell Phillips, "Philosophy of the Abolition Movement," *SLL,* 119, 152; "Address of the Executive Committee of the American Anti-Slavery Society to the Friends of Freedom and Emancipation in the U. States," in *The Constitution a Pro-Slavery Compact: or Selections from the Madison Papers &c* (New York: American Anti-Slavery Society, 1844), 101. See also "Political Cant," *Liberator,* April 4, 1845, and the praise for Hildreth's *Despotism* in *Liberator,* February 14, 1840.

13. Garrison, *Selections,* 250.

14. For recent narratives of the Dorr War, see Ronald P. Formisano, *For the People: American Populist Movements from the Revolution to the 1850s* (Chapel Hill: University of North Carolina Press, 2008), 160–76; Christian G. Fritz, *American Sovereigns: The People and America's Constitutional Tradition before the Civil War* (New York: Cambridge University Press, 2008), 246–76; Wilentz, *The Rise of American Democracy,* 539–45; Erik J. Chaput and Russell J. DeSimone, "Strange Bedfellows: The

Politics of Race in Antebellum Rhode Island," *Common-Place* 10, no. 2 (January 2010), www.com mon-place.org/vol-10/no-02/chaput-desimone/. On abolitionist responses in the state, see Deborah Bingham Van Broekhoven, *The Devotion of these Women: Rhode Island in the Antislavery Network* (Amherst: University of Massachusetts Press, 2002), 38–46.

15. "The Civil War in Rhode Island," *Liberator*, July 22, 1842; "Rhode Island," *Liberator*, October 29, 1841. See also "The Civil War in Rhode Island," *Liberator*, July 8, 1842; August 5, 1842; WLG to EQ, November 9, 1841, *LWLG* 3:38; "Free Suffrage," *Liberator*, October 29, 1841. For the Garrisonians' endorsement of the Whigs' compromise constitution, see *Eleventh Annual Report, presented to the Massachusetts Anti-Slavery Society, by its Board of Managers* (Boston: Oliver Johnson, 1843), 19–20.

16. "Rhode-Island Affairs," *Liberator*, August 19, 1842; "The Rhode-Island Controversy," *Liberator*, September 30, 1842; "Free Suffrage," *Liberator*, December 10, 1841; WLG to George W. Benson, July 8, 1842, *LWLG* 3:95. See also the criticism of the "Charterist" party in *Liberator*, August 26, 1842.

17. "Rhode-Island Affairs"; "Free Suffrage," *Liberator*, December 10, 1841. See also "Rhode Island," *Liberator*, October 29, 1841; "'Democracy,'" *Liberator*, February 25, 1842.

18. For previous discussions of abolitionists' relationships with Chartists, see Betty Fladeland, "'Our Cause Being One and the Same': Abolitionists and Chartism," in *Slavery and British Slavery, 1776–1846*, ed. James Walvin (Baton Rouge: Louisiana State University Press, 1982), 69–99; and Betty Fladeland, *Abolitionists and Working-Class Problems in the Age of Industrialization* (Baton Rouge: Louisiana State University Press, 1984); Seymour Drescher, "Cart Whip and Billy Roller: Antislavery and Reform Symbolism in Industrializing Britain," *Journal of Social History* 15, no. 1 (1981): 3–24; Patricia Hollis, "Anti-Slavery and British Working-Class Radicalism in the Years of Reform," in Christine Bolt and Seymour Drescher, eds., *Anti-Slavery, Religion, and Reform: Essays in Memory of Roger Anstey* (Folkestone, U.K.: Dawson, 1980), 295–315. For two other historians who have briefly noted the Garrisonians' sympathy for Chartism and connected it to the political dimension of the Chartists' demands, see Douglas B. A. Ansdell, "William Lloyd Garrison's Ambivalent Approach to Labour Reform," *Journal of American Studies* 24, no. 3 (December 1990): 402–7; Turley, *The Culture of English Antislavery*, 184–87.

19. On Chartism and parliamentary reform, see Malcolm Chase, *Chartism: A New History* (Manchester, U.K.: Manchester University Press, 2007); Wahrman, *Imagining the Middle Class*, part 3; Dorothy Thompson, *The Chartists: Popular Politics in the Industrial Revolution* (New York: Pantheon Books, 1984); Derek Beales, "The Idea of Reform in British Politics, 1829–1850," *Proceedings of the British Academy* 100 (1999): 159–74; Gareth Stedman Jones, "Rethinking Chartism," in *Languages of Class: Studies in English Working Class History, 1832–1982* (Cambridge, U.K.: Cambridge University Press, 1983), 90–178; Dorothy Thompson, "The Early Chartists," in *Outsiders: Class, Gender and Nation* (London: Verso, 1993), 45–76; James A. Epstein, *Radical Expression: Political Language, Ritual, and Symbol in England, 1790–1850* (New York: Oxford University Press, 1994); Philip Harling, "Parliament, the State, and 'Old Corruption': Conceptualizing Reform, c. 1790–1832," in *Rethinking the Age of Reform: Britain, 1780–1850*, ed. Arthur Burns and Joanna Innes (New York: Cambridge University Press, 2003), 98–113; Iorwerth Prothero, *Radical Artisans in England and France, 1830–1870* (Cambridge, U.K.: Cambridge University Press, 1997), 22–45; Edward Royle and James Walvin, *English Radicals and Reformers, 1760–1848* (Brighton, Sussex: Harvester Press, 1982), 108–23, and a useful historiographical essay by Miles Taylor, "Rethinking the Chartists: Searching for Synthesis in the Historiography of Chartism," *Historical Journal* 39, no. 2 (June 1996): 479–95.

20. On Chartists' rich movement culture, see Chase, *Chartism*.

21. Venturi, *William Henry Ashurst*, 3–4; "The Struggle for Equal Rights in England." See also *Oxford Dictionary of National Biography*, online ed., s.v. "Ashurst, William Henry"; Rasor, "Ashurst, William Henry, Senior," in *Biographical Dictionary of Modern British Radicals*, ed. Baylen and Gossman, 21.

22. See Marcus Cunliffe, *Chattel Slavery and Wage Slavery: The Anglo-American Context, 1830–1860* (Athens: University of Georgia Press, 1979); Rugemer, "The Southern Response to British Abolitionism," 221–48.

23. "Great Public Meeting of the Glasgow Emancipation Society; Reception of the American Delegates," *Liberator*, August 28, 1840, rpt. from the Glasgow *Argus*. See Alexander Wilson, *The Chartist Movement in Scotland* (Manchester, U.K.: Manchester University Press, 1970), 35–41, 114–25; Fladeland, "'Our Cause being One and the Same,'" 85–86; Alexander Wilson, "Chartism in Glasgow," in Asa Briggs, ed., *Chartist Studies* (London: Macmillan, 1959), 249–87. On debates in the GES, see Rice, *Scots Abolitionists*, 59–114; GES Minute Books, William Smeal Collection (reel 1), vol. 2:173–74; 3:183–201. For examples of Chartists comparing slaves and British workers, see "The Black and the White Slave," *Chartist Circular* (Glasgow), June 7, 1840; "The Land of Freedom," *Chartist Circular*, June 27, 1840; "The White Slave's Murmurs," *Chartist Circular*, December 5, 1840; "White and Black Slaves," *Chartist Circular*, January 2, 1841.

24. Garrison and Garrison, *Garrison* 2:401n.

25. "Great Public Meeting."

26. "Great Public Meeting."

27. "The London Convention," *Liberator*, October 23, 1840.

28. "Address to John A. Collins, Esq.," *Liberator*, May 28, 1841; "Mr. Collins in Scotland," *Liberator*, May 28, 1841; "Anti-Slavery Meeting," *Liberator*, June 4, 1841. See Rice, *Scots Abolitionists*, 110–13.

29. WLG to EQ, August 14, 1846, *LWLG* 3:372, with the evening of conversation cited in 374n7; "The New Anti-Slavery League," London *Universe*, August 21, 1846, rpt. in *Liberator*, September 19, 1851. See also WLG to HEG, September 3, 1846, *LWLG* 3:392–94; Richard Bradbury, "Frederick Douglass and the Chartists," in Rice and Crawford, eds., *Liberating Sojourn*, 169–86; Perry, *Childhood, Marriage, and Reform*, 267.

30. "Dissolution of the American Union: Letter from Henry C. Wright," *Liberator*, January 30, 1846; William Lloyd Garrison, *American Slavery: Address on the Subject of American Slavery, and the Progress of the Cause of Freedom throughout the World, delivered in the National Hall, Holborn . . .* (London: Richard Kinder, 1846), 4. See also "Dissolution of the Union," *Liberator*, January 2, 1846.

31. Garrison, *American Slavery*, 4–6, 22–23. See also WLG to RDW, September 5, 1846, *LWLG* 3:396–97.

32. "Letter from Richard Allen," *Liberator*, July 1, 1842.

33. JBE to SMJr, October 1, 1846, *BAA*, 290–92, qtd. on 290, 291. See also JBE to SMJr, November 2, 1846, *BAA*, 296.

34. For critics at home, see SMJr to Mary Carpenter, December 29, 1845, *BAA*, 245; "Abolitionists Vindicated," *Liberator*, July 14, 1843; "Who Are the European Abolitionists?" *Liberator*, October 3, 1845. On Sturge's attempted alliance between Chartists and middle-class reformers, see Alex Tyrrell, *Joseph Sturge and the Moral Radical Party in Early Victorian Britain* (London: Christopher Helm, 1987), 85–134; Fladeland, *Abolitionists and Working-Class Problems*, 49–73; "Letter from Elizabeth Pease," *Liberator*, May 26, 1843.

35. SMJr to JBE, December 4, 1846, *BAA*, 302; Garrison, *American Slavery*, 21.

36. William Lovett and John Collins, *Chartism: A New Organization of the People* (1840; rpt., Leicester, U.K.: Leicester University Press, 1969), v, 5, 21; Wendell Phillips, "Chartism" (A. Ms.), HL, bMS, Am 1953 (1585).

37. WP to EPN, August 12, 1842, *BAA,* 179; EPN to WP, September 29, 1842, *BAA,* 182–83; EPN to WP, October 31, 1842, BPL, Ms.A.1.2.12.2.101.

38. EPN to AWW, June 24, 1841, *BAA,* 154; EPN to WP, September 29, 1842, *BAA,* 183; EPN to AWW, December 30, 1841, *BAA,* 159; "Pro-Slavery Church—The Old Platform," *Liberator,* October 15, 1841. On Pease's Chartism, see also Midgley, *Women against Slavery,* 151–53; Chase, *Chartism,* 193. See also EPN to unknown recipient, February 28, 1842, *BAA,* 169–70; EPN to WP, January 31, 1843, *BAA,* 186; EPN to NPR, November 11, 1840, Haverford College Special Collection 806, Box 1.

39. "Struggle for Equal Rights." See also "From our English Correspondent," *Liberator,* August 23, 1844. In the years mentioned, Ashurst published over 130 dispatches. In the same period there were about 680 issues of the *Liberator* published. For only a few examples of Ashurst columns that returned to these themes, see articles by "Edward Search" in *Liberator,* March 10, 1843; March 29, 1844; March 28, 1845; June 30, 1848; October 3, 1845; October 9, 1846; March 12, 1847; September 22, 1848; November 10, 1848; September 28, 1849. See also the reports by another Chartist in "Present Condition of England—The Chartists," *Liberator,* March 3, 1843; "Chartism in England," *Liberator,* June 21, 1844.

40. "British Chartism: Lecture of Wendell Phillips before the Boston Lyceum," New-York *Tribune,* December 26, 1842.

41. WP to EPN, December 30, 1842, BPL, Ms.Am.123 (32); EPN to WP, January 31, 1843, *BAA,* 185; "British Chartism." Although Phillips did not receive all the tracts from Lovett in time to incorporate them into the first iteration of his speech, he told Pease the letters he received in time "were amply sufficient."

42. "The English Chartists," *Liberator,* June 17, 1842; "Letter from Thomas Davis," *Liberator,* June 24, 1842; "Letters from Henry C. Wright," *Liberator,* July 28, 1843. On Wright's reservations, see Perry, *Childhood, Marriage, and Reform,* 267. On Douglass, see Blassingame, ed., *Frederick Douglass Papers,* 1:134; Blackett, *Building an Antislavery Wall,* 18–25.

43. "State of Things in England," *Liberator,* March 10, 1843; "The Pro-Slavery Church—The Old Platform—The Anti–Corn Law Convention—George Thompson," *Liberator,* October 15, 1841; MWC to Elizabeth Pease, March 31, 1843, *BAA,* 190. See also "English and American Insanity of Legislation," *Liberator,* March 3, 1843; "Slavery—Land Monopoly," *Liberator,* July 2, 1847; EPN to MWC, September 13, 1844, BPL, Ms.A.9.2.20.60; Chase, *Chartism,* 50.

44. "Parliamentary and Financial Reform," *Liberator,* November 23, 1849. See also "Skeleton of a Lecture by George Thompson M.P. of England," Concord Antiquarian Society Collection, Box 3, Folder 43, Concord Free Public Library; "Representative Reform Movement in England," *Liberator,* November 2, 1849; "Great Movement in England for Representative Reform," *Liberator,* November 9, 1849; "George Thompson," November 30, 1849; "Grand Reform Meeting," *Liberator,* November 30, 1849; "[Letter from George Thompson]," *Liberator,* December 14, 1849; "Representative Reform Movement in England," *Liberator,* December 14, 1849; "George Thompson and Parliamentary Reform," *Liberator,* December 21, 1849. On parliamentary reform after Chartism and Thompson's role, see Nicholas C. Edsall, "A Failed National Movement: the Parliamentary and Financial Reform As-

sociation, 1848–1854," *Bulletin of the Institute of Historical Research* 49, no. 119 (May 1976): 108–31; Gifford, "George Thompson and Trans-Atlantic Antislavery," 268–69; Taylor, *Decline of British Radicalism*, 158–73.

45. "The Chartists of Scotland," *Liberator*, December 18, 1840. On Garrisonians' unwillingness to endorse the idea of wages as a form of slavery, see Jonathan A. Glickstein, "'Poverty Is Not Slavery': American Abolitionists and the Competitive Labor Market," in Perry and Fellman, eds., *Antislavery Reconsidered*, 195–218.

46. "The Chartists of Scotland." See Lovett and Collins, *Chartism*.

47. Lovett and Collins, *Chartism*, 5. See also Eugenio Biagini and Alistair J. Reid, *Currents of Radicalism: Popular Radicalism, Organised Labour, and Party Politics in Britain, 1850–1914* (Cambridge, U.K.: Cambridge University Press, 1991), 1–19.

48. "Address to Mr. Collins, Esq."; EPN to WP, September 29, 1842, *BAA*, 183. See also EPN to unknown recipient, February 28, 1842, *BAA*, 169–70; EPN to WP, January 31, 1843, *BAA*, 186.

49. "The Question of Labor," *Liberator*, July 9, 1847. See also "Working Men," *Liberator*, January 7, 1831.

50. "Question of Labor"; "British Chartism"; WP to EPN, August 12, 1842, BPL, Ms.A.1.2.12.2.77. On Phillips's later labor radicalism, see Timothy Messer-Kruse, "Eight Hours, Greenbacks, and 'Chinamen': Wendell Phillips, Ira Steward, and the Fate of Labor Reform in Massachusetts," *Labor History* 42, no. 2 (2001): 133–58.

51. "Wendell Phillips," *Liberator*, February 9, 1844; "The Question of Labor."

52. Wendell Phillips, "Idols," *SLL*, 246.

53. Phillips, "Woman's Rights," *SLL*, 27–29.

54. Phillips, "Woman's Rights," 28. For Mill's ambivalence about participation, see Zakaras, "John Stuart Mill," 221–49.

55. Phillips, "Woman's Rights," 22.

56. "Another Workingmen's Opinion," *Liberator*, July 29, 1864; "Shakerism—Death of J. W. Walker," *Liberator*, April 21, 1854. For Walker's activities in the West, see John W. Quist, *Restless Visionaries: the Social Roots of Antebellum Reform in Alabama and Michigan* (Baton Rouge: Louisiana State University Press, 1998), 419, 420.

57. *Liberator*, May 12, 1848; "First of August at Abington," *Liberator*, August 4, 1854. See also "John C. Cluer at Nantucket," *Liberator*, August 1, 1845; "Twentieth Annual Meeting of the Massachusetts A. S. Society," *Liberator*, February 6, 1852; "Twenty-Ninth Annual Meeting of the Massachusetts Anti-Slavery Society," *Liberator*, January 31, 1862. On Cluer's labor activism in New York and New England, see Mary H. Blewett, *Constant Turmoil: the Politics of Industrial Life in Nineteenth-Century New England* (Amherst: University of Massachusetts Press, 2000), 84.

58. "First of August at Abington," *Liberator*, August 4, 1854.

59. "Class Legislation—The Fee Simple in Land," *Liberator*, February 26, 1847; "Letters from Richard D. Webb and Elizabeth Pease," *Liberator* April 25, 1845; "From our Dublin Correspondent," *NASS*, August 22, 1850. See also "Letter from our English Correspondent," *Liberator*, March 29, 1844; "State of Things in England," *Liberator*, March 10, 1843.

60. HCW-BPL, vol. 22:146 (September 6, 1843); Phillips, "Disunion," *SLL*, 362–63; Phillips, "Public Opinion," 52.

CHAPTER SEVEN

1. Leonard L. Richards, *The Slave Power: The Free North and Southern Domination, 1780–1860* (Baton Rouge: Louisiana State University Press, 2000), 3.

2. Smith qtd. in Richard H. Sewell, *Ballots for Freedom: Antislavery Politics in the United States, 1837–1860* (New York: Oxford University Press, 1976), 85.

3. Phillips, "Public Opinion," 50.

4. Blassingame, ed., *Frederick Douglass Papers* 2:395, 396.

5. "First Annual Meeting of the New England Non-Resistance Society," *Non-Resistant,* December 7, 1839; WLG to the Editor of the *Emancipator,* May 31, 1839, *LWLG* 2:481. On the difference between "power" and "influence," see Wendell Phillips, *Can Abolitionists Vote or Take Office Under the United States Constitution?* (New York: American Anti-Slavery Society, 1845), 28. See also WLG to Gerrit Smith, March 27, 1840, *LWLG* 2:572; WLG to Oliver Johnson, August 5, 1839, *LWLG* 2:525; WLG to Smith, May 8, 1840, *LWLG* 2:598–600.

6. Phillips qtd. in Stewart, *Wendell Phillips,* 133.

7. I am grateful to Dorothy Ross for suggesting this last phrase.

8. WLG to MWC, July 19, 1848, *LWLG* 3:568.

9. Wendell Phillips, *SLL,* 51 (Peter the Hermit), 128 (Martin Luther), 229 (quote about Socrates); Stewart, *Wendell Phillips,* 28–29.

10. Wendell Phillips Commonplace Book, BPL; Phillips, "Philosophy of the Abolition Movement," *SSL,* 104–105. For some of the extra-parliamentary movements Phillips mentioned, see the still useful Patricia Hollis, ed. *Pressure from Without in Early Victorian England* (London: Edward Arnold, 1974).

11. "The London Convention," *Liberator,* October 23, 1840. See also WLG to EPN, December 1, 1840, *LWLG* 2:730. For doubts about petitions, see Susan Zaeske, *Signatures of Citizenship: Petitioning, Antislavery, and Women's Political Identity* (Chapel Hill: University of North Carolina Press, 2003), chap. 7.

12. Blassingame, ed., *Frederick Douglass Papers* 2:221. See also Phillips, *Can Abolitionists Vote,* 3–4; Parker Pillsbury, "Why the American Abolitionists Do Not Vote in their Government," *Antislavery Advocate* (December 1854).

13. For an overview of the ACLL, see Paul A. Pickering and Alex Tyrrell, *The People's Bread: A History of the Anti–Corn Law League* (New York: Leicester University Press, 2000).

14. "Elizabeth Pease," *Liberator,* July 30, 1841; Pickering and Tyrrell, *People's Bread,* 191–212; Gifford, "George Thompson and Trans-Atlantic Antislavery," 228–36; Sarah Pugh to EPN, September 20, 1842, *BAA,* 181; "The Pro-Slavery Church—The Old Platform—The Anti–Corn Law Convention—George Thompson," *Liberator,* October 15, 1841; "Presentation of Plate to George Thompson," *Liberator,* April 29, 1842; "Speech of George Thompson," *Liberator,* August 19, 1842; EPN to Edward M. Davis, November 30, 1841, HL, bMS, Am 1054 (140–45); Richard Allen to WP, February 3, 1842, HL, bMS, Am 1953 (201); EPN to Unnamed, February 28, 1842, *BAA,* 169–70.

15. See RDW to MWC, June 30, 1845, BPL, Ms.A.1.2.15.42; "Our Cause in Ireland," *Liberator,* November 28, 1845; WP to RDW, May 30, 1845, BPL, Ms.A.1.2.15.34; WP to SHG, August 12, 1845, Gay Papers; GT to MWC, October 2, 1845, *BAA,* 238–39; RDW to EPN, May 26, 1844, *BAA,* 220–21; Richard Allen to MWC, June 2, 1844, BPL, Ms.A.9.2.20.36B. See also Simon Morgan, "The Anti–

Corn Law League and British Anti-Slavery in Transatlantic Perspective, 1838–1846," *The Historical Journal* 52, no. 1 (2009): 87–107; Temperley, *British Antislavery*, 137–67.

16. See Lucretia Mott to RDW and Hannah Webb, March 17, 1843, BPL, Ms.A.1.2.13.15; AWW to EPN, February 25, 1846, BPL, Ms.A.1.2.16.19; WP to EPN, January 31, 1846, BPL, Ms.A.1.2.16.11; "Horrible," *Liberator*, May 21, 1841; "The News from England," *Liberator*, July 24, 1846; "Letter from Richard Allen," *Liberator*, January 6, 1844; "Edward Search," *Liberator*, March 27, 1846; WP to EPN, April 1844, BPL, Ms.A.1.2.14.25; WP to EPN, October 1844, BPL, Ms.A.1.2.14.60; Frances Armstrong to SMJr, February 16, 1846, *BAA*, 252; Fladeland, *Abolitionists and Working-Class Problems*, chap. 6; Elizabeth A. Ashurst to Elizabeth Neall, October 1841, Gay Papers.

17. Jacob Bright to John Bright, April 18, 1853, Maloney Collection of McKim-Garrison Family Papers, New York Public Library, Box 2-MGF 13. Rice, *Scots Abolitionists*, 44; Chambers-Schiller, "The Cab," 88; WLG to EPN, March 1, 1841, *LWLG* 3:16–18; "Great Anti–Corn Law Meetings," *Liberator*, March 10, 1843; HCW-BPL, vol. 20:212 (September 27, 1843); George Thompson, *Corn Laws: Lectures, delivered before the Ladies of Manchester* (Manchester: Haycraft, [1841]), 3.

18. "Letter from James N. Buffum," *Liberator*, December 12, 1845; Thompson qtd. in Pickering and Tyrrell, *People's Bread*, 191.

19. Pickering and Tyrrell, *People's Bread*, 14–40.

20. Pickering and Tyrrell, *People's Bread*, 1–3; *Oxford Dictionary of National Biography*, online edition, s.v. "James William Massie"; "Anti-Slavery Feeling at Perth" and "Public Meetings," *Liberator*, November 13, 1840.

21. "The National Anti-Slavery Bazaar," *Liberator*, December 19, 1845. On the ACLL bazaars, see Pickering and Tyrrell, *People's Bread*, 124–27; Archibald Prentice, *History of the Anti–Corn-Law League* (London: W. & F. G. Cash, 1853), vol. 1:298–301; Peter Gurney, "'The Sublime of the Bazaar': A Moment in the Making of a Consumer Culture in Mid-Nineteenth Century England," *Journal of Social History* 40, no. 2 (2006): 385–405; F. K. Prochaska, *Women and Philanthropy in Nineteenth-Century England* (Oxford, U.K.: Clarendon Press, 1980), 47–72. Chapters from *Dawn Island* were published in the *National Anti-Slavery Standard*, as well; see the issue for September 25, 1845. Fair organizers in the United States made the comparison between the *Liberty Bell* and *Dawn Island* themselves; see "The Twelfth Massachusetts Anti-Slavery Fair," *Liberator*, September 19, 1845.

22. See *National Anti–Corn Law Bazaar: To be Held in the Theatre Royal, Covent Garden, London, May, 1845* (Manchester, U.K. [1845]), 3, 4, 9, 12. For George Thompson's participation in the first ACLL bazaar publicity, see GT to George Wilson, January 15, 1842, George Wilson Papers, Manchester Central Library, M20/5.

23. "The Fourteenth National Anti-Slavery Bazaar," *Liberator*, January 14, 1848; Isabel Jennings to MWC, November 30, 1845, BPL, Ms.A.4.gA, vol. 1, nos. 93–95; "Nineteenth National Anti-Slavery Bazaar," *Liberator*, January 28, 1853. For evidence that abolitionists solicited surplus items from the Covent Garden bazaar for sale at their own fairs that year, see Nathaniel Barney to MWC, July 8, 1845, BPL, Ms.A.9.2.21.30; RDW to MWC, June 30, 1845, BPL, Ms.A.1.2.15.42. For the Massies' contributions, see "Nineteenth National Anti-Slavery Bazaar," *Liberator*, January 28, 1853; "Twentieth National Anti-Slavery Bazaar," *Liberator*, January 20, 1854.

24. EPN to AWW, December 30, 1841, *BAA*, 159; JBE to SMJr, October 29, 1844, *BAA*, 231. For early application of the term "bazaar" to the antislavery fairs, see "Ninth Massachusetts Anti-Slavery Fair," *Liberator*, July 29, 1842; "The Mass. A. S. Fair," *Liberator*, December 2, 1842; "The Anti-Slavery

Fair at Armory Hall," *Liberator,* December 22, 1843. To trace the name change, cf. "The Twelfth Massachusetts Anti-Slavery Fair," *Liberator,* September 19, 1845, and "The National Anti-Slavery Bazaar," *Liberator,* December 19, 1845. By 1846, the latter name had stuck. See "Twelfth National Anti-Slavery Bazaar," *Liberator,* January 23, 1846, and every subsequent annual report on the bazaar in the *Liberator.*

25. "Letter from Edward Search," *Liberator,* May 10, 1844; "Power of Opinion—Free Trade," *Liberator,* May 15, 1846. See also "The Anti–Corn Law," *Liberator,* March 27, 1846; "Democratic England and Oligarchic America," *Liberator,* August 27, 1847; "Letter from London," *NASS,* May 7, 1846.

26. "Great Anti–Corn Law Meetings," *Liberator,* March 10, 1843; "Reform Liberality," *Liberator,* February 13, 1846.

27. See Kevin B. Nowlan, "The Meaning of Repeal in Irish History," in *Historical Studies IV: Papers Read before the Fifth Irish Conference of Historians,* ed. G. A. Hayes-McCoy (London: Bowes and Bowes, 1963), 1–17; Kevin B. Nowlan, *The Politics of Repeal: A Study in the Relations between Great Britain and Ireland, 1841–50* (London: Routledge, 1965); Lawrence J. McCaffrey, *Daniel O'Connell and the Repeal Year* (Lexington: University Press of Kentucky, 1966); K. Theodore Hoppen, "Riding a Tiger: Daniel O'Connell, Reform, and Popular Politics in Ireland, 1800–1847," *Proceedings of the British Academy* 100 (1999): 121–43.

28. RDW to MWC, October 1, 1843, BPL, Ms.A.1.2.13.59. On Webb, see McDaniel, "Our Country Is the World," chap. 6; Douglas C. Riach, "Daniel O'Connell and American Anti-Slavery," *Irish Historical Studies* 20, no. 77 (March 1976): 3–25, esp. 9; Riach, "Richard Davis Webb and Antislavery in Ireland," 149–67.

29. RDW to WP, April? 17, 1843, HL, bMS, Am 1953 (1277/1).

30. "The Only Alternative—Dissolution of the Union, or the Abolition of Slavery," *Liberator,* April 29, 1842. On timing, see Walters, *The Antislavery Appeal,* 130. For the larger context of Garrison's calls for disunion, see Varon, *Disunion!*

31. See *Cong. Globe,* 27th Cong., 2nd Sess., 168–215 (1842), quotes on p. 168. A typographical error in the *Globe* provides Monday, January 25, as the date; January 24 is correct. See also William Lee Miller, *Arguing about Slavery: John Quincy Adams and the Great Battle in the United States Congress* (New York: Vintage, 1998), 429–44.

32. *Cong. Globe,* 27th Cong., 2nd Sess., 168, 181 (1842). See also 170–74.

33. "Meeting of the Essex County A.S. Society," *Liberator,* February 25, 1842; "Dissolution of the Union," *Liberator,* March 11, 1842.

34. "Address to the Young People of Ohio," *Liberator,* October 12, 1849. See also Walters, *The Antislavery Appeal,* 180n2; "Repeal of the Union," *Liberator,* May 6, 1842; Varon, *Disunion!,* 301; "Speeches at the Annual Meeting of the American Anti-Slavery Society," *Liberator,* June 1, 1860. See also WLG to the Executive Committee of the AASS, May 9, 1842, *LWLG* 3:71–72; "Repeal of the Union," *Liberator,* May 13, 1842; *Eleventh Annual Report,* 4–10; Phillips, "Disunion," in *SLL,* 352. On precedents for disunionist rhetoric, see Mason, *Slavery and Politics,* 228–32.

35. WLG to Charles L. Corkran, February 27, 1842, *LWLG* 3:54; WLG to RDW, February 27, 1842, *LWLG* 3:53. Other Garrisonian abolitionists had also been keeping British correspondents informed about recent clashes over the "gag rule." See John A. Collins to RDW, January 1, 1842; Edward M. Davis to EPN, February 15, 1842; Collins to RDW, April 2, 1842; Elizabeth Neall to EPN, June 18, 1842, all in *BAA,* 161–62, 166, 173, 175–76.

36. "The Annual Meeting at New-York," *Liberator*, April 22, 1842; WLG to George W. Benson, March 22, 1842, *LWLG* 3:62; WLG to Abel Brown, March 18, 1842, *LWLG* 3:57; WLG to James B. Yerrinton, May 7, 1844, *LWLG* 3:256. See also Garrison and Garrison, *Garrison* 3:98; "The Irish Repeal Movement," *Liberator*, September 8, 1843. WLG to George W. Benson, May 13, 1842, *LWLG* 3:74; "Daring Abolition Movement—Repeal of the Union Proposed—Treason Organized at Last," *Liberator*, May 20, 1842; "Expulsion of Mr. Giddings from the House of Representatives," *Liberator*, April 1, 1842; "Repeal of the Union," *Liberator*, May 6, 1842; WLG to the Executive Committee of the AASS, May 9, 1842, *LWLG* 3:71; "Cheering Meetings in New York," *Liberator*, May 20, 1842; "The Union," *Vermont Telegraph* (rpt.), *Liberator*, June 24, 1842; "In the Conflict," *Liberator*, January 20, 1843; "The Case of John L. Brown," *Boston Morning Chronicle* (rpt.), *Liberator*, March 17, 1844; "Repeal!" *Herald of Freedom* (rpt.), *Liberator*, June 14, 1844; WLG, "Address to the Slaves of the United States," in Stanley Harrold, *The Rise of Aggressive Abolitionism: Addresses to the Slaves* (Lexington: University Press of Kentucky, 2004), 178; *Eleventh Annual Report*, 10; *Twelfth Annual Report, Presented to the Massachusetts Anti-Slavery Society, by its Board of Managers* (Boston: Oliver Johnson, 1844), 86. Previously the simultaneity of disunionism and Repeal has been noted only in passing. See introduction to Taylor, ed., *British and American Abolitionists*, 7; Noel Ignatiev, *How the Irish Became White* (New York: Routledge, 1995), 17; Mayer, *All on Fire*, 314.

37. "Letter from Richard Allen," *Liberator*, July 1, 1842; "This Slaveholding Union," *Liberator*, August 5, 1842; RDW to WP, June? 2, 1842, HL, bMS, Am 1953 (1277/1); WP to EPN, June 29, 1842, BPL, Ms. A.1.2.12.2.62; EQ to RDW, June 14, 1844, BPL, Mss. 960, 1:6.

38. HCW to WP, September 26, 1843, HL, bMS, Am 1953 (1349/1); "Letter from Richard Allen," *Liberator*, July 7, 1843; "Letter from Richard Allen," *Liberator*, July 1, 1842. See also James Haughton to WP, September 10, 1843, HL, bMS, Am 1953 (710).

39. "Great Anti-Slavery Meeting in Faneuil Hall," *Liberator*, February 4, 1842.

40. "The Irish Repeal Movement," *Liberator*, September 8, 1843. The most complete analysis of the Irish American Repeal movement and its contentious relationship with abolitionists is Murphy, *American Slavery, Irish Freedom*.

41. "The Irish Repeal Movement"; "Letter from Amasa Walker," *Liberator*, September 8, 1843.

42. "O'Connell," *Liberator*, August 18, 1843. See also "The Irish in America," *Liberator*, December 15, 1843.

43. "O'Connell," *Liberator*, August 18, 1843; *Disunion: Address of the American Anti-Slavery Society; and F. Jackson's Letter on the Proslavery Character of the Constitution* (New York: American Anti-Slavery Society, 1845), 21.

44. WP to RDW, June 29, 1842, BPL, Ms.A.1.2.12.2.61. See also WLG to Daniel O'Connell, December 8, 1843, *LWLG* 3:231. On tensions between O'Connell and the Garrisonians, see "Irish Repeal—American Slavery—O'Connell," *Liberator*, June 17, 1842; James Haughton to Daniel O'Connell, October 1, 1842, and Haughton to O'Connell, August 5, 1843, both in O'Connell, ed., *Correspondence* 7:176–77, 217–18; "The O'Connellites and the Hibernian Anti-Slavery Society," *Liberator*, June 16, 1843; James Haughton to Edward M. Davis, August 16, 1843, HL, bMS, Am 1054 (89); "O'Connell and the American Pro-Slavery Repealers," *Liberator*, September 8, 1843; "James Haughton to his Brother Repealers," *Liberator*, September 8, 1843; "Mr. O'Connell and Mr. Garrison," *Liberator*, October 6, 1843. On improved relations between Garrisonians and O'Connell, see "Repeal Movements," *Liberator*, July 14, 1843; James Haughton to WP, August 13, 1842, HL, bMS, Am

1953 (710); "Irish Repeal and American Slavery," *Liberator*, November 17, 1843; "Grand Meeting in Faneuil Hall," *Liberator*, November 24, 1843; EQ to RDW, November 27, 1843, BPL, Mss. 960, vol. 1, no. 4; EPN to Anne Warren Weston, January 27, 1844; O'Connell to James Haughton, February 4, 1845, O'Connell, ed., *Correspondence* 7:305.

45. For "kill repeal by kindness," see Hilton, *Mad, Bad, Dangerous People*, 541. For the repression of Repeal, see McCaffrey, *Daniel O'Connell and the Repeal Year*, 135–213.

46. RDW to Quincy, October 16, 1843, *BAA*, 199–202, qtd. on 202; Abby Kimber to RDW, June 18, 1844, BPL, Ms.A.1.2.14.38–39. For more examples of Webb's softening attitude towards O'Connell, see RDW to Phillips, December 14, 1842, HL, bMS Am 1953 (1277/1); RDW to MWC, July 3, 1843, BPL, Ms.A.1.2.13.35; RDW to MWC, February 29, 1844, BPL, Ms.A.1.2.14.16; RDW to MWC, November 16, 1843, BPL, Ms.A.1.2.13.82; RDW to EQ, August 16, 1843, BPL, Mss. 960, vol. 2, 7–9. For other expressions of outrage about his treatment, see EPN to WP, January 30, 1844, BPL, Ms.A.1.2.14.10; Richard Allen to MWC, June 2, 1844, BPL, Ms.A.9.2.20.36B; Sarah Pugh to Richard and Hannah Webb, March 27, 1844, BPL, Ms.A.1.2.14.21; James Haughton to MWC, July 18, 1844, *BAA*, 222–23; EPN to Anne Warren Weston, January 27, 1844, *BAA*, 211; NPR to RDW, September 5, 1844, BPL, Ms.A.1.2.14.52; HCW-BPL, vol. 24:29. For positive reactions to O'Connell's release, see EPN to MWC, September 13, 1844, BPL, Ms.A.9.2.20.60; RDW to MWC, September 17, 1844, BPL, Ms.A.1.2.14.57; James Haughton to MWC, October 14, 1844, BPL, Ms.A.9.2.20.71. On Webb's interview with O'Connell in prison, see RDW to EQ, August 17, 1844, BPL, Mss. 960, vol. 2:13–14; RDW to MWC, September 2, 1844, BPL, Ms.1.2.14.51.

47. Rapport, *1848*, 96–97.

48. On Peel's political motives, see, for example, Jonathan Parry, *The Rise and Fall of Liberal Government in Victorian Britain* (New Haven, Conn.: Yale University Press, 1993), 163–66.

49. WP to EPN, January 31, 1846, BPL. See also WLG to William Ballantyne Hodgson, July 17, 1848, *LWLG* 3:562; WLG to the *Liberator*, October 20, 1846, *LWLG* 3:437ff; WLG to HEG, September 10, 1846, *LWLG* 3:402ff; WLG to HEG, September 17, 1846, *LWLG* 3:410ff; WLG to RDW, March 1, 1847, *LWLG* 3:468ff; RDW to MWC, October 31, 1846, BPL, Ms.A.9.2.22.109.

50. Foner, ed., *Life and Writings of Frederick Douglass* 1:238; "Anti-Slavery Convention," *Liberator*, June 25, 1847; Blassingame, ed., *Frederick Douglass Papers* 2:86.

51. "American Slavery—Anti-Slavery League," *Daily News* (London), August 19, 1846. For the first League Council, see *The First Report, Adopted at the General Meeting of the Anti-Slavery League, at Finsbury Chapel* (London: A. Munro, 1847). Simon Morgan also notes the Anti-Slavery League's "direct imitation" of the Anti–Corn Law League in Morgan, "The Anti–Corn Law League," 106.

52. WP to EPN, February 19, 1850, BPL, Ms.A.1.2.19.6. On the antislavery arguments in favor of free trade, see Richard Huzzey, "Free Trade, Free Labour, and Slave Sugar in Victorian Britain," *Historical Journal* 53, no. 2 (2010): 359–79.

53. Phillips, "Public Opinion," 43.

54. "American Anti-Slavery Society," *Liberator*, May 16, 1845.

55. RDW to [Caroline Weston?], February 22, 1849, BPL, Ms.A.9.2.24.63a. On accounts of the politics of the period that emphasize internal changes in aristocratic government, see Anthony Howe, *Free Trade and Liberal England, 1846–1946* (Oxford: Oxford University Press, 1997), 7; Boyd Hilton, *Corn, Cash, Commerce: Economic Policies of the Tory Governments, 1815–1830* (Oxford, U.K.: Oxford University Press, 1977); Philip Harling, *The Waning of "Old Corruption": The Politics of Economical*

Reform in Britain, 1779–1846 (Oxford, U.K.: Clarendon Press, 1996); Peter Mandler, *Aristocratic Government in the Age of Reform: Whigs and Liberals, 1830–1852* (Oxford, U.K.: Clarendon Press, 1990).

56. Roberto Romani, "The Cobdenian Moment in the Italian Risorgimento," in Howe and Morgan, eds., *Rethinking Nineteenth-Century Liberalism*, 128; Cobden qtd. in Howe and Morgan, eds., *Rethinking Nineteenth-Century Liberalism*, 80; Phillips, "Public Opinion," 37. See also Hilton, *Mad, Bad, and Dangerous People*, 311–21; Howe, *Free Trade and Liberal England*, 1–37.

57. WLG to George W. Benson, March 22, 1842, *LWLG* 3:62; JMM to RDW, October 23, 1843, BPL, Ms.A.1.2.13.66. See also "Abolitionists Vindicated," *Liberator*, July 14, 1843; John F. Quinn, "The Rise and Fall of Repeal: Slavery and Irish Nationalism in Antebellum Philadelphia," *Pennsylvania Magazine of History and Biography* 130, no. 1 (January 2006): 45–78.

58. Lydia Maria Child to MWC, April 26, 1842, in *Lydia Maria Child: Selected Letters, 1817–1880,* ed. Milton Meltzer and Patricia G. Holland (Amherst, Mass.: University of Massachusetts Press, 1982), 170.

59. Perry, *Radical Abolitionism*, 183; "The Non-Voting Theory," *NASS*, January 1, 1846.

60. WP to RDW, August 12, 1842, BPL, Ms.A.1.2.12.2.76.

61. Wyatt-Brown, *Lewis Tappan*, 271.

62. "Disunion Pledge," *Liberator*, June 27, 1845; Henry Clarke Wright Journals, HL, vol. 48 (March 28, 1842): 51; "The Annual Meeting at New-York"; "The Union," *Tocsin of Liberty* (rpt.), *Liberator*, May 20, 1842.

63. Nowlan, "Meaning of Repeal," 4–5, O'Connell qtd. on 5; "Letters from Richard D. Webb and Elizabeth Pease," *Liberator*, April 25, 1845. See also EPN to Anne Warren Weston, January 27, 1844, *BAA*, 211; K. Theodore Hoppen, *Ireland since 1800: Conflict and Conformity* (2nd ed., London: Longman, 1999), 30.

64. "Breakfast to Garrison and Thompson," *Liberator*, November 27, 1846. See also Edward M. Davis to WP, May 27, 1844, HL, bMS Am 1953 (471/1).

65. *Disunion: Address of the American Anti-Slavery Society*, 12–22, qtd. on 21, 22.

66. "Letter from Richard Allen," *Liberator*, July 1, 1842; Neall to EPN, June 18, 1842, *BAA*, 177.

67. On Giddings and Garrison, see Stewart, *Holy Warriors*, 106; Stewart, *William Lloyd Garrison and the Challenge of Emancipation*, 147–49; James Brewer Stewart, *Joshua R. Giddings and the Tactics of Radical Politics* (Cleveland: Press of Case Western Reserve University, 1970), 75; "The National Intelligencer—Mr. Giddings," *Liberator*, April 15, 1842; "Sundry Items, Showing the Desperate Condition of Slaveholders," *Liberator*, April 22, 1842; "Extracts of a Letter from J. R. Giddings to his Constituents, in Vindication of His Course in Congress," *Liberator*, May 6, 1842; "Joshua R. Giddings," *Liberator*, July 22, 1842; "The Free States Fighting to Protect Slavery," *Liberator*, July 29, 1842.

68. On the Texas meeting, see Garrison and Garrison, *Garrison* 3:136–38; Mayer, *All on Fire*, 341–42; Charles Sumner to WP, February 4, 1845, HL, bMS, Am 1953 (1188/1); Stewart, *Holy Warriors*, 113. On Wilson and the Garrisonians, see Richard H. Abbott, *Cobbler in Congress; the Life of Henry Wilson, 1812–1875* (Lexington: University Press of Kentucky, 1972), 23–27. See also "Remarks of Mr. Wilson, of Middlesex," *Liberator*, March 21, 1845; "Waltham Picnic," *Liberator*, August 8, 1845; "Middlesex County Anti-Texas and Anti-Slavery Convention," *Liberator*, September 26, 1845; and list of signatures in "To the Public," *Liberator*, January 30, 1846.

69. WP to EPN, February 24, 1845, BPL, Ms.A.1.2.15.17; Phillips qtd. in Stewart, *Wendell Phillips*, 133; RDW to MWC, March 2, 1845, BPL, Ms.A.1.2.15.20.

70. WLG to HEG, August 20, 1847, *LWLG* 3:515; Garrison qtd. in Richard H. Sewell, *John P. Hale and the Politics of Abolition* (Cambridge, Mass.: Harvard University Press, 1965), 64; AWW to EPN, February 25, 1846, BPL, Ms.A.1.2.16.19.

71. WP to EPN, August 29, 1847, BPL, Ms.A.1.2.17.66.

72. Phillips, *Can Abolitionists Vote*, 6.

73. Wendell Phillips, "Lincoln's Election," *SLL*, 307.

CHAPTER EIGHT

1. Wyatt-Brown, "William Lloyd Garrison and Antislavery Unity," 22.

2. "The Meeting at Framingham"; Conway, *Autobiography* 1:185.

3. NPR to RDW, September 5, 1844, BPL, Ms.A.1.2.14.52; NPR to RDW, January 29, 1844, BPL, Ms.A.1.2.14.9; Rogers qtd. in Stewart, *Wendell Phillips*, 132.

4. Garrison qtd. in McKanan, *Identifying the Image of God*, 90.

5. "Poetry: Verses, Suggested by the Present Crisis," *Liberator*, December 19, 1845. See also "Free Speech and Free Inquiry," *Liberator*, April 2, 1847. On wartime uses of the poem, see A. J. Aiséirithe, "Piloting the Car of Human Freedom: Abolitionism, Woman Suffrage, and the Problem of Radical Reform, 1860–1870," Ph.D. diss., University of Chicago, 2007, 90.

6. For a useful summary of these events, see Rapport, *1848*.

7. See Roberts, *Distant Revolutions*; Michael A. Morrison, "American Reaction to European Revolutions, 1848–1852: Sectionalism, Memory, and the Revolutionary Heritage," *Civil War History* 49, no. 2 (2003): 111–32; Paola Gemme, *Domesticating Foreign Struggles: The Italian Risorgimento and Antebellum American Identity* (Athens: University of Georgia Press, 2005); Larry J. Reynolds, *European Revolutions and the American Literary Renaissance* (New Haven, Conn.: Yale University Press, 1988); Adam-Max Tuchinsky, "'The Bourgeoisie Will Fall and Fall Forever': The *New-York Tribune*, the 1848 French Revolution, and American Social Democratic Discourse," *Journal of American History* 92, no. 2 (2005): 470–97.

8. "The American Republic a Liar and a Hypocrite," *Liberator*, May 12, 1848; Alphonse de Lamartine to MWC, March? 1849?, BPL, Ms.A.9.2.4.2; "Letter from Paris," *NASS*, September 20, 1849; "Reformatory: Letter from Maria W. Chapman," *Liberator*, September 28, 1849; Victor Schoelcher to MWC, February 19, 1852, BPL, Ms.A.9.2.26.9; Schoelcher to MWC, July 22, 1852, BPL, Ms.A.9.2.26.47; "Letter from Mrs. M. W. Chapman," *NASS*, July 10, 1851; Taylor, *Women of the Anti-Slavery Movement*, 68–78; WLG to EPN, July 31, 1849, *LWLG* 3:645–46. For early reports on the news abroad in Garrisonian newspapers, see "General Intelligence—Foreign," *NASS*, March 23, 1848; "Important from Europe," *Liberator*, March 24, 1848; "Fourteen Days Later from Europe—France a Republic—The Spirit of Freedom Spreading!" *Liberator*, March 31, 1848; "Further Intelligence from France—All Europe in Commotion," *Liberator*, April 14, 1848; "The News from Paris," *NASS*, July 20, 1848.

9. See letters from Eliza Ashurst to Elizabeth Neall Gay in Gay Papers, especially dated July 31, 1848, November 25, 1848, August 30, 1849, and September 19, 1849. On Anne Knight, see MWC to EPN, November 29, 1848, BPL, Ms.A.1.2.18.41; EPN to [MWC], 15 May 1849, Ms.A.9.2.25.90; Bonnie S. Anderson, "*Frauenemancipation* and Beyond: The Use of the Concept of Emancipation by

Early European Feminists," in Sklar and Stewart, eds., *Women's Rights and Transatlantic Antislavery*, 92–93. For Chapman's article on Deroin, see "Letter from Mrs. M. W. Chapman," *Liberator*, May 18, 1849.

10. "European Politics," *Liberator*, April 21, 1848; "Letter from Edward Search," *Liberator*, April 27, 1849. See also "Letter from Edward Search," *Liberator*, October 20, 1848; "Rome—Land Monopoly," *Liberator*, August 31, 1849. On Emilie Ashurst's clandestine work as a courier and close friend of Mazzini, see Smith, *Mazzini*, 93, 187–88, 211.

11. "Fourteenth Annual Meeting of the American Anti-Slavery Society," *NASS*, May 18, 1848; "Letter from London," *NASS*, April 6, 1848. For abolitionist references to French emancipation, see, from many examples, "French Republic: Liberty—Equality—Fraternity," *NASS*, April 6, 1848; "Meeting of the American Anti-Slavery Society—French Revolution," *NASS*, April 13, 1848; "Abolition of Slavery in the French Colonies," *Liberator*, April 14, 1848.

12. "The American Republic a Liar"; "Speech of Lucretia Mott," *North Star*, May 26, 1848; "Lucretia Mott," *North Star*, June 23, 1848; Phillips, "Welcome to George Thompson," *SLL: Second Series*, 29.

13. "From our Dublin Correspondent," *NASS*, April 12, 1849; "France—England—Ireland," *Liberator*, July 7, 1848. For Estlin's skepticism, see JBE to SMJr, April 7, 1848, BPL, Ms.B.1.6.2.70; May 26, 1848, BPL, Ms.B.1.6.2.75; August 30, 1848, BPL, Ms.B.1.6.2.78.

14. Mary Carpenter to MWC, March 19, 1848, BPL, Ms.A.9.2.24.50; "Fourteenth Annual Meeting of the American Anti-Slavery Society." On African Americans' reactions to the revolutions of 1848, see Mitch Kachun, "'Our Platform Is as Broad as Humanity': Transatlantic Freedom Movements and the Idea of Progress in Nineteenth-Century African American Thought and Activism," *Slavery and Abolition* 24, no. 3 (December 2003): 1–23.

15. "Annexation—Jamaica—Cuba—Yucatan," *NASS*, June 8, 1848.

16. "The Manifest Destiny," *NASS*, April 6, 1848; SMJr to JBE, May 2, 1848, BPL, Ms.B.1.6.2.74. On the escape attempt, see Harrold, *Subversives*, 116–45; Josephine F. Pacheco, *The Pearl: A Failed Slave Escape on the Potomac* (Chapel Hill: University of North Carolina Press, 2005). See also "The Spirit of Liberty Contagious," *Liberator*, April 21, 1848; "Annual Meeting of the American Anti-Slavery Society," *Liberator*, May 19, 1848; "Letter from Henry C. Wright," *Liberator*, June 23, 1848; "The Conviction of Drayton," *Liberator*, August 18, 1848.

17. "Meeting of the American Anti-Slavery Society—French Revolution," *NASS*, April 13, 1848; Blassingame, ed., *Frederick Douglass Papers* 2:116; "Russia and Hungary at Home," *NASS*, September 13, 1849; JBE to SMJr, May 26, 1848, BPL, Ms.B.1.6.2.75. See also "From our Boston Correspondent," *NASS*, May 11, 1848; "The Revolution in France—Slavery Abolished in the French Colonies—Anti-Slavery Celebration in the Old Cradle of Liberty," *Liberator*, March 31, 1848.

18. James Russell Lowell, *The Anti-Slavery Papers of James Russell Lowell* (2 vols., Boston: Houghton Mifflin and Co., 1902), vol. 1:106; see also 1:52–59, 2:105–11; James Russell Lowell, *The Complete Poetical Works of James Russell Lowell* (Boston: Houghton Mifflin Co., 1897), 91–94, 100–101. On Higginson, see Butler, *Critical Americans*, 22–25.

19. "This Hour," *NASS*, July 20, 1848; "Ohio Senator," *NASS*, March 1, 1849. See also "Selections," *NASS*, March 30, 1848; Charles Francis Adams to Committee of the AASS, April 3, 1848, HL, bMS Am 1953 (189); "Giddings Speech," *NASS*, March 30, 1848.

20. "People's Convention at Worcester," *NASS*, July 13, 1848; "The Cause of Liberty Advancing," *Liberator*, July 14, 1848. On the People's Convention, see Laurie, *Beyond Garrison*, 153–88.

21. MWC to EPN, November 29, 1848, BPL, Ms.A.1.2.18.41; "The Voting Mania," *NASS*, November 8, 1849. See also "The Abolitionists and the Free Soil Party," *Liberator*, August 11, 1848; "The Free Soil Movement in America," *Liberator*, November 17, 1848.

22. R. J. M. Blackett, *Beating Against the Barriers: Biographical Essays in Nineteenth-Century Afro-American History* (Baton Rouge: Louisiana State University Press, 1986), 87–137; William Edward Farrison, *William Wells Brown: Author and Reformer* (Chicago: University of Chicago, 1969), 142–47. For "European branch," see SHG to RDW, December 10, 1849, Gay Papers.

23. John Ernest, ed., *Narrative of the Life of Henry Box Brown, Written by Himself* (Chapel Hill: University of North Carolina Press, 2008), 45.

24. WLG to EPN, June 20, 1849, *LWLG* 3:625.

25. "The New Issue," *NASS*, August 17, 1848; MWC to WP, September 28, 1848, HL, bMs, Am 1953 (394/2). See also "The Liberty Party," *NASS*, July 20, 1848. On the concern sparked among abolitionists about Chapman's decision, see WLG to Helen Garrison, July 18, 1848, *LWLG* 3:564; WLG to MWC, July 19, 1848, *LWLG* 3:568; RDW to EQ, March 31, 1848, BPL, Ms. 960, vol. 2:35.

26. "From our Dublin Correspondent," *NASS*, July 13, 1848; George Armstrong to SMJr, January 23, 1849, BPL, Ms.B.1.6.3.56. See also "The Free Soil Movement in America," *Liberator*, November 17, 1848; "From our London Correspondent," *Liberator*, November 24, 1848; "From our London Correspondent," *Liberator*, December 15, 1848.

27. Bartlett, *Wendell Phillips*, 136; WLG to SMJr, December 2, 1848, *LWLG* 3:604. See also WLG to HEG, July 26, 1848, *LWLG* 3:574.

28. For a similar point made about Garrison's later embrace of Republicans, see Mayer, *All on Fire*, 456.

29. "Liberty Party Nominations," *Liberator*, November 11, 1842; "The Meeting of Freemen," *Liberator*, December 2, 1842.

30. SMJr to RDW, February 6, 1849, BPL, Ms.B.1.6.3.58. See also SMJr to JBE, May 2, 1848, BPL, Ms.B.1.6.2.74.

31. RDW to MWC, June 15, 1849, BPL, Ms.A.9.2.24.78. See also "Affairs in Europe," *Liberator*, June 15, 1849.

32. RDW to MWC, December 31, 1851, *BAA*, 385. See also "France and Italy," *Liberator*, June 1, 1849; SMJr to JBE, September 7, 1849, *BAA*, 341.

33. See Rapport, *1848*, 327–34; Geoffrey Ellis, "The Revolution of 1848–1849 in France," in H. Hartmut Pogge Von Strandmann and R. J. W. Evans, eds., *The Revolutions in Europe, 1848–1849: From Reform to Reaction* (Oxford, U.K.: Oxford University Press, 2000), 27–53, esp. 44–52.

34. Elizabeth Bates Chapman to WP, November 28, 1848, HL, bMS, Am 1953 (797); Caroline Weston to SMJr, December 2, 1848, BPL, Ms.B.1.6.3.55.

35. MWC to EPN, November 29, 1848, BPL, Ms.A.1.2.18.41.

36. SMJr to JBE, November 10, 1850, *BAA*, 352–54; JBE to SMJr, May 2, 1851, *BAA*, 377–78; WP to EPN, March 9, 1851, BPL, Ms.A.1.2.20.10–11.

37. "Shall We Ever Be Republican?" *NASS*, April 20, 1848. On "finality," see David M. Potter, *The Impending Crisis, 1848–1861* (New York: Harper & Row, 1976), 121–22.

38. Roberts, *Distant Revolutions*, 135–38.

39. "Review of Daniel Webster's Speech," *Liberator*, March 22, 1850; "Proceedings of the New England Anti-Slavery Convention," *Liberator*, June 7, 1850.

40. The best-known cases of northern resistance to the Fugitive Slave Law are well summarized in Don E. Fehrenbacher, *The Slaveholding Republic: An Account of the United States Government's Relations to Slavery* (New York: Oxford University Press, 2001), chap. 8. See also Gary Lee Collison, *Shadrach Minkins: From Fugitive Slave to Citizen* (Cambridge, Mass.: Harvard University Press, 1997); R. J. M. Blackett, "Dispossessing Massa: Fugitive Slaves and the Politics of Slavery After 1850," *American Nineteenth Century History* 10, no. 2 (2009): 119–36.

41. "Respectability," *Liberator*, November 28, 1851. See also Thomas P. Slaughter, *Bloody Dawn: The Christiana Riot and Racial Violence in the Antebellum North* (New York: Oxford University Press, 1991).

42. Phillips qtd. in Stewart, *Wendell Phillips*, 153; "Speech of Wm. Lloyd Garrison," *NASS*, June 27, 1850.

43. "George Thompson in Boston!" *Pennsylvania Freeman*, rpt., *Liberator*, December 6, 1850. See also "Congratulatory Meeting to Geo. Thompson, Esq., M.P., in Faneuil Hall," *Liberator*, November 22, 1850.

44. Allan Nevins and Milton Halsey Thomas, eds., *The Diary of George Templeton Strong* (New York: Octagon, 1974), vol.2:76. On Kossuth's visit, see Roberts, *Distant Revolutions*, 146–67; Morrison, "American Reaction to European Revolutions, 1848–1852"; Donald S. Spencer, *Louis Kossuth and Young America: A Study of Sectionalism and Foreign Policy 1848–1852* (Columbia: University of Missouri Press, 1977).

45. "The Fugitive Kossuth," *Liberator*, November 14, 1851; "Kossuth and Slavery," *Liberator*, December 26, 1851; "Kossuth: Speech of Wendell Phillips," *Liberator*, January 2, 1852; "Preaching in Syracuse," *NASS*, October 23, 1851. For other examples of abolitionists comparing Kossuth to fugitive slaves, or comparing the architects of the Fugitive Slave Law to Kossuth's enemies in Europe, see Garrison and Garrison, *Garrison* 3:341; "Speech of Frederick Douglass, at the Tabernacle," *NASS*, May 23, 1850; "Speech of C. C. Burleigh," *NASS*, June 6, 1850; "Speech of Parker Pillsbury," *Liberator*, August 29, 1851; W. E. Channing, "The American Slave to Kossuth," *Liberator*, December 19, 1851; "From Our Dublin Correspondent," *NASS*, December 11, 1851.

46. William H. Ashurst to RDW, November 13, 1851, BPL, Ms.A.1.2.20.153. See also RDW to AWW, December 19, 1851, BPL, Ms.A.9.2.25.139; SMJr to JBE, November 4, 1851, *BAA*, 383; "Kossuth, Tell Him of American Slavery! Save Him! Save Him!" *Liberator*, November 7, 1851; "Kossuth—England—France," *Liberator*, November 7, 1851; Eliza Wigham to [AWW,] November 12, 1851, BPL, Ms.A.9.2.25.137; "Kossuth and Hungary," *Liberator*, December 12, 1851; Garrison and Garrison, *Garrison* 3:343.

47. On the invitation from the Motts, see Anna Davis Hallowell, ed., *James and Lucretia Mott: Life and Letters* (Boston: Houghton, Mifflin and Co., 1884), 333–34.

48. "Kossuth Fallen!" *Liberator*, December 19, 1851; "Kossuth: Speech of Wendell Phillips." See also "Kossuth's Apology for His Silence in Regard to American Slavery," *Liberator*, December 26, 1851; Edmund Quincy, "Policy of M. Kossuth," *NASS*, January 1, 1852; "The Eighteenth National Anti-Slavery Bazaar," *Liberator*, January 30, 1852; RDW to MWC, December 31, 1851, *BAA*, 384–85; "New England Anti-Slavery Convention," *NASS*, June 3, 1852; Charles Hovey to [AWW?], January 5, 1852, BPL, Ms.A.9.2.26.1; EPN to [AWW?], February 9, 1852, BPL, Ms.A.9.2.26.9; Mary Estlin to AWW, February 20, 1852, BPL, Ms.A.9.2.26.11; "Kossuth—Phillips," *Liberator*, February 13, 1852.

49. The *Letter to Kossuth* is reprinted in its entirety in *LWLG* 4:97–199, qtd. on 103 and 176.

50. *Kossuth in New England: A Full Account of the Hungarian Governor's Visit to Massachusetts* (Boston: John P. Jewett, 1852), 92. For more sympathetic abolitionist responses, see "The American and Foreign Anti-Slavery Society and Kossuth," *NASS*, January 1, 1852; William H. Furness to WLG, December 30, 1851, BPL, Ms.A.1.2.20.158; "A Plea for Kossuth," *Liberator*, January 2, 1852; "Kossuth," *Liberator*, January 9, 1852; "Defence of Kossuth," *Liberator*, March 12, 1852.

51. "Kossuth: Speech of William Lloyd Garrison, at the Melodeon, Thursday evening, Jan. 29, 1852," *Liberator*, March 5, 1852; *LWLG* 4:102, 152; "Kossuth: Speech of Wendell Phillips"; "Kossuth and the Great American Lie," *Liberator*, March 19, 1852. See also MWC to Mary Estlin, January 24, 1852, *BAA*, 286; "Kossuth and His Mission: Its Object Not Liberty, but Nationalism," *Liberator*, March 26, 1852.

52. "Bloodhounds Turning Spaniels," *Liberator*, December 19, 1851.

53. "Policy of M. Kossuth," *NASS*, January 1, 1852; "Kossuth and Slavery," *NASS*, December 18, 1851; *LWLG* 4:155. See also HCW-BPL, February 27, 1852, Ms.Am.1869 (1). For abolitionists' criticism of Father Mathew along similar lines, see John F. Quinn, *Father Mathew's Crusade: Temperance in Nineteenth-Century Ireland and Irish America* (Amherst: University of Massachusetts Press, 2002), 159–69.

54. "Anti-Slavery Celebration at Abington," *Liberator*, July 15, 1853. See the catalog of fugitive slave cases in Samuel May Jr., *The Fugitive Slave Law and its Victims* (New York: American Anti-Slavery Society, 1856), 15–25. The Kostza affair is mentioned in "Celebration of W. I. Emancipation at Abington, August First, 1854," *Liberator*, August 11, 1854. See also Larry Gara, *The Presidency of Franklin Pierce* (Lawrence: University Press of Kansas, 1991), 106–7; Gautham Rao, "The Federal *Posse Comitatus* Doctrine: Slavery, Compulsion, and Statecraft in Mid-Nineteenth-Century America," *Law and History Review* 26, no. 1 (Spring 2008): 1–56, esp. 32–37.

55. "Anti-Slavery Celebration at Abington."

56. "The Island of Cuba—the Determination of the American People," *Liberator*, November 26, 1852. For quote, see editorial note just above the article. See Robert E. May, *The Southern Dream of a Caribbean Empire, 1854–1861* (Baton Rouge: Louisiana State University Press, 1973).

57. "Speech of Wendell Phillips," *Liberator*, May 27, 1853. See Robert E. May, *Manifest Destiny's Underworld: Filibustering in Antebellum America* (Chapel Hill: University of North Carolina Press, 2002).

58. For evidence that some expansionists inside and outside the administration did see the Crimean War as a moment of opportunity, see May, *Southern Dream*, 39–40; and Gara, *Presidency of Franklin Pierce*, 136–37. See also Frank A. Golder, "Russian-American Relations during the Crimean War," *American Historical Review* 31, no. 3 (April 1926): 462–76.

59. "Anti-Slavery Celebration at Abington." On the Washington *Union* and its relationship to the Pierce administration, see Gara, *Presidency of Franklin Pierce*, 52.

60. SMJr to RDW, July 21, 1854, *BAA*, 406; SMJr to JBE, July 30, 1854, *BAA*, 406. See also May, *Southern Dream*, 66–68.

61. On Soulé, see May, *Southern Dream*, 41–43, 70; Potter, *The Impending Crisis*, 182–86.

62. On Sanders in Europe, see Eyal, *The Young America Movement and the Transformation of the Democratic Party*, 93–115; Yonatan Eyal, "A Romantic Realist: George Nicholas Sanders and the Dilemmas of Southern International Engagement," *Journal of Southern History* 78, no. 1 (February 2012): 107–30; Potter, *Impending Crisis*, 178. For the Sanders-Kossuth correspondence about Mazzini's letter, see articles in the *Liberator*, July 21, 1854; "Mazzini, Kossuth, and Mr. Sanders," *Liberator*,

August 11, 1854; "Celebration of W. I. Emancipation at Manchester, England," *Liberator,* September 1, 1854; Francis Bishop to Mary Estlin, August 1, 1854, BPL, Ms.A.9.2.28.19; Joseph Rossi, *The Image of America in Mazzini's Writings* (Madison: University of Wisconsin Press, 1954), 123–29.

63. Richard Hildreth, *Despotism in America: An Inquiry into the Nature, Results, and Legal Basis of the Slave-Holding System in the United States* (Boston: John P. Jewett, 1854); "Fugitive Slave Bill and Manhood Suffrage," in *BAA,* 357–58, qtd. on 357. For the *Liberator's* endorsements of Hildreth, see "New Publications," *Liberator,* May 12, 1854; "The Anti-Slavery Movement and the Dissolution of the Union," *Liberator,* May 19, 1854. See also, from a wealth of examples of the use of the term "despotism," R. Smith, "Letter from London," *NASS,* April 6, 1848; "Despotism at Home," *NASS,* August 2, 1849; "American Slavery and Turkish Freedom," *NASS,* August 30, 1849; "Celebration at Abington, July 4, 1850," *NASS,* July 25, 1850; "Letter from William P. Powell," *NASS,* May 8, 1851; "Meeting of the American Anti-Slavery Society, at Syracuse," *NASS,* May 22, 1851; "The Rights of Freemen under Despotisms," *NASS,* July 31, 1851; "Letter from Parker Pillsbury," *Liberator,* July 28, 1854; "The Fellow-Feeling between Autocrats and Slavocrats," *Liberator,* December 26, 1851.

64. WP to EPN, August 7, 1854, *BAA,* 407.

65. WP to EPN, August 7, 1854, *BAA,* 407.

66. "The Meeting at Framingham." See Potter, *The Impending Crisis,* 190–93; William W. Freehling, *The Road to Disunion,* vol. 2: *Secessionists Triumphant, 1854–1861* (New York: Oxford University Press, 2007), 145–67; Albert J. Von Frank, *The Trials of Anthony Burns: Freedom and Slavery in Emerson's Boston* (Cambridge, Mass.: Harvard University Press, 1998).

67. "The Meeting at Framingham."

68. Conway, *Autobiography* 1:185.

69. "Debate in Congress, on the Boston Petition," *Liberator,* July 7, 1854.

70. "The Meeting at Framingham."

71. "The Meeting at Framingham."

72. "The Meeting at Framingham."

73. "The Meeting at Framingham."

74. Temperley, *British Antislavery,* 237–40; Stacey M. Robertson, *Parker Pillsbury: Radical Abolitionist, Male Feminist* (Ithaca, N.Y.: Cornell University Press, 2000), 91–114; Lucretia Mott to RDW, April 5, 1852, BPL, Ms.A.1.2.21.13; Sarah Pugh to RDW, April 9, 1852, BPL, Ms.A.1.2.21.15, and April 28, 1852, BPL, Ms.A.1.2.21.18; Maloney Collection of McKim-Garrison Family Papers, New York Public Library, Box 1; Pennsylvania Anti-Slavery Society Executive Committee, Minute Book (1846–56), 181, Pennsylvania Abolition Society Papers, Series 5, Reel 31, Historical Society of Pennsylvania; Edward M. Davis to WP, July 21, 1852, HL, bMS Am 1953 (471/1).

75. On the Crystal Palace incident, see Lisa Merrill, "Exhibiting Race 'under the World's Huge Glass Case': William and Ellen Craft and William Wells Brown at the Great Exhibition in Crystal Palace, London, 1851," *Slavery and Abolition* 33, no. 2 (2012): 321–36; Blackett, *Beating Against the Barriers,* 101–2; Farrison, *William Wells Brown,* 148–51, 186–88; Joan D. Hedrick, *Harriet Beecher Stowe: A Life* (New York: Oxford University Press, 1994), 233–71.

76. See "Anti-Slavery Conference in Manchester," *Liberator,* August 11, 1854, for an announcement, and all of the articles in *Liberator,* September 1, 1854.

77. "Celebration of W. I. Emancipation at Manchester, England," *Liberator,* August 25, 1854; "Celebration of W. I. Emancipation at Manchester, England," *Liberator,* September 1, 1854; "Com-

memoration of W. I. Emancipation in the Manufacturing Metropolis of Great Britain," *Liberator*, August 25, 1854. See also "Great Manchester Anti-Slavery Conference," *Liberator*, October 6, 1854.

78. "The Anti-Slavery Meetings in Manchester," *Liberator*, September 1, 1854; "Letter from London," *NASS*, October 25, 1849; "Speech of William Lloyd Garrison," *Liberator*, August 26, 1853.

79. "Anti-Slavery Celebration at Abington"; "Letter from Joseph Barker, No. II," *Liberator*, July 7, 1854; "The Meeting at Framingham." For Cluer's involvement in the failed Anthony Burns rescue, see Von Frank, *The Trials of Anthony Burns*, 93, 137. For another reference to "European liberalism," see "Eighteenth National Anti-Slavery Bazaar," *Liberator*, January 30, 1852.

80. WLG to Charles Sumner, June 27, 1854, *LWLG* 4:301.

81. "Anti-Slavery Celebration at Abington."

CHAPTER NINE

1. WP to EPN, November 21, 1852, BPL, Ms.A.1.2.21.124; Phillips, "Philosophy of the Abolition Movement," *SLL*, 138. On Hale, see, for example, "Kossuth: Speech of Wendell Phillips," *Liberator*, January 2, 1852.

2. Abraham Lincoln, "Speech at Peoria, Illinois," in *The Collected Works of Abraham Lincoln*, ed. Roy P. Basler (New Brunswick, N.J.: Rutgers University Press, 1953), vol. 2:276; "Mr. Soule's 'Vulgar Turbulence'—George Sanders," *New York Times*, September 29, 1854. I am unable to discover where Lincoln read the *Daily News* editorial, originally published September 12, 1854. But it was reprinted in American newspapers. For full discussion of the quote, see Caleb McDaniel, "New Light on a Lincoln Quote," *Offprints*, April 2, 2011, mcdaniel.blogs.rice.edu/?p=126.

3. Lincoln, "Speech at Peoria, Illinois," in Basler, ed., *Collected Works of Abraham Lincoln*, 2:275, 276.

4. JMM to RDW, November 1, 1856, BPL, Ms.A.1.2.26.78; JMM to RDW, April 4, 1856, BPL, Ms.A.1.2.26.11; "What is the Duty of Abolitionists?" *Liberator*, September 12, 1856. See also David Brown, "William Lloyd Garrison, Transatlantic Abolitionism and Colonisation in the Mid Nineteenth Century: The Revival of the Peculiar Solution?" *Slavery and Abolition* 33, no. 2 (June 2012): 233–50.

5. Abby Kelley to WP, November? 29, 1858, HL, bMS, Am 1953 (556/4). See also Parker Pillsbury to EPN, February 27, 1859, BPL, Ms.A.1.2.29.23; Abby Kelley to WP, December 9, 1860, HL, bMS, Am 1953 (556/5). On Kelley's disaffection, see Aiséirithe, "Piloting the Car of Human Freedom," 59–72.

6. Phillips, "Philosophy of the Abolition Movement," 113, 114, 138; Stewart, *Wendell Phillips*, 210. On Seward's faults, see, for example, SMJr to RDW, March 9, 1860, BPL, Ms.B.1.6.8.11.

7. Wendell Phillips, "Disunion," *SLL*, 352. See also "Thirty Years Completed," *Liberator*, January 4, 1861; "Speech of Charles C. Burleigh," *Liberator*, February 22, 1861; "Speeches at the Annual Meeting of the American Anti-Slavery Society," *Liberator*, June 1, 1860. The day before Phillips spoke, Georgia had adopted articles of secession, but on January 20, Phillips only knew of the secession of South Carolina, Alabama, Florida, and Mississippi—hardly the bulk of the South.

8. Phillips, "Disunion," 344; MWC to EPN, December 10, 1860, BPL, Ms.A.1.2.30.169.

9. Phillips, "Disunion," 346, 347, 354. See also "The Dissolution of the Union and the 'Southern Confederacy,'" *Liberator*, January 4, 1861.

10. Wendell Phillips, "Progress," *SLL,* 386; Phillips, "Disunion," 355.

11. WLG to Oliver Johnson, April 19, 1861, *LWLG* 5:17; Wendell Phillips, "Under the Flag," in *SLL,* 411; "New Occasions Teach New Duties," *Liberator,* May 3, 1861. See also "New Allies for Freedom," *Liberator,* November 6, 1863; "New Occasions Teach New Duties," *Liberator,* May 26, 1865. On the northern response to Lincoln's call for troops, see James M. McPherson, *Battle Cry of Freedom: The Civil War Era* (1988; New York: Oxford University Press, 2003), 274. On Phillips's transformation, see Melinda Lawson, *Patriot Fires: Forging a New American Nationalism in the Civil War North* (Lawrence: University Press of Kansas, 2002), 132–41.

12. James Haughton to WLG, May 29, 1861, BPL, Ms.A.1.2.31.50b; Eliza Wigham to WLG, May 31, 1861, BPL, Ms.A.1.2.31.53b; JMM to RDW, August 16, 1861, BPL, Ms.A.1.2.31.60A. See also RDW to [AWW], July 16, 1861, BPL, Ms.A.9.2.30.70; RDW to AWW, August 25, 1861, BPL, Ms.A.9.2.30.75.

13. Edward M. Davis became "Captain Davis," and Samuel May Jr.'s son also joined the army as a paymaster, beginning a series of enlistments by second-generation Garrisonians that would later include Garrison's own son. For enlistments of May Jr.'s son and Davis, see SMJr to RDW, September 30, 1861, BPL, Ms.B.1.6.8.77; EQ to RDW, October 25, 1861, BPL, Mss. 960, vol. 1, 25. See also Sarah Pugh to RDW, August 11, 1863, BPL, Ms.A.1.2.32.46A. On shifting views of insurrection among abolitionists in the 1840s, see Harrold, *The Rise of Aggressive Abolitionism;* Stanley Harrold, "Romanticizing Slave Revolt: Madison Washington, the *Creole* Mutiny, and Abolitionist Celebration of Violent Means," in John R. McKivigan and Stanley Harrold, eds., *Antislavery Violence: Sectional, Racial, and Cultural Conflict in Antebellum America* (Knoxville: University of Tennessee Press, 1999), 89–107; Merton Dillon, *Slavery Attacked: Southern Slaves and their Allies, 1619–1865* (Baton Rouge: Louisiana State University Press, 1990), 215–16, 224–26; Friedman, *Gregarious Saints,* 196–222; Perry, *Radical Abolitionism,* 231–67. On reactions to the Indian revolt, see RDW to [AWW?], November 17, 1857, BPL, Ms.A.9.2.29.36; Gray, "Whisper to him the word 'India,'" 398.

14. "Orsini and Pierri Meeting," *Liberator,* May 7, 1858; Mischa Honeck, "'Freemen of All Nations, Bestir Yourselves': Felice Orsini's Transnational Afterlife and the Radicalization of America," *Journal of the Early Republic* 30, no. 4 (Winter 2010): 587–615.

15. "The Relation of the Anti-Slavery Cause to the War," *Liberator,* May 10, 1861; WLG to Henry T. Cheever, September 9, 1861, *LWLG* 5:35.

16. James Haughton to WLG, May 29, 1861, BPL, Ms.A.1.2.31.50B. For other letters from confused British correspondents, see Eliza Wigham to WLG, May 31, 1861, BPL, Ms.A.1.2.31.53b; Wigham to SMJr, June 28, 1861, BPL, Ms.B.1.6.8.64; Wigham to SMJr, December 5, 1861, BPL, Ms.B.1.6.8.90; RDW to AWW, July 16, 1861, BPL, Ms.A.9.2.30.70; RDW to AWW, August 25, 1861, BPL, Ms.A.9.2.30.75. On the tensions in Garrisonian networks more generally, see R. J. M. Blackett, *Divided Hearts: Britain and the American Civil War* (Baton Rouge: Louisiana State University Press, 2001).

17. Garrison qtd. in Mayer, *All on Fire,* 531.

18. "Letter," *Liberator,* July 31, 1863.

19. Phillips, "Under the Flag," 413; WLG to Henry T. Cheever, September 9, 1861, *LWLG* 5:35.

20. RDW to [AWW?], July 1861, BPL, Ms.A.9.2.30.70; Eliza Wigham to WLG, May 13, 1861, BPL.

21. JMM to RDW, November 2, 1857, BPL, Ms.A.1.2.27.68.

22. SMJr to RDW, May 6, 1860, BPL, Ms.B.1.6.8.23; SMJr to RDW, November 6, 1860, BPL, Ms.B.1.6.8.39. See also "Twenty-Seventh Anniversary of the American Anti-Slavery Society," *Liberator,* May 18, 1860; JMM to RDW, June 23, 1860, BPL, Ms.A.1.2.30.78; "Fraternity Lecture: Wendell

Phillips upon the Presidential Election," *Liberator,* November 16, 1860; MWC to EPN, December 10, 1860, BPL, Ms.A.1.2.39.169.

23. Phillips, "Lincoln's Election," *SLL,* 305, 306.

24. "Non-Voting Theory: Reply to Messrs. White, Earle, and Bowditch."

25. *Sixth Annual Report of the Executive Committee of the American Anti-Slavery Society* (New York: William S. Dorr, 1839), 51. For pointing me to this quote, I am indebted to Loughran, *The Republic in Print,* 502n120.

26. "Annual Meeting of the Massachusetts Anti-Slavery Society," *Liberator,* February 1, 1861.

27. James M. McPherson, *The Struggle for Equality: Abolitionists and the Negro in the Civil War and Reconstruction* (1964; Princeton, N.J.: Princeton University Press, 1992), 86–87.

28. See McPherson, *Struggle for Equality,* chaps. 1 and 4, and the discussion of Phillips's Cooper Union speech on p. 82.

29. Phillips, "Under the Flag," 398.

30. Matthew J. Clavin, *Toussaint Louverture and the American Civil War: The Promise and Peril of a Second Haitian Revolution* (Philadelphia: University of Pennsylvania Press, 2010), 1–4, 87–94.

31. SMJr to RDW, March 27, 1862?, BPL, Ms.B.1.6.7.34; "Twenty-Ninth Annual Meeting of the Massachusetts Anti-Slavery Society," *Liberator,* February 7, 1862; Phillips, "Progress," 379.

32. Phillips, "Under the Flag," 397, 398, 399.

33. Eliza Wigham to SMJr, June 28, 1861, BPL.

34. JMM to RDW, December 19, 1861, BPL, Ms.A.1.2.31.86A; SMJr to RDW, May 3, 1861, BPL, Ms.B.1.6.8.56; SMJr to RDW, November 26, 1861, BPL, Ms.B.1.6.8.87.

35. Cf. Gary W. Gallagher, *The Union War* (Cambridge, Mass.: Harvard University Press, 2011); Chandra Manning, *What This Cruel War Was Over: Soldiers, Slavery, and the Civil War* (New York: Alfred A. Knopf, 2007); Eric Foner, "Why the North Fought the Civil War," *New York Times,* April 29, 2011, www.nytimes.com/2011/05/01/books/review/book-review-the-union-war-by-gary-w-gallagher.html.

36. WLG to Oliver Johnson, April 19, 1861, *LWLG* 5:17; WLG to Aaron M. Powell, May 14, 1861, *LWLG* 5:27. See also "New Occasions Teach New Duties," *Liberator,* May 3, 1861.

37. Phillips, "The War for the Union," *SLL,* 420.

38. Phillips, "The War for the Union," 421.

39. Phillips, "The War for the Union," 415–16, 417, 420.

40. "Our Duty," *Liberator,* April 26, 1861; "The Relation of the Anti-Slavery Cause to the War," *Liberator,* May 10, 1861.

41. Phillips, "The War for the Union," 419.

42. "Resistance to Slaveholders Obedience to God," *Liberator,* July 13, 1860. See also "Speech of William Lloyd Garrison," *Liberator,* December 16, 1859; "Brown and Garibaldi," *Liberator,* November 23, 1860; "Non-Resistance and Anti-Slavery," January 13, 1860. When James Redpath wished to include an autograph of Hugo's to put in a volume of "the best utterances called forth by the Invasion of Virginia," he approached Chapman, assuming she would have an original letter from Hugo. See Redpath to MWC, January 12, 1860, BPL, Ms.A.4.6A.2.12.

43. Phillips, "Harper's Ferry," *SLL,* 263, 274; Phillips, "The Puritan Principle and John Brown," *SLL: Second Series,* 297, 301.

44. Phillips, "Harper's Ferry," 272, 285–86.

45. Phillips, "Harper's Ferry," 274, 275, 282, 285, 287; "Under the Flag," 400, 414.

46. William Robson, December 7, 1861, BPL, Ms.B.1.6.13.85; Martineau, *Writings on Slavery and the American Civil War*, 150–53, qtd. on 152.

47. SMJr to RDW, October 11, 1861, BPL, Ms.B.1.6.8.78; JMM to RDW, August 16, 1861, BPL, Ms.A.1.2.31.60A. On British opinion, see Blackett, *Divided Hearts*; Amanda Foreman, *A World on Fire: Britain's Crucial Role in the American Civil War* (New York: Random House, 2010).

48. RDW to the Westons, n.d., *BAA*, 459; RDW to Unknown Correspondent, November 6, 1861, BPL, Ms.A.9.2.30.82; JMM to RDW, December 19, 1861; RDW to [AWW?], January 21, 1862, BPL, Ms.A.9.2.31.1. See also JMM to RDW, August 16, 1861, BPL, Ms.A.1.2.31.60A; RDW to EQ, January 31, 1862, BPL, Mss. 960, vol. 2:77–79; JMM to RDW, October 1, 1861, BPL, Ms.A.1.2.31.71B; SMJr to RDW, October 11, 1861, BPL, Ms.B.1.6.8.78; JMM to RDW, December 19, 1861, BPL, Ms.A.1.2.31.86A; SMJr to RDW, December 20, 1861, BPL, Ms.B.1.6.8.94; JMM to RDW, December 30, 1861, BPL, Ms.A.1.2.31.89B; EQ to RDW, 1862, BPL, Mss.960, vol. 1, no. 28; SMJr to RDW, January 12, 1862, BPL, Ms.B.1.6.9.2; SMJr to RDW, February 25, 1862, BPL, Ms.B.1.6.9.10; SMJr to RDW, March 1862, BPL, Ms.B.1.6.7.74; SMJr to RDW, BPL, January 16, 1863, BPL, Ms.B.1.6.9.58; SMJr to RDW, July 1, 1863, BPL, Ms.B.1.6.9.97; SMJr to RDW July 7, 1863, BPL, Ms.B.1.6.9.96; SMJr to RDW, *BAA*, 511–12 RDW to [Caroline Weston?], December 31, 1861, BPL, Ms.A.9.2.30.89; Eliza Wigham to SMJr, January 24, 1862, BPL, Ms.B.1.6.9.7; RDW to EQ, April 3, 1863, BPL, Mss. 960, vol. 2:81.

49. SM Jr. to RDW, May 23, 1863, BPL, Ms.B.1.6.9.93; McKim to RDW, February 1, 1862, BPL, Ms.A.1.2.31.97A. See also RDW to EQ, BPL, Mss. 960, vol. 2:77–79; EQ to RDW, 1862, Mss. 960, vol. 1, no. 28; May Jr. to RDW, January 12, 1862, BPL, Ms.B.1.6.9.2.

50. EQ to RDW, March 26, 1843, Quincy Papers, Massachusetts Historical Society, Reel 47.

51. "From our Dublin Correspondent," *NASS*, July 30, 1846; "From our Dublin Correspondent," *NASS*, November 25, 1847.

52. SMJr to RDW, October 11, 1861, *BAA*, 461; JMM to RDW, August 16, 1861, BPL.

53. See Brown, *Moral Capital*; Huzzey, *Freedom Burning*.

54. JMM to RDW, December 31, 1861, BPL; MWC to Anne Greene Chapman, November 22–23, 1862, BPL, Ms.A.9.2.31.27.

55. MWC to Anne Greene Chapman, November 22–23, 1862, BPL; Phillips, "Under the Flag," 397.

56. WP to RDW, August 13, 1862, BPL, Ms.A.1.2.31.143A. See also Lucretia Mott to RDW, September 10, 1862, BPL, Ms.A.1.2.31.147A.

57. See *Letters on American Slavery from Victor Hugo, De Tocqueville, Emile de Girardin, Carnot, Passy, Mazzini, Humboldt, O. Lafayette—&c.* (Boston: American Anti-Slavery Society, 1860); "Henry Vincent on the American War," *Liberator*, December 30, 1864; RDW to [AWW], December 24, 1861, BPL, Ms.A.9.2.30.85.

58. WLG to Oliver Johnson, December 6, 1861, *LWLG* 5:46–48; WLG to Charles B. Sedgwick, May 20, 1862, *LWLG* 5:93. See also SMJr to RDW, September 30, 1861, BPL, Ms.B.1.6.8.77; McPherson, *Struggle for Equality*, 108; WLG to George Julian, April 13, 1862, *LWLG* 5:91; "The War for the Union of Liberty with Slavery," *Liberator*, September 13, 1861.

59. Abby Kimber to RDW, February 22, 1863, BPL, Ms.A.1.2.32.12A; JMM to RDW, March 17, 1864, BPL, Ms.A.1.2.33.28A; RDW to [AWW?], November 6, 1861, BPL, Ms.A.9.2.30.82. See also Mary Carpenter to Samuel J. May, April 16, 1864, in Carpenter, *The Life and Work of Mary Carpenter*, 301.

CHAPTER TEN

1. "Letter from John Stuart Mill," *Liberator,* March 20, 1863; "Address to President Lincoln," *Liberator,* January 6, 1865. On eased transatlantic relations, see SMJr to RDW, September 23, 1862, BPL, Ms.B.1.6.9.46; Caroline Weston to Mary Estlin, April 21, 1863, BPL, Ms.A.7.3, pp. 120–21; SMJr to RDW, April 21, 1863, *BAA,* 505. For examples of Union support on both sides of the Atlantic after the Emancipation Proclamation, see "New French View of the 'Rebellion,'" *Liberator,* January 8, 1864; SMJr to RDW, February 17, 1863, BPL, Ms.B.1.6.9.85; "The New Birth of the Nation," *Liberator,* May 8, 1863. Important pro-Union British pamphlets include W. E. Adams, *The Slaveholders' War: an Argument for the North and the Negro* (London: J. Snow, 1863); and Francis W. Newman, *The Good Cause of President Lincoln: a Lecture by Professor F. W. Newman* (London: the Emancipation Society, [1863]).

2. Qtd. in Stewart, *William Lloyd Garrison and the Challenge of Emancipation,* 180; "Address of Wendell Phillips," *Liberator,* July 11, 1862. On the debates among abolitionists about Fremont, who ultimately left even Phillips disillusioned, see McPherson, *Struggle for Equality,* 266–80; Stewart, *Wendell Phillips,* 250–53.

3. Aiséirithe, "Piloting the Car of Human Freedom," 223. Aiséirithe offers a different but still insightful account of the split between Phillips and Garrison that argues for dramatic evolution in their thinking and objectives during the war. My account attempts to acknowledge subtle adjustments in both men's thinking but primarily emphasizes the important continuities between the antebellum decades and the war years, even when it came to their differences. For a concise statement of the divide between Phillips and Garrison that resembles, in part, my own account, see Stewart, *William Lloyd Garrison and the Challenge of Emancipation,* 179–80. For transatlantic correspondence about the split, see Marianne Neill to WLG, July 14, 1864, BPL, Ms.A.1.2.33.67A; MWC to EPN, July 18, 1864, BPL, Ms.A.1.2.33.68B; Harriet Martineau to WLG, August 10, 1864, BPL, Ms.A.1.2.33.77A; EPN to WLG, September 1, 1864, BPL, Ms.A.1.2.33.90B; Thomas Hughes to WLG, September 9, 1864, BPL, Ms.A.1.2.33.90A; EPN to [MWC?], September 28, [1864?], BPL, Ms.A.9.2.22.90; RDW to EQ, October 12, 1864, BPL, Mss. 960, vol. 2:87; Francis W. Newman to WLG, October 14, 1864, BPL, Ms.A.1.2.33.94B; John Estcourt to WLG, November 9, 1864, BPL, Ms.A.1.2.33.101B.

4. See McPherson, *Struggle for Equality,* 103, 289–90; Stewart, *Wendell Phillips,* 244.

5. "Speech of Wendell Phillips," *Liberator,* February 5, 1864. See Stewart, *Wendell Phillips,* 246–48.

6. "New England A.S. Convention," *Liberator,* June 10, 1864; "Speech of Wendell Phillips, Esq.," *Liberator,* February 5, 1864. For similar outrage about Lincoln's 10-percent plan, see also Gerrit Smith to WLG, March 14, 1864, BPL, Ms.A.1.2.33.26; Parker Pillsbury to Theodore Tilton, May 22, 1864, New-York Historical Society.

7. WLG to Oliver Johnson, June 17, 1864, *LWLG* 5:213; Stewart, *William Lloyd Garrison and the Challenge of Emancipation,* 183–84.

8. "New England A.S. Convention."

9. "Massachusetts Anti-Slavery Society Annual Meeting," *Liberator,* February 17, 1865. For Garrison's criticism of the Amnesty Proclamation, see "Annual Meeting of the Massachusetts Anti-Slavery Society," *Liberator,* February 5, 1864. On the principled agreements between them, see Friedman, *Gregarious Saints,* 270; Mayer, *All on Fire,* 566. Cf. Stewart, *William Lloyd Garrison and the Challenge of Emancipation,* 184.

10. "Thirty-First Anniversary of the American Anti-Slavery Society," *Liberator*, May 20, 1864; WLG to Oliver Johnson, July 14, 1863, *LWLG* 5:165. See Jennifer L. Weber, *Copperheads: The Rise and Fall of Lincoln's Opponents in the North* (New York: Oxford University Press, 2006), 136–42; Aiséirithe, "Piloting the Car of Human Freedom," 138–43; Mayer, *All on Fire*, 564.

11. Weber, *Copperheads*, 10; WLG to Gerrit Smith, October 31, 1863, *LWLG* 5:170–71. On the "Copperhead" movement and its firm opposition to the Republicans' adoption of emancipation as a war policy, see McPherson, *Battle Cry of Freedom*, 493–94, 506–7.

12. "Annual Meeting of the Massachusetts Anti-Slavery Society," *Liberator*, February 5, 1864. For defenses of Lincoln's record, despite its faults, see "Thirty-First Anniversary of the American Anti-Slavery Society," *Liberator*, May 27, 1864; SMJr to RDW, September 13, 1864, BPL, Ms.B.1.6.10.9; WLG to Francis W. Newman, [July 15, 1864,] *LWLG* 5:222–27.

13. "New England A.S. Convention." See also "New England Anti-Slavery Convention," *Liberator*, June 3, 1864. Garrison visited Washington, D.C., and was clearly moved by the plaudits he received there from Republican officials in Congress and at the White House. See WLG to Helen E. Garrison, June 9, 1864, *LWLG* 5:209–11; Henry Wilson to WLG, February 11, 1864, BPL, Ms.A.2.33.11. Wilson's letter reported a private conversation he had with the secretary of war, who had "remarked there was *one person whom he wished to see* before he died, and *that person was yourself.*" For Thompson's speech, see BPL, Ms.A.1.2.33.38A–39.

14. "Annual Meeting of the Massachusetts Anti-Slavery Society," *Liberator*, February 5, 1864.

15. WP to SMJr, September 19, 1864, BPL, Ms.B.1.6.10.10; "New England A.S. Convention."

16. John Stuart Mill, "Considerations on Representative Government," in *CWJSM* 19:449, 455, 456.

17. See Mill's exposition of Hare's scheme in "Considerations on Representative Government," 453–61. See also F. D. Parsons, *Thomas Hare and Political Representation in Victorian Britain* (Houndmills, Basingstoke, Hampshire, U.K.: Palgrave Macmillan, 2009), 43–75; Duff Spafford, "Mill's Majority Principle," *Canadian Journal of Political Science / Revue canadienne de science politique* 18, no. 3 (September 1985): 599–608; Paul B. Kern, "Universal Suffrage without Democracy: Thomas Hare and John Stuart Mill," *The Review of Politics* 34, no. 3 (July 1972): 306–22.

18. Mill, "Considerations on Representative Government," in *CWJSM* 19:456, 459, 460.

19. "Address of Wendell Phillips," *Liberator*, July 11, 1862.

20. "Address of Wendell Phillips," *Liberator*, July 11, 1862.

21. "Address of Wendell Phillips," *Liberator*, July 11, 1862.

22. Moncure Conway to Wendell Phillips, August 2, [1865], HL, bMS, Am 1953 (437/2); John Stuart Mill to Moncure Daniel Conway, October 23, 1865, *CWJSM* 16:1105, 1106. Mill would later cite Wendell Phillips's support for Hare's system when trying to convince English liberals to adopt it. See Mill to John Elliot Cairnes, September 1, 1867, *CWJSM* 16:1314.

23. "Address of Wendell Phillips," *Liberator*, July 11, 1862.

24. "Address of Wendell Phillips," *Liberator*, July 11, 1862.

25. "Address of Wendell Phillips," *Liberator*, July 11, 1862.

26. "Washington and the West: Speech of Wendell Phillips," *Liberator*, April 25, 1862; "Speech of Wendell Phillips," *Liberator*, July 12, 1861.

27. "Thirty-First Anniversary of the American Anti-Slavery Society," *Liberator*, May 20, 1864.

28. "Annual Meeting of the Massachusetts Anti-Slavery Society," *Liberator*, February 5, 1864.

29. "New England A.S. Convention."
30. "New England A.S. Convention."
31. "New England A.S. Convention."
32. "New England A.S. Convention."
33. "New England A.S. Convention."
34. WLG to Charles Eliot Norton, January 13, 1865, *LWLG* 5:249.
35. "Washington and the West: Speech of Wendell Phillips."
36. WP to SMJr, September 19, 1864, BPL; Aiséirithe, "Piloting the Car of Human Freedom," 134. For more on the bitter exchange between May Jr. and Phillips, see Aiséirithe, "Piloting the Car of Human Freedom," 197–98. On 144–200, Aiséirithe also offers the fullest discussion to date of why Phillips saw his involvement in the Fremont campaign as compatible with his commitments as a reformer. But also see the interpretation of Phillips and Fremont in Stewart, *Wendell Phillips,* 251–53. On the strain between Ann and Wendell Phillips, see Stewart, *Wendell Phillips,* 232–35.
37. "Thirty-First Anniversary of the American Anti-Slavery Society," *Liberator,* May 20, 1864.
38. On abolitionist censure of Louisiana's early reconstruction, see McPherson, *Struggle for Equality,* 243–44. The accounts of Louisiana's troubled reconstruction in 1864 provided by McPherson and Peyton McCrary generally agree with the abolitionists' depiction of Banks and the state government he installed. See McCrary, *Abraham Lincoln and Reconstruction: The Louisiana Experiment* (Princeton, N.J.: Princeton University Press, 1978). My understanding of Banks's regime is informed, however, by the useful and persuasive corrective in Ted Tunnell, *Crucible of Reconstruction: War, Radicalism, and Race in Louisiana, 1862–1877* (Baton Rouge: Louisiana State University Press, 1984).
39. WLG to Francis W. Newman, July 22, 1864, *LWLG* 5:229; "New England Anti-Slavery Convention," *Liberator,* June 3, 1864. See also WLG to Francis W. Newman, July 15, 1864, *LWLG* 5:220–27; and Wright's support of Garrison's arguments in "The President and the Reconstruction Policy," *Liberator,* January 29, 1864. On northern states' suffrages, see Keyssar, *Right to Vote,* 69.
40. WLG to Francis W. Newman, July 22, 1864, *LWLG* 5:228–29.
41. "Speech of Wendell Phillips," *Liberator,* February 5, 1864. Phillips's idea that Lincoln should use the "thunderbolt" of war to enfranchised freedpeople most closely resembled the arguments of Radical Republicans who believed Congress should use its war powers to extend suffrage in reconstructed states. See Michael Les Benedict, *Preserving the Constitution: Essays on Politics and the Constitution in the Reconstruction Era* (New York: Fordham University Press, 2006), 3–22.
42. "Massachusetts Anti-Slavery Society Annual Meeting," *Liberator,* February 17, 1865; "New England Anti-Slavery Convention," *Liberator,* June 3, 1864.
43. Tunnell, *Crucible of Reconstruction,* 26–41, qtd. on 49. Phillips's criticisms of Banks were evidently influenced by the biased accounts of Thomas J. Durant, a disillusioned Louisiana Unionist who gained the admiration of Phillips and other northern abolitionists after Banks had severely limited his power in the state. See his reference to Durant in "Massachusetts Anti-Slavery Society Annual Meeting," *Liberator,* February 17, 1865. Cf. Joseph G. Tregle Jr., "Thomas J. Durant, Utopian Socialism, and the Failure of Presidential Reconstruction in Louisiana," *Journal of Southern History* 45, no. 4 (November 1979): 485–512.
44. "Equal Political Rights," *Liberator,* January 13, 1865.
45. WLG to Francis W. Newman, July 22, 1864, *LWLG* 5:229; WLG to Francis W. Newman, July 15, 1864, *LWLG* 5:224.

46. WLG to Francis W. Newman, July 22, 1864, *LWLG* 5:230.

47. Phillips qtd. from 1865 and 1866 in Stewart, *Wendell Phillips*, 266, 272.

48. WLG to Charles Eliot Norton, January 13, 1865, *LWLG* 5:249.

49. "Massachusetts Anti-Slavery Society Annual Meeting," *Liberator*, February 17, 1865.

50. "Equal Political Rights," *Liberator*, January 13, 1865; *LWLG* 5:382ff.

51. "Thirty-Second Anniversary of the American Anti-Slavery Society," *Liberator*, May 19, 1865; Alonso, *Growing Up Abolitionist*, 213–16; Stewart, *Wendell Phillips*, 232–36.

52. On the Conway debacle, see John Bright to RDW, June 23, 1863, BPL, Ms.A.1.2.32.38; Chesson to RDW, June 23, 1863, BPL, Ms.A.1.2.32.38; GT to RDW, June 23, 1863, BPL, Ms.A.1.2.32.39; Maria Martineau to RDW, June 26, 1863, BPL, Ms.A.1.2.32.37B; WLG to Horace Greeley, June 30, 1863, *LWLG* 5:161ff.

53. "Thirty-First Anniversary of the American Anti-Slavery Society," *Liberator*, May 27, 1864; "Massachusetts Anti-Slavery Society Meeting," *Liberator*, February 10, 1865. See also WP to SMJr, September 19, 1864, BPL, Ms.B.1.6.10.10; SMJr to WP, September 20, 1864, BPL, Ms.B.1.6.10.11; Thomas Wentworth Higginson to WLG, January 2, 1865, BPL, Ms.A.1.2.34.1.

54. See McPherson, *Struggle for Equality*, 161; Friedman, *Gregarious Saints*, 260–61. Cf. Aiséirithe, "Piloting the Car of Human Freedom," chapter 5, which sees the disputes among abolitionists about freedmen's aid as signs of "shifts in both their conceptions or definitions of freedom and their ideas and attitudes toward the enslaved" (201).

55. "Letter from J. Miller McKim," *Liberator*, December 30, 1864.

56. See *Proceedings of the American Anti-Slavery Society, at Its Third Decade* (New York: American Anti-Slavery Society, 1863).

57. For an insightful recent study of the debates over the dissolution of the antislavery societies, see Francesca Gamber, "The Public Sphere and the End of American Abolitionism, 1833–1870," *Slavery and Abolition* 28, no. 3 (December 2007): 351–68.

58. "Thirty-Second Anniversary of the American Anti-Slavery Society," *Liberator*, May 26, 1865; "Massachusetts Anti-Slavery Society Annual Meeting," *Liberator*, February 17, 1865. See also "Elective Franchise," *Liberator*, April 21, 1865; WLG to Francis W. Newman, July 22, 1864, *LWLG* 5:228. McKim made a similar argument in March 1864, writing to Webb that, while he was "in favor of universal suffrage, without respect to color," he thought that goal was separate from his tasks "as a member of the American Anti-Slavery Society." "I am a democrat but not because I am an abolitionist. Abolitionism tends to but does not include democracy," McKim said, primarily to stress the semantic distinction between the movements (JMM to RDW, March 17, 1864, BPL, Ms.A.1.2.33.28A).

59. "Thirty-Second Anniversary of the American Anti-Slavery Society," *Liberator*, May 26, 1865.

60. "The Renovation of the South," *Liberator*, August 4, 1865; "The Renovation of the South," *Liberator*, August 11, 1865.

61. WLG to Theodore Tilton, February 3, 1866, *LWLG* 5:379. See also WLG to Charles Sumner, February 11, 1866, *LWLG* 5:383–84; WLG to Armenia S. White, December 21, 1868, *LWLG* 6:88–91.

62. JMM to RDW, March 27, 1865, BPL, Ms.A.1.2.34.36A; SMJr to RDW, February 9, 1866, BPL, Ms.B.1.6.10.38. See also SMJr to RDW, February 14, 1865, BPL, Ms.B.1.6.10.14; JMM to RDW, March 2, 1866, BPL, Ms.A.1.2.34.130; "To the People of the United States and the Friends of Freedom Everywhere," *Liberator*, April 7, 1865.

63. John Stuart Mill to Moncure Daniel Conway, October 23, 1865, *CWJSM* 16:1106.

64. Moncure Conway to Wendell Phillips, October 7, [1865?,] HL, bMS, Am 1953 (437/2).

65. "Negro Suffrage," *Liberator,* January 20, 1865; "Massachusetts Anti-Slavery Society Annual Meeting," *Liberator,* February 10, 1865.

66. "Massachusetts Anti-Slavery Society Annual Meeting," *Liberator,* February 10, 1865; "Thirty-Second Anniversary of the American Anti-Slavery Society," *Liberator,* May 19, 1865.

67. "Thirty-Second Anniversary of the American Anti-Slavery Society," *Liberator,* May 19, 1865; "Massachusetts Anti-Slavery Society Annual Meeting," *Liberator,* February 17, 1865. See also Stewart, *Wendell Phillips,* 255–56.

68. "Massachusetts Anti-Slavery Society Annual Meeting," *Liberator,* February 17, 1865.

69. "In the Majority," *Liberator,* January 27, 1865; "Be of Good Cheer," *Liberator,* July 14, 1865. See also "General Butler on the Crisis," *Liberator,* May 12, 1865; "An Argument on Universal Suffrage," *Liberator,* May 12, 1865; "Letter from Robert Dale Owen," *Liberator,* July 7, 1865; "Gen. Banks on Suffrage," *Liberator,* July 28, 1865; "Restoration of the Rebel States," *Liberator,* August 4, 1865; "Equal Political Rights," *Liberator,* August 4, 1865; "Gen. Garfield on Negro Suffrage," *Liberator,* August 11, 1865; "Gen. Meagher's Views," *Liberator,* August 18, 1865; "Safeguards of Personal Liberty," *Liberator,* August 25, 1865; "Reconstruction," *Liberator,* August 25, 1865.

70. Phillips, "Public Opinion," 52, 53. For more on abolitionists' reactions to Garrison's seeming relaxation, see Aiséirithe, "Piloting the Car of Human Freedom," 188–93, 198–99.

EPILOGUE

1. "Nature of the Struggle," *Liberator,* April 7, 1865.

2. "Letters from New York," *Liberator,* August 4, 1865. See also "The British Aristocracy and the Slaveholders," *Liberator,* August 18, 1865; Mentia Taylor to SMJr, January 1865, BPL, Ms.B.1.6.10.30; "Unqualified Suffrage," *NASS,* March 24, 1866; "John Bright on the British Reform Bill," *NASS,* April 21, 1866. "Notes from Abroad," *NASS,* July 28, 1866; "John Bright," *NASS,* September 22, 1866; "The Reform Question in England," *NASS,* September 7, 1867. For identification of "Maladie du Pays," I am indebted to Alonso, *Growing up Abolitionist,* 262.

3. "Freedom Triumphant!"; *Special Report of the Anti-Slavery Conference, Held in Paris . . . on the Twenty-Sixth and Twenty-Seventh August, 1867,* 38. See also "Letter from Hon. N. H. Whiting," *Liberator,* August 11, 1865; "Anti-Slavery Celebration at Framingham," *Liberator,* July 14, 1865.

4. "Speech of Wendell Phillips, Esq., at the Brooklyn Academy of Music," *NASS,* February 24, 1866.

5. "Letter from Mazzini," *Liberator,* July 7, 1865. See also letter by Louis Kossuth in *Liberator,* July 7, 1865; "Letter from President Lincoln to Count Gasparin," *Liberator,* August 18, 1865; John Stuart Mill to Max Kyllmann, May 30, 1865, *CWJSM* 16:1062–63; "Gen. Thompson on Reconstruction," *NASS,* January 20, 1866; "Europe to America," *NASS,* June 23, 1866; "The Liberals of Europe," *NASS,* July 7, 1866; Bender, *A Nation among Nations,* 123–24; Butler, *Critical Americans,* chaps. 2–3.

6. Mazzini to "Mr. Conway," October 30, 1865, in Alice de Rosen Jervis, trans., *Mazzini's Letters* (1930; Westport, Conn.: Hyperion Press, Inc., 1979), 195–96. On Godkin, see Alonso, *Growing up Abolitionist,* 264; Butler, *Critical Americans,* 121–27. See also Henry Clarke Wright, *The Ballot: What Does It Mean? Who Shall Use It?* (n.p.: n.d.). Wright argued for the enfranchisement of black Americans and women by rhetorically asking readers whether they were better equipped to vote

than drunkards or immigrants. On "capacity," see Alan S. Kahan, *Liberalism in Nineteenth-Century Europe: The Political Culture of Limited Suffrage* (Houndmills, Basinstoke, Hampshire, U.K.: Palgrave Macmillan, 2003).

7. Samuel J. May to Estlin, June 26, 1865, BPL, Ms.A.7.2.103; "Celebration of West India Emancipation," *Liberator*, August 11, 1865. These questions would later preoccupy the liberals surveyed in Butler, *Critical Americans.*

8. Qtd. in Garrison and Garrison, *Garrison*, 137; WLG to James Russell Lowell, January 1, 1867, *LWLG* 5:442ff.

9. For Chesson's account of his American trip, see *Dinner to Mr. F. W. Chesson, at the National Liberal Club, on Friday, July 16th, 1886* (n.p., n.d.), xv, REAS; *Oxford Dictionary of National Biography,* online ed., s.v. "Chesson, Frederick William (1833–1888)." On *The Empire,* see Gifford, "George Thompson and Trans-Atlantic Antislavery," 313–17.

10. Diary of F. W. Chesson, 1854–66, REAS 11/1–13. On writing Cobden's biography, see entry for August 1, 1865 in REAS, 11/12; Chesson, ed., *The Political Writings of Richard Cobden.*

11. *Proceedings at the Public Breakfast*, 70; Diary of Frederick Chesson, 1866, September 1866–May 1867, May 1867–April 1868, REAS 11/13–15; *Oxford Dictionary of National Biography,* online ed., s.v. "Jamaica Committee (act. 1865–1869)." On the Morant Bay Rebellion, see Rugemer, *The Problem of Emancipation,* 291–301; Thomas C. Holt, *The Problem of Freedom: Race, Labor, and Politics in Jamaica and Britain, 1832–1938* (Baltimore: Johns Hopkins University Press, 1992), chap. 8.

12. "Thirty-Second Anniversary of the American Anti-Slavery Society," *Liberator*, May 26, 1865.

13. On Garrison's providentialism as the end of the war, see Nicholas Guyatt, *Providence and the Invention of the United States, 1607–1876* (New York: Cambridge University Press, 2007), 309–11, qtd. on 310.

14. James Brewer Stewart emphasizes Garrison's desire for personal vindication and retirement in Stewart, *Wendell Phillips,* 243–69; Stewart, *William Lloyd Garrison and the Challenge of Emancipation,* 175–98. See also Friedman, *Gregarious Saints,* 256–70. Henry Mayer argues, less persuasively, that the schism was caused by Phillips's haughtiness and pursuit of personal glory. See Mayer, *All on Fire,* 562–71.

15. "Thirty-Second Anniversary of the American Anti-Slavery Society," *Liberator,* May 19, 1865; Aiséirithe, "Piloting the Car of Human Freedom," 119, 223, 332–33, qtd. on 119. See also Friedman, *Gregarious Saints,* 274; Stewart, *Wendell Phillips,* 293–95. For debates about whether the AASS should take up woman suffrage, see Aiséirithe, "Piloting the Car of Human Freedom," chapter 6.

16. "Nothing Venture, Nothing Have," *NASS*, February 9, 1867; Phillips qtd. in Stewart, *Wendell Phillips,* 294–95. For abolitionists' initial optimism about Johnson, see McPherson, *Struggle for Equality,* 316–18.

17. Guyatt, *Providence and the Invention of the United States,* 321–25, qtd. on 324. See, for an example of Garrison's comments on Reconstruction, "Our National Situation," *NASS,* March 9, 1867.

18. Wendell Phillips, "William Lloyd Garrison," in *SLL: Second Series,* 459, 460.

19. Phillips, "William Lloyd Garrison," 459–72. Phillips had also praised O'Connell four years before as an icon of "agitation." See "Daniel O'Connell," in *SLL: Second Series,* 384–417.

20. *Proceedings at the Public Breakfast,* 35.

21. Phillips, "Daniel O'Connell," 398–99.

22. Wendell Phillips, "The Scholar in a Republic," in *SLL: Second Series,* 330–64, qtd. on 338.

23. Phillips, "The Scholar in a Republic," 342–57, qtd. on 342, 344, 350.

24. Phillips, "The Scholar in a Republic," 361.

25. Butler, *Critical Americans*; Elizabeth Cady Stanton, *Eighty Years and More (1815–1897): Reminiscences of Elizabeth Cady Stanton* (New York: European Publishing Co., 1898), 332–34, qtd. on 333.

26. Wendell Phillips, "Harriet Martineau," in *SLL: Second Series*, 473. On Crete, see "The Cretan Revolution," *NASS*, January 19, 1867; David Prior, "'Crete the Opening Wedge': Nationalism and International Affairs in Postbellum America," *Journal of Social History* 42, no. 4 (Summer 2009): 861–87.

27. On the renewal of correspondence and friendship, see RDW to MWC, January 18, 1865, BPL, Ms.A.9.2.32.29; Mary Estlin to [Caroline Weston], February 23, 1865, BPL, Ms.A.9.2.32.32; Mary Carpenter to WLG, October 26, 1865, BPL, Ms.A.1.2.34.94B; SMJr to RDW, July 3, 1866, BPL, Ms.B.1.6.10.46. On the British visitors mentioned, see SMJr to RDW, April 2, 1867, BPL, Ms.B.1.6.10.47; SMJr to RDW, May 15, 1868, BPL, Ms.B.1.6.10.54; Mary Estlin to WLG, May 22, 1868, BPL, Ms.A.1.2.36.31B. Webb's visit was unfortunately blighted by a steamboat accident in Detroit that kept him from seeing many of his friends. See RDW to SHG, February 26, 1869, Gay Papers. On the Fenians, see RDW to AWW, May? 23, 1867, BPL, Ms.A.9.2.32.70; SMJr to RDW, [1870?], *BAA*, 543–44; RDW to Unknown Correspondent, [1870?], BPL, Ms.A.9.2.16.25; RDW to EQ, March 12, 1870, BPL, Mss. 960, vol. 2:102; RDW to EQ, March 15, 1870, BPL, Mss. 960, vol. 2:101. On woman suffrage, SMJr to RDW, June 28, 1869, BPL, Ms.B.1.6.10.84; SMJr to Mary Estlin, February 12, 1870, BPL, Ms.A.7.2.107; Mott to RDW, February 24, 1870, BPL, Ms.A.1.2.36.109; Pugh to RDW, April 8, 1870, BPL, Ms.A.1.2.36.115; Pugh to RDW, February 6, 1871, BPL, Ms.A.1.2.37.4. On the Franco-Prussian War, Lucretia Mott to RDW, January 22, 1870, BPL, Ms.A.1.2.36.104A; EQ to RDW, August 2, 1870, BPL, Mss. 960, vol. 1, no. 34; RDW to EQ, August 18, 1870, BPL, Mss. 960, vol. 2:103; RDW to EQ, September 3, 1870, BPL, Mss. 960, vol. 2:104; Gerrit Smith to RDW, November 18, 1870, BPL, Ms.A.1.2.36.130; SMJr to RDW, January 12, 1871, BPL, Ms.B.1.6.11.7; RDW to SMJr, January 24, 1871, BPL, Ms.A.9.2.32.79; RDW to [MWC?], September 15, 1871, BPL, Ms.A.9.2.32.82. On labor and civil service reform, SMJr to RDW, August 24, 1870, BPL, Ms.B.1.6.11.3; SMJr to RDW, November 5, 1868, BPL, Ms.B.1.6.10.67; Quincy to RDW, April 30, 1871, BPL, Mss. 960, vol. 1, no. 36; SMJr to RDW, November 8, 1871, BPL, Ms.B.1.6.11.20; SMJr to RDW, November 29, 1871, BPL, Ms.B.1.6.11.21. On the Liberal Republicans and Godkin, RDW to JMM, February 5, 1872, Garrison Family Papers, HL, bMS, Am 1906 (646); SMJr to RDW, March 22, 1872, BPL, Ms.B.1.6.11.24. On Webb's cooperation with Mill, see JSM to Thomas Joseph Haslam, August 17, 1867, *CWJSM* 32:182; JSM to John Elliot Cairnes, September 1, 1867, *CWJSM* 16:1314; JSM to RDW, February 24, 1868, *CWJSM* 32:189.

28. Jane Addams, *Twenty Years at Hull-House* (New York: Penguin Books, 1998), 19–20. See also Jonathan M. Hansen, *The Lost Promise of Patriotism: Debating American Identity, 1890–1920* (Chicago: University of Chicago Press, 2003).

29. Webb qtd. in Bruce Nelson, "'My Countrymen Are All Mankind': Ireland, Slavery and Abolition," *Field Day Review* 4 (2008): 255; Alonso, *Growing Up Abolitionist*, 288–91, qtd. on 290.

INDEX

Index

racial amalgamationism, riots against, 55
racial equality: Dorrites and, 142–43; Garrison on, 38–41; suffrage and, 137–38. *See also* suffrage
Radical Republicans, 328n41
rational deliberation, 94–96, 109
Reconstruction: Amnesty Proclamation and 10 percent plan, 234, 235, 237; Louisiana and black suffrage issue, 233, 246–51, 256
Reform Act of 1832 (U.K.), 40, 144
reign of terror (1830s): "foreign interference" charge and, 53–56; French Revolution, allusion to, 62; nationalism and, 116–17; public opinion and, 90; revolutionary stories and, 63; schisms of 1840 and, 66; unintended results of, 58–60
religion: abolitionist schisms and, 69; Boston evangelical reformers and Garrison, 31; Garrisonians and politics vs., 183–85. *See also* non-resistance
Remond, Charles Lenox, 67–68, 71, 79, 164, 170
Republican Party: 1860 electoral victory, 218; compromise and, 213; Garrison on, 223; Radical Republicans, 328n41; sympathy with, 211–12
republican revolutions, European, 185–89, 193–94
"responsibility," 155–56
revolutions: American Revolution, 22, 28–29; European counterrevolutions, 193–94; European republican movements, 185–89; Garrison on European revolutions, 40–41, 43–44. *See also specific places*
Richards, Leonard L., 159
riots and violence: against black abolitionists (1842), 100; justified violence, 215–16; majoritarian tyranny and, 100–101; schism of 1840 and, 72–73; Tremont Temple (1860), 106, 107. *See also* reign of terror (1830s)
Rogers, Nathaniel P., 70, 74–75, 111, 121, 125–26, 184
Romantic poetry and heroism, 27–30, 43, 45–46, 129
Ross, Dorothy, 278n43
Roy, Ram Mohun, 83
Russia, 26, 27, 201–2

Sanders, George N., 202, 208, 211
Schoelcher, Victor, 2, 6, 10, 186, 232
Scoble, John, 58, 71
Scotland, 57, 75
Search, Edward (pseud.). *See* Ashurst, William Henry
secession movement, southern, 212–13
Seward, William Henry, 212, 213

Shaen, William, 2
shame, patriotic mobilization of: Atlantic crossings of 1850s and, 206–7; continuity of strategy of, 80–81; England and, 48; expansionism and, 188–89; foreign appeals and, 47; Fugitive Slave Law and, 197; Lundy, Garrison, and, 34–37; "moral Lafayettes," 53, 54, 67, 199; NEASS and, 47–48; Thompson tour and, 51
"The Shipwreck" (Garrison), 27
Sims, Thomas, 196
slave insurrections, fear of, 54–55
Slave Power: agitation vs. political action and, 159–61; aristocracy and, 140–42, 148, 157–58; expansionism and, 203; Grew on defeat of, 259; Pierce and, 200; Sanders and, 202
slavery: 1850 Compromise, 194–95; as cause of Civil War, 230; Emancipation Proclamation (1863), 232, 253; escaped slaves, 190–91; Fugitive Slave Law, 101, 102, 194–97, 200, 204–5; Missouri Crisis (1819–21), 33; other forms of oppression vs., 254; problems revealed by, 225; Tallmadge thesis, 33–34; Thirteenth Amendment, 232, 251, 253–54, 260; "white" or "wage" slavery, 151, 152, 154. *See also* emancipations
Slidell, John, 227
Smith, Gerrit, 159, 210
Smith, James McCune, 59–60
Smith, Robert, 209
sobriety, 105–6
Society in America (Martineau), 61
Socrates, 110, 161
Soulé, Pierre, 201, 202, 208, 211
"South America" (Garrison), 25–26, 28
southern aristocracy. *See* aristocracy; Slave Power
Spain, 24, 25, 27, 48, 201–2
speech, freedom of, 73–74, 111–12
Stanton, Edwin, 262
Stanton, Elizabeth Cady, 71, 267
Stanton, Henry B., 71
Stevenson, Andrew, 59
Stewart, James Brewer, 331n14
Story, Joseph, 11
Stowe, Harriet Beecher, 207
Strong, George Templeton, 197
Sturge, Joseph, 61, 71–72, 149
suffrage: 1855 state of, 4–6; black, 137–38, 246–50, 251, 254, 261; Chartism and, 155–56; debate on abolition vs., 329n58; Dorrites and, 142–43; educational qualifications for, 155–56, 255–56; Fifteenth Amendment, 264; in France, 4,

342